RAPID DESCENT

Deregulation and the Shakeout in the Airlines

Barbara Sturken Peterson
and James Glab

SIMON & SCHUSTER
New York   London   Toronto
Sydney   Tokyo   Singapore

SIMON & SCHUSTER
Rockefeller Center
1230 Avenue of the Americas
New York, New York 10020

DESIGNED BY BARBARA MARKS
Manufactured in the United States of America

10 9 8 7 6 5 4 3 2 1

Library of Congress Cataloging-in-Publication Data
Peterson, Barbara Sturken.
    Rapid descent : deregulation and the shakeout in
the airlines / Barbara Sturken Peterson and James
Glab.
        p.   cm.
    Includes bibliographical references and index.
    1. Aeronautics, Commercial—United States—
Deregulation.   2. Airlines—United States—
Deregulation.   3. Competition.
I. Glab, James.   II. Title.
HE9803.A3P48   1994
387.7′1—dc20   94-5526   CIP
ISBN 0-671-76069-6

Acknowledgments

Many thanks to our friends and colleagues who assisted and encouraged us during the writing of *Rapid Descent*—Deborah Gaines, Richard Severo, Justin Lin, Alan Fredericks, Charles Taylor, Nadine Godwin, Joe Brancatelli, Tracey Smith, Phil Turner, Mike Driscoll, Jim Brown, Bill Poling, and Joe Scott—and to the late Coleman Lollar for his friendship and inspiration.

We are also grateful for the help we received from the staffs at the Northwestern University Transportation Center, the Columbia University business school library, and the New York Public Library. John Eichner and Beth Geltman at SH&E and Marian Mystic and Bill Jackman at the Air Transport Association provided assistance in researching the book. There are many other individuals we would like to thank, although some would prefer not to be mentioned by name, who generously gave up hours of their time to talk candidly about what happened in the airline business.

Our agent, Julie Castiglia, provided critical support at every stage. In that regard we want to thank our editor at Simon & Schuster, Bob Bender, who devoted much time and attention to shaping our manuscript, and his assistant Johanna Li. Maggie Drucker provided excellent legal advice, and Gypsy da Silva, thoughtful copy supervision.

To Bill and Leigh

B. S. P.

To my family and friends

J. G.

Contents

INTRODUCTION

"How was your flight?"

*"Well, aeronautically it was a
great success. Socially it left
quite a bit to be desired."*
—NOEL COWARD

Noel Coward's words have never seemed more fitting. Whatever
the merits of the federal government's deregulation of the
airlines in 1978, one thing is certain: It forever changed air
travel from an elegant and exotic experience into fodder for late-night
comics. Airlines have gone from one of the nation's most admired
and stable industries to one of the most chaotic and reviled. This is
the story of that transformation.

Today's airline passengers face illogical air fares, cramped and
suffocating aircraft cabins, and cattle-car treatment at "hub" airports
that do to humans what postal sorting centers do to our mail. Those
whose careers depend on noticing such things have picked up the
near-universal disgust with the business of flying. In his presidential
campaign, Bill Clinton claimed that "we've wrecked the airline industry," with no fear of contradiction. Ralph Nader, one of the first
proponents of deregulation, now says the airlines should be regulated
like public utilities. Even Alfred Kahn, the economist and former
Civil Aeronautics Board chairman, jokes that whenever he is introduced as the father of deregulation, "People think I'm going to demand a blood test."

Public opinion surveys show that most Americans believe airline
deregulation was a mistake; ironically, they are also traveling by air

in numbers never thought possible twenty years ago. Every day more than a million people board a flight operated by major United States airlines. Deregulation made that possible, changing air travel from an elitist to a populist mode of transport.

Yet deregulation, as everyone knows, did not live up to its advance billing. Fares did go down, as promised, and a whole new generation of airlines came forth to challenge the incumbents; but fifteen years later the airline industry is dominated by a handful of large companies, and American and United still hold the number one and two positions, just as they did during the forty years of regulation.

In writing this book we chose to focus on a few people and companies that made a difference. Robert Crandall, the only one still holding his job after the rambunctious 1980s, is the acknowledged father of many of the most successful corporate strategies of recent times. Frank Lorenzo is also an outsize character who, aside from his notoriety as labor's nemesis, is as much the personification of deregulation as Crandall. Then there is Don Burr, Lorenzo's close associate, whose individualistic People Express was the fastest growing company of any kind in American history. Dick Ferris, who led United Airlines when it liked to call itself the Largest Airline in the Free World, made deregulation possible by breaking up the airline club that had run the business since the late 1930s.

The careers of these men frequently intersected with the sagas of the airlines once known as the Big Four—American, Eastern, TWA, and United. They, along with Pan American, were the largest airlines in the country when the business was deregulated in 1978. Some flourished and others perished, and their stories illustrate the essential changes deregulation wrought.

Many people see the results—the failed companies, the astonishing losses the airlines racked up in recent years, the service woes—as part of a broader failure of deregulation itself. But in a deregulated environment, the success or failure of individual airlines has much to do with the caliber and personalities of the people at the top. In a free market, poorly managed companies should be allowed to fail—at least that's what the purists argue. Still, a lingering mystique clings to the airlines—the legacy of a Golden Age of air travel few of us ever experienced. The public still apparently believes flying ought to have more allure than a bus ride. Whatever the reasons, the call to do something about air travel persists to this day, fifteen years after the law was passed.

As airline reregulation is debated, however, there is a danger that people will have forgotten how badly the old system of price and route controls worked—not just for consumers, but for many of the airlines as well. Surely no one can suggest a return to the days when the government spent tax dollars on absurdities like a straight-faced study into the optimum size of an in-flight sandwich or a system of subsidies that rewarded airlines for flying empty planes.

Kahn once wrote that competition, even with all its imperfections, is nearly always preferable to regulation. Yet it may not be the fruits of competition but the imperfections of the regulations still remaining—or the government's failure to enforce them—that cause much of the distress to travelers today. The wave of mergers in the mid to late 1980s resulted in large part from the government's refusal to apply the antitrust laws to stop the more egregious combinations. And its failure to stop blatant predatory pricing by big airlines against newcomers may have encouraged more of the same, ultimately driving some companies out of business.

The story is not yet over; every so often there is yet another flurry of upstart airlines demonstrating—as someone once said of a second marriage—the triumph of hope over experience. But the outcome is already clear: Despite the intentions of the architects of deregulation, many airlines have gone bankrupt, leaving a half-dozen large airlines to dominate the field. This is an account of how we got there.

1

How Did
It Come
to This?

T he chief executives of America's biggest airlines and airplane-makers did not return to their offices after Labor Day in 1990. By midday on Tuesday, September 4, many of them were heading in private jets for an obscure airstrip in the Wyoming wilderness. And by the time the sun dipped behind the Medicine Bow Mountains that evening, they were no longer dignified deans of an industry but ersatz cowboys in ill-fitting jeans and ten-gallon hats, huddling before a campfire in the chill air. For the next five days, their whereabouts would be kept secret from all but their closest associates.

They were there for the annual meeting of the "Conquistadores del Cielo," Spanish for Conquerors of the Sky, a mysterious society of aviation executives founded in 1937 by TWA chief Jack Frye. At first a casual social club, it evolved into an exclusive, and increasingly secretive, fraternity, membership in which connotes elite status within the tight universe of the commercial airline and aerospace industries. Their playground, as in years past, was the A Bar A Ranch owned by Lear Gates chairman Charlie Gates, a vast 20,000-acre spread near the small Wyoming hamlet of Encampment.

That the club's members have been close-mouthed to the point of paranoia is not surprising, for its existence seems to mock the competition that deregulation was intended to create. Not only does

it evoke the cozy club that ran the airlines in the past, but its continuing appeal suggests that the club was never quite disbanded.

By Wednesday, September 5, they were more than one hundred
strong, all men, for women had never been admitted into their ranks.
This year, as always, found men like Bob Crandall of American and
his archrival Stephen Wolf of United bunking together with other
leaders of America's aviation industry in humble wooden cabins.
Crandall was the unofficial dean of the airline business. He had
groomed almost more senior airline executives than anyone else. Some
of his former protégés were now his rivals; Wolf in fact had worked
for Crandall. Now they publicly reveled in the role of tough competitors, battling each other for scarce overseas routes, stealing one
another's top executives. Yet in Wyoming they were friends; a pho-
tographic album of the Conquistadores meetings shows Crandall and
Wolf, along with Northwest Airlines chairman Al Checchi, laughing
together in a moment of unrehearsed gaiety.

In spirited contests, many involving knives and guns, they acted
out a parody of the cutthroat competition the public sees.

Present among them were many men who had lost the positions
that had qualified them for the club. Dick Ferris, the charismatic
leader of United Airlines for thirteen years, was there, although he
had been out of work since his humiliating ouster from the airline
three years before. He was still drawing his half-million-a-year salary
from United (which he had been guaranteed for five years); it was
almost as if nothing had happened.

And Frank Lorenzo was there, too, a gaunt apparition, a reminder
of the Conquistadores' success in defying the vicissitudes of their
business. Lorenzo had weeks before ended his twenty-year airline
career, selling all his holdings in Continental Airlines, because his
notoriety was hurting the company. He came to Wyoming with his
longtime lieutenant, Phil Bakes, now another unemployed airline
executive. Bakes was the Zelig of airline deregulation, who had helped
write the law as an aide to both Edward Kennedy and Alfred Kahn,
and then spent ten years at Lorenzo's Texas Air. Bakes had just left
his last job, as chief executive of troubled Eastern Airlines.

The Conquistadores were sympathetic. Back home, Lorenzo and
his family were accosted by picketers. Here, he was accorded respect,
even sympathy, for his battle with the unions at Eastern. Even those
who had crossed swords with Lorenzo were cordial. Lorenzo had
fired fellow conqueror Tom Plaskett, now Pan Am chairman, three
years earlier—an experience Plaskett shared with Steve Wolf, who'd
lasted just nine months working for Lorenzo. All was forgotten in

the quiet of their mountain redoubt—although when Lorenzo injured his eye in a rifle shoot, some noted that the man organizing the event was none other than Hollis Harris, a veteran Delta executive who'd just been hired to erase the trauma of the Lorenzo years at Continental.

By Thursday evening everyone was anticipating the "initiation," the hoary rituals that remove the Conquistadores from the realm of a mere trade association. After dinner, a chosen few quietly retreated to prepare. The Conquistadores have a complex membership structure: Every year a few aspirants are admitted to the inner sanctum of lifetime membership. Herb Kelleher, the irrepressible chairman of Southwest Airlines and Crandall's good friend, was among the half-dozen or so to be tapped this year. Along with the others, he slipped into one of the velvet and brocade costumes that had been purchased years before from the Spanish Opera. Lips were rouged, a crude goatee and thick black mustache crayoned on his face. Grinning malevolently, he appeared a low-rent Cyrano de Bergerac. Dave Hinson, head of Midway Airlines, was a rouge-cheeked monk. Delta chairman Ron Allen wore plum-colored velvet and a feathered cap.

Torches were lit, drawing the rest of the group to witness the ceremony. A procession of armor-clad knights rode into view. There, as everyone stared, was the cream of the aviation business unrecognizable under their vaudeville garb.

Crandall—the man who built American into the country's number-one airline, whose public persona is that of a gruff, ruthless competitor—was here a comic sight, his face crinkled into a lipsticked grin, a thin mustache penciled onto his cheeks. He wore a tunic of blinding scarlet and gold, thigh-high red boots, and a red-and-gold cap sprouting pink feathers. Brandishing a saber, Crandall approached the kneeling aspirants to anoint them. Kelleher, Crandall's putative competitor in his Dallas backyard, was now his fellow Conquistador.

Perhaps nowhere, not even in California's Bohemian Grove, is there so secret a group whose members all hail from the same business. The remote site of their meeting and their public silence naturally have fueled suspicion even more. Some conquerors have reportedly yielded to the temptation to talk business; Frank Lorenzo is said to have approached Continental Airlines chairman Robert Six in a discussion about merging their airlines years ago, when Lorenzo had only tiny Texas International to his name. "Sure, we talk about business," says one Conquistador, who, like all of them, requests anonymity when talking about the group. But he, like others, insists it is all innocent enough (although Northwest later charged Crandall with violating antitrust laws, in part by talking about pricing at one Conquistadores meeting).

On Sunday, the Conquistadores boarded their jets to return to their normal jobs the next morning. This year, however, they faced a situation that was far from normal. Iraq's invasion of Kuwait just weeks before had already pushed up oil prices and threatened to scare off passengers with renewed fears of terrorism. The airlines were in fact hurtling toward such an unprecedented disaster that some analysts drew an analogy to the troubles of the savings and loan industry. The difference was that the government would not step in and seize control of the nation's airlines.

SAM SKINNER, PRESIDENT BUSH'S TRANSPORTATION secretary, was troubled by what he saw in the most visible industry under his watch. Early on in his tenure he had promised to breathe a "spirit of competitiveness" into the airline business. Instead the industry was consolidating rapidly in a wave of bankruptcies and mergers.

He called the airline chiefs to Washington that fall, and one by one they dutifully trekked to the capital to tell Skinner what their survival would require. Skinner was not pleased by what he heard. The airline bosses wanted an old-fashioned government handout to cover their losses. In the past, a bailout in some form would have been forthcoming; the government would not have allowed airlines with the high profiles of a Pan Am or an Eastern to simply shut down. This was no longer the case. Deregulation had erased the mystique from the business; airlines that could not make it on their own would perish.

Skinner, a former Illinois prosecutor known as Sam the Hammer for his toughness on crime, was uncomfortable with the lack of an obvious solution. The answer came one October morning, somewhat tentatively, in one of the sessions he liked to convene in the dining room just off his tenth-floor office in the hulking Transportation Department headquarters. His visitors that day were some of the leading Wall Street airline analysts.

Skinner delighted in entertaining guests with a computer terminal he kept in a corner. It connected him with the government's system for monitoring air traffic and allowed him to see what was happening anywhere in the nation's airspace.

He clicked the computer control in his hand: Up came a map of the United States. Tiny white pulsating dots emerged. Each dot was an airplane that was at that moment moving from one point to another somewhere over the United States. It was, as many witnesses would remark, a breathtaking display. The machine could, if asked, tell onlookers anything they wanted to know about any one of those planes aloft at that instant.

Watching the secretary play with the computer was absorbing. He'd zero in on a dot, press a few keys, and the computer would identify it as United Airlines flight 635 from Chicago to Los Angeles, at twenty-three thousand feet, flying 350 miles an hour. A few more keystrokes, and he would know how many minutes it was from its destination.

He could focus it, too, on just one airport. Chicago's O'Hare, where twenty-two hundred jets lifted off the runways every day, was a big bright spot on the map, like a cluster in a galaxy.

The entire U.S. commercial airline industry was on display in that one machine—all the giant hubs, glowing brightly, where airlines had learned to herd passengers in mass numbers from one plane to another, sending them back out to other destinations, like shuffling a deck of cards. It was a system that the surviving airlines had learned to exploit well.

Skinner's exercise revealed, too, that American and United owned more of those dots than their rivals, though Delta was close behind. The spot on the map that was Atlanta glowed every bit as brightly as O'Hare. Atlanta was the hub of hubs, the original model that had spawned so many others. Those three aviation giants commanded a huge share of the dots on his screen, carrying, on average, more than half of all the passengers in the U.S. skies.

After Skinner had performed his keyboard drill, it appeared there were some questions the machine couldn't answer.

"Will it tell us which airlines are going to go under?" asked one of Skinner's guests. When Skinner, quite seriously, invited them to list the airlines about to fold, the group huddled. Michael Derchin, a respected Wall Street analyst working for a British merchant bank, put the list of endangered companies at five and a half: "Eastern, Pan Am, TWA, America West, Continental." The half, he said, was the Trump Shuttle, the bauble that real estate tycoon Donald Trump had bought at an inflated price from Frank Lorenzo two years before.

"You are going to preside over the bankruptcy of the entire U.S. airline industry," Derchin told Skinner.

When Skinner asked what he could do, someone jokingly replied, "Get another job." Skinner had his hands tied.

The analysts were convinced there was only one choice for the deregulated industry: allowing foreign ownership of airlines. Politicians would squawk, of course, about national pride, and unions would be outraged at more jobs going to foreign owners.

Yet in just a few weeks, Skinner would take the first big step toward doing just that.

ON FEBRUARY 2, 1991, the airline CEOs gathered again. This time the setting, for a banquet hosted by the New York brokerage firm of Shearson Lehman, was the gilded ballroom of the Ritz-Carlton Hotel in Naples, Florida. This, too, was an annual tradition, combining an agreeable spell of socializing with a little business. The airline men would spend a few days at the resort, where each would take a turn delivering an unvarnished sales pitch for his company before a flock of attentive stockbrokers and pension fund managers. Shearson had thoughtfully planned a corny revue to enliven the evening, and the emcee was the puckish Herb Kelleher. He would suit the role perfectly. He had shamelessly spurred his workers to new heights of productivity with his buffoonery. He had gyrated in an Elvis costume at a company staff meeting and, wearing a bunny suit, handed out peanuts to startled passengers in flight. He was a paragon of unhealthy living: He smoked five packs of cigarettes a day and delighted onlookers that night by swigging bourbon with abandon.

That night, Kelleher's Southwest Airlines was the only major airline in the room that could claim to be making any money, in part because Kelleher had sagely avoided provoking the big airlines. And tonight their predicament would make fine comedy material.

Puffing on a Merit, squinting out into the room, Kelleher stared into the crowd and drawled: "I'd like to salute all those ass-kissers over there." There were Bob Crandall, Steve Wolf, USAir chief Ed Colodny, and other chiefs at the side of Sam Skinner. Kelleher in fact was getting even with them for deserting his table for that of the transportation chief. But if Skinner's dinner companions appeared to be groveling that night, they had reason to. By then, they knew their survival depended in part on their ability to sell or buy assets that would mean hundreds of millions of dollars for their companies. All of these deals would have to come to Skinner's agency for approval.

One of these transactions would allow Bob Crandall to take over much of TWA's transatlantic operations; the other would give United's Wolf permission to buy Pan Am's London operation. That would make American and United international titans and would cripple the companies they were replacing.

All this was stoking dissatisfaction in some quarters over the results of airline deregulation, as Skinner had heard from a number of unhappy congressmen lately. The airlines' woes had set off a morbid feeding frenzy, with the richer companies feasting off what remained of weaker rivals. "The airline business is the closest you can get to war in peacetime," was a favorite Kelleher line.

But the business still retained the old clubbiness suggested by the Conquistadores. In the whole crowd of airline managers that night, there was only one true outsider. Carl Icahn, although he chaired TWA, had never given up the unorthodox habits he'd acquired as an arbitrager. He rarely fraternized with his peers from other airlines and frequently mocked his competitors as complacent and poorly managed. He'd shown up at the party that night at the urging of a longtime Shearson airline analyst.

"I see Carl Icahn is sitting here, and this reminds me of these two guys up in New York, Irving and Morris," Kelleher said in an ersatz Texas twang. The two men, Kelleher continued, had been in business together for years. Morris retired to Miami Beach and when they met a few years later, Irving inquired how Morris was enjoying retirement.

"Fine. I'm raising bees," Morris said. "Bees?" his friend answered. "You've got an apartment. How do you raise bees?" Morris responded, "I stick them in a shoebox and put them in a closet." Irving's response was, of course: "That's crazy—don't they die?" Morris shrugged. "Yeah, sure—but fuck 'em, it's a hobby."

Kelleher smiled at Icahn. "Yep, Carl, this is the way some people run an airline."

Icahn, the others suspected, would not be at TWA much longer. The TWA chief was a gambler who visibly twitched at the chance to buy or sell an asset. It was Icahn's hostile raid on TWA in 1985, a battle in which he had bested Lorenzo, that had symbolized the turning point for the airlines. Since then, dozens of once-independent airlines had disappeared from the skies, leaving air travel in the control of a half-dozen big companies that had erected formidable barriers to any challengers. Even with the advantages of their huge size, a number of those that remained were in abysmal shape. It was beginning to strike some people—like Sam Skinner—that the future of the entire U.S. airline industry might be in doubt.

BY THE END OF THE YEAR, Pan Am would disappear from the U.S. skies. A number of foreign airlines would offer to buy sizable chunks of their U.S. counterparts. Others would soon be flying under bankruptcy court protection.

Over the next two years, the astronomical losses—about $7 billion or $8 billion—would wipe out the airlines' entire profits of the previous sixty years.

Where did it all go so wrong?

2

THE
CLUB

From its beginnings, the airline business was run like a club. The first airlines began to appear after World War I as minor appendages to large Wall Street holding companies. Flying was seen as a dangerous activity: By the mid-1920s, over twenty years after the Wright brothers' flight at Kitty Hawk, the airlines were carrying barely six thousand passengers a year. Pilots were regarded as foolhardy showmen by a public that was nonetheless entertained by their barnstorming antics.

One of these barnstorming performers would radically alter the public's perception of flying. Charles Lindbergh's solo transatlantic flight in 1927 awakened the country to the vast potential of commercial aviation. And his future father-in-law, Dwight Morrow, prominent banker and adviser to President Calvin Coolidge, opened a steady stream of capital to the industry. Morrow proposed giving private airline companies handsome subsidies to carry the U.S. mail. His ideas became law in 1926, transforming the postmaster general into a commercial aviation czar who could funnel millions of dollars to the fledgling airlines.

So was born a long tradition of coziness between federal government officials and the airlines. The inevitable scandal soon followed.

It began one day in May 1930, when President Herbert Hoover's postmaster general, Walter Folger Brown, called the country's top airline executives to a private session to divide up the nation's principal air routes. Brown believed that the United States would be better off with a few large airlines than with many little competitors. His guests at the secret session, he had decided, would control America's airways.

Brown showed his visitors a map of the United States with a few lines zig-zagging across the continent and up and down the East Coast. In short order, he awarded three plum cross-country routes to United Air Lines, American Airways, and Transcontinental Air Transport, the corporate predecessors of United Airlines, American Airlines, and Trans World Airlines. The East Coast went to Eastern Air Transport, later Eastern Airlines. All this was blatantly illegal; the law required that air routes be awarded through competitive bidding. So, to comply with the letter of the law, there was a formal bidding process. The airlines simply agreed not to bid against each other.

These airlines soon became known as the Big Four, and they were to dominate U.S. air travel for nearly sixty years. In fact, shortly after Brown's "spoils conference," independent Western Air Express rushed into a merger with Transcontinental, adding the "W" in TWA. The word was out that the little guys could forget about getting any decent contracts from Brown, who routinely ignored bids that undercut those from his favored airlines. By 1933, these airlines were raking in virtually all of the $20 million the federal government annually paid out to airmail contractors. Pan American World Airways was the other airline to emerge around this time, and under Brown's patronage it won an effective monopoly on all international routes.

As it turned out, one of Brown's guests had recorded his suspicion that such a meeting of competitors might violate the Sherman Antitrust Act. When federal agents started sniffing around the odd circumstances of the airmail contract awards, they discovered the torn fragments of the man's scribbled account in his trash and pieced them together.

The press trumpeted the story as the "Airmail Scandal." The Senate held highly publicized hearings in the winter of 1934, chaired by Alabama senator Hugo Black, the future Supreme Court justice. Franklin Roosevelt was in the White House, and he responded to this embarrassing affair by canceling all existing domestic airmail contracts, turning over the job of flying the U.S. mail to the Army Air Corps. But the Army had slacked off in its training after the war and its pilots were ill-prepared. In three months, dozens of planes crashed, killing twelve people. "Legalized murder!" was how Eastern chief Eddie Rickenbacker described it. The cost of airmail transport quadrupled.

The airlines then turned for help to Charles Lindbergh, who conveniently was already on their payroll: He had been working for both TWA and Pan American as a consultant, test pilot, and route explorer since his historic transatlantic flight. Lindbergh publicly criticized Roosevelt for putting the airmail delivery system into jeopardy. Chastened, Roosevelt caved in to the pressure. The postal contracts once again went out to the commercial airlines, but this time under a competitive bidding process. No airline whose earlier, tainted contracts had been canceled would be allowed to bid. So the big airline companies did the simplest thing: They slightly altered their corporate names (changing Airways to Airlines, for instance, or adding an Inc.), becoming "new"—and airmail-eligible—companies. After all the dust had settled and a new round of contracts had been issued, the three transcontinental routes were held once again by United, American, and TWA, and the East Coast routes by Eastern. They would hold nearly exclusive rights on these choice routes until deregulation came along.

IN A BRIEF BURST OF reform, right after the airmail scandal, Congress forced the big Wall Street holding companies out of the airline industry, severing the ties between the sellers of airplanes and the buyers, although they would carry on together at the Conquistadores. Over the next few years, the combine of Boeing and United Aircraft split off its United Airlines operation; Aviation Corporation sold off its American Airlines unit; and North American Aviation, which was controlled by General Motors, got rid of its interest in TWA and Eastern.

Around this time a generation of flamboyant flyboys rose to take over the controls of the country's largest airlines. The early pioneers were occasionally ridiculed as "the scarf and goggles set," better at flying planes than at managing companies. However, they would prove adept at getting their way in Washington.

One of the first aviation entrepreneurs was Cyrus Rowlett Smith, who was born into poverty in a small Texas town. He went to work at the age of nine, eventually landing at a small airmail carrier called Texas Air Transport, which was merged into American Airways in 1931. Smith's paternalism and folksy managerial style made him a legend at American, where he became president in 1934. He remained at the helm of the company for thirty years. He was a blunt-spoken man of modest habits, sometimes choosing to fly in coach so he could give his first-class seat to someone else. On flights to the airline's base in New York City, he'd invite the entire crew over to his Park Avenue apartment for dinner afterward. He later served as Commerce Secretary under President Lyndon Johnson.

The chief at United Airlines was W. A. "Pat" Patterson, perhaps the most mild-mannered of the bunch, a former Wells Fargo banker who got into the airline business in 1929, when the founders of Boeing and United Aircraft put him in charge of a West Coast airline they owned that became a part of United. He stayed with the company until the late 1960s. While he built United into the biggest airline in the western world, Patterson was an old-fashioned moralist at heart. Although he hired the first stewardesses, he refused at first to allow them to serve liquor, saying that would turn them into "cocktail waitresses."

American and United grew up as paternalistic and stable as the men who ran them. But at other lines, the eccentric styles of the executives caused trouble.

Eastern, for example, was headed by the autocratic World War I flying ace and Medal-of-Honor winner Eddie Rickenbacker, who had started working for the airline when it was owned by General Motors. In 1938 he acquired Eastern with financial backing from Wall Street investors and ran it with a tight fist and a military command structure. Rickenbacker had a wholly unsentimental view of the airline business, describing it as "putting bums on seats." He never understood that he was running a service business, and his flight crews were notoriously surly. The airline developed such a reputation for poor service that its passengers actually formed a protest group: WHEAL, or We Hate Eastern Airlines.

TWA also suffered from often indifferent leadership. In its early years it was piloted by Jack Frye, a former stunt pilot and poker-playing pal of Harry Truman. Frye was frustrated by a series of absentee owners, however: first by former Yellow Cabs owner John Hertz, and then by multimillionaire Howard Hughes, whom Frye helped to bring into the company in 1940. A mercurial manager at best, Hughes liked to fly inaugural flights himself, often in his bare feet to "get the feel" of the plane. Like Rickenbacker, he did not care much for the needs of the average passenger; he would occasionally dislodge paying customers from a flight to make room for his movie star friends. And as the tycoon became increasingly irrational and isolated, TWA's fortunes began to suffer. In the 1950s Hughes refused to buy the new jets that would revolutionize airline travel. His board of directors finally ousted him in 1960. TWA was the last of the Big Four to enter the jet age.

The paradigmatic airline boss was Pan Am founder Juan Trippe, a domineering, manipulative, and exceptionally charming individual. A former Navy pilot and New York investment banker, he acquired the fledgling airline in 1926 and ran it with a small group of old college friends from Yale, including Cornelius Vanderbilt Whitney, who was chairman of the airline until after World War II. Their first coup was to secure a contract to carry mail from Florida to Cuba, even though they had no plane or crew. But with license in hand, Trippe hurriedly leased a German-made Fokker Trimotor and began the ninety-mile mail run with a flight from Key West to Havana in a hurricane one October day in 1927. It was the nation's first international route.

Over the years, Trippe established route networks all over the world, operating milk runs in South America, Africa, and the South Pacific. Before he retired in the late 1960s, he had met nearly every head of state, and he could always count on a friendly reception at the White House. But Trippe's notorious arrogance cost him dearly. Largely because he had alienated Civil Aeronautics Board appointees, Pan Am was barred from flying any domestic routes—a situation that was to devastate the company after deregulation.

BY THE MID-1930S THE BIG airlines were still recovering from the air mail scandal, and their capital base was drying up. So they turned once again to the U.S. government, which had been so helpful before, setting up an office near the White House for the Air Transport Association, a trade group that ultimately grew into a heavily funded industry lobbying arm.

Safety had continued to be a problem. In 1935 a popular senator, Bronson Cutting of New Mexico, had been killed in an air crash, and the public was clamoring for the government to do something. It was the time of the New Deal and new federal agencies were the rage. The solution was obvious: Create a new government body whose sole function would be to watch over the safety and economic health of the airlines.

Few new agencies have been established with as much help from the industry to be regulated. American's C. R. Smith, Eastern's Eddie Rickenbacker, and United's Pat Patterson huddled with Air Transport Association chief Colonel Edgar Gorrell to draft an industry version of regulatory legislation. They leaned on a congressional ally, House Commerce Committee chairman Clarence Lea, and he gave the airline executives a chance to look over the legislation to check that it met their interests.

Some observers, however, saw potential abuse in the bill. Amelia Earhart testified at a Senate hearing that she worried that the aviation agency might not let anyone new enter the industry. At a later session, then-Senator Harry Truman dismissed the famous aviatrix's concerns as "ridiculous." Although he didn't want "any Tom, Dick, and Harry getting into the business," Truman said that there was no intent to throttle competition. "My God, you have to trust someone, don't you?" he asked.

Truman's side prevailed. The Civil Aeronautics Act of 1938 created a five-member bipartisan board to oversee virtually all aspects of the airline business. The Civil Aeronautics Board had power to license new airlines, grant new routes, approve mergers, and investigate accidents, although safety matters were later transferred to another new agency, the Federal Aviation Administration. The legislative record shows that Truman and other congressional sponsors truly believed that the act would encourage competition except where it would threaten safety. But the trust they had invested in the agency had already been undermined. Colonel Gorrell had persuaded lawmakers to give all eighteen airlines with existing mail contracts permanent rights to stay on the routes they held, supposedly to protect them from "cutthroat" competition. In fact, the law gave them a stranglehold on the most valuable markets in the country. Within a year, most of the major airlines that had been losing money were in the black once again, and new investment capital was flowing into the industry.

Amelia Earhart's prediction proved correct. The CAB would not allow a new major scheduled airline to come into existence for forty years.

AFTER WORLD WAR II, THE tight little clique that ran the airlines—C. R. Smith, Patterson, Rickenbacker—expanded to include a few others who had risen to prominence, such as Continental's Bob Six and Delta's C. E. Woolman. "It was U.S. Airlines, Inc.," said American chief Bob Crandall later, with the CAB as a board of directors that determined the shape of the industry. Applications for admission were inevitably denied.

One came from former Air Force pilot Ed Daly, who was working as a low-paid airport ticket agent when he scraped up fifty thousand dollars to buy the certificate of a moribund line called World Airways in 1950. World was licensed to fly as an "irregular," as charters were called, which meant they could operate special flights for groups but could not sell individual tickets. These airlines tended to be thinly financed, erratically run companies, whose owners would never be Conquistadores. They did not threaten the status quo.

But Daly and his compatriots had noticed something the established airlines had ignored. The public desire for affordable air travel could not be contained. By 1951, airline passenger volume for the first time surpassed first-class rail traffic. That was the only meaningful comparison, since the airlines sold only one type of fare—first class—priced at a level that would keep ordinary citizens earthbound.

Daly eventually became the largest charter operator in the country, one of a hardy band of ex-soldiers who took on the airline establishment. A former prize fighter, he packed a pistol wherever he went, and his exploits soon drew attention. When the Soviets crushed the Hungarian uprising in 1956, Daly personally flew out refugees, and later he took on risky rescue missions out of Vietnam and Cambodia. Daly built up a fortune flying these daring military charters with handsome contracts from the U.S. government. At the same time the government denied him what he wanted most: a chance to fly a scheduled bargain-priced airline.

But Daly was obsessed. Charters proved that a wide consumer market existed for air travel at the right price. The fares on charters were about half those on scheduled flights, based on the simple principle that passengers would split the cost of flying a nearly full plane, while scheduled flights had to operate no matter how many seats were filled. Charter passengers had to form groups and put up with all kinds of restrictions, and they couldn't change flights or get full refunds. Daly wanted to transcend this airline underclass. With his secondhand planes and low costs, he could fly people for a lot less than the big airlines.

This, in essence, was the fundamental concept underlying deregulation. By the mid-1950s, others were trying to test it. An outfit called North American Airlines offered almost daily transcontinental flights, with fares at 40 percent off scheduled prices, a feat the company had pulled off simply by pooling the flight authorities of several charter lines. Soon it was carrying nearly three hundred thousand passengers annually and making a profit, until the CAB, under pressure from the scheduled airlines, shut it down for some technical rule violations.

In 1958, Boeing brought out the 707; the jet age had begun. The jets doubled the speed and passenger capacity of their propeller-driven predecessors and promised to bring down the airlines' costs dramatically. There was no reason the scheduled airlines could not sell at least some of their tickets at affordable prices.

Paradoxically, the entrenched airlines seemed to band together even more, entering into agreements that would have been illegal in any other business. One of the worst was concocted just as the first jets were rolling off the assembly line. C. R. Smith was its author. The airline pilots had struck the year before, and the growing power of unions posed a new threat to the industry's profits. So each airline pledged to contribute a share of its own revenues to any rival that suffered a strike. The CAB approved the pact with full immunity from the antitrust laws. In one step, the airlines had negated the effectiveness of the unions' right to strike and declared that, even as competitors, they would unite whenever it suited their interests. Since airlines had no incentive to settle labor disputes, strikes were often long, drawn-out affairs. By the mid-1970s, airlines had paid out a handsome $350 million in mutual aid to each other.

American under Smith was widely regarded as the industry leader, but in 1961, United Airlines acquired Washington-based Capital Airlines, ousting American from the number-one spot it had held for years. The merger was the last and by far the largest of a series that had eliminated some independent lines from the skies: Western Air Lines acquired Inland Airways and Braniff took over Mid-Continent Airlines in 1952; Delta picked up Chicago & Southern in 1953; Continental bought out Pioneer Airlines in 1955; and Eastern absorbed Colonial Airlines in 1956.

Patterson's coup in grabbing Capital set off an enduring rivalry between United and American and a long-time grudge on Smith's part. Smith tried to catch up, proposing a merger with Eastern, but other airlines lined up against it and the CAB rejected it on anticompetitive grounds. Mergers was one area where the CAB exercised its considerable powers, and when American tried to acquire Western it was rejected again. Pan Am and TWA also applied for permission to merge in 1962, but were turned down, as this would have virtually eliminated international competition among U.S. airlines.

BUT THE CAB STILL REFUSED to let new companies in. In 1967 Ed Daly formally proposed scheduled coast-to-coast service at seventy-five dollars one-way, less than half the going rate. The CAB proceeded to sit on his application for eight years, then dismissed it as stale.

Around that time, the airline pioneers were retiring, leaving a host of problems for their successors. Juan Trippe receded to the background, although he continued to meddle in company affairs at Pan Am's Park Avenue headquarters; Pat Patterson turned over United's reins to Edward Carlson, a hotel man; and Eastern endured a series of short-lived reigns by executives who tried to fill Rickenbacker's shoes. TWA was led by Charles Tillinghast, a respected financier, but he was close to retirement himself. C. R. Smith formally retired from American in 1968, remarking, "These days no one can make money in the goddamn airline business. The economics represent sheer hell."

He was right: By the 1970s, five airlines—the Big Four and Pan Am—still had not figured out how to make money. They were among the nation's largest companies, each with annual revenues topping $1 billion. Yet in profitability, air carriers ranked thirtieth among thirty major U.S. industries.

This was in part because of the bizarre behavior regulation inevitably produced. There was, for example, the strange case of the "sandwich wars," which began in the late 1960s when airlines started to overload their busiest routes with extra flights to try to grab market share. All that happened was that everyone's flights took off half-full. The airlines then added on-board frills, competing for passengers with fancy sandwiches and picnic baskets. As the culinary competition spread through the industry, CAB members were forced into making straight-faced rulings on whether Northeast Airlines' steaks were "cooked to order," as its ads promised, or were simply reheated, as rival Delta Air Lines charged. The result was the same—no one gained any competitive edge, everyone just lost more money.

Something had to be done, and in 1970, another closed-door meeting was convened with the blessing of the government. The executives of American, TWA, and United met privately and agreed to cut back on the number of flights from coast to coast—a market where they had no other competition—thus guaranteeing fuller planes. This was a blatant violation of antitrust laws, but the CAB granted one-year approval of this "capacity control" agreement with antitrust immunity, which encouraged similar agreements on many other routes.

Richard Nixon was president and his appointees would carry the mandate to protect the airlines much further than their predecessors, stretching and even violating the law. A couple of blundering bureaucrats—Secor Browne, a lawyer and businessman, and Bob

Timm, a wheat farmer with expensive tastes, unintentionally made the case for reform.

An appointment to the CAB was a nice sinecure and often led to a higher-paying job in the airline business. Sitting on the five-member board itself was not particularly challenging. Once, when Lyndon Johnson's confidant and agriculture secretary Charles Murphy came to him to say he was overworked and wanted to resign, Johnson responded that he needed him in Washington and would find him a less demanding job. Murphy was appointed chairman of the CAB.

Murphy's successor, CAB chairman Browne, summarized his attitude toward new route awards for airlines by saying "ain't nobody going no place." His logic was simple: The economy was slowing, and the airlines were not going to be carrying many additional passengers, so any growth in airline capacity should simply be halted until demand caught up.

Browne may only have been a knee-jerk defender of big business. But Bob Timm, who followed him, was to go down as a disaster, even by the mediocre standards of the board. He was as eager to join the airline club as its members were to induct him. Timm loved golf, and soon was a regular guest of airlines or airplane manufacturers for weekend golfing trips to Bermuda. TWA's Tillinghast invited Timm on a grand tour of Europe, thoughtfully arranging golf outings at every stop along the way. It was heady stuff for a fifty-three-year-old wheat farmer whose only previous government experience had been as a state utilities commissioner.

Timm's golf trips attracted the attention of consumer activist Ralph Nader, by then the patron saint of aggrieved passengers. Nader went after the airlines when he was bumped from an Allegheny Airlines flight on April 18, 1972, missing an important speaking engagement. He responded by suing Allegheny for $250,000, charging that it misled passengers by deliberately selling more seats than it operated. Nader's lawsuit laid the groundwork for the eventual regulation of the airlines' overbooking practices. But Nader saw this as just one piece of a broader pattern of industry abuses. He formed a watchdog group, the Aviation Consumer Action Project, and demanded that the CAB investigate ownership of the nation's airlines, charging that a handful of banks and insurance companies secretly controlled much of the industry.

As the CAB's regulation of the industry grew more ham-handed, an airline underground sprang up. Travelers banded together in phony groups that existed only to charter a flight. Authorities became suspicious when organizations like the Czechoslovakian Radio Hour Friendship Club started showing an unlikely interest in globe-trotting. The CAB assigned gumshoes to stand at airports and check charter passengers' IDs. The campaign reached hilarious heights in 1971, when the government's air fare police raided a plane carrying members of the "Left Handed Club," a group they accurately suspected included many right-handed passengers in search of inexpensive air travel.

As these absurdities mounted, Congress took notice. California Democratic congressman John Moss formed a group of two dozen legislators known as the Moss Group, whose sole purpose was to stop the CAB from allowing airlines to gouge consumers. Moss went to court to get the airlines to cough up $265 million in refunds to consumers, who he claimed had been overcharged when the CAB improperly approved fare increases in 1969. The courts agreed and sent the matter back to the board. But the CAB, ever solicitous of the airlines, simply refused to order any refunds.

This kind of arrogance embarassed even some of the CAB's own staff. A quiet rebellion was building among some of the agency's younger employees. Some had even printed up bumper stickers that said "Ground the CAB—Deregulate the Airlines." But the idea was still radical enough that the renegade staffers were quick to hide their stickers when a senior official strolled by.

Deregulation would come sooner than the government rebels thought, thanks in large part to the excesses of their bosses. Some observers started noticing that the CAB had not given out a single new route in five years, despite scores of requests from airlines. Not only were Daly and other aspirants blocked from scheduled service, even the existing scheduled lines could not expand. Browne and Timm had in fact carried out a secret agreement to protect the airlines that possibly violated the law and that would, when revealed, make it impossible to defend the status quo.

3

THE

TRIAL

riday, September 27, 1974, promised to be an unseasonably hot day in the nation's capital and, judging from the newspapers that morning, a dull one as well. Watergate was over, and the city, habituated as it was to a daily dose of scandal, was adrift. A new distraction was needed.

At a few minutes past 11:00 A.M., Stephen Breyer, a law professor on the staff of Senator Edward Kennedy, slipped into a private meeting of airline executives on the tenth floor of the marble colossus that houses the Department of Transportation. Breyer was not the friendly observer from Capitol Hill his hosts imagined him to be. His visit, as they would soon learn, was more in the spirit of a district attorney out to catch a band of robbers plotting a break-in.

Breyer's quest had begun early that day. As he scanned *The Washington Post,* he noticed a short item in the business section about a meeting that morning in the office of Transportation Secretary Claude Brinegar. OPEC's quadrupling of oil prices, combined with a faltering economy, had pushed a couple of airlines close to bankruptcy, and Brinegar had summoned them to Washington to find a way to aid them without a direct handout. The story mentioned that Pan Am was in trouble. The venerable airline weeks before had asked the White House for $10 million a month in emergency aid, which to the president's advisers had sounded ominously like the recent bailout of the Penn Central railroad, a billion-dollar fiasco. A more palatable solution had been found: Brinegar would help the airlines agree on higher "minimum rates" on flights to Europe, where the scheduled airlines were taking a beating from charter competition.

To the average reader this sounded reasonable enough. But Breyer was shocked. Raising minimum rates, he knew, was simply a euphemism for a fare hike, which according to law had to be approved in public hearings. If he had read the article correctly, a high official of the U.S. government was about to conspire in private with some of the nation's airlines to fix prices. Breyer decided he had better be there as a witness. He had taught antitrust law for years, but he had never imagined he would actually enter the proverbial smoke-filled room.

Claude Brinegar was a longtime oilman; he was senior vice-president of Union Oil when President Nixon gave him the transportation portfolio in his cabinet. He was a loyal Republican who had stayed on through Watergate and Nixon's resignation. That morning he had joined other advisers to President Gerald Ford at a summit meeting to tackle the country's soaring inflation rate. Yet minutes later, he was able to march into a private office at Transportation and tell his airline guests they ought to raise fares.

Breyer confessed to a secret delight at Brinegar's clumsy backroom dealing. "Raise your prices! What's wrong with you airlines?" Breyer later recalled the secretary saying. The point of the exercise was to stop charter companies from taking business away from the big lines. As long as charters were charging low prices, the scheduled airlines felt they couldn't raise fares. Pan Am and TWA had each lost around $70 million on their international operations in the last year, largely because they were flying too many gas-guzzling jumbo jets. But they believed if the charters raised their prices, they could too. No matter that this stood the law of supply and demand on its head—that the airlines, with all their empty seats, should have been cutting fares instead.

Breyer was amazed at his luck in stumbling upon such a textbook case of price fixing. He was even more pleased, in fact, when Brinegar shooed the outside visitors away to allow the airline representatives to come to an agreement themselves. He had enough to regale Senator Kennedy with the fruits of his spying. "It was a cartel, a simple cartel being organized by the government," he said. Kennedy was also pleased. He had lured Breyer down from Harvard Law School for a year's sabbatical in order to inject some spark into a judiciary subcommittee he chaired. The two, in fact, had already begun preparing some exhaustive hearings into economic regulation that weren't scheduled to convene until spring.

But Breyer did not want to wait for the following year to expose his conspirators. He convinced Kennedy that they should haul the hapless bunch before his panel for a quick grilling, as a dry run for the real work that lay ahead.

Just as a postmaster's secret meeting with airlines had touched off a wave of reform forty years before, so would the discovery of a similar closed-door session bring about the most sweeping change to hit the industry since its inception.

This time, the reform would be carried along by a unique confluence of forces: the public's distrust of government after Watergate and Vietnam, rising panic over the economy, and Kennedy's desire to seem worthy of the presidency. By the time it was over the inquiry that was originally intended as an academic exercise would veer into scandal, occasional flashes of humor, and tragedy.

STEPHEN BREYER, AT AGE THIRTY-SIX, seemed an unlikely person to unleash the forces that would upend an industry. He was a thoughtful, scholarly man, with a more intellectual bent than the typical congressional recruit. He had excelled at Stanford and Harvard Law School, won a Marshall Scholarship to Oxford, and clerked for Supreme Court Justice Arthur Goldberg. Breyer's gifts would one day make him a serious candidate for a seat on the highest court himself.

Aside from a stint as an assistant Watergate prosecutor under his colleague from Harvard, Archibald Cox, Breyer had spent most of his life in academia. That was to suit Kennedy's inquiry fine. Had a more politically minded person been in charge, the outcome would have been far different. For years, the established airlines had cultivated friends in Congress with the same blandishments they lavished on government regulators. An experienced staffer would have been sensitive to the dangers of alienating such powerful industry friends. Breyer's only real interest in the airlines was as a laboratory subject. He had written papers on economic regulation, with the thesis that it often led to waste, inefficiency, and worse in the industries involved.

But as Breyer later admitted, the airlines were not a high priority when he arrived in the capital in 1974 to preside over the staff of Kennedy's subcommittee on administrative practices and procedures. His official job was to find something of substance for the panel to do; his unofficial mission was to convince the Washington elite that

Kennedy was presidential material. Although Kennedy was the front-runner for his party's nomination in 1976, his peers regarded him as an intellectual lightweight. And recent events had further damaged the prospects for his candidacy.

In the fall of 1972, Kennedy's supporters had urged him to claim jurisdiction for his subcommittee over the growing Watergate scandal. Capital insiders were dazzled by the prospect of a Kennedy leading the charge against Nixon: Columnist Stewart Alsop wrote that it would be "the biggest political television show since the McCarthy hearings." Kennedy's subcommittee held three months of closed-door hearings on the burglary of Democratic National Committee headquarters at the Watergate complex, producing enough findings for the Senate to create a special select committee to investigate the misdeeds of the Nixon re-election effort.

But Nixon supporters countered by linking Watergate with another scandal, Chappaquiddick. Questions had continued to linger about Kennedy's role in the drowning of Mary Jo Kopechne in a car he was driving on the island on July 18, 1969. Nixon's men responded to the senator's interest in Watergate by trying to get the FBI to investigate whether Kennedy himself had been guilty of obstruction of justice in delaying his report of the accident.

The episode caused great embarrassment to Kennedy. Republican senator Barry Goldwater, violating senatorial courtesy, said Kennedy "is the last person in the country who should lecture us" on Watergate. Columnist Tom Wicker of *The New York Times* wrote that it was widely accepted that "of all Democrats, Kennedy [is] the one least able to make the moral case against the Nixon Administration."

Many opinion-makers agreed that Watergate was dragging down Kennedy along with Nixon by reviving memories of Chappaquiddick. The two scandals were linked in other ways. It turned out that Watergate burglar Howard Hunt had been dispatched by Nixon to snoop around Chappaquiddick the previous summer to dig up fresh dirt on his nemesis. Nixon's dark obsession with the Kennedys, his aides intimated, had led him into the Watergate mess in the first place. What all this meant was that Kennedy had to stay on the sidelines during his party's hour of triumph.

This humiliation was still fresh when Kennedy brought Breyer to his home in suburban Virginia one afternoon in the middle of 1974. The idea was to find a serious subject for his panel to explore, preferably one that would rise above the political partisanship of Watergate.

"In some ways it was chance," Breyer said. "The first thing I thought of was to get a list of things, to find something for the panel to do, to give it substance. That's what was on my mind, not deregulation. The airlines had nothing to do with it.''

But out of a list of ten items, all aimed at giving substance to the committee and, by implication, Kennedy himself, regulation of the airline industry was plucked from obscurity. Breyer recalled that he felt compelled to point out to Kennedy why no one in Congress had gone near the subject—it was too technical and dull to generate much press coverage. But the more they chatted, the more Kennedy perceived the advantages of such an exercise. Relaxing regulations on airlines would inevitably lower fares, Breyer said. Kennedy would appear as a champion of the consumer at a time of raging inflation and soaring oil prices. And economists had been arguing for years that airlines could operate much more efficiently without regulation.

Breyer soon went back to Cambridge but agreed to return that fall to prepare the hearings. Meanwhile, Nixon resigned on August 8, 1974, and the newspapers were again full of speculation about Kennedy's presidential ambitions and the lingering mysteries of Chappaquiddick. On September 23, Kennedy held a news conference in Boston to put the rumors to rest. "I will not be a candidate for president or vice-president of the United States in 1976," he said. "My decision is firm, final, and unconditional." Kennedy gave as his reason "family responsibilities," saying "I simply cannot do that to my wife and children." That led to more painful rehashing of personal ordeals: his son's bout with bone cancer and his wife's recent drunk-driving arrest. Kennedy undoubtedly was eager for a respite from unwelcome media scrutiny.

A few days later, *Washington Post* columnist Joseph Alsop wrote a poignant account of Kennedy's plight. "I want to see what I can really do as a free senator," Alsop quoted Kennedy as saying. "When everyone thinks you may be going after the White House, you can't take a single step . . . that isn't interpreted in terms of presidential politics. I've got a lot to do, and I have a better chance of getting something done that really needs to be done."

Alsop positively gushed about the new, cerebral Kennedy the capital seemed to demand. "Kennedy means to attempt serious legislative work . . . with the patience to do all the needed homework." As much of official Washington was reading these words, Breyer had already found the issue that would raise Kennedy's standing.

• • •

THE AIRLINES AND THEIR ALLIES over at Transportation were furious
when they heard about Kennedy's plans to stage a hearing on the
charter rate scheme. Brinegar dispatched his aide-de-camp, a lawyer
named Robert Binder, to have a talk with Breyer. The encounter
quickly grew unpleasant. "If you go ahead with these hearings, Pan
Am will fail," Binder said, warning that the negative publicity would
cause bankers to cancel Pan Am's line of credit. When Breyer politely
disagreed, Binder called him a "lunatic college professor" and
stormed out.

Pan Am then leaned on its friends in Congress to start questioning
the senator's jurisdiction to poke into airline matters. The chairmen
of the relevant committees were especially close to the industry; many
congressmen liked to fly as VIP guests on the "inaugural flights" that
launched new services. The key senators in charge of the airlines
were Commerce Committee chairman Warren Magnuson, a grizzled
Democratic pol from the state of Washington, and Howard Cannon
of Nevada, a reliable industry "friend" who headed the aviation
subcommittee. The two began pleading with Kennedy to back off,
warning that if he proceeded, Pan Am's failure would be on his
conscience.

Kennedy was taken aback. If Pan Am was indeed so fragile,
perhaps they should reconsider. But a few calls to friends in the
financial community allayed his fears.

Kennedy's staff needed a compelling witness for their side. They
needed someone to speak for the victims of Brinegar's arrogance,
those who would be denied a chance to travel by the higher rates.
So Kennedy's staff asked around and decided to invite on opening
day a hot-headed, loud-mouthed English charter operator who'd long
been a critic of the Pan Ams and TWAs of the world: Freddie Laker.
He was already a folk hero abroad for his long battle to start up a
no-reservations Skytrain service across the Atlantic for the unheard-
of price of about ninety dollars each way.

The night before his November 7 testimony, Laker dined at the
home of Tom Susman, who was then chief counsel to the subcommittee, along with a few members of Kennedy's staff. Everyone was
anxious to hear what this eccentric entrepreneur might say about the
parlous state of the business. But he didn't arrive alone. Clinging to
the arm of the portly, fiftyish Briton was a young bouffant-coiffed
blonde in a tight miniskirt. Laker was clearly enjoying his celebrity.

Laker, like Ed Daly, was truly the personification of deregulation,
but about twenty years ahead of his time. The son of a Canterbury
scrap dealer, he entered the airline business at age sixteen, peddling

tea for a penny a can at Short Brothers aircraft manufacturing. He started his aircraft-leasing business after the war, buying up used Halton planes with a loan from his former employer. This somewhat dubious investment took off in 1948, when the Russian blockade of West Berlin sparked a massive airlift from the West. Suddenly Laker's fleet of clunky planes was in demand. Once the blockade was lifted, he used revenues from government contracts to start Laker Airways and became a highly successful packager of what the British call "cheap holidays": jam-packed charters to places like Tenerife.

In the 1960s, Laker realized there would be an important market for frequent scheduled transatlantic flights at discount prices. Using wide-bodied jets, of which there was a surplus, and offering no amenities, Laker would make profits simply by lowering the fares to the point where planes would fill to capacity. His idea was so simple that it was, given the tenor of the times, doomed to defeat. His applications to launch Skytrain were rebuffed by government authorities on both sides of the Atlantic.

Laker had another axe to grind. He had been fighting a running battle with the CAB, which had slapped him with a huge fine for technical rule violations. Laker was well aware of the U.S. plan to try to boost prices on transatlantic charters. The Civil Aeronautics Board by then had embraced the higher prices as minimum charter rates. Laker refused to abide by them.

He was every bit the colorful witness that Kennedy's staff had imagined. "We are now suffering from a disease I call Panamania," he said. "People seem to have lost their senses over what will happen to Pan Am, TWA, and British Airways." Laker had obviously not succumbed to this illness. He said the big airlines were to blame for their own problems. "These carriers are taking advantage of the problems, which in large measure they have brought upon themselves, to attempt to destroy a segment of the air travel business in which they don't belong."

The press loved the spectacle: on one side the full weight of the government and the airline industry; on the other, masses of backpacking students and working-class people who wanted a once-in-a-lifetime trip to Europe they couldn't afford without Skytrain.

Panamania had indeed been rampant. As Laker noted, the administration would do nearly anything to prevent a Pan Am failure on its watch. The White House mounted a jingoistic "Fly America" campaign to discourage Americans from flying on British Air, Air France, or other foreign lines. It even encouraged a bizarre bailout offer from the shah of Iran, who said he would shell out $300 million for a 13 percent stake in Pan Am, a plan that one critic said "would be like asking Chairman Mao to take over the Pennsylvania Railroad."

Pan Am had found that its close ties to the White House could be a mixed blessing. After Juan Trippe's retirement, Najeeb Halaby, a Washington socialite and federal aviation administrator under President Kennedy, had a brief spell as Pan Am chief. Halaby's Kennedy connections did not help him with the Nixon administration. Juan Trippe, who was still on the airline's board, told aides about getting a phone call one day from an angry Richard Nixon. Halaby had apparently annoyed the president by criticizing the administration for the airlines' problems. Nixon, according to this account, screamed: "If you don't get rid of Halaby, your airline will never get another foreign route!"

But Halaby resigned and the president's men obligingly came up with something better than a route: They actually promoted a courtship between Pan Am and TWA, the same combine the CAB had earlier rejected as flagrantly anticompetitive. American and Eastern were also enlisted as suitors. Donald Farmer, an attorney in the antitrust division of the Justice Department, got so concerned about all this that he wrote up mock merger proposals between all the Big Four and Pan Am, and then sat back and waited for the real ones to roll in.

Nixon's attorney general John Mitchell did his part, by playing matchmaker in the proposed Pan Am–TWA merger. After a visit from a Pan Am emissary, he sent a message to underlings in the Justice Department, saying that the merger, which hadn't even been formally filed, ought to be approved. An account of this blatantly improper approach eventually made its way into a Jack Anderson column, but the capital was too riveted by the Watergate revelations to pay much attention to this minor footnote to the whole affair.

But after Nixon, Pan Am was out of luck. Joining Laker on the first day of Kennedy's hearings was a top Justice Department official, Keith Clearwaters, who said flatly that the plan hatched in Brinegar's office and later rubber-stamped by the CAB was illegal. Clearwaters said the decision would be reversed, immediately. The news made the front page of *The New York Times* the next day. Airline reform, it seemed, was not too boring to generate headlines.

MOST ECONOMISTS BELIEVED THAT THE trucking industry was the logical place to begin deregulation. Ground transportation costs affected the prices of virtually all consumer goods; air travel was primarily a middle-class concern. But now airlines appeared the best place to start. Not only was their whole system of regulation ripe for reform, but air fares promised to provide consumers tangible evidence of deregulation's benefits: Increase competition, and prices would come tumbling down. It would be harder to demonstrate that an item at Sears Roebuck was cheaper because of trucking deregulation. In fact, the retailing giant was one of a number of strange bedfellows that formed a group to push for deregulation, ranging from Ralph Nader's aviation consumer group to the right-wing National Conservative Union. Sears's Washington lobbyists hoped that if airline deregulation was a success, trucking reform would be next.

Breyer first had to build his case, and he described it as a trial: He would gather the kind of evidence that a high-powered prosecutor might take into court, to leave no doubt in the mind of the jury—in this case, the traveling public—that grave injustices were being committed at their expense. The Senate had rarely attempted such an exhaustive inquiry into a government agency. Breyer recalled that its last attempt—a huge inquiry into the Federal Communications Commission—led to the resignation of one commissioner and the suicide of another. He could hardly have foreseen that Kennedy's airline hearings would see both suicide and scandal before they were through.

Breyer pulled in a couple of talented investigators to snoop around the CAB. He recruited Phil Bakes, a twenty-eight-year-old assistant Watergate prosecutor and Harvard Law School graduate and editor of the law review. He also hired Jim Michie, a former investigative reporter who'd covered New Orleans district attorney Jim Garrison's probe of the JFK assassination back in the late 1960s. The team had no contact with the vested interests trying to block their investigation and had, in fact, gleefully watched when Senate aviation subcommittee chief Howard Cannon, loyal as ever to the airlines, used his clout as head of the powerful Rules Committee to try to kill the budget for Kennedy's hearings. (He failed, but a joke circulated that "Kennedy may find himself parking out in Maryland if he doesn't lay off.") Turf is always a sensitive matter on Capitol Hill and Kennedy arguably had trespassed on Cannon's territory, but up to that point, Cannon had taken no action with respect to the airlines' improprieties.

Jim Michie and Phil Bakes began spending a lot of time at the CAB's drab headquarters at 1825 Connecticut Avenue, sifting through boxes of papers. Then Michie had a stroke of luck. He found a mole in the agency, a quiet thirty-six-year-old man named William Gingery, who had studied for the priesthood before becoming a civil servant. Gingery had been the agency's head of enforcement for about a year, and was embarrassed enough by CAB chairman Bob Timm and his golf junkets to help Kennedy's quest.

Michie heard whispers about a politically sensitive investigation being squelched to protect the airlines. Soon Gingery was doing a fair amount of snooping himself. He secretly provided Michie with confidential files, dashing out for middle-of-the-night photocopying sessions and then returning the documents to their proper place before morning.

Gingery was expected to testify on February 19 before Kennedy, who had resumed his hearings that month. "He was our star witness," Michie said, for Gingery could provide much detail about misuse of power by the political hacks at the aviation agency.

But a few days before he was scheduled to appear, Gingery vanished. He failed to call Michie as promised on the weekend and didn't answer repeated calls to the small apartment where he lived alone. Michie was frantic. None of Gingery's colleagues seemed to know where he had gone. After several days, Michie finally located someone who would check with the superintendent at Gingery's suburban Virginia apartment building.

Around eleven o'clock on the night of February 18, Michie's phone rang. Gingery had been found dead on the floor of his living room. He had apparently placed a high-powered hunting rifle in his mouth and pulled the trigger. A blood-spattered letter was found nearby.

Kennedy received Gingery's suicide note by mail a few days later. It was rambling and at times emotional. For twenty pages, Gingery spewed out rage and frustration at what he felt was an outright attempt by higher-ups at the board to deceive him. "Last Friday I learned that I am a fool," began one typical sentence. What Gingery knew was even worse than what Michie had suspected.

The story grew out of Watergate. The committee to re-elect President Nixon had twisted a few arms in the airline business, and two companies, Braniff and American, had made large, secret cash contributions in a manner right out of a spy novel. Braniff poured forty thousand dollars into the re-election coffers via its regional manager in Panama, Camilo Fabrega, who collected the money by selling Braniff tickets off the books and then sending the cash stuffed in envelopes on a plane to Dallas. American was even more agreeable, since it would need White House approval for its plan to merge with Western Air Lines. George Spater, successor to C. R. Smith, arranged through a Lebanese agent, Andre Tabourian, to raise seventy-five thousand dollars, all of it in hundred-dollar bills, again concealing the loot as on-board luggage. American later pleaded guilty to making an illegal campaign contribution in 1973, and Spater resigned and retired quietly to the English countryside, where in a sudden career change he became a scholar and an authority on Virginia Woolf. Despite its generous gift to the president, American's merger was turned down.

What would ultimately cause Gingery to take his life was the way in which this sordid matter was handled by the CAB. The full story had not come out. It turned out that the carriers maintained slush funds of hundreds of thousands of dollars—Braniff had amassed nearly $1 million by selling more than three thousand unreported tickets and funneling the income to a secret bank account. But the CAB launched an ineffectual investigation of its own and then abruptly ended it. The word came down from Chairman Timm's office that the investigation was officially closed.

There it sat until Gingery came along some months later. "He began to dig and he found it," Michie recalled. "His suicide note indicates he felt betrayed by the people whom he had trusted."

A week before his scheduled congressional testimony, Gingery had opened a CAB safe containing documents related to the airline industry. He then realized the case of the secret slush funds went well beyond the American and Braniff disclosures. Other airlines too had made questionable contributions but had never been charged. The case was dropped simply to protect the airlines from criminal prosecution. Gingery would have to tell this whole story before the Senate committee if he testified under oath.

Kennedy's staff was shocked. Michie, in particular, never quite accepted the man's suicide. "The guy seemed to be level-headed . . . he didn't give me any impression that he was going to blow his brains out." The rest of the staff was eager to avoid the unsavory implication that they had triggered the death by pressuring the man to appear, and had little to say in public. But the press was intrigued. Michie remembers the hearing right after Gingery's death was "packed" with journalists, fifteen or twenty television cameras, network crews, and dozens of newspaper reporters.

Kennedy felt, however, that this was a matter for the Watergate special prosecutor. Gingery's suicide note was turned over first to prosecutor Henry Ruth, and then to the Justice Department. About a year later, Justice announced, with no explanation, that the case was closed. The accepted version of events was that Gingery was a troubled man who would have taken his life anyway. One theory was that Gingery had a very close relationship with a man who was counsel at the CAB; the two men had gone to seminary together. Perhaps Gingery was distraught over the possibility, largely imagined, that he might somehow betray his close friend in his Senate testimony.

The public revelations of the CAB as a political instrument with its business conducted largely in secret were to dramatize the case for radical change. Ralph Nader stated that many airlines saw the Civil Aeronautics Board as "an instrument of political blackmail and extortion." And Senator Sam Ervin, who had led the congressional investigation into Watergate, observed that of all the industries in the United States, the airlines were "peculiarly susceptible" to political pressure. This was hardly what Harry Truman had envisioned when he had urged skeptics of the new CAB to "have faith" in the system back in 1938.

A much more serious abuse of power had been unearthed as well, a mysterious policy to freeze the growth of the nation's airline service by withholding any new route awards, a policy Breyer believed illegal.

Poking through the files up at the agency, Phil Bakes had found what Breyer would call the "smoking gun," a document that proved the existence of a secret arrangement begun under chairman Secor Browne, famous for his creed of "ain't nobody going no place." It was a memo written by one of the CAB's hearing judges, explaining why he couldn't take up a route case "pursuant to the instructions from the chairman's office" regarding new route authority. In effect, it confirmed that such a policy was being carried out. Breyer believed that the route freeze had more serious implications than even the airline slush funds, for it totally perverted the intent of the law.

Kennedy began questioning the board members about the alleged moratorium soon after the hearings resumed in 1975. By then Bob Timm had so embarrassed the White House with his golf junkets that he was asked to step down as chairman, although he remained a board member. The new chairman of the agency was Richard O'Melia, a one-time aide to red-baiting senator Joseph McCarthy.

O'Melia and Timm told Kennedy, under oath, that there was no truth to this tale of a route moratorium. They were apparently sure that there was no written record of it, as it was implemented only by inaction. But they were ignorant of the evidence that had fallen into the committee's hands.

Kennedy brought O'Melia and Timm back to the hearings and confronted the flustered pair with the written evidence of the scheme. O'Melia stunned the panel by abruptly blurting out: "The route moratorium is over, right now." He had confirmed the existence of an allegedly illegal scheme by ending it. "Deregulation began at that moment," Breyer would later say.

Just a few months later, the CAB formally ended the freeze by opening a proceeding—the first such in five years—to award new rights between Kennedy's hometown, Boston, and Detroit. A few days after that, a federal appeals court ruled that the CAB had acted improperly in approving the blatantly anticompetitive agreement among United, American, and TWA to jointly cut back their flights on certain routes. Soon Bob Timm was gone from the board for good. The rationale upholding the regime had begun to crack. "Once they departed from their perfect regulatory system, they were in a system that made no intellectual sense. From that moment on it was chaos," said Breyer.

Kennedy's aides had the nagging feeling that the inquiry into the airlines might be straying too far from the senator's traditional blue-collar Democratic constituency. After all, what were the problems of airline passengers to people without jobs, who had never been able to contemplate taking a flight on American or Pan Am? "There was no clamoring for this," Bakes recalled. "Inflation was the big problem then, the cost of energy; nobody was saying there was this over-whelming need for low-cost air travel."

That question came up one day when Kennedy moved his committee to Boston for a field hearing. Kennedy was immediately beset by protesters over his stand in favor of school busing, some of whom squeezed into the hearing room to listen to the testimony. Finally, one woman stood up and angrily demanded of Kennedy: "Why are you having these hearings? I can't buy an airline ticket!"

Kennedy was ready with a quick comeback. "That's why we are having these hearings," he said. "It's so that people like you can afford to fly."

The CAB, Kennedy said, spent almost all of its enforcement budget stamping out low fares, while ignoring complaints about price gouging. Kennedy found many examples of unsavory attempts to stamp out competition. One was the case of the "pirate flights," as CAB insiders dubbed it. In 1974, Beverly Hills press agent Erman Pessis proposed affordable flights from the West Coast to Europe. To circumvent inevitable rejection from the CAB, he planned to fly between Tijuana, Mexico, and Luxembourg, putting the operation outside the reach of the U.S. government—or so he thought. Those eager for the low fares he'd charge on his Air Europe flights would simply board a bus in California and cross the border.

CAB officials were not amused, and began an unseemly campaign to block the flights. They planted a story in the press that U.S. marshals were planning to board the first flight departing from Tijuana so they could force the plane down somewhere over Iowa, presumably to see how many Americans were aboard. The story may in fact have been false, but it had the desired effect of scaring away the company's customers. The outfit was forced to fold.

A panel of airline customers testified that they were forced to pay the highest fare possible, and the airlines ignored their complaints or needs.

Airline witnesses protested, but again, Kennedy was ready with an embarrassing piece of evidence, an American Airlines staff training manual that stated in bold letters: "American's basic sales policy is to sell the highest priced product that the customer is willing to buy to obtain the service he prefers."

The airlines had their day before Kennedy's panel. But since most of the senior executives in the business did not take the senator's threat of reform very seriously, they dispatched junior managers to make what they felt was a simple case for maintaining the status quo.

Lined up on the other side was a host of influential economists from the nation's most prestigious universities. They were virtually unanimous in arguing that airline regulation had to go. "If you poked an economist then and said 'airlines,' they'd say 'deregulate,' " said Mike Levine, then a law professor at Cal Tech and the University of Southern California.

Cornell professor and New York State utilities regulator Alfred Kahn came along to articulate this view, and Kennedy's staff was dazzled. Every bit the ham that Laker had been, Kahn displayed the levity of a Borscht Belt comedian and a peerless grasp of the subject. He was, someone joked, a "standup economist."

Kahn possessed an unusual blend of brilliance and humility. The son of Russian immigrants, he had been a child prodigy, graduating first in his class from New York University at age eighteen, later getting his Ph.D. in economics from Yale. What brought him to the attention of Kennedy's committee was his two-volume work entitled *The Economics of Regulation*. His main thesis was that regulation is imperfect and that where possible, even imperfect competition is preferable. Regulators naturally tend to protect the companies they are regulating, he wrote, and that in turn breeds inefficiency and excessive prices, whereas industries like the airlines might normally be competitive in the absence of regulation. The airlines' "sandwich war" was a classic case of this syndrome.

Other economists had started to write about the airlines as well. The airline regulatory system had grown up around the idea that air transportation was a public utility like the rails or electricity or telephones, and that its rates must reflect a reasonable rate of return so that capital could be plowed into building for increased needs.

But economists had noticed something the CAB hadn't: The airlines were not really a natural monopoly, in the way railroads or power companies were—the skies, unlike pipelines, could admit many newcomers. In theory, the only things needed to enter the airline business were a plane, people to fly it, and permission to land it somewhere. This led to the theory called "contestability of markets," which held that if airlines were free to enter and exit markets at will, fares would go down, if not through actual competition, then through the threat of competition. Given the mobility of airplanes, the ease of entry into a given market would always pose the possibility of a new company coming in and challenging inadequate service or exorbitant fares, thus keeping the incumbents honest. A corollary to this notion was the economists' belief that there were no economies of scale in the airline business; a small company could compete just as effectively as a larger one, because there were no inherent advantages to huge size.

One argument frequently raised against deregulation, however, was uncertainty about what would result. Critics, including most of the major airlines, said it was too risky to tamper with the system, which was at least delivering most people safely to their destinations.

This defense had one glaring flaw. Airlines could already operate free of CAB regulation within Texas and California, the only states large and populous enough to support exclusively intrastate service. The federal government only regulated airlines that flew across state borders, so those two states provided a test kitchen for the deregulation theory.

By the time Kennedy's hearings began, a number of exclusively intrastate lines had sprung up, such as Pacific Southwest Airlines in California and Texas's Southwest Airlines. They managed to charge about half the fare that the rest of the airlines charged for an interstate trip of the same distance. Between Dallas and Houston the fare was fourteen dollars on off hours, but it was double that between Washington and New York, although the mileage was the same.

Mike Levine had been the first to study this anomaly as a student at Yale Law School in the 1960s. Levine had spent a few weeks in California researching the state's airline business and won a prize for his paper, which was published by the *Yale Law Journal*. It was soon noticed by Kahn and other more senior economists who were writing about deregulation.

Witnesses for American, United, and other major airlines had trouble explaining to Kennedy's satisfaction the discrepancy between the intrastate fares and those charged elsewhere. The weather is worse in the Northeast, they argued, and the routes had more traffic. "That was ridiculous," said Levine. "The only reason air travel worked so well in California was because it wasn't regulated."

When it was all over, Stephen Breyer returned to Harvard and retreated into his office. He emerged three months later with a massive report, a blueprint for opening the airline industry to competition. It was, in today's terms, a modest proposal. It recommended that airlines have greater freedom to enter new routes, and even that was called "controversial" in press reports, showing just how entrenched the system had become. The CAB members were not spared; the report said the hearings "reveal a strong likelihood of highly improper and possibly criminal behavior on the part of the Board members themselves," although the Justice Department never pursued the matter. Breyer did not want to become a permanent fixture on Capitol Hill, and he eventually went back to teaching full-time. A few years later he was appointed a judge on the federal appeals court in Boston. His involvement in deregulation was never to get the prominence it deserved.

President Ford introduced an airline "regulatory reform" bill, and Kennedy soon proposed his own bill. Newspaper columnists were agog. One pundit described the investigation as "Kennedy's finest hour," and indeed it seemed he was already reaping the benefits. Abroad, Kennedy was considered heir apparent to the White House. When he took a swing through the Middle East and Europe, he was feted by kings and heads of state as if he had taken his rightful place in the Oval Office. His excursion into airline regulation had enhanced his stature: He'd been hailed as a champion of consumers, had succeeded in reversing an odious government policy, and had won warm notices from the press. And Pan Am was still flying. The airline would continue to defy reports of its imminent demise for years.

It was only a little while before Alfred Kahn would say: "We are going to get the airline eggs so scrambled that no one is ever going to be able to unscramble them."

4

THE
UNITED FRONT
CRUMBLES

*Deregulation will be the greatest
thing to happen to the airlines
since the jet engine.*
—RICHARD FERRIS

J ust as they had right after the airmail scandal of the early 1930s,
the chiefs of the nation's biggest airlines journeyed to Washington in the mid-1970s to kill the nascent reform movement.
One typical response came from Donald Nyrop, the crusty old-time
chairman of Northwest Airlines, who just looked bored during the
airlines' strategy sessions. "He looked up and said, 'Well, we'll just
form a committee to get rid of it,' " recalled a witness. "Then he
went right back to reading *The Wall Street Journal.*"

Not all the airline executives were as sanguine as Donald Nyrop,
however. Airline deregulation had demonstrated enormous appeal to
the voters in the 1976 elections. "Remember, low fares get votes
without costing the politician a single cent," said Freddie Laker,
voicing an irresistible pitch to a candidate for high office. On a spring
day in 1977, in a hushed Senate hearing room, it finally became too
much for one staunch airline defender to bear.

As a panel of airline witnesses finished testifying, Phil Bakes,
whom Kennedy had promoted to Breyer's old position, looked up
from his seat to see a tough-looking man approaching him.

"You fucking academic pinhead!" the man shouted at Bakes.
"You don't know shit. You can't deregulate this industry, you're going
to wreck it. You don't know a goddamn thing!"

Bakes sat speechless as the wild-eyed stranger continued his harangue. "Who the hell is this?" he wondered. And so it was that he and other startled onlookers were treated to some of the first public utterances on deregulation from Robert Crandall, the man who would so personify its aftermath.

Crandall, despite the temper so crudely displayed that day, was at age forty-one a highly regarded senior vice-president of marketing at American Airlines. His peers even considered him the company's future chairman, although he hardly was the model of a smooth CEO. He wore his hair in a slicked-back pompadour and his angular features could at times seem menacing. Some colleagues even called him "Fang," in an unkind reference to his crooked teeth, which he later had fixed.

Crandall had traveled to Washington to help his boss, American chairman Al Casey, make the case that deregulation would be a dangerous step and would cause chaos for air travelers. They also believed it would cost them their jobs.

American had reason to be worried. At the time, the company was in awful shape. In 1975 it lost $20 million, battered by the recession and the energy crisis, and the long-term outlook was even worse. It had a fleet of aging, gas-guzzling jets that left it even more vulnerable to the whims of the OPEC oil cartel; its jet fuel bill alone had ballooned by $180 million in one year. The airline served the kinds of long-distance routes that would immediately be jammed by newcomers once the government opened up the industry to competition.

The company also had other, largely self-inflicted problems. After the Watergate scandal had carried off George Spater, C. R. Smith came back to American for a brief spell as interim chairman. He found a very different airline from the one he'd left in 1968. Spater, at least, had tried to bring the carrier's management into the modern age, hiring a host of young MBAs. Smith, a traditionalist, fired some of the bright young recruits, replacing them with his cronies. The company floundered as it was hit with some of the worst economic times since the industry's beginnings in the 1930s. One former executive said, "The airline in one year lost five years—it was a big step back." Smith finally retired for good, and the board hired Casey, then the respected CEO of the Times Mirror Company. By then Bob Crandall, a former TWA executive with the very sort of competitive streak that regulation had discouraged, had arrived on the airline's financial side. When the top position opened in American's moribund marketing department, Crandall, who had virtually no relevant experience, convinced Casey to give it to him.

Crandall soon assembled a staff he drove mercilessly. He became notorious for his marathon Monday staff meetings, at which every department head reporting to him made presentations. The session would start before noon and often go, with barely a break, until midnight. Each manager would be called to go over the events of the previous week; it seemed, said one former manager, that each delayed flight and lost bag would have to be accounted for and dissected in detail. People wondered where Crandall got his energy; he seemed to fuel himself by chain-smoking cigarettes and drinking endless cups of coffee.

He would push others as hard as he drove himself. One day, a passenger sales manager made what was obviously an incomplete presentation. "Everyone sank down in their chairs" as Crandall kept probing and failing to get answers, one witness recalled. The next day, the hapless manager was transferred out of headquarters to a low-level sales job in an undesirable station referred to as East Armpit. A popular refrain around the office was: "Crandall eats nails for breakfast."

Some American employees began to feel Crandall's hard-driving style was taking a toll on their personal lives. When he began holding weekend staff meetings with increasing frequency, the wives of his subordinates drew straws to choose an emissary to beg Crandall to go a little easier. He reportedly did back off a bit, on others, but not on himself. Crandall had such an inhuman appetite for work that employees would concoct ways of distracting their boss; they took to constantly refilling his ever-present coffee cup in the hope that he would take more frequent bathroom breaks.

Crandall's rise could not be attributed totally to obsessive work habits. He had an extraordinary ability to absorb information and spew out analyses, almost like the computers he'd developed as a specialty early on. Several times a month, he would try to visit American workers in the field. On one of these trips, a former subordinate recalled, one employee stood up and asked Crandall a "ridiculously obscure" question about some statistic—"How many available seat-miles do we have between Pittsburgh and Los Angeles for the month of April?" Crandall began to blurt out the answer. "I looked up and I could see what was happening: He realized he was sounding like an automaton," the former colleague said. "He caught himself, he faked a struggle: 'Oh, wait a minute, let me think about that,' and then he gave the answer. And I was thinking, 'Come on, how could you possibly know that?' "

Close associates observed that Crandall did not seem to be propelled by a desire for riches or power; in fact he was adept at delegating and sharing responsibility. Early on he showed an urge to lead. His youth may have forged his intense and somewhat aloof manner. His father was a peripatetic insurance salesman who moved his family so frequently that Crandall attended fourteen schools in twelve years. The family finally settled in Barrington, Rhode Island, long enough for young Crandall to finish high school and begin a romance with a classmade, Jan Schmults. The two married several years later.

His combativeness stood out early. High-school friends recall that even on social occasions Crandall would turn the conversation into a loud debate on politics or philosophy, punctuating his arguments by pounding the table, determined to wear down his opponents. "He's an enormously, intensely competitive guy—the kind of competitiveness you normally see in athletes," said one old acquaintance.

After attending Wharton Business School, Crandall worked at Eastman Kodak and, later, Hallmark Cards, where he first learned about the nascent computer business. The airlines intrigued him; he served a brief stint as a low-level accountant at the Air Transport Association in Washington. Crandall got his first high-ranking airline job at age thirty-one, as assistant treasurer at TWA, where he was in charge of data processing. There he established a monkish work routine. He would rise at 5:00 A.M., run a few miles, board the commuter train from his home in New Jersey, and be at his desk in midtown Manhattan by seven. He would normally stay there until 8:00 or 9:00 P.M. His workaholic habits did not advance him as fast as he had hoped, however, and when he was passed over for the job of chief financial officer, he left the airline for a treasurer's job at Bloomingdale's. He later said he was "bored stiff" by retailing, and in 1973 he moved twenty blocks south to American's headquarters at 633 Third Avenue.

Crandall was part of a new generation of executives who would bring the airlines out of their hidebound ways. But the vestiges of the club would prove hard to shake. Until the late 1970s, four of the country's five largest airlines were based within a few blocks of each other in midtown Manhattan, a geographical reality that underscored the industry's closeness. Eastern was headquartered at Rockefeller Center at Fifth Avenue and Forty-ninth Street, reflecting its long association with the Rockefeller family, the company's largest shareholder. Pan Am had the top floors of its namesake skyscraper on Park

Avenue and Forty-fifth, and American and TWA were right across the street from each other at Third Avenue and Fortieth Street. American and TWA employees could even look in each other's windows.

Airline executives would meet for lunch nearly every day at the Wings Club, an exclusive aviation fraternity located in the Biltmore Hotel right next to the Pan Am Building. Often, they were busy trying to merge their companies. At some time or another, each of the four New York–based majors had discussed a merger with the other three. One of Crandall's first projects had been the proposed combine of American and Pan Am.

United Airlines was different. Not only was it separated from the industry club by its Chicago location, but its top management had trained in an unregulated industry, the hotel business. Its chairman, Eddie Carlson, had been the chairman of Seattle-based Western International Hotels (later known as Westin) when the chain was bought by United in 1970. Carlson went onto United's board and shortly thereafter was named chairman.

Like the fabled Pat Patterson, Carlson was a paternalistic manager who traveled often to the airline's stations, carrying his little leatherbound notebooks called "Ready Eddies," in which he'd jot down questions from employees with promises to get back soon with an answer—which he invariably did. He had a remarkable memory, and would remember not only the names of the workers he visited once a year but their families' names and the ages of their children.

In 1971, Carlson brought over to the airline a young executive named Dick Ferris, who had once been his personal assistant at the hotel company.

If Bob Crandall appeared too raffish for the executive suite, then Ferris was quite the opposite. Tall and conventionally handsome, always impeccably dressed, Ferris would dominate any group he walked into, like a smiling politician.

Ferris grew up in Berkeley, California. After graduation from high school, he joined the Army and wound up as the manager of a club for noncommissioned officers in Tokyo. Once discharged, Ferris headed to Ithaca, New York, to enroll in the Cornell Hotel School, working his way through as a cook and bartender at the local Statler Inn. He had gone on to manage several Western International hotels, in such places as New York City and Johannesburg, South Africa.

Ferris, his colleagues thought, was obviously being groomed for better things. "He wasn't some guy who climbed out of a monkeywrench job," said a United veteran. "He had class. Ferris wore the best suits; sometimes people had to tell him, 'Don't wear the gold cufflinks when you're talking to the mechanics.' "

Early on, Ferris traveled around with Carlson and tried to adopt his boss's folksy style. He would drop into the cockpit and chat with the flight crews; he'd politely inquire after employees' spouses. But he lacked Carlson's amazing memory for detail, and his efforts to imitate Carlson seemed forced. Some of the pilots were suspicious of this smooth young man who was Carlson's heir apparent.

Ferris became the president of United Airlines in 1974 and soon found a way to ingratiate himself with the pilots: He'd be a flyboy himself. The idea first came up on a trip to Hawaii when Ferris, as usual, slipped into the cockpit to chat up the crew. The pilot, a longtime United captain named Jack Starr, took note of Ferris's obvious interest in the controls of the 747 and asked him if he'd ever wanted to learn how to fly. Ferris confessed that he had, but had never found the time.

A few weeks later, Captain Starr showed up unannounced at Ferris's office and told the president that if he was serious about learning to fly, he would be glad to teach him. Ferris begged off, saying he was just too busy. A few weeks later, Starr tried again, this time giving Ferris a few books on the subject.

When he was sitting next to Eddie Carlson on a flight not long after that, Ferris pulled out one of the piloting books and started to leaf through it.

"What are you doing?" Carlson said.

"I'm just starting to read about flying," Ferris replied.

"You haven't got time for that," the chairman warned him.

"That decided it for me," Ferris recalled. When the persistent Captain Starr showed up once again, Ferris scheduled him for a series of lessons at 7:00 A.M. on Sundays—the only time he could spare. After seven hours flying with Starr in a single-engine Cessna 172 from little Palwaukee Airport outside Chicago, Ferris soloed. But he didn't stop there; after he got his pilot's license, Ferris went on to earn a multiengine rating and then learned how to fly a Lear jet.

Ferris often flew himself to the airline's far-flung stations, sometimes covering three or four of them in a day, and his flying skills gave him new insights into many of the technical issues an airline chief ought to know about. Eventually, he would test-fly aircraft that United was considering purchasing, such as the advanced 767 jet from Boeing. But flying also helped him to win acceptance from United's pilots, most of whom were long-term veterans—members of a tight fraternity who had been skeptical about this former hotel executive who was making decisions about their lives. The leaders of the Air Line Pilots Association at United did warm up to Ferris after that, and even jokingly awarded him a union seniority number.

Carlson and Ferris, with their hotel background, soon began questioning the need for regulation. United's position as the nation's largest airline had put it at a severe disadantage under the CAB's peculiar regulatory logic. The board refused to let United fly across the Pacific, simply because it was a "domestic" carrier, yet it would not give United any more domestic routes either, because it already had more than anybody else. Instead, the board routinely awarded them to smaller airlines, such as Continental, Northwest, or Western, to create a more balanced distribution of route rights.

United's Washington lobbyist was Monte Lazarus, a former aide to CAB chairman Secor Browne, putative author of the infamous route moratorium. By the mid-1970s, however, Lazarus was a born-again deregulator, and he set about convincing his superiors at United that they could do much better without regulation. Many observers believed it was the CAB's route freeze and United's belief that it would never be able to expand that ultimately broke up the club and ensured the passage of the deregulation law that so many of its members feared.

The import of United's defection could not be underestimated. It left the airlines without the unanimity that would have allowed the Air Transport Association to pour lots of money into a lobbying campaign to stop deregulation. To Senator Kennedy's deregulation-minded staff that was exciting news. United's independence meant that Kennedy's chief opposition would be rendered toothless.

Ferris and Lazarus came to the Senate to talk to Phil Bakes about what they wanted in the legislation. "They were the first ones through the door," Bakes said. "And it's sort of like being a prosecutor—the first ones in the door can negotiate the best deal with us." United not only was barred from entering new routes, it couldn't shed the money-losers that were dragging down profits. But to allow airlines to desert communities willy-nilly would be political suicide. So Bakes and the United officials got down to political horse trading, with Bakes offering more liberal route entry and exit provisions and pricing freedoms in exchange for United's understanding about the need to maintain service to some communities dear to the hearts of certain senators.

When a smaller pro-deregulation airline—Denver-based Frontier—tried playing the game, it was rebuffed. The company would have clout disproportionate to its size because of the many small communities it served, and would continue to serve. At least, that was the trump card put down by two senior Frontier executives who called on Bakes. They wanted something in exchange for their support, however—money. "What they wanted was unconscionable," Bakes said. Specifically, they wanted a provision in the bill that would guarantee Frontier several million dollars in retroactive federal subsidies. Bakes turned them down. "We already had United," he said. "We didn't need Frontier."

Ferris chose to declare his support for deregulation at the Wings Club in New York City on March 16, 1977, as if to taunt his rivals by breaking ranks on their home turf. First, though, Ferris went to Washington for a private meeting in Senator Kennedy's office. Kennedy was impressed by the good-looking airline chief, who seemed to be the perfect pitchman for his deregulation cause. But while Ferris's action set off a furor, in hindsight his ideas were conservative compared with what ultimately came about. Ferris thought that perhaps fares could go up or down by 10 percent each year, and that route franchises should be continued. Ferris also warned that consumers shouldn't be gulled by promises of cheap fares forever. "In the long term, air fares are going to go up," he predicted.

Casey publicly berated Ferris soon after that, claiming that his ideas would "mean much higher prices for the average customer," the opposite of what the deregulators claimed would happen. Casey, however, believed that American would not even be around long enough to raise fares if deregulation came to pass.

United and American did agree on one thing. Something had to be done about the airline industry's poor financial performance. United reckoned that the industry would need $5 billion to buy the next generation of aircraft. The airlines' profits had been pathetic, with the industry earning a return on investment of around 3 percent a year. Ferris knew that the days of government handouts were over and feared the industry could be strangled by well-meaning regulators. "There is a real danger that unless something is done, the airlines may soon be in the same position as the Northeast passenger railroads . . . to be a ward of the state," he told a Senate committee.

Still, the people at American thought United was a turncoat, motivated simply by greed. Ferris and Crandall, who in the 1980s would pilot the two largest airlines in the United States, soon became personal rivals. Ferris, in fact, liked to do imitations of Crandall whenever he could, pounding his fists in parody and growling in a gravelly voice. The two men would carry on the tradition of C. R.

Smith and Pat Patterson, trying to beat each other out at any opportunity.

CRANDALL AND OTHER DEREGULATION FOES finally recognized they were beaten when they lost the ever-reliable friend of the industry, Senator Howard Cannon. The Nevada Democrat had been their best hope, since his powerful aviation subcommittee could block any reform effort by simply refusing to release a bill. Cannon knew all the airline chiefs personally and occasionally flew as a guest on their planes. He had dutifully raised a fuss when Kennedy had traipsed on his airline turf, yet the airlines overlooked an obvious point. While Cannon may have been their man in Congress, his re-election depended on the support of his home state. And his state's casinos wanted more of the cheap charter flights the scheduled airlines so vigorously opposed.

Another reason for Cannon to reconsider was that Kennedy was clearly going to make hay out of the airline reform matter, and the only way Cannon could share the glory would be to jump aboard and claim the jurisdiction that was rightfully his.

One day Cannon gave a luncheon speech for the Aero Club in Washington, an assortment of aviation lawyers, lobbyists, government regulators, and military men. No one was quite sure what the senator would say, so when Cannon opened with a few choice insults aimed at regulatory reform and Ted Kennedy, "the smiles on the faces of the airline people in the room were very large," recalled Mary Schuman, an aide to Senator Warren Magnuson. Some people even got up in midspeech and left the room to call back to their headquarters to give them the news: "Howard's not going to do anything crazy."

Cannon got to the very end of his speech and in one brief paragraph said he was going to draft a bill, introduce it, and reform regulation of the airlines. Everyone was stunned. Cannon did in fact submit the bill himself and it later became known as the Cannon-Kennedy Airline Deregulation Act or, occasionally, as the Kennedy-Cannon act, depending on one's allegiance.

FOR A TIME, CRANDALL WAS absorbed in his battle against Washington, ordering his staff to put together a slide show to accompany his diatribes. His favorite illustration showed Ted Kennedy, Gerry Ford, Ralph Nader, and Jimmy Carter side by side, with the tag line: "There has to be something wrong when these men can agree on something." Yet that image spoke volumes about why Crandall was losing: Even before Ferris's official defection, he couldn't fight an issue with such bipartisan appeal. Instead he channeled his rage into a management tactic he called "competitive anger."

President Ford had installed a soft-spoken lawyer named John Robson as chairman of the Civil Aeronautics Board after the Timm fiasco. Robson was hardly a rabid free-trader, and during his confirmation hearing he quoted Winston Churchill's famous remark: "I did not come here to preside over the dissolution of the British Empire." Yet it seemed to Bob Crandall that Robson could very well cause the dissolution of American Airlines. Robson had picked up on the signals from Capitol Hill and in one of his first tentative steps toward competition, had decided to give charter airlines freedom to sell tickets to anyone who wanted them.

One day in 1976 Crandall decided to get even. He convened a large meeting in the boardroom at American Airlines' Third Avenue headquarters in New York. About three dozen executives crowded around the big table—from marketing, from finance, from the planning and pricing departments. Their mission was to come up with a way to compete with the charter operators who, thanks to the CAB, were draining the backs of American's planes of passengers, with their low unrestricted prices on flights coast to coast.

As the meeting started, Crandall walked up to a blackboard and sketched two airplanes side by side.

"This guy over here is the charter guy," Crandall told the group as he pointed to one of his drawings. "He has the advantage of very low costs—he has low labor costs, he has low overheads." A charter airline, he noted, can operate at a much lower level of fixed costs than a scheduled airline, which keeps its aircraft going most of the time and must have a large infrastructure to support those operations. The charter carrier's cost per seat was substantially lower than the scheduled airline's. Crandall then turned to the other airplane on the board, the scheduled carrier. "Now, here's an airplane flying in the same airspace, five miles away from the charter airplane, and it has some empty seats on it," he said. "What is the cost of those seats?"

Crandall and his team considered the cost of operating that flight and divided it by the total number of seats on their airplane. The result indicated their operating cost per seat was substantially higher than the charter airplane's. But as they debated the cost analysis, they concluded that they didn't have to consider the average cost of all the seats but only the cost of operating the empty seats on their airplane. About five or six of every ten seats on their plane would have paying passengers in them, enough to cover most of the cost of operating the flight.

Since American already had covered many of its costs with the customers it had, the cost of its empty seats was considerably lower than the charter carrier's. If American sold its empty seats with the same restrictions imposed by the charter operator, it would actually have lower costs.

American's staff later looked back on that day as a watershed in the company's fortunes. For the next six months Crandall's staff worked sixteen-hour days, seven days a week, on the concept that emerged from that meeting. In early 1977 it knocked more than a third off its coach prices and called them "Super Savers," and with the government's blessing put them on sale all over the country. The move had the desired effect. Without a price advantage, the no-frills charters could hardly compete against the perceived superiority of scheduled service. "It ultimately drove the charters out of business," according to executive Wes Kaldahl, one of Crandall's closest associates at American. Crandall admitted he had been given a push by the reformers in Washington. "We never would have thought about it at all, absent the stimulus of the free market in the form of that charter operator." Deregulation, at least in spirit, had already begun.

The advent of discounts also meant that airlines had to start keeping track of how many seats they sold at different fares. Using the computers just appearing in airline offices, the carriers could allocate their space and quickly adjust fare type to demand. "Yield management"—the arcane art of juggling and rejuggling the number of airline seats available at different prices on a specific flight—had arrived. The system would make it possible for one passenger paying $399 for a ticket to find himself seated next to someone who'd paid $99.

Critics would later label it the "dark science," charging that yield management was really another name for bait-and-switch. It was the objective so bluntly expressed in the old American training manual used by Kennedy in his hearings: "to sell the highest priced product that the customer is willing to buy." It could be accomplished much more efficiently without regulation.

American had gotten a jump on United with its Super Savers, although United was quick to respond. But then Crandall started getting a flood of complaints from an unlikely source, his best customers.

Regulation, after all, had encouraged the kinds of inefficiencies that benefited business travelers: Half-empty planes meant they could always count on having an extra seat or two to themselves. After Super Savers, angry letters poured in from regular customers alarmed that the extra seat was filled, especially when its occupant was a garrulous tourist or an unruly toddler.

Crandall jokingly called his budget customers "the pukes," but he realized that this new market could threaten his old one. It was simply inequitable. The infrequent flyers were getting the benefit of the low fares, while the business travelers paid more for worse service.

Sometime after Super Savers took off, Crandall asked Michael Derchin, who was working for him as head of marketing planning, to find a way to reward repeat customers. "We knew that deregulation was coming," said Derchin. "We had to do two things: lock in the frequent flyer so the other guy couldn't steal him; and two, reward him for his patronage."

Derchin sent Crandall what became the blueprint for the first frequent-flyer plan, based on the principle that the more you flew, the more credits you got. Crandall, who wrote terse comments in the margin of whatever he received, scrawled on Derchin's voluminous report: "excellent job."

Yet when it was brought up at a managers' meeting, the proposal was openly ridiculed by some of those present. "The reaction was 'what are these guys smoking?' It was just that they had all worked under regulation. Nobody did stuff like that back in those days," recalled Derchin.

"It was hardly Einsteinian thinking" that went into the nation's first frequent-flyer plan, Crandall cracked. It was an unabashed ripoff of the Green Stamps formula. The aim would be to give airline passengers a financial incentive to stick with one company. American's people had noticed that United had something called the Million-Mile Club: For every hundred thousand miles the customer flew, he got a star. But all United gave these peripatetic travelers was a tacky wall plaque on which to display their stars. One day, American executive Thomas Plaskett paid a sales call on a big customer. "He was so proud of himself, he had ten stars on his plaque." Plaskett thought that this was incredible—the man had flown a million miles on United and that was all they could do for him. "Whatever we did, we decided it had to capitalize on the basic human emotion—greed," said Plaskett. Work on the program, however, would take four years, because the airline lacked the necessary computer technology.

• • •

THE MOST POWERFUL AND BY far the most controversial of the airline innovations was invisible to customers.

To sell discount seats, and to keep track of all the air fares deregulation would produce, the airlines needed advanced computers. As late as the 1960s, airlines were still doing many tasks manually and when taking reservations relied heavily on such rudimentary tools as the telephone and scratch pad. For example, United reservations offices in major cities used a primitive "iron wheel" to keep track of bookings. Reservations clerks sat at large round tables, and in the middle of each was a big iron wheel that revolved like a giant Lazy Susan. Attached to the rim of the wheel were reservations sheets for United's various flights from that city for the next thirty days. As the clerks answered phone calls from passengers or travel agents, they spun the wheel until they found the appropriate flight sheet and checked off the number of passengers being booked on that flight. That night, the various offices would exchange reservations data by telemeter.

In the early 1960s, American had begun work on an in-house computer reservations system called Sabre, and was waiting to see which of the competing vendors being tested at rival carriers would come to provide the industry's standard software. But by the time he got to American, Crandall recalled, the company had fallen well behind the rest of the Big Four in data processing: Instead of using modern computer terminals, most of its reservations offices were still using outmoded machines that were essentially glorified typewriters. Crandall was shocked to learn that two thousand state-of-the-art computer terminals American had purchased years before were sitting in a warehouse in Tulsa, gathering dust. He immediately had them installed at American's reservations offices.

The airlines faced an enormous investment if each was to build up a powerful computer reservations system, capable of taking reservations not only on their own flights but on all other airlines', since many itineraries involved more than one carrier. The airlines' low profit margins would barely permit them to acquire needed planes, much less embark on such ambitious projects. In 1970, the biggest airlines got together and decided it made more sense to have one jointly owned industry system that would be installed in their own offices and in travel agencies all around the country. They presented the plan, called ATARS, to the appropriate people in Washington, and to their shock, the Justice Department said it would take the airlines to court for violating the Sherman Antitrust Act if they proceeded.

This little-remembered episode would have grave consequences. The threat of antitrust action would ultimately kill this and repeated efforts by the airlines to form a single, unbiased reservations system. That made it inevitable that each airline would go its own way—and that the strongest and biggest companies would naturally develop the best systems. Back in 1970, few foresaw the enormous power these systems would confer on their owners, allowing them, in some cases, to dominate a market and ultimately, some charged, to drive competitors out of business. Arguably, all the problems with the airline computer reservations systems thereafter would not exist had that joint plan gone forward. Said Charles Rule, head of the Justice Department's antitrust division during the mid-1980s: "It is one example where antitrust enforcement actually led to more antitrust problems later on."

In 1975, major airlines banded together again, this time with the American Society of Travel Agents, whose role as industry middlemen was increasing. The CAB gave them immunity from antitrust prosecution, but only to "talk"—and there was some question whether the actual system they proposed would ever be blessed. But the joint industry computer project was doomed in any event when, in July of that year, United's Dick Ferris broke ranks with the industry, pulling his company out of the talks with little explanation.

His motives became clear six months later, when United dropped a bombshell: It was going to get a big jump on its competitors by selling its own computer reservations system—Apollo—to travel agencies, revolutionizing the way air travel was sold. Agents who could afford to lease the equipment from United could make reservations electronically for hundreds of airlines, even for some hotels and rental car companies. It was a major advance: Travel agents then had to look up schedules and fares in weighty "flight guides" and write out airline tickets by hand.

American, Eastern, and TWA were furious. Crandall had believed that a joint system still had a chance; now he'd have to respond to Ferris. Crandall had a computer wizard on his staff named Max Hopper who had joined American after previous jobs at Shell Oil, Electronic Data Systems, and United Airlines. So important was Hopper's Sabre system to American that he eventually became the airline's second-highest-paid executive. Hopper worked feverishly to make sure American's Sabre system could compete with United's. TWA soon joined the fray. The battle for electronic control of the airlines' distribution system had started.

But Ferris made a blunder. A few weeks later, an organization called the Woodside Group, which included many of the nation's largest commercial travel agencies, held a meeting at Atlanta's Peachtree Plaza Hotel to listen to the three airlines describe their new travel agency automation systems. United, apparently convinced it easily would dominate the automation market, refused to attend. TWA executives arrived unprepared.

When American's turn came, Crandall put on a bravura performance. In style, Crandall was a descendant of the legendary John Patterson, the late-nineteenth-century founder of National Cash Register, who invented "organized, hyperthyroid, high-pressure salesmanship in the United States," wrote chronicler Nicholas von Hoffman. Patterson's banshee-style pitches, with shouts of "Kill them—crush them," would be admirably evoked by Crandall in his sales presentations. At the Atlanta session, Crandall pounded the podium, battering into the heads of his listeners that they need look no further than Sabre for their computer needs. Max Hopper had produced a slick slide show illustrating how Sabre would bring the agencies out of the dark ages, how it would display all airline schedules and fares, make reservations, and even print tickets.

"All the major commercial agencies of the country on that day went with Sabre," said Woodside Group director Thornton Clark, and that gave American an edge that it still commands today. Ferris's arrogance had cost United dearly.

At first, United, American, and TWA believed that no more than a few hundred of the largest agencies would ever order the computer equipment. After all, the airline vendors were charging agencies hundreds of dollars a year for each computer terminal, as well as a small fee for each ticket they issued. But they were quickly proven wrong. The cost of hardware was dropping dramatically and deregulation produced such a bewildering variety of discount air fares and purchase conditions that travel agents needed computers to stay current with all the prices available to their customers, as well as the constantly changing airline flight schedules. The price the airlines charged kept coming down.

So United figured out a way to recover from American's initial success in the travel agency competition: It gave some agents the equipment free, and reportedly even paid some valued agency customers to go with Apollo rather than Sabre. Soon this would become another arena for cutthroat competition, conducted away from public view.

Thus, well before Alfred Kahn arrived in Washington in mid-1977, the biggest airlines already were working on the sophisticated means that they would later use to thwart the intent of the deregulators. The reformers were oblivious to all this, and some would later confess that they blundered in not recognizing earlier how the computers would threaten competition. What the deregulators did see at the time was all good: that even the most tentative encouragement from Washington had produced a rash of low fares.

One of the more original plans had emanated from an outfit down in Texas, run by a pair who would wield as much influence as Crandall and Ferris on the deregulated airlines of the 1980s.

5

THE NEW
FLYBOYS

rank Lorenzo met Donald Burr at a party in New Orleans
sometime in 1969. Both were young Manhattan investors
specializing in airlines. At age twenty-eight, Burr was vice-
president of the National Aviation Corporation, a well-known aviation
finance firm. The twenty-nine-year-old Lorenzo had just formed an
investment company called Jet Capital and had picked up a few clients
in the Caribbean.

The two were immediately drawn to each other. As Burr recalled,
they shared a fascination with the airlines that went beyond sensing
opportunities for profitable stock trading. Burr had been president
of his flying club at Stanford University, and Lorenzo had always
wanted to fly. They'd been at Harvard Business School two years
apart, and had each ventured into the ailing airline business, which
had rarely attracted the best business school graduates. The two also
harbored fantasies of running an airline themselves.

They were in New Orleans scouting investment possibilities at a
meeting of "Local Service Airlines." These were the wallflowers of
the industry—airlines like Ozark, Mohawk, and Allegheny, whose
names suggested their regional limitations. Deregulation was a few
years away, but it would definitely spell the end for this breed of
airline, which fed on fat federal subsidies that guaranteed air service

to places ignored by the big airlines. For Lorenzo and his friends, however, this endangered airline category would provide entree into the business.

Soon after they returned to Manhattan, Lorenzo and his partner, Robert Carney, teamed with Burr in an unsuccessful attempt to take over Mohawk Airlines. But then they found the chance they had been waiting for. Bankers were about to put a small Houston line, Texas International, into receivership. Burr had invested in the money-losing company, and faced with the loss of his capital, he urged that Lorenzo and Carney be brought in to resuscitate the airline, which had a $7 million negative net worth.

In the fall of 1972 Lorenzo suddenly found himself president of what was quite possibly the worst airline in America. It had begun as Trans Texas Airlines, serving places like Texarkana, Waco, and Wichita Falls. By virtue of a milk-run flight across the Mexican border, it had turned itself into Texas "International" by the early 1970s. The public was not fooled and nicknamed the operation "Tree Tops" and "Try Try Again." It had been supported for years by millions of dollars in federal subsidies and had little incentive to innovate. "Everyone in Texas had had their bag lost by us at least once. It was a thoroughly disregarded airline," said Don Burr.

Yet with a relatively small amount of their own money, they had their own airline, albeit one that was an industry joke. Lorenzo and Carney agreed to raise $1.15 million in equity to invest in a $35 million recapitalization of the airline, gaining voting control of 60 percent of the company's shares. They also convinced Burr to join them in Houston. Burr was the only member of the trio who was married at the time, and his family objected to being uprooted from their home in the tony New York suburb of Tuxedo Park. Lorenzo promised Burr that if he quit his job as National Aviation president he would get a similar position at Texas International.

When Burr arrived in Houston, however, Lorenzo had changed his mind, and declared that only one person could be in charge. Burr rejected every title Lorenzo offered him and "pouted for months," Burr recalled. Burr eventually accepted the nebulous post of "chairman of the executive committee."

For years Texas International had been headed by a complacent group of former military men who averaged about sixty years in age, had gone to small southern colleges, and judging from the results, had lacked any demonstrable business sense. Lorenzo, Carney, and Burr quickly pushed them aside and started recruiting other young

Ivy League graduates to turn the company around. For them Lorenzo was an attractive role model—the youngest president of a jet airline in U.S. aviation history.

Burr and Lorenzo soon became inseparable. Burr was best man at Lorenzo's 1972 wedding to Sharon Murray, daughter of a Florida real estate developer. The two were godfathers to each other's children, and they often took vacations together.

Yet they sometimes resembled siblings in the way they fought. "They were constantly at each other's throats," one associate recalled. "It was something out of Sigmund Freud." Lorenzo's older brother, Olegario Jr., or Larry, as he was called, only recently had died of a heart attack at age thirty-three. Lorenzo became obsessed with his health soon after that, and Burr convinced him to take up jogging. They ran marathons all over the country together.

They were an odd couple—the moody Lorenzo, with his dark Latin good looks, and the boyishly handsome Burr, a Mayflower WASP. "We were always the two young assholes who were going to redo the industry," Burr recalled later. "And we were arrogant, thumbed our nose at the industry, and said 'these guys are dinosaurs.' "

Lorenzo soon earned his pilot's license and, as Burr saw it, the two would be just like the old flyboys, but with MBAs.

They put in orders for new jets and started attacking Texas International's service problems, but the airline could not shed its image as a loser. One day in mid-1976, as Lorenzo sat in a meeting of managers, Gerry Gitner, a marketing whiz whom Lorenzo had lured down to Houston from TWA, entered the room with a smile. "I've got good news," he said. "Today the airlines got a major fare increase through." The CAB had just let the airlines raise a family plan fare that allowed heavily restricted discounts for relatives traveling together.

Normally, this would have been good news for the airline's bottom line. But Lorenzo had just bought some tickets for his brother and his family to fly down to Texas. That cost him $650, and when Lorenzo recalculated the price at the new rates the tab shot up to more than $800. "This is ridiculous," he said. "Here we are all losing money, complaining about how traffic is so bad . . . Everyone is blaming it on the economy. And here you had these guys coming proudly into a staff meeting saying, 'We just got a big fare increase today.' "

Lorenzo's solution may have been somewhat less sophisticated than that produced by Bob Crandall's brain trust, but the result was the same: The notion that low fares would fill planes—and thus pay off by the increase in volume—had just dawned on the scheduled airline industry.

But Lorenzo's inspiration came from Washington, not from his customers. He often traveled to the capital to vent his frustrations about his airline's dismal fortunes. "I was pulling my hair out, trying to find a way we could be more competitive. And one day, somebody suggested to me 'why don't you try an experiment? There is a rage called deregulation going on.' "

The idea came, in fact, from CAB chairman John Robson, whose liberal leanings had already prodded Bob Crandall into action. The "experiment," as Lorenzo laughingly recalled later on, was intended "to test this notion the public would fly more if the fares were less."

Lorenzo correctly perceived this was his chance to break out of the doldrums. He ordered his staff to come up with a new discount fare. "I kept pushing. I got mad. I could really sense the people in Washington were pushing for some little outfit like us to take the first step."

Aides finally came up with the idea of offering "no-frills" flights, serving only peanuts instead of a meal, in exchange for which passengers would pay only "Peanuts" fares. But Lorenzo had trouble selling the idea to his board. "One of our directors said he thought the fare was the stupidest thing he'd ever heard of. It was the name in particular he objected to. And yet the name—it was so memorable—really lifted Texas International out of obscurity."

In Washington that December, they held a news conference at the Hay-Adams Hotel to announce they'd sell tickets on their less popular flights at half price. Jimmy Carter had not yet moved into the White House across the street, but a stylized cartoon of the newly elected Georgia peanut farmer was produced for the occasion. "Everybody should be able to fly for Peanuts," it said. It was the first genuine fare cut ever that was available without a lot of restrictions; Crandall's Super Savers had not yet appeared.

The beauty of the fare was its simplicity—no restrictions, no advance purchase limits, just a flat 50 percent off one flight each day in certain markets. The fares went into effect at the end of January 1977, and the affected flights were immediately sold out. "God, we'd never carried three people and a dog between here and Salt Lake City and all of a sudden planes were full," said Don Burr. Suddenly Texas International, the basket case of the business, was turning a profit.

• • •

LORENZO HAD LONG COVETED HIS own airline. He grew up in Rego Park, Queens, close to the approach to La Guardia Airport, but it was not proximity to the planes that excited his interest. He perceived early on that aviation would be a growth industry.

His father, Olegario Lorenzo, had immigrated to New York from Galicia, a rugged and impoverished region on the Atlantic coast of Spain. The elder Lorenzo became a hairdresser and prospered as a small business owner, and eventually opened his own beauty parlor in Manhattan. One of his son's early jobs was to help out with the business after school and "take the pins out of the hair," Lorenzo recalled later.

Frank Lorenzo made his first airline investment at the age of fifteen. After his first airline trip on TWA to London he bought a few shares in the company. By the time he won a scholarship to Columbia University, he'd been dabbling in the stock market for years. In college he joined a fraternity, waited on tables in the faculty club, and got involved in campus politics. His charm and eagerness to be accepted at Columbia led some of his peers to call him "Frankie Smooth-Talk."

Lorenzo's eagerness got him in trouble. In the spring of 1959, he joined other sophomore class leaders in a plot to rig the outcome of student elections by voting twice. Lorenzo was the only one caught in the act of stuffing the ballot box, and at first he denied everything, calling it a "stunt." His fellow plotters disavowed Lorenzo, and he "cracked" under questioning by the student board, according to an account in the *Columbia Daily Spectator*. He was banned from voting in future Columbia elections.

His escapade brought him his first negative publicity, but strangely, it impressed some of his fraternity brothers, who admired his stoic handling of the scandal. This would be a pattern throughout his career; the same hubris that so alienated his workers and the traveling public also brought him admiration from his peers in the business world.

After graduation, Lorenzo went to Harvard Business School, where he was influenced by a popular professor on campus, Roland Christianson, whose field was business strategy—specifically, how to turn companies around. He encouraged his students to "distill a company down to its simplest terms," Lorenzo recalled. Lorenzo's fascination with taking a dying company and making it profitable led him inexorably to the airlines, where sick companies were legion.

After earning his MBA in 1963, Lorenzo went to work for TWA in New York as a financial analyst. He moved two years later to a better-paying job at Eastern Airlines' Rockefeller Center headquarters. Leaving his office one day, Lorenzo bumped into a Harvard classmate, Robert Carney, who was working at S. G. Warburg, the investment firm right across the street. The two started having lunch together and soon decided to quit their jobs and go into business together. In 1966, the pair formed a consulting and investment company, Lorenzo and Carney, together putting up thirty-five thousand dollars of their own money. In 1969, they set up Jet Capital, a holding company with Lorenzo as chairman, and through a public stock offering were able to raise $1 million in operating funds. Carney was a silent partner, who would be in on most of Lorenzo's business dealings but usually remained in the background when Lorenzo faced the cameras.

PEANUTS FARES HAD CURED TEXAS International's immediate problem of how to convince the public to buy its much-maligned product. But this early success pointed up some of the problems that would come with competition. Many airlines were accustomed to flying planes half-full, and so were their flight crews. When the same flights suddenly were carrying double the number of passengers, the now overworked staff rebelled. And even odder problems developed.

At Denver, Texas International's planes had rarely departed with more than fifty people aboard, and given its poor service, overcrowded flights were rarely a problem. The altitude at Denver meant that planes had to achieve a certain payload before the aircraft could lift off, and Texas International's planes had to be balanced with thousands of pounds of lead jammed in the tail fin and nose cone to take off. The planes were always balanced to fly half-full.

Post-Peanuts, the airline found the flights were so full that they literally could not take off. It took the lead out but the planes still had trouble lifting off and eventually the old heavy airplane seats had to be replaced with lighter ones.

Low fares were soon a media phenomenon, and Washington lawmakers started to take notice. Constituents were demanding to know why all the airlines weren't charging less. But one group did not see the appeal of these cheap tickets; Texas International employees grumbled that they couldn't be expected to serve one hundred cups of coffee on a one-hour flight. Don Burr recalled that workers asked him: "Why don't you just raise the fare a bit?"

WHILE PEANUTS FARES HAD GIVEN him a reputation as a maverick, Lorenzo was just as scared of deregulation as Crandall. "If there was a carrier deregulation was meant to destroy, it was Texas International," he said. When he'd bought it, the airline had only six jets and nineteen prop planes, and annual sales of about $70 million, a far cry from the $1 billion plus raked in by American and United. It had relatively high costs, yet it had to compete with small, low-cost Southwest Airlines in its Texas backyard and lacked the resources and capital base to expand into the big leagues. Dick Ferris recalled sitting next to Lorenzo on a flight in 1977 when both were en route to a Conquistadores meeting. Lorenzo, Ferris said, spent much of the flight sounding off on deregulation. "Frank was very much against it," Ferris recalled, although Ferris's airline was largely the reason. The only way for Lorenzo to compete with United and other big lines would be to expand by buying another airline. But that was an option he did not mention when he went to Washington to testify against deregulation.

What he did mention was nonetheless disconcerting. When Lorenzo joined the other CEOs fighting the idea on Capitol Hill, his remarks before Senator Howard Cannon's aviation subcommittee were prescient. He warned that under total deregulation, the nation would eventually wind up with "a couple of very large airlines," and that smaller regional carriers like his own "will shortly become history."

And when Cannon asked him if he thought deregulation would constitute "an attack on the labor movement" in the airline industry, Lorenzo said that yes, he believed it would. Little did anyone realize the extent to which Lorenzo would lead that attack.

LORENZO WAS FIRST EXPOSED TO organized labor as a graduate student at Harvard Business School. He found a summer job driving a truck for Coca-Cola, which required him to join the Teamsters Union. Later in his career he would often produce his old union card as proof he did not deserve his labor-bashing reputation, but in fact that experience helped form his hard-line views.

"All of us kids didn't particularly like the union because the union didn't do anything for us. The union's real role was making life easier for the older guys, and in fact what the union really tried to do was to keep the young kids down on the farm," he said.

Lorenzo had no patience for the work rules enforced by his union seniors, he said, since they cut into his commissions, which was how most of the part-time employees were paid. Sometimes he'd sneak out and work during his lunch hour, putting in extra hours to earn more, until he'd get caught and be "written up" by the shop steward.

"It would drive us crazy. You were not allowed when you hit your lunch hour to work from twelve to one. I liked to, and so we'd go out and do things like put up signs to help the stores sell more Coke, and they all liked that—except the unions, they would climb the walls."

Lorenzo claimed that at the time he simply brushed aside such irritations. But nearly thirty years later, he still talked about the episode with apparent feeling. "You know, we got exposed to a lot of the kinds of stuff that is going on today—the work rules, the inefficiencies, all that. It was all there," he said.

By 1974, some of his airline's unionized employees had started demanding wage increases up to the levels enjoyed by their counterparts at airlines like United. Lorenzo refused, and in December of that year one of the airline's unions, the Air Line Employees Association, went out on strike. The pilots honored the picket lines, effectively grounding the airline. The strike went on for nearly five months, and Lorenzo's new jets sat idle.

The battle was notable for its hostility. Union leaders charged Lorenzo with refusing to bargain in good faith and asked the CAB to strip the carrier of its operating rights. Lorenzo responded by calling the union's demands "absurd" and accusing it of engaging in publicity stunts. When federal mediators finally brought the two camps together, the talks were nearly derailed when the pilots accused Lorenzo of attempting to arrange with a nonunion charter airline to fly the company's lucrative route between Houston and Mexico City. A settlement was soon reached, but Lorenzo's first battle with labor set him apart from the rest of the industry, where such public bickering was then quite unusual.

It was labor, in fact, that would cause a rift in Burr's friendship with Lorenzo. The reasons stemmed from Burr's unusual background.

As a youth, Burr got caught up in religion. His father, an engineer, was semiretired by ill health and was a leader in the local Congregational church. The family resided in South Windsor, Connecticut, the same area their forebears, who included Aaron Burr, had settled in 1630. They lived modestly, and Burr recalled that while his mother was a Whitney, "they were the poor Whitneys."

Burr became a junior proselytizer for his church's Pilgrim Youth Fellowship, traveling around the state and signing up converts. He was such a persuasive representative that one summer the church sent him to the Union Theological Seminary, hoping he would make it his life's vocation. Instead, Burr found that he hated religious studies and the idea was dropped. But he never lost the missionary zeal it inculcated in him, which he later displayed in his Billy Sunday–like sales pitches.

A life in business was unthinkable. "My church background instilled in me the idea that business was dirty," Burr said. His high-school yearbook listed his probable occupation as "English professor." But at age twenty, Burr learned that his girlfriend Brigit, a pretty blonde cheerleader whom he'd dated since high school, was pregnant. They hastily married and Burr's father cut off his support. The corporate world suddenly looked a lot more inviting. It was on to Harvard for his MBA.

Despite his conversion to a more mercenary calling, Burr never quite shed his religious beliefs. Ever the proselytizer, Burr began pushing Lorenzo to accept the theory that you could unleash workers' potential by allowing them to move back and forth between different jobs within the company. This was known as cross-utilization, but Burr had a new twist to it: All employees should be required to own stock in the company so they would be more motivated.

In a unionized airline company, where labor contracts dictated hours and job responsibilities in minute detail, such a concept would have to remain largely theoretical. But Burr thought that at least among the nonunion personnel such an idea could be tested. He convinced Lorenzo to invest a sizable budget in developing a new program to encourage employee productivity, and Burr threw himself into it, spending months fine-tuning the plan.

One day, Burr stepped up to present his new "human resources" program before a group of managers. Lorenzo walked out after fifteen minutes, fuming "this is bullshit." Burr felt he had been humiliated in front of his employees. He was despondent, and he began to think seriously about having his own airline.

Robert McAdoo, who worked in the finance department at Texas International, privately agreed with Burr. He described Lorenzo less than flatteringly as a "true economic man" who "wouldn't cross the street unless it was to his economic advantage to do so.

"If he had a choice between keeping $1.00 in his pocket and being liked by his employees or keeping $1.50 but not being liked, he'd keep the $1.50," said McAdoo.

LORENZO REALIZED THAT DEREGULATION, INSTEAD of ruining him, might enrich him. Jimmy Carter's new chairman at the CAB would give Lorenzo, Laker, and other mavericks opportunities they had been denied.

Alfred Kahn would become a national celebrity through his work in deregulating the airlines, but he came to it reluctantly. When President Jimmy Carter first offered him the post of CAB chairman early in 1977, Kahn turned him down. Kahn was then on leave from the faculty of Cornell, running the New York State Public Service Commission, regulating 500 public utilities, 365 water companies, and 50 telephone companies. He felt that the matters he oversaw were far more important to the average citizen than airline fares. "It's not my highest aspiration to make it easy for people to jet around the world," he said. And he also wondered if the president would support him if his actions helped to push some of the weaker airlines into bankruptcy. "What if we do deregulate, and Eastern or Pan Am goes bankrupt?" he asked Stu Eizenstat, the president's domestic policy adviser. Eizenstat assured Kahn the president would stand by him.

But a confidential memo to Carter written by members of his transition team warned of severe disruptions to the airline system that could cause political problems for the Democrats. "There could be visible dislocations which could be blamed on you," they said. Experts were predicting that one or more airlines could go under in the next two years. The reformers did not mention this publicly. Airline deregulation was just too popular.

Kahn was sworn in as the chairman of the Civil Aeronautics Board on June 10, 1977. His philosophy was simple: Allow airlines to fly as many routes as possible, and at the lowest fares they could afford to charge.

The cause-and-effect relationship between reduced regulation and lower air fares was soon strikingly clear. "I have only to open my mouth and the fares come tumbling down," Kahn quipped, and indeed during the summer of 1977 travel was booming. Freddie Laker's Skytrain finally won permission to take off, and discount fares proliferated. Many of these fares had been approved under the previous regime, but Kahn's CAB got most of the credit, and a string of adulatory articles confirmed the notion that he was responsible for the airlines' sudden generosity toward their customers. Kahn was the most compelling advocate for competition that the press had witnessed in years.

Yet Kahn first had to get rid of the ossified regulatory regime that had built up over forty years. "No one could blow his nose without getting my permission," he said. "It was insane."

Kahn was amused by some of the strange matters that came before him. Working late one night, Kahn answered the phone to hear the irate voice of a man who said he was a sheepherder from Virginia. "What happened to my petition? It's an emergency! I put in a request to carry sheep from here to Ireland and it was three weeks ago and I haven't heard anything." Kahn asked the man what the urgency was. "My sheep—they're in heat!" the man shouted. It turned out that each board member was supposed to sign off anytime someone wanted to carry animals by air. To Kahn, this was yet another reminder of a system so rigid and illogical that its reach extended even to animal husbandry.

Soon after Kahn took over, the CAB got a petition from Eastern Airlines. The airline was short of cash, and it proposed as one solution that it be allowed to pay for advertising with free tickets. Kahn liked the idea, until the staff he had inherited from the previous regime told him that simply couldn't be done because it was a "deviation from tariff."

Then United Airlines came in with the very type of creative marketing idea that Kahn had been awaiting. The airline wanted to promote its winter flights to Denver by offering skiers "snow guarantees," a promise to refund a passenger's ticket if there was no snow. Kahn failed again to persuade the experts on his staff. "Deviation from tariff," he was again informed.

Kahn brought in as many deregulation allies as he could round up to fight the unexpected resistance he was getting from within. Phil Bakes came in as general counsel, along with a staff of other reform-minded lawyers and advocates. Kahn enthusiastically backed the appointment to the board of economist Elizabeth Bailey, who filled one of the Republican slots. Bailey was the first woman to have earned a Ph.D. in economics from Princeton University and held a prestigious post at Bell Labs in New Jersey. She, like Kahn, firmly believed that free market forces were preferable to regulation.

But Kahn saved most of his persuasive powers for a long-distance campaign to woo Mike Levine, the lawyer and academic who had written the pioneering study of air service in California in the sixties. Levine, spending a year at the London School of Economics, turned

Kahn down until, after yet another entreaty from Kahn, Levine's wife added her voice. "What are you doing? You are a guy who said for ten years you've got to deregulate, and now here's a guy who really wants to do it. He will either try and fail and you won't have helped him—or worse, he'll try and succeed and you won't have been there." That was too much for Levine's ego to bear. He called Kahn and told him he would soon be there to help him at the CAB.

Unlike the other deregulators—Breyer, Bakes, and Kahn—Levine had a genuine love of aviation. As a child growing up on Long Island in the 1950s, he often rode his bicycle out to Idlewild (later Kennedy) Airport to watch the first jets touch down on the runway. By age twelve, he was reading aviation trade magazines, dense stuff like *Aviation Week and Space Technology,* and learning about the regulation of airlines.

Levine had worked at the CAB right out of Yale Law School in 1965, but quit in disgust at the "intellectual corruption" he found there. After his law review article on California and Texas airline regulation attracted much attention, he continued to write and speak out about the airlines wherever he could. When Levine was on the faculty at CalTech, American chairman Al Casey, who was a trustee of the university, once threatened to go to Levine's superiors to get him to stop sounding off about deregulation.

Levine moved into the plum spot of top adviser to Alfred Kahn, functioning as Kahn's chief of staff. His zealous devotion to deregulation in its purest form was such that some of his peers nicknamed him the Ayatollah. But while Kahn appeared to be more comedian than bureaucrat, behind the scenes he and Levine were seriously figuring out how to do as much as possible within the parameters of the law. Levine thought of it in garment industry terms: He was Mr. Inside, cutting the suits, and Kahn was Mr. Outside, peddling the clothes. Kahn relied heavily on Levine's legal advice, and they overrode the in-house critics who had earlier slowed his progress.

They swiftly got to work destroying as much of the regulatory machinery as they could. They allowed airlines to file fare changes with little notice, instead of waiting months for approval, figuring that airlines would be more likely to experiment if they got a jump on their competitors. Then, in an otherwise routine case for service to Albany, New York, Kahn's board issued an order saying for the first time in history that airlines proposing to offer lower fares on a route would have an advantage in winning new route authority. Then Kahn did something even more far-reaching. Two carriers wanted permission to fly the same route, a Washington-to-Cincinnati run, and the board said they could both go in if they chose. "In one swoop, we undermined the traditional character of certification," said Kahn.

While all this may seem tame today, at the time it was radical. In the past, the CAB had moved at a glacial pace; Kahn in a few months had made more changes than the old board would have made in decades. His facility for one-liners helped to defuse much of the airlines' opposition. "I'm tempted to tell Pan Am to go to hell, and I don't mean a new route," Kahn quipped in typical fashion.

Kahn was never one to shy from debate, and when the AFL-CIO invited him over to their headquarters, he accepted. The unions made it clear they were strongly opposed to deregulation. Kahn listened politely. "It was, after all, a Democratic administration," he said. "They were right to be worried. I said, 'Look, we Democrats believe in an expanding economy, expanding demand, and that's what makes for higher employment.' "

But then Kahn added the kicker. "On the other hand, protection from competition permits strong unions and a wage/price spiral where pilots are earning six-digit salaries and flying only forty hours a month, with a second business on the side and beautiful houses and two places in the country!" Few people in Washington could have gotten away with such candor.

Television crews began showing up, and wherever he went, Kahn seemed to attract a flock of reporters seeking pithy quotations. At a demonstration of new, quieter aircraft staged by Eastern Airlines at an airfield outside Washington, Kahn was asked what he thought of the noise levels of the various planes he'd just heard. "I really don't know one plane from the other. To me they are just marginal costs with wings." Frank Borman, Eastern's ex-astronaut chief executive, was left speechless.

Faced with this brilliant crew of deregulating bureaucrats, the airlines, as Bob Crandall confessed later, "simply did not know what to do." Delta Air Lines ran to the federal appeals court at every opportunity, accusing Kahn of violating the law, prompting Kahn to quip later: "Delta wasn't ready when I was." Delta chief executive Thomas Beebe even started jetting up from Atlanta to Washington to talk to his former governor about how dreadful deregulation would be for scores of little communities in his home state. But Carter brushed him off.

Mary Schuman, who was then in charge of the airline deregulation issue in the White House staff, remembers talking to Carter one day about Delta and being surprised to find that the president was immune to the pleas of one of the biggest employers in Georgia. Delta made one or two other efforts to block deregulation in Congress, but, like American, finally gave up.

Frank Lorenzo, on the other hand, had a clear vision of what he needed to do. He kept it to himself, but one day he couldn't resist testing his idea on one of the government regulators who would have to approve it.

In the summer of 1978, Lorenzo played host to Mike Levine, who had taken to traveling around the country to visit airline headquarters. The two spent an afternoon in Houston chatting about the industry and dined together at a local country club. Afterward, Lorenzo thoughtfully offered Levine a ride to the airport.

As they drove along, Lorenzo casually turned the conversation to CAB policies. He was interested, he said, in how the board might react if one airline tried to acquire another in a hostile takeover. Most mergers proposed among airlines had been friendly affairs, and there was little in the record that would indicate just how such aggression would be received by federal regulators. "I said I thought the board would have no view one way or another," Levine remembered. "I told him that the board would analyze it the way it would any other transaction, that we would assess the competitive implications." Lorenzo simply smiled and changed the subject.

To Levine, it had been a hypothetical query and he thought no more about it. A few weeks later, Lorenzo announced that he had bought 9.2 percent of the stock of National Airlines and that he would launch a fight to gain control of the Miami-based company.

6

MERGER FEVER

I f there was a single event that awakened the business community
and the public to Frank Lorenzo, it was his unexpected announcement that little Texas International had quietly purchased
a sizeable interest in National Airlines, a company with nearly four
times its revenues. Lorenzo's bid for National earned him a profile
in *Forbes* magazine headlined "Lorenzo the Presumptuous." He was
unmoved, and soon announced plans to increase his stake from just
under 10 percent to 25 percent.

The news came as a nasty surprise to National Airlines chairman
Bud Maytag. It was, after all, the first "non-negotiated acquisition,"
or unfriendly takeover attempt, in U.S. airline history. Conscious of
his duties to shareholders, Maytag politely responded to Lorenzo's
announcement by saying that the National board would carefully
consider any merger offer from Texas International, although none
had yet been presented.

Lorenzo clearly had studied the move for a while, and those close
to him were not surprised at all. "Everyone who knew him knew he
was obsessed with being a big player," said Bob Ginther, Cannon's
aviation subcommittee aide, who in the late seventies became the
president of the trade association for the Local Service Airlines, a

job which put him in close contact with Lorenzo. "We saw him as a guy who wanted to go somewhere fast."

To Washington opinion-makers, however, Lorenzo presented his audacious move as the inevitable result of deregulation. The two airlines would be a "perfect fit," he said, a label he would subsequently pin on nearly any merger that caught his fancy. He made his pursuit of National sound like the height of reason, noting that National had wanted to build a hub in Houston—an asset his plan would conveniently supply. National also lacked smaller planes like Texas International's fleet of DC-9s, which Lorenzo argued would be the workhorses of the deregulated industry. In other words, he would rescue both airlines from inevitable oblivion once competition set in.

Lorenzo's lunge was in fact a direct result of deregulation, though not necessarily for the reasons he suggested. A merger was likely the only quick fix for Texas International in a competitive landscape.

Lorenzo couldn't sell his idea to National's chairman, however, because Maytag wouldn't return his phone calls. Lorenzo believed Maytag's reluctance to talk to him was part of the still-pervasive club mentality among CEOs of the larger airlines.

"It was a big club," Lorenzo said, "and we were always outside the club—the eighteenth out of eighteen airlines. We were very low status, and the industry was very clubby and status-oriented." At any rate, since he considered National's shares seriously undervalued, Lorenzo kept buying them. "The fact is, we didn't know where it was going to lead us," Lorenzo remarked. "We just knew it was a good stock, it was potentially a good merger, and maybe Maytag would turn around and pay attention to us."

Pan Am, on the other hand, was a charter member of the club, so when Pan Am decided it, too, wanted National, Maytag was only too happy to talk.

The old order was crumbling, however. The chairman of Pan Am, General William Seawell, surveyed a vastly different scene from his forty-sixth-floor office than had Juan Trippe. Eastern moved its headquarters from New York to Miami in 1976, and by 1978 American was already planning to leave New York City for Dallas, returning to C. R. Smith's Texas roots. American's move was a big shock to New York, where Al Casey had established his credentials as a civic leader. American's move would signal the end of the cozy aviation community in mid-Manhattan.

Pan Am was in much worse shape than any of them. By the late 1970s, the Transportation Department had set up an informal operation called "Project Pan Am Watch," sort of a deathbed vigil intended to alert the White House if the company was indeed about to expire.

The carrier's troubles originated in 1966, when Trippe in typical fashion placed a $600 million order with Boeing for twenty-five of its new 747 jumbo jets, a radical design innovation that would eventually open a new world of international air travel to the mass market. But by the time First Lady Pat Nixon christened the first 747 to enter service in 1970, the international market was turning sour and Pan Am had a lot of unfilled seats on its hands.

As early as 1973, a secret Pan Am internal management study concluded that its prospects for survival as an airline were so dismal that the company should consider getting out of passenger transportation altogether and use its worldwide network of offices, personnel, and overseas contacts to build a Japanese-style international trading company. Although the study was sparked by concern about fuel prices and availability during the 1973 oil crisis, it concluded that the biggest threat to Pan Am was the tendency of the government to give more international routes to "domestic" airlines while continuing to deny Pan Am access to routes within the United States.

Trippe had left the airline's sprawling international route network dangerously overextended, for reasons that had nothing to do with profitability. "They'd collect [route] authorities and fly them without any economic pretext whatsoever—there was a nonstop route between Bangkok and Sydney that was flown just because they won it, and I don't think that plane ever had more than twenty people on it," said Sky Magary, a former Pan Am executive.

Seawell got an early taste of the problem when he tried to cut back some less-traveled international routes to Europe and the Caribbean. A junior executive assigned to examine traffic figures noticed that Pan Am was operating several 727s a day from Miami to Rock Sound, Eleuthera, with barely enough traffic to support a tiny commuter plane. The aide, thinking he'd be praised for ferreting out such waste, dropped the service from Pan Am's schedule. Soon he was summoned to the chairman's office by an ashen-faced Seawell. Trippe, who was still on the Pan Am board, was "very interested" in the Rock Sound service, was how Seawell delicately put it. Trippe and a group of friends had bought property on the island; the service was, in effect, their private jet shuttle.

Pan Am also suffered from unrelenting internal turmoil among its top layers of management. This went back to the Trippe years, when "people promoted themselves into power by claiming a close association with Trippe even if they might not have had one," one former manager said. Trippe retired in 1968 and was succeeded briefly by a former Pan Am pilot, Harold Gray, and then by Najeeb Halaby. (Halaby would later gain fame as the father-in-law of Jordan's King Hussein.) The infighting continued, however. When Halaby appointed four group vice-presidents to spread out the power, the result was not a smoothly running machine, but a series of turf battles among the four. They became known as the Groupies—"They clawed at each other constantly," said one subordinate. The airline lost $364 million from 1969 to 1976; by 1970, its long-term debt exceeded $1 billion.

This was the situation Seawell faced when he was brought to Pan Am in 1971 as president, succeeding Halaby as chairman in 1972. At age fifty-three, Seawell was "tall, wavy-haired and just good-looking enough to meet the Pan Am tradition of photogenic executives," wrote Trippe chronicler Marylin Bender. Seawell had worked at American Airlines under C. R. Smith, and then became North American president of Rolls-Royce, a leading aircraft engine manufacturer. A West Pointer and Harvard Law School graduate, a decorated World War II veteran and former Air Force general, he liked to be referred to as "the general."

Pan Am had long ago lost its status as the only U.S. carrier on international routes, thanks to a treaty the United States signed with Great Britain in 1946 that allowed TWA and another American line onto the North Atlantic routes. In the late 1970s it faced even greater competition. The Carter administration was negotiating more liberal aviation treaties with other countries, which opened all kinds of new overseas air service and gave traditionally domestic U.S. lines new routes. In turn, foreign-flag lines, which were often owned and subsidized by their governments, were allowed to serve additional points in the United States. Pan Am had always depended on domestic carriers to feed passengers to New York or Miami or Los Angeles, where they would transfer to a Pan Am flight for their overseas trip. The more international routes and new U.S. gateways the government assigned to other companies, the less "feed" Pan Am would get for its own flights.

It became increasingly obvious that Pan Am would need a substantial domestic route system to provide it with the passengers who previously traveled to Pan Am's gateway airports on United, American, Delta, Eastern, and other mainly domestic carriers, which all had elaborate U.S. route networks and now would apparently be granted liberal opportunities to expand overseas as well.

Many at Pan Am believed their airline would be unfairly disadvantaged under deregulation. "When the cards in deregulation were dealt, not everyone had an equal hand," said Martin Shugrue, an executive of Pan Am in the 1970s and 1980s. "Some people got four aces and some got four kings and some people got garbage. Pan Am, uniquely at the time, got garbage," he said.

The "garbage" was Pan Am's abysmal lack of domestic routes. While this may have sounded like sour grapes—after all, American and United could rightfully complain about their exclusion from foreign markets—Pan Am, surprisingly, won sympathy for its view from Alfred Kahn. Kahn did believe that because of peculiar circumstances some airlines would be disproportionately affected by unfettered competition and should be given some form of protection—a notion that often put Kahn at odds with deregulation zealots on his staff. Kahn tried to give Pan Am more domestic services—allowing it "fill up" rights—that is, permission to carry passengers on the domestic portion of an international itinerary.

Then when a new route from Dallas to London opened up, Kahn persuaded his fellow board members to award it to Pan Am. However, where international routes were concerned it was still politics as usual. Dallas-based Braniff fought back with a heavily funded lobbying campaign and persuaded Jimmy Carter to reverse the decision and give the plum route to a Texan airline. Pan Am was defeated by the very forces Juan Trippe had so cleverly manipulated for years.

Kahn was furious at Carter and in a rare fit of pique he publicly threatened to resign. He knew that if Pan Am's international franchise was eroded without a corresponding improvement in its domestic rights the airline was doomed. Kahn openly fretted about how much "nibbling" Pan Am could stand. He called it his "St. Sebastian theory," explaining that while "each arrow is not fatal," the cumulative effect would be slow death.

Seawell continued to seek out overseas opportunities for Pan Am. For instance, he took a deep personal interest in winning the new air routes to the People's Republic of China. But he was mainly preoccupied with getting his own domestic route network.

Although it was clear in 1978 that deregulation was likely to become law soon, Seawell couldn't be sure just how quickly Pan Am could make a wholesale move into the domestic market until Congress passed a final version. Besides, an airline needs more than route authority to add new service; it also needs the planes and employees to fly the routes. A merger with a sizable domestic partner would provide a quick fix. Seawell soon settled on National as an attractive candidate, since it was based at one of Pan Am's key gateway cities,

Miami, and its stock was trading at a reasonable eighteen dollars a share in the spring of 1978.

While Lorenzo waited for CAB approval to increase his stake in National in August 1978, Pan Am started buying National stock, and when the price had risen to around thirty dollars in the last week of August, said it would buy all outstanding shares at thirty-five dollars pending CAB approval. In early September, Maytag and Seawell cut a deal. With National trading at thirty-four dollars, they agreed that Pan Am would buy all National's outstanding common stock for $350 million, or forty-one dollars a share.

Lorenzo and Texas International, who had been buying shares at eighteen and nineteen dollars, suddenly found themselves and their National stock on a fast ride. When they had accumulated about $15 million worth, "We thought a merger with National at maybe twenty-five dollars a share was an interesting deal," Lorenzo remembered. "Well, it went through twenty-five so fast we didn't know what hit us. So from the time it got into the thirties, we lost interest as far as a deal we could do, but on the other hand, we were marking up our value, so we had a tremendous stake in where the company went."

After the CAB approved his application to buy more stock, Lorenzo raised his stake to 20.1 percent by mid-September. After all, Pan Am and National's merger plan still had to win CAB approval— by no means a sure thing, since the rules at the CAB were changing under Alfred Kahn, and would change even more when Congress voted on the Airline Deregulation Act.

KAHN AND THE CAB WERE facing not just one but three airline mergers in the summer of 1978. In addition to the battle for National, Continental Airlines and Western Air Lines had filed for approval to merge, and two local service carriers—North Central Airlines and Southern Airways—also wanted to combine forces.

Kahn was deeply puzzled by all this merger activity. After all, the CAB had in practice given carriers virtual carte blanche to serve any domestic markets they wanted. "This is the last time in the world anyone needs to merge to gain new routes," the CAB chairman told a reporter later that summer. "We are strongly motivated to let anyone fly wherever they want. But instead of grasping the opportunities we're offering, this disease, this psychology, is getting abroad that airlines ought to merge."

But others were not surprised at all. A number of airline witnesses had testified that once economic restraints were lifted, the industry would be rocked by the same upheaval—bankruptcies and mergers—that often occurs in unregulated industries. Some congressmen were already warning that the deregulators could not have it both ways by lifting controls but preventing airlines from entering into business agreements.

As the deregulation bill moved through Congress, it was clear that the airlines had gotten the message across to certain legislators. In the Senate floor debate much discussion concerned mergers. Several senators indicated that they intended the bill to make it easier for airlines to merge in order to survive. "We must . . . permit the firms that are attempting to do business in this field to make the kind of responses that they may need to in order to succeed in an unregulated environment," said Senator Warren Magnuson.

Kahn may have inadvertently contributed to the airlines' merger fever by his penchant for flippant comments. After only a few months in his CAB job, he told a group of aviation lawyers: "I feel like the Red Queen of *Alice in Wonderland,* executing the sentence first, then getting around to holding the trial." It was this metaphoric trial that had the airlines worried—the uncertainty of what would follow Kahn's mad rush to undo forty years of regulation.

Seawell also turned to Lewis Carroll for an image to defend his plan for a merger with National. "I'm tired of playing the role of the White Queen," Seawell told a Senate subcommittee in August 1978, "who is told that there is jam tomorrow, jam yesterday, but never any jam today. At Pan Am we believe we ought to get some today . . . Pan Am doesn't have the time to wait and build our own domestic system."

Kahn was not the only one troubled by the merger applications on his desk. The top antitrust official at the Justice Department, John Shenefield, worried publicly that the airline industry was moving into a merger "panic" and speculated that approval of all the pending applications might send other carrier CEOs rushing into each other's arms as a defensive measure. Shenefield said in late summer of 1978 that "it would be ironic if the dawn of the new era were to produce a merger wave reducing the number of competitors and the amount of competition."

Ralph Nader, in fact, had tempered his enthusiastic support for deregulation in an especially prescient warning in 1977. "It is absolutely essential that the Justice Department's role in monitoring and enforcing the antitrust laws be significantly upgraded and adequately funded to provide protection for the public as the CAB's authority is being reduced," he said.

"We don't want to transfer the faith of airline passengers from the CAB to an industry overwhelmingly dominated by United Airlines and two or three major airlines. The public should not be forced to trade deregulation for tight oligopoly in the air transport industry," he concluded.

But Kahn's CAB, in the spirit of deregulation, was generally loath to interfere in the actions of the marketplace. The Board told Pan Am, as it had told Lorenzo, to go ahead and buy more National stock. Shenefield urged Kahn to put a halt to the buying until the antitrust implications of both potential mergers could be evaluated, but Kahn refused. Shenefield had been right that the merger frenzy would spread.

In December 1978, Frank Borman of Eastern Airlines was getting worried about the prospect of competing against a combination of Pan Am and National. He decided as a defensive measure that Eastern ought to buy National, and he jumped into the bidding, too—at fifty dollars a share. By Borman's account, Seawell "was furious—he had his hand on the pot, ready to rake it in, when I suddenly raised the ante."

CONGRESS PASSED THE DEREGULATION BILL that October. Some praised it as a model of legislative probity; others criticized its various "Christmas tree" provisions designed to appease special interests. The main thrust of the bill was still pure deregulation: It gave airlines the right to enter new routes without CAB permission, and with some limitations, to exit any market they chose; it allowed them to raise and lower fares within a certain percentage range, with all pricing controls—and the CAB itself—scheduled to "sunset," or shut down entirely, by 1985. It was the first time in history that the federal government's role in the economic regulation of an industry was actually abolished.

The sunset provision was there almost by accident. It had been slipped in earlier by Congressman Elliot Levitas of Atlanta, the so-called "Deltacrat" who ably represented the interests of his hometown airline. Levitas thought he'd kill the bill with such a radical idea, but the tactic backfired when the professional staffs on the Hill seized on its symbolic appeal. Several staffers admitted it was a somewhat cynical move, since most believed Congress would intervene to extend the agency's life. It didn't, of course, and as a result, a politically oriented cabinet member, rather than a bipartisan board, would soon preside over the greatest wave of consolidation the industry had ever seen.

The law also included some provisions that helped bring a lopsided victory in both houses. One was a fat subsidy program to continue air service to small communities that might otherwise be abandoned by profit-minded airlines. The law also had a provision for "labor protection" to ensure that anyone who lost a job because of deregulation—even because of deregulation-related bankruptcies or mergers—would be given priority in hiring at another line or adequate compensation. And the act also eliminated the notorious Mutual Aid Pact that had blunted the effectiveness of the unions' right to strike.

The first tangible evidence that deregulation had begun was an arrest by the Washington, D.C., police on the weekend of October 21, 1978.

A minor provision of the deregulation act gave airlines the right to claim hundreds of "dormant" routes—where an incumbent carrier's authority had gone unused—on a first-come, first-served basis once the president signed the bill. Often routes were dormant because they were not likely to produce profits. However, that was not the whole picture, because the route moratorium had left the airlines starved for new opportunities.

After Congress passed the law, it sat on Jimmy Carter's desk for days, as his aides planned a signing ceremony. Meanwhile, a representative of United planted himself out on the sidewalk outside the CAB, thus claiming the first place in line for the dormant route grab. Other carriers then sent their own representatives to stand in line. Soon the line snaked around the corner, and television crews showed up to record the first public skirmish of deregulation.

As the round-the-clock vigil wore on, tempers frayed. A messenger representing Continental Airlines was arrested for packing a handgun. A messenger for Ozark left for a bathroom break; when he returned, he was denied his former place in line. He threatened to pull a gun on his adversaries.

Early the next morning, Mike Levine got a call at home. "You've got to get down here fast," he was told. He rushed down to the CAB building and saw the unruly mob that deregulation had produced. "You guys are wasting your time," he said. "You're going to get all the routes you want—you don't have to do this." Levine's first implementation of deregulation was ruling on bathroom visits by airline surrogates.

President Carter signed the law on October 24, 1978. Few airline CEOS were in attendance. But the next day the throng of airline representatives bolted through the door at 1825 Connecticut Avenue. To everyone's surprise, United only asked for a single route, Orlando–Buffalo, while Braniff, the flamboyant Texas airline, staked a claim to some four-hundred-odd markets.

Alfred Kahn was not around to see his handiwork stitched into law. As Carter was putting his signature on the new law, Kahn was moving into new quarters in the White House, to take up an ill-fated assignment as the president's inflation czar. He had been at the CAB for less than a year and a half, yet he would forever be identified as the father of deregulation. The pending merger applications he had left behind at the CAB went to his successor, Marvin Cohen, an Arizona lawyer who was even more reluctant than Kahn to interfere in the workings of the marketplace.

Even so, the Justice Department urged the dismissal of both Pan Am's and Texas International's applications on antitrust grounds, claiming that under the new merger approval standards mandated by the Deregulation Act, both would be anticompetitive. Justice lawyer Shenefield wasn't alone in opposing the merger proposals. The CAB's own Consumer Protection Bureau also urged the board to block both Pan Am and Lorenzo from buying National, and so did the CAB law judge.

Yet, despite all the urging to the contrary, the CAB approved an acquisition of National by either Pan Am or Texas International (the Eastern merger application for National was being considered separately). This curious decision stemmed purely from the board's desire to "let the market work," according to CAB member Elizabeth Bailey. In 1979, the CAB approved the North Central–Southern merger, creating Republic Airlines (a year later, Republic again expanded by merger, acquiring Hughes Airwest).

But just when it was starting to appear that the new post-deregulation CAB was going to close its eyes to a wave of industry consolidation, the board startled everyone by overturning its staff law judge's recommendation and rejecting the merger application of Continental and Western Air Lines, saying the merger was anticompetitive. Continental and Western were head-to-head competitors in much of the country. A merger would subject consumers in those cities to "the danger of tacit cooperation between the merged carrier and United," the only other airline in many of the markets, CAB Chairman Cohen said in dismissing the application.

In September 1979 the CAB also rejected Eastern's request to acquire National. The two competed on too many routes, the board said. In some markets, the combined airline would have controlled up to 94 percent of the traffic. By that time, the board's decision was moot, however. Two months before the CAB acted on the Eastern application, Seawell had already come to terms with Lorenzo, agreeing to pick up Texas International's 24.5 percent of National for the same fifty dollars a share that Eastern had offered, subject to President Carter's approval of a Pan Am–National merger. (Mergers and international routes are subject to White House review.)

Eastern's Borman was disappointed by his failure to win National. He had also picked up a case of merger fever. In the months following the National battle, he approached Northwest, Braniff, and TWA about a merger with Eastern. All three turned him down. Of the Big Four, Eastern was possibly in the worst shape, loaded with debt after a jet-buying binge, with a history of labor acrimony, and with a route system extremely vulnerable to attack from new low-fare airlines.

Eastern had also never been able to shake its reputation for poor service, a legacy of Eddie Rickenbacker's damn-the-passenger philosophy. CAB member Bailey experienced this attitude firsthand one day when she was rudely denied a seat in the nonsmoking section of an Eastern flight, even though the law required the airline to accommodate her. Bailey found a passenger who volunteered to change seats with her, but as the flight taxied down the runway, the flight attendant got on the loudspeaker and welcomed all the passengers on board "except for that woman in the back." When the plane landed, Bailey revealed her identity to the flight attendant and showed her the complaint she had composed, at which point, Bailey said, "You should have heard what she called me." A few days later, Frank Borman flew up to Washington to offer his personal apology to Bailey.

MEANWHILE, AFTER MORE THAN A year-long battle, Lorenzo walked away from National Airlines. Texas International had turned a pretax profit of $46 million on the National stock it sold to Pan Am, nearly four times its net worth before the bidding started.

General Seawell won a Pyrrhic victory in the battle for National Airlines: He had paid too much. By Pan Am's own reckoning, the $436.7 million that it paid for National exceeded the net assets of that company by $228.6 million. The additional debt could hardly have come at a worse time. By 1980 it was clear that the economy was heading into recession, and the cost of fuel was escalating. From 1979 to 1980, Pan Am's fuel bills jumped by 60 percent; fuel costs went from 25 percent of the airline's operating expenses to 32 percent.

There was some feeling within Pan Am that the National system should be kept separate and operated as a domestic sister company at least for a while, and only gradually absorbed into the parent airline. Others advocated a quick combination of the two companies.

Typical of Pan Am, this disagreement escalated into a major political battle in the executive ranks. President Dan Colussy argued for a fast absorption of National into Pan Am, while executive VP Bill Waltrip advised a much slower pace of integration.

Colussy won. In the spring of 1980, Martin Shugrue—who had come up through the ranks at Pan Am from his first job as a flight engineer—was assigned the thankless task of merging the two airlines' labor contracts. "I said then and there, 'Don't do this,' " Shugrue recalled. "Let's have Pan Am Domestic and Pan Am Overseas and operate them as separate businesses. Let's take the next ten years to integrate."

But Seawell wouldn't listen to Shugrue. The general had issued his orders and expected them to be carried out. "He wouldn't hear of anything else once he made his mind up. I couldn't talk to him about it, he threw me out of his office," Shugrue remembered. In Shugrue's opinion, "That cost Pan Am its future."

The labor contracts were merged, with horrible repercussions for the company's cost structure. "Basically what happened is that Pan Am ended up capitulating and paying all the National people at the higher Pan Am rates—which was suicide," a former senior official of Pan Am said. "That ensured they could never, ever run a successful domestic system."

Pan Am's union work rules also were extended to National, raising costs even more. Because of its long history as an international carrier with long overseas flights, Pan Am's unions had exacted unique work rules. For example, the rules specified that a Pan Am pilot had to go off duty whenever he passed through his point of origin—a reasonable expectation for a pilot bringing a plane back from Europe to New York, but a serious productivity constraint for a pilot who makes a thirty-minute flight to Boston and back in a domestic route network.

Shugrue took many months to come to terms with the various unions on both sides, and the results were higher costs and a disgruntled workforce.

The merger set off a corporate culture clash that made it difficult if not impossible for former National staffers to get along with their new overseers and colleagues from Pan Am. "The National people thought they had a better way to do things than the Pan Am people did, and the Pan Am people thought the National people were country bumpkins," one executive remarked. The merger agreement had originally promised that everyone at National would keep their jobs under the new regime, but some managers ended up being fired by their new Pan Am bosses, or quitting in disgust.

Aside from problems of personnel and style, the difficulties of combining the operations of two such different airlines turned out to be monumental. During one week, for instance, an estimated 154,000 phone calls to the merged airline's reservations centers were simply not answered by anyone. When calls were answered, the reservations agents often found themselves unprepared to cope with the caller's request.

"If someone said they wanted to book a flight to Melbourne, for example, a Pan Am agent would just assume they were talking about Melbourne, Australia, and someone who had been a National agent would assume they meant Melbourne, Florida," a former Pan Am staffer noted.

"The reservations system was a complete and total disaster," Shugrue agreed. "And it was all part of this integration process. The phones weren't talking to each other, the computers weren't talking to each other, and employees weren't talking to each other."

The flying public also had to be educated about the fact that National Airlines—which was known for the orange sunburst on the tail of its planes and for the feminist outrage it stirred with its "Fly Me—I'm Judy" TV commercials, featuring its female flight attendants—was now part of Pan Am, and that Pan Am no longer flew only overseas. Pan Am's ad agency whipped up a TV ad in which the camera showed a National Airlines DC-10 in its traditional livery, and then panned around the front of the plane to show the other side, which was painted in Pan Am colors.

"It was brilliant, and it should have run for three years," Shugrue maintained. "Instead, it ran for six months," he noted, because Seawell and Pan Am's top management were determined "to smash them together."

The two airlines also had incompatible fleets of aircraft. It is axiomatic in the airline industry that the fewer different aircraft types a company has, the better. A variety of different planes from different manufacturers always means higher costs, more specialized mechanics, a greater range of replacement parts, more complicated record-keeping, and perhaps even entirely separate maintenance bases for each aircraft type. Seawell had already complicated the Pan Am fleet when he decided to supplement its 747s with an order for the smaller L-1011 widebodies produced by Lockheed. But when National joined the fold, it added a third type of twin-aisle aircraft: McDonnell Douglas DC-10s.

The costs of the National merger to Pan Am in a year of rising fuel prices and soft traffic showed dramatically on the company's balance sheet. Pan Am suffered a record operating loss of $129.6 million in 1980. The company was faced with serious liquidity problems. Seawell needed to raise money fast and he realized that the only way to do that was to sell assets. The company's airline was deemed sacrosanct, so he turned first to real estate and then to the airline's sister hotel company, both of which had been profitable investments.

Deregulation's first victim, arguably, was the glass and steel skyscraper at Forty-fifth Street and Park Avenue. By the end of the 1970s, the Pan Am Building had become a fitting metaphor for the company's festering problems. When the Walter Gropius–designed structure had gone up in 1963, blocking what had been a sweeping vista along Park Avenue, it was derided as a "monument to greed and irresponsibility." Those were the days when Trippe and his Yale cronies literally looked down on their competition, secure in the knowledge that the logo emblazoned atop their aerie was the best-known corporate name in the world after Coca-Cola. Now this dubious landmark would have to go on the block.

In 1980, Pan Am agreed to sell its majority ownership of the building to Metropolitan Life Insurance for $400 million, turning a profit of $294 million. The next year Pan Am sold its Inter-Continental Hotels unit to the United Kingdom's Grand Metropolitan conglomerate for $500 million. Eight of Pan Am's 747s also were sold for $200 million, and then immediately leased back so the airline could keep using them. These infusions of capital helped Pan Am's balance sheet in 1981 but had no impact on the now-combined airline's miserable operating picture: 1981 operating results were even deeper in the red, a record deficit of $359 million.

One member of the Pan Am board said that by the time the hotel chain was sold, Pan Am's situation was much worse than many people—even inside the company—realized. "The very day they agreed to make the sale, Pan Am bounced a couple of checks," he recalled. "They just didn't have any cash." Pan Am apparently had been drawing on some of Intercontinental's accounts, to the tune of almost $20 million, which it had no right to do.

Internecine warfare in the executive suite reached record levels.

Seawell and Colussy went for days without speaking to each other. Although the chairman had sided with his president in agreeing to a quick absorption of National, he was now paying more attention to executive vice-president Waltrip, and the executive corps on the forty-sixth floor was quick to line up behind one of the two contenders—especially as speculation began to grow that the Pan Am board of directors might be getting fed up with General Seawell's battle plans under deregulation.

As tempers grew more heated, Seawell fired off a broadside at the Colussy forces, firing a number of executives who were considered Colussy people, longtime Pan Am executive Sky Magary remembered—but he didn't call them into his office to do it. "They found out about it by reading *The Wall Street Journal,*" Magary recalled.

By 1981, Seawell and Colussy met in combat one final time, and in the ensuing shouting match, Colussy either quit or was fired. Waltrip became president, but by this time the Pan Am board of directors—an august group that included such luminaries as Frank Stanton and Walter Cronkite of CBS, Jack Parker of General Electric, Donald Kendall of Pepsico and Akio Morita of Sony—had had enough. Cronkite would, in fact, soon resign, so concerned was he at Pan Am's direction.

Seawell probably saw it coming. Insiders report that the general's stiff upper lip was beginning to quiver by this time, and his shoulders began to slump from his normal ramrod-straight military posture.

Seawell had always been somewhat aloof from his staff—"a little bit too dependent on the pomp and circumstance of being the general," one aide recalled. "He's a very autocratic guy, and seemed very formal and distant. But I think he was just a fairly shy person, maybe unwilling to let anybody see his weakness or lack of resolve."

By 1981, though, Pan Am's misadventure with the National acquisition and its continuing heavy losses were taking their toll, and Seawell's facade started to crumble. That same year, Seawell agreed to step down, Waltrip became president, and the board began a search for a new post-deregulation chairman for Pan Am.

One year later, even the CAB—which had allowed and even encouraged the merger—deemed the Pan Am–National alliance an abject failure. Pan Am, said an internal CAB study, was stuck with fixed operating costs at a level that was "enormously higher than the majors' [i.e., the major carriers'] average, and climbing."

"In general," the CAB study observed, "Pan Am's operating costs are far above its competitors', and the coming of intense competition under deregulation has left it unable to compete profitably.

This has been aggravated by the increasing costs and decreasing revenues from its newly acquired domestic system, and by the division and discord which hampered the former management."

Frank Lorenzo, on the other hand, had only just begun. He had testified before the CAB that he would not look for another airline to acquire if the agency ruled against his National bid, saying that National was "an unusual situation." Those words were quickly forgotten. With his purchasing power suddenly enhanced by tens of millions of dollars and his leveraging skill giving him access to many times that amount, Lorenzo set his sights even higher. He turned his gaze on TWA, where he'd begun his airline career as a lowly assistant nearly twenty years before.

TWA was part of a larger holding company, Trans World Corporation, which also owned Hilton International Hotels, Canteen Corporation, and other subsidiaries. Lorenzo quietly bought up 4.9 percent of Trans World's stock, and on September 13, 1979, asked TW Corporation's Chairman, Ed Smart, to breakfast at the Carlyle Hotel on Manhattan's Upper East Side.

TWA at the time was in financial distress. Like Pan Am, it had rushed out at the beginning of the decade and bought dozens of 747s, which by this point were flying around with empty seats. Lorenzo was unfazed by the fact that TWA was about fourteen times the size of his own carrier.

"We told Ed Smart that what would make the most sense for him was to spin off TWA out of Trans World Corporation," Lorenzo said. From Texas International's perspective, "TWA did not have a southern hub. The hub we could provide in Houston, plus our access to Mexico, plus our DC-9s all made great sense, and a great fit with TWA," he pointed out. "But Smart didn't have any interest."

"Smart basically told him, 'Screw off, no deal,' " a former TWA executive said. "He cut it short right there." According to one account, Smart actually walked out of the meeting.

Lorenzo's reputation as a renegade was spreading through the industry club. "The other guys in the industry regarded him as a pirate, more as a speculator than as someone who wants to operate an airline," said one industry analyst. Lorenzo's obsession with deal making was also noticed by his own associates at Texas International. Gerry Gitner put it this way: "If Lorenzo sat next to the queen of England, he'd ask her, 'How much do you want for Wales?' "

7

THE UPSTARTS

Frank Lorenzo couldn't savor his spectacular profit from the sale of Texas International's National stock for long. On the morning of January 7, 1980, he found a letter lying on his desk from Don Burr. After eight years, Burr wrote, he was resigning from Texas International Airlines. Even though Lorenzo had just given him the title of president and raised his pay to $150,000, Burr was still unhappy.

The rift between the two former friends had grown so wide that they had gone their separate ways over the previous holidays, breaking their tradition of spending Christmas together at Burr's Utah ski home. Burr had instead spent his vacation sulking and complaining to his mother, who had flown in from Connecticut. He had never forgotten Lorenzo's rude rejection of his cherished plan to motivate employees. He now wanted to strike out on his own. Burr's mother told him he was being foolish. "You've got a big job, lots of responsibility, prestige, and status," she said. "You are very well off. I think it's crazy."

But Burr was hardly being impulsive. Along with Lorenzo, he had been watching the progress of the deregulation law and the ease with which new airlines were raising capital. The situation seemed to call for just the sort of entrepreneurial endeavor he envisioned.

Lorenzo did not realize the extent to which he'd given Burr his opening. Although Texas International now had annual sales of $240 million and a fleet of thirty-five planes, it was not really a player. As his lunges at National and TWA had shown, Lorenzo wanted to run an airline of consequence. He'd often disappear for weeks in pursuit of a mysterious deal, leaving Burr to run the company. Burr, meanwhile, had cultivated a small group of transplanted New Yorkers like himself, intelligent, well-educated people who had migrated to Texas to try something different. Burr was confident that he could attract the best talent away from Lorenzo.

Burr kept all this to himself when Lorenzo phoned and asked him to reconsider his resignation. "Come on back," Burr recalls Lorenzo as saying. "This is nonsense." The two met for a final stab at reconciliation, but Burr left, saying "it just isn't going to work."

Burr's decision was final. A few weeks after his letter had arrived in Lorenzo's office, Burr packed his belongings into a van and pulled out of the parking lot at Texas International's drab airport headquarters. He still had no idea where he was going, but he did have several other disaffected employees with him. One was Melrose Dawsey, his thirty-two-year-old secretary, who had worked closely with him for years. The talented Gerry Gitner, by then Lorenzo's top marketing man, also immediately quit when he learned of Burr's resignation.

The three pulled all the money out of their savings. Burr reaped a nice after-tax profit from selling the 125,000 shares he'd accumulated in Texas International, which was then trading at eighteen dollars per share. Burr also sold two condominiums he owned in Park City, Utah. Altogether he scraped up $355,000. Gitner came up with $175,000 and Dawsey scrounged $20,000. That gave them a total of $550,000; they could not even get half a plane for that.

Yet Burr's investment banking experience had taught him that virtually anyone with a compelling business plan could raise money. He set up shop in a small suite of offices in a nondescript shopping center in downtown Houston and spent days batting around ideas with Dawsey and Gitner. For inspiration, all they had to do was to look 250 miles north to Dallas. Southwest Airlines' formula of short flights, low fares, and no frills was wildly successful. In fact, Southwest had just started its first flights outside Texas, thanks to the new deregulation law, but it was staying within the regional boundaries its name suggested.

The concept could easily be transplanted to other parts of the country, and Southwest clones began to spring up. Two Chicago airline men, Hughes Airwest executive Irwin Tague and a former Air Force pilot named David Hinson, moved into the virtually abandoned Midway airfield right near the center of their hometown. In November of 1979, they started no-frills Midway Airlines, unabashedly cribbing the Southwest formula. By flying short distances and offering one-class, low-fare service, Midway could theoretically stay out of the way of the giants across town at O'Hare, United and American.

Kahn's CAB had almost giddily welcomed this newcomer in. This, not mergers of existing carriers, was what deregulation was supposed to be about. The experience of Air Florida, a dinky intrastate line quickly expanding into a major airline under dynamic financier and former Braniff executive Ed Acker, was also encouraging.

Burr wanted to get in on the excitement. Upstarts were poised to be the new darlings of Wall Street. Midway raised $33 million for capital funding. With their low labor costs and lean structures, these newcomers seemed to have an enormous advantage over the Big Four. Financial institutions that had long nurtured their ties to the TWAs and Americans of the world were now contemplating bankrolling the very companies that proposed to take on the big guys.

This reflected deregulation theory distilled to its basic tenets: There were no economies of scale in the airline business. The advantage simply went to the company with the lowest costs. Don Burr recalls that he viewed United, American, and the other big airlines as "sheep being led to slaughter." The press soon picked up the war cry, dismissing the Big Four as "Flying Dinosaurs."

In fact, just after deregulation, United and American acted like wounded animals, pulling back rather than stomping all over their competition. United even abandoned many of the eastern routes it had picked up in its Capital merger, and American also dropped some of its northeastern markets. Times were hard: The cost of jet fuel shot up by 88 percent in 1979, followed by another 23 percent increase in 1980, and the nation was heading into recession. The two airlines tried to cut costs, laying off workers and jettisoning their older, fuel-guzzling 707s and DC-8s.

"A good new entrant can clean their clock anytime," said an industry analyst. Bob Crandall and Dick Ferris countered by referring to the upstarts as "cream skimmers" who were going to swoop down on their most profitable routes, slash fares, and take their business away. Their complaints did not engender much sympathy.

One day that spring of 1980, Burr called Southwest's Herb Kelleher, who was delighted that his success had already spawned a flattering number of imitators. "Sure, come on up," he said. Burr had encouraged a few more of his Texas International friends to defect, and he sent a team up to Dallas to spend a few weeks observing Kelleher's operation. Kelleher had perfected the art of the "fifteen-minute turnaround"—unloading an arriving jet and reboarding new passengers within a quarter-hour, a practice that drastically cut costs. Kelleher's low costs meant he could charge less, and his cut-rate fares had filled his planes to capacity. So had his trademark flamboyance. Among other things, the uniform for Southwest's female flight attendants consisted of hot pants. Since his little airline had started up at Love Field in 1971, the traffic between Dallas and Houston alone had doubled.

To Burr and his team, the most obvious market to exploit was the northeast. The Boston-to-Washington air corridor was the busiest in the country by far, traveled by two and a half million flyers a year. The only competition was the Eastern Shuttle, which for years had provided its captive clientele an unattractive mix of high fares and surly service.

Still, no one knew quite how to begin. Burr's thinking went something like this: "We've got nothing. I've got to get a few planes, find someone to fly them, and get a place to land . . . then I guess I'll have an airline." He saw himself as the modern incarnation of early pioneers like Juan Trippe who could, literally overnight, round up a couple of ten-seater craft and simply take off.

That was difficult in the northeast, however. The prime space at airports was locked up by the incumbents under long-term leases. Burr sent his new staffers to scout for locations. Gerry Gitner came back with the suggestion they look at the underused airport at Newark, New Jersey. Burr gagged. "Newark, God, that's the dog hole of the world," he said, "who's going to finance us at Newark?" Gitner later said that Burr preferred Baltimore as a base, apparently because he wanted to settle down on Maryland's swank Eastern Shore.

But Burr couldn't ignore all the numbers—New York was sitting there practically untapped. Even with its unglamorous image, Newark was just fourteen miles from Manhattan and had an abandoned terminal building that would do just fine. Burr reconciled himself to the idea of settling in the New Jersey suburbs. He eventually found a community to his liking, the wealthy town of Bernardsville. Curiously, Burr's forebears were founding fathers of the city of Newark. Numerous generations later, Don Burr was proposing to revive its airport.

Later that spring Burr approached prominent Boston venture capitalist Thomas Lee. Burr was convinced he could rake in millions in profits. "Take a 737 airplane—that's got 118 seats," he'd say. "Put it on a short hop say, Buffalo to New York, about an hour's trip. You charge thirty-five dollars a ticket, less than the cost of driving, and that gets you $4,130. The fixed costs of the trip—fuel, crew, and other essentials—total $2,000 or so. So you have over $2,000 gross profit per hour—a profit margin of nearly 100 percent." There was no question that fares that low would fill the plane to capacity.

The key to Burr's plan was his astonishingly low operating costs. Employees would be trained in several jobs so that they could move easily back and forth among them, boosting productivity. Workers' base salaries would be set far lower than those of their unionized counterparts, but they'd get stock in the company at attractive prices, giving them further motivation. No source of revenue had been overlooked: Passengers would even pay fifty cents for soft drinks and five dollars for each checked bag. The high costs of manning service counters at airports would be cut by collecting fares in flight. And the airline would save millions of dollars in travel agency commissions by selling tickets directly to consumers. In all, Burr could operate his carrier at a fraction of the cost of the established carriers.

Lee liked his idea, but told Burr that he couldn't sell it without a name. Burr was stumped at first; his first tries, like Sundance, drew groans from his colleagues. Finally, he sat down with his team and played a word-association game. Lorenzo had always been amused by Don's "people ideas," so they came up with "People Express." But when they tried it out before the Wall Street investment crowd, the reaction was occasionally bemused. "That sounds like some communist airline," said Michael Derchin, who by then had left American for an airline analyst job with Oppenheimer. Burr would occasionally startle investors by saying he wanted simply to "make a better world." His plan—with its concept of worker ownership and bringing air travel to the masses—did strike some as a cross between socialism and Harvard B-School do-goodism. People Express would indeed offer a flying experience closer to Aeroflot than to Pan Am, but its low-fare, high-volume formula would, Burr said, make them all rich.

Burr's unorthodox sales pitch soon paid off. In August, Burr had lunch in New York City with William Hambrecht, a dynamic partner in the San Francisco investment firm of Hambrecht and Quist and one of the people responsible for the flow of risk capital into Silicon Valley during the seventies. Hambrecht, who'd had success in getting

Apple Computer started, readily agreed to help Burr raise the $12 million he was seeking. Burr then applied for CAB approval.

Later that month, Burr arrived for his first inspection of the dreary, neglected North Terminal he'd leased at Newark. He found a squalid, rat-infested horror. "Whatever didn't fall on your head, bit you in the ankle," he said. He rushed to the phone to call Bill Hambrecht in a panic. Hambrecht reassured him that they had a deal, no matter what the airport space looked like. They made an initial offering of stock and, to their surprise, raised $25 million in a matter of weeks, more than double their goal.

Burr offered to refurbish the decrepit terminal out of his own pocket. At first he was rebuffed by the Port Authority, which seemed to take the view that the brash newcomer was too weird to succeed. Burr recalled that one day a particularly truculent official tried to dissuade him from proceeding. "Let me show you what happened to the last guy who tried to operate out of here," said the man, who guided Burr up some stairs to an abandoned office with broken windows, peeling paint, and furniture lying in a heap. On the wall was a yellowing poster depicting the previous occupant, Colonial Airways, which had long faded into aviation history. Burr cleaned up the mess and made it his office.

The officers by then included former Lorenzo employees Robert McAdoo, who'd apprenticed in the financial department at TWA; Lori Beaman, a personnel officer; and Harold Pareti, an effusive young lawyer who'd worked at the CAB before joining Texas International. Burr, typically, organized them along democratic lines: All executives earned the same salary, forty-eight thousand dollars a year. No one had secretaries or expense accounts; even the CEO answered his own phone. All were in their late twenties or thirties; Burr, at thirty-nine, was the oldest of the lot. Together they'd plunked down nearly $1 million of their own money to invest in the fledgling organization, in exchange for 1.3 million shares of stock. Burr was insistent that everyone own stock in the enterprise, no matter what their status; even the lowest-paid clerks were still required to buy a few shares in the company, usually by having part of their salaries withheld.

Back in Houston, the exodus of management talent from Texas International perplexed Lorenzo. In all, fifteen of Lorenzo's top managers defected to People Express. Those who remained thought that Lorenzo "acted like a jilted lover," said one colleague.

Then when Neal Meehan, a longtime Lorenzo associate, said he was leaving to join Burr, Lorenzo exploded. Meehan at first was unmoved by Lorenzo's pleas; he willingly played the guest of honor at a party at Burr's Houston home for this newest People's recruit.

But a few days later, Meehan suddenly stopped taking Burr's calls. There was no contact for weeks. Finally, Meehan told Burr that Lorenzo had made him a counteroffer he could not refuse. Meehan had been chosen to head a brand-new airline Lorenzo was starting, one that would compete on the same turf as Burr's, New York Air.

For years Burr argued that New York Air was dreamed up as Lorenzo's revenge on him for forming People Express. Lorenzo insisted that New York Air was already in the works when Burr left, implying that Burr in effect stole the idea from him. The rupture between the two went deep, and the once inseparable friends didn't speak for years. A tentative rapprochement came in 1984 at the Conquistadores' Wyoming retreat. By then the two were certified members of the club. They resumed their friendship, and it was to prove more durable than either of their new airline companies.

BY THE FALL OF 1980 Lorenzo was quickly moving to overtake Burr in the race to be the first to create a deregulation-proof airline, and the effort seemed to revive his spirits. He was, like Burr, inspired by the entrepreneurial spirit he saw around him, and more likely, by the money he saw rolling in from Wall Street. Lorenzo wanted a big airline company. He, too, wanted low labor costs, but without the "touchy-feely" veneer of People's. If Burr fancied himself a latter-day flyboy, Lorenzo likely drew his inspiration from Henry Frick, Andrew Carnegie, and the other robber barons whose biographies he'd studied as a boy. They had created large holding companies to build railroads and steel mills, and Lorenzo would do the same to build an airline empire.

In the summer of 1980, Lorenzo set up the Texas Air Corporation, which, despite its name, would never fly a plane. It had plenty of cash—about $35 million after taxes from the National raid, plus a like amount that was already sitting in Texas International's coffers. Lorenzo had already built up Texas International's war chest through a series of what an associate described as "creative financings." In 1978 Jet Capital did a unit offering of subordinated debentures and common stock. At the time, it was regarded as "a new kind of deal for an airline," said Jet Capital director Douglas Tansill.

"This increased Frank's awareness that there was money out there, money that could be used, if he chose, to acquire the undervalued assets that he also saw," Tansill said. Such thinking was unusual for the airline, and Lorenzo's sophistication in financial matters was already setting him apart from his peers. The new holding company would be his vehicle for establishing new airlines or acquiring existing ones. The Texas Air umbrella embraced the existing Texas International Airlines, a unionized carrier in the Southwest; and New York Air, which would be a separate, nonunion, low-frills outfit in the Northeast. At the top of this corporate pyramid would be Jet Capital, the original firm cofounded by Lorenzo and Carney, which would own a controlling interest in Texas Air. It was, as analysts would remark, an extremely clever setup, one that gave Lorenzo and his partners an inordinate amount of influence for the money that they had put in.

To replace the talent drained by Burr, Lorenzo went on a recruiting binge. "He hired deregulation," was how one observer put it, using big salaries to lure some of the stars who'd helped write the law. He recruited Phil Bakes, who'd worked as deputy manager for Ted Kennedy's ill-fated presidential campaign after leaving the CAB in 1979. Lorenzo persuaded the father of deregulation himself, Alfred Kahn, to sit on New York Air's board of directors, flattering Kahn by telling him that this low-fare airline was the embodiment of his ideas. Clark Onstad, general counsel of the Federal Aviation Administration during deregulation, also signed on. Not long after that, even deregulation "ayatollah" Mike Levine succumbed to Lorenzo's entreaties and joined Texas Air.

Lorenzo's new team would give the company a not entirely accurate image as a darling of deregulation. For on September 8, 1980, just weeks after Lorenzo had announced his plan to create New York Air, the Texas International directors authorized a plan to explore a merger with another airline. Lorenzo had failed to acquire National and TWA, but now he seized on Continental as a choice target. This next takeover battle would make Lorenzo's lunge at National seem friendly. But it would remain behind the scenes over the next six months as plans to start up New York Air progressed.

Bakes, Lorenzo's cicerone through the politics of deregulation, was assigned to make sure that New York Air was airborne before the end of 1980. That would give the fledgling company a healthy jump on People Express, scheduled to make its debut the following April. Both airlines had a capital base of around $25 million. By late October, both New York Air and People Express had obtained the blessing of the CAB.

Lorenzo next took the provocative step of asking for an unprec-

edented number of highly desirable takeoff and landing positions at
Washington's National Airport. Unlike most other airports in the
United States, which are controlled by local authorities, the Washington facility came under the jurisdiction of the Federal Aviation
Administration. Space there was extremely hard to come by, and
Lorenzo couldn't break in unless he could pry some "slots" loose
from the existing airlines, which had every reason to preserve their
turf and deny space to any aggressive newcomer. In New York, Lorenzo bid for gates at La Guardia, rather than staking out abandoned
territory as Burr had at Newark. Lorenzo was eyeing some of the
nation's most desirable landing fields.

The conventional wisdom at the time was that no airline executive
in his right mind would voluntarily hand over any space at National
to a low-fare competitor. A *Business Week* article in September took
an especially jaundiced view of Lorenzo's chances. "An upstart carrier called New York Air plans to challenge Eastern Air Lines' ham-
merlock on the busy New York–Washington air corridor," the story
began, "even though it has no place to land and little chance of getting
the 20 daily operating slots it needs at . . . close-in National Airport."

However, Phil Bakes knew firsthand that politicians were concerned the deregulation experiment might fail. If newcomers were
blocked at the departure gate, it would make a mockery of the new
ease of entry the law was supposed to encourage. The argument
worked: The FAA gave Lorenzo's airline a king's ransom in slots that
would allow it to start nearly hourly service between New York and
Washington, striking directly at the Eastern Shuttle, which had been
one of Eastern's few consistent moneymakers.

Burr said later that he assumed Frank Lorenzo had bagged the
slots through some "chicanery." But Burr had other worries—his
terminal was still a wreck and he lacked planes, a workforce, and
other necessities. Meanwhile, thousands of applicants were showing
up to apply for work at his new People Express. Burr had had the
idea of calling every employee a "manager." Successful applicants
had to demonstrate an aptitude for handling multiple functions. Psychological exams were administered to all applicants and those with
airline experience were nearly always disqualified as too accustomed
to rigid job definitions. At People's a person might be a flight attendant one day, work on reservations the next, and sort baggage
another time. The new airline, as it turned out, would be run by a
group of former schoolteachers, recent college graduates, and other
neophytes.

Lorenzo, too, would have nonunion workers who would earn far less than their counterparts at Texas International. New York Air was hiring captains at salaries of thirty thousand dollars, about half the rate at major lines. And he had one huge advantage over Burr: He already owned airplanes. To launch New York Air, he simply took six of Texas International's DC-9 jets and repainted them in bold red colors, splashing a red apple on the tail fin.

This "advantage" had one drawback, however. The unions were enraged, especially the Air Line Pilots Association, which saw this as a transparent bid to spin off assets of a unionized airline into a nonunion sister company. To ALPA, Lorenzo again was proving himself a nemesis of organized labor.

All this was ignored as New York Air prepared to make a splashy debut in New York in early December, to cash in on the Christmas travel rush. It set air fares of twenty-nine and forty-nine dollars one-way, depending on the time of day. That was just a few dollars more than the bus fare, and well below Eastern's sixty-dollar ticket price.

The first New York Air flights were set to take off on December 14, but Lorenzo did not anticipate the depth of the pilots' animosity. ALPA filed a lawsuit to block the airline, and the court issued a stay to consider the pilots' arguments. As December 14 passed and New York Air planes sat grounded, the unions kept up the attack. On December 16, Captain John O'Donnell, an Eastern pilot and president of ALPA, delivered a blistering attack on Lorenzo before a group of Wall Street securities analysts. He warned that New York Air could start an ominous trend, which he named the "runaway airline." Once other airlines saw what Lorenzo was up to, he said, there would be similar spinoffs from major unionized carriers, giving management a new weapon against labor: Either give us concessions or we'll siphon off more assets into the nonunion sister company.

The court, however, soon waived the temporary restraining order and on December 19, New York Air's first flight lifted off. But the celebration was dampened by noisy disruptions outside the terminal. Protesting pilots had lined up outside the art deco Marine Air Terminal building at La Guardia Airport, where a cocktail party was being held to celebrate the new airline's debut. The hostility was palpable. One of the VIP guests, the widow of the beloved New York City mayor Fiorello La Guardia, declined to cross the picket line. Harry Hoglander, a pilots' leader at TWA, was one of the picketers, and recalled their anger that Lorenzo was being heralded as a "hero of deregulation, the darling of the Yuppie Right." Ronald Reagan's inauguration was just weeks away, and the prospect of a conservative Republican in the White House was hardly good news for the pilots.

The new administration's dedication to the labor protection provisions in the deregulation law was questionable at best.

Union leaders had also been disturbed by the tenor of the CAB's order formally approving New York Air's startup. If it was a test of how the board would interpret the new law's labor provisions, they had reason to be worried. Although the law specifically directed the CAB to consider "the need to encourage fair wages and equitable working conditions" for employees of new airlines, the agency simply brushed off union objections, saying it could not "expand (our) presence in the labor field." Although New York Air would be flying Texas International planes without Texas International pilots, the CAB said that Lorenzo was, in effect, within his rights to shift his aircraft to the nonunion spinoff.

Over the next few weeks more pilots from other airlines joined the protest against the newcomer at La Guardia. The cockpit crews at the new line often withstood verbal harassment from other pilots over the radio as they taxied down the runway. It gradually died down but left a sour taste, as if the promise of deregulation had already been perverted.

For his part, Burr would not threaten the status quo. His modest plan was not to assault a fortress like Washington National but to start off with flights to Buffalo, New York, and Norfolk, Virginia, with some used 737s he picked up from Lufthansa German Airlines. And his flyspeck operation was, then, of little interest to the unions.

At the last minute, he too was dealt a setback. The Newark terminal lacked not only charm, but also heat, functioning restrooms, and places for passengers to sit. "What's going to happen if we have all these people showing up here and the toilets don't work?" Burr fumed. He decided he couldn't wait for the Port Authority to act, so he hired workmen to go in at night and make the repairs without permission from the authorities. "The next morning they would come in and rip it all out," he said. He began to despair of ever taking off, and although he had assembled every other piece of the airline with amazing ease, the airport side was an enormous and unexpected stumbling block.

But People Express made its deadline, starting operations on a balmy April 30, 1981, with twenty-three-dollar flights to Buffalo, a price that would beat the cost of driving. As Burr boarded that first flight, he panicked. Only a few of the 118 seats were filled. "I've put every cent I have into this airline and it's going to fail," he remembered thinking.

Within a few days newspapers had picked up on the remarkable low fares the airline was offering. With virtually no advertising, People Express's reservations lines were jammed. Soon the airline was flying to five cities, including Columbus, Ohio, Jacksonville, and Boston. On its Norfolk runs, it offered a thirty-five-dollar one-way fare while its main competitor, Piedmont, charged eighty-two dollars. Piedmont soon dropped its fare to thirty-five dollars.

PEOPLE EXPRESS, NEW YORK AIR, and other upstarts had become a bona fide media phenomenon. "The Great Airline Revolution of the 1980s," was what some pundits called it.

Other newcomers rushed in once they saw the welcome extended by Washington. Charter operator World Airways began scheduled coast-to-coast service at ninety-nine dollars one-way, ending Ed Daly's long war of attrition against the CAB; it was joined by another irregular, Capitol Airlines. Brand-new Columbia Air and Air Chicago joined the fray. Muse Air was an upstart with a curious history: It was formed by former Southwest Airlines chief Lamar Muse, whose acrimonious split with Herb Kelleher a few years earlier led some to call his new airline "Air Revenge." After a year it seemed deregulation was working.

Just months after People Express's debut, however, the much-ballyhooed "airline revolution" was dealt a serious setback. What the media had been ignoring in their effusiveness was a long-simmering crisis in Washington that threatened dire consequences for the future of the deregulation experiment.

Air traffic controllers had been threatening to strike since the beginning of the year, but few took them seriously. As federal employees, they were barred from walking off the job. When the controllers' union contract with the FAA expired in mid-March, there was relief when nothing happened. In all likelihood an eleventh-hour agreement would be reached, the airlines thought. It was a vast miscalculation, in retrospect, and it revealed how unprepared the industry was for the Reagan administration's hard-line approach to labor.

The thirteen-thousand-member Professional Air Traffic Controllers Organization was regarded as the most militant of the federal employee unions. Worn down by years of high-stress conditions, the controllers were angry at what they perceived as the government's insensitivity to their needs. When their demands for a shorter work week and higher pay were rejected, they took the unprecedented step of walking off the job on August 4, 1981.

The air travel system was immediately thrown into chaos, with massive flight cancellations. President Reagan ordered the controllers to return to work. Their leader, Robert Poli, urged his members to hold out.

Sometime later that day, President Reagan placed a phone call to Dick Ferris at United, to find out what the chief of the nation's largest airline would think if he fired all the striking controllers. Reagan reminisced to Ferris about how he'd been head of the Screen Actors Guild at the time when public employees were first allowed the right to be represented by a union. He remembered when they pledged never to strike as part of that agreement.

Ferris told Reagan he had his support. "The law is the law," he said, "we don't feel the controllers should hold the whole nation hostage." Reagan issued an ultimatum—return to your jobs within three days or you're fired. Most chose the latter alternative.

Right after the controllers were fired, leaving the system drastically short-handed, the Federal Aviation Administration took what it thought was the logical, even-handed step: It ordered all airlines to temporarily ground about a third of their fleets. But it was not the Uniteds and Americans that would suffer the most from the strike. Thanks to the recession, they had excess capacity and could more easily idle their planes. It was their nonunion competition, the off-spring of deregulation, airlines like People Express, New York Air, and Midway, that were hurt most. The Reagan administration had in one blow turned back the progress of the deregulation law that espoused the free enterprise Republicans held so dear. Don Burr and Frank Lorenzo got no personal phone calls from the president.

In the weeks that followed, New York Air was blown out of most of its markets. It had to eliminate all flights between New York and Boston, forcing it to abandon the shuttle concept less than a year after its startup. It would take years to recover.

Although a number of people later urged Reagan to grant amnesty to the controllers, the president would not budge, even though it took much longer than expected to rebuild the air traffic control system with newly trained replacements. "Yes, perhaps they deserved to be fired," said Alfred Kahn. "But I remember going around and saying: They pardoned Nixon after one year. These guys had a life sentence. And we needed them."

Another victim of the controllers' strike was former Pan Am president Dan Colussy, who had been about to launch a new low-fare carrier in the eastern United States called Columbia Air. He had airplanes and crews ready to go, but suddenly lost the airline's landing slots at La Guardia and Pittsburgh; this put the venture out of business before its first flight.

Midway and other small fry were also affected disproportionately to their size. People Express found itself shut out of dozens of airports. Burr rushed down to Washington to plead personally with Federal Aviation Administrator Lynn Helms to make an exception for his company. At that point People flew only six planes, which were brimming to capacity. To retire two of them would devastate the airline.

Burr told Helms flatly: "We are clearly going to go out of business. We have no staying power. We're different from American and the other guys. We are what deregulation is all about and we are going to go under."

As Burr recalled the conversation, Helms's response was essentially, "This is not my problem. Why don't you sell your planes? You think I'm going to give you a break?"

It was, said Burr, "One of most straightforward rejections I'd ever had in my whole life."

People had indeed come close to expiring, losing $6 million in the weeks right after the PATCO strike. Burr quickly put his idled planes into cities like Syracuse, New York, and Burlington, Vermont, and charged rock-bottom fares for flights down south. As soon as the snow fell, the flights were full. Yet Burr was still frozen out of the big markets—Chicago, Denver, Dallas, and Washington.

The advantages of size, supposedly nonexistent in the airline industry, were starting to become apparent. The 1981 controllers' strike and its aftermath certainly prevented the newcomers from growing as quickly as they otherwise might have. And although the controller force was rebuilt, it wasn't restored to prestrike levels for several years. Landing slots at the four busiest airports—New York's La Guardia and Kennedy, Chicago's O'Hare, and Washington's National—remained restricted.

The problem for new or growing airlines was that those four airports provided access to some of the best air travel markets in the country; as long as the new entrants couldn't win access to those markets, the promise of deregulation would be delayed. Long after the controllers' strike, new entrant America West Airlines, for example, fought unsuccessfully for several years to win slots at Washington National and La Guardia. The ability of the old airlines to cling tenaciously to what they saw as their established property rights in terms of gates and slots at these key airports was another flaw in the deregulators' original theory.

"It's a question of allocating them fairly," an attorney for one new airline told *The New York Times* in 1984. "The incumbent carriers do not want any new carrier in there—it's more competition. The bottom line is that the ability of a new carrier to get in is impossible."

In the wake of the controllers' strike it was becoming clear that airline deregulation couldn't succeed unless the government recognized the barriers to entry that still existed, and did something to remove them.

8

DIRTY TRICKS

O n a Friday morning in the middle of February 1982, Elliott
Seiden, a lawyer in the antitrust division of the Justice Department in Washington, switched on his desk tape recorder.
His colleagues wanted him to listen to a recording of a phone call
that had just arrived in their office. They suspected it might contain
damaging evidence on a prominent business personality.

The raspy voice Seiden heard betrayed a lifetime of chainsmoking.

"I think it's dumb as hell, for Christ's sake, all right, to sit here
and pound the shit out of each other and neither one of us making
a fucking dime," said the man.

"Goddamn, what the fuck is the point of it?"

Seiden was shocked. The speaker was Bob Crandall, the president
of American Airlines. He was talking to his counterpart at rival
Braniff Airlines, Howard Putnam.

The call took place on February 1. That morning, Crandall exploded when he saw a Braniff ad in the paper showing two checklists,
which compared Braniff's and American's passenger amenities.
There were check marks on each line in the Braniff column and none
in the American column.

Crandall, the tape made clear, was even more furious at Braniff's
persistent price slashing. American had been adding flights out of

Braniff's home base at the giant Dallas/Fort Worth Airport, and Delta Air Lines was also moving in. Braniff had responded by cutting fares almost in half. Crandall matched the price cuts, but it galled him to do it; it cost American an estimated $7 million a month in passenger revenues.

"Nobody asked American to serve Harlingen. Nobody asked American to serve Kansas City," Putnam told Crandall, referring to Braniff routes where American had moved in.

"The [American hub] complex is here," Crandall shot back, "ain't gonna change a goddamn thing, all right? We can both live here, and there ain't no room for Delta. But there's no reason I can see—all right?—to put both companies out of business."

"But if you're going to overlay every route of American's on top of every route that Braniff has—I just can't sit here and allow you to bury us without giving our best effort," Putnam argued.

Crandall then pointed out to Putnam that Eastern and Delta managed to coexist at Atlanta without destroying each other, implying that American and Braniff could do the same.

"Do you have a suggestion for me?" Putnam asked.

"Yes, I have a suggestion for you," Crandall barked. "Raise your goddamn fares 20 percent. I'll raise mine the next morning. . . . You'll make more money, and I will too."

"We can't talk about pricing," Putnam warned.

"Oh, bullshit, Howard, we can talk about any goddamn thing we want to talk about," Crandall insisted.

"God, this is bad stuff," Seiden said to his colleagues. Clearly, he said, it was attempted price-fixing, and unlike the old days, it wasn't being done with the help of the government. The following Monday morning, the Justice Department convened a grand jury investigation into the possible criminal behavior revealed by the call. As Crandall would learn months later, Putnam, on the advice of lawyers, had taped their conversation and turned it over to the federal government.

As the months of grand jury proceedings wore on, Seiden saw a problem. There had, in fact, been no agreement to fix prices; Putnam had turned Crandall down. Merely attempting to fix prices is no crime. "What do we have?" Seiden wondered. "Was it an actionable offense or just stupid conduct on the part of Crandall?" Seiden and the other antitrust lawyers realized there was a larger issue here as well. American had been building a hub at Dallas, acquiring gates and adding flights. The lawyers figured that if Braniff had agreed to Crandall's suggestion, it would not only have been price fixing, it would have been monopolization. The two airlines combined would have controlled Dallas/Fort Worth, with about 98 percent of the airline traffic out of the region. Seiden decided to slam Crandall and American for the equally serious crime of attempted monopolization, a violation of another section of the Sherman Antitrust Act.

IN EARLY 1982, OFFICIALS IN Washington were watching with interest as the once gentlemanly airline business deteriorated into an undignified brawl. Airlines, it seemed, were getting good at playing dirty.

Crandall's tough talk had earned him a dubious reputation in the industry. In early 1982, at a conference on new airline companies at Wall Street's Oppenheimer and Company, a story made the rounds about the American president's alleged reaction to an incursion into Detroit, where New York Air and Midway had moved in with low fares. At an American staff meeting, Crandall had reportedly blurted out, "I want 'em out of Detroit." The message had made it back to Crandall's intended targets.

"You guys have to be careful," Michael Derchin, then an analyst at Oppenheimer, warned Don Burr and the other confident leaders of the upstart airlines. "The big guys will lose money as long as it takes to get rid of you."

Bob Crandall saw the situation differently. Deregulation had set off a Darwinian struggle, and to survive, the industry had to get rid of its old clubby decorum.

"We all went out and started to behave like aggressive competitors, and that includes bopping the enemy on the head, which is what they do in every other business," Crandall said later. "But the fact of the matter is, that wasn't considered kosher in our business. . . . It was a newly competitive industry, and [the Justice Department] wanted to set tight constraints around competitive behavior."

Other airline chiefs, while less blunt, were using their might to strike back at their low-cost competition. United Airlines took the unusual step of abruptly severing its "interlining" agreement with New York Air, which meant the two airlines no longer would sell tickets for each other's flights. That could deprive New York Air of revenue from joint ticket sales. United refused to explain the move; observers noticed it happened right after New York Air went into United's Cleveland turf.

There were other disturbing incidents coming to light. United had demanded the right to approve New York Air's schedules out of La Guardia Airport as a condition of its contract to provide ground support services to the newcomer there. United refused to approve New York Air's schedule one month, however, when the airline proposed a big increase in flights to Boston.

United and American said they were simply displaying the tough competitiveness a free market demanded. Both airlines had had a rough time in 1980: United's operating loss reached $67 million and American's ballooned to nearly twice that amount. Both had shed many money-losing services: United pulled out of 123 short-distance routes. Ferris, like Crandall, was struggling to find a workable strategy, building up service at Chicago, Denver, and San Francisco, and toying with—but later abandoning—smaller hubs at Cleveland and Kansas City. Their recovery depended on how well they exploited the advantages they did have.

"This was survival—taking advantage of a competitor's vulnerability, putting economic pressure where you can put economic pressure, and I don't think there's anything wrong with that," said Tom Plaskett, who at the time was American's top marketing executive. "It sometimes gets to be painful and ugly, and some people may say unfair, but that's what the [capitalist] system is all about."

Plaskett had a point: The airlines were exhibiting just the sort of entrepreneurial energy that regulation had suppressed for years. The problem was that much of this ingenuity was going into erecting barriers to competition.

For all that Crandall and his colleagues wrapped themselves in the mantle of capitalism, the history of American business was rife with examples of anticompetitive conduct. Among the first people to be tried and convicted under the criminal section of the Sherman Antitrust Act in the early twentieth century was National Cash Register founder John Patterson, the archetype of the ruthless free-marketeer, whose sales pitches so eerily prefigured Crandall's. He was so obsessed with dominating the market for his machines that he arranged to open distribution outlets next to secondhand dealers to force them to sell out or declare bankruptcy. Sometimes Patterson would open two "dummy stores" on either side of his intended target, cutting prices and underselling until the "enemy" closed down. He'd spy on his competitors and sometimes sabotage them. The airline business of the 1980s sometimes resembled Patterson's world—only the transgressions would be accomplished electronically. The evidence, such as it was, was often ephemeral.

Alfred Kahn had foreseen the dangers. Before he left the CAB, Kahn predicted that bigger lines would respond to the upstarts with predatory pricing—that is, cutting prices to unprofitable levels to push irritating newcomers out of the way, only to raise them again when the deed was accomplished. When World Airways chief Ed Daly finally won the right to fly scheduled flights coast to coast in the fall of 1978, Kahn openly fretted about the response from the major lines. Capitol, another reborn charter line, was coming into that market too, and Kahn, in one of his last memos to his CAB staff, wrote:

"World and Capitol are going to come in with a $99 fare, and we have to think about whether or not we're going to put any restrictions on the competitive response of the established carriers. They will certainly come down to $99, and is there any doubt that this will drive out World and Capitol, and is there any doubt that the fares will then go up? And will others come in after they've seen what happened to World and Capitol?"

Kahn was right. In 1980, Eastern started flying between New York and Los Angeles, and for the first time in their history, all of the Big Four were competing coast to coast. Suddenly their fares sank to the ninety-nine dollars charged by World. Eastern ultimately lost so much money it had to pull out of the cross-country market. A few years later, World went bankrupt. Daly died in January 1984, "a disillusioned man," according to chronicler Ronald Davies.

The big airlines also ganged up on People Express. Dick Ferris, for instance, drew up a scheme called "Friendship Express," although it was hardly a gesture of friendship to Don Burr. United ripped galleys out of some of its 737s, cramming more seats in cattle-car style, and slashed fares to People's levels. It signed an agreement with its pilots to work longer hours and loosen costly work rules. United launched this ersatz upstart on June 12, 1981, installing the no-frills service on almost a sixth of its route network. But "Friendship" bombed. United still had too high a cost structure to compete with the upstarts. The endeavor was purged from the company's collective memory; Ferris ten years later claimed total ignorance of it.

The lesson, however, was not lost on the Big Four. They simply could not compete above board; they would never be able to match People's or New York Air's cost structure. The big lines would find it much more effective to capitalize on their size, exploiting the economies of scale that supposedly didn't exist in the airline business.

The simple premise behind predatory pricing is that a larger competitor usually has the wherewithal to outlast his challenger. Any losses incurred in the battle can be quickly recouped once the opponent is out of the way. A textbook case came in 1983, when People Express started service from Newark to the Twin Cities, Northwest's main hub, with a $99 fare. Northwest, whose lowest fare from New York at the time was $263, didn't just match the upstart, but undercut it with a $95 fare. Then it boosted its flight frequencies, sandwiching extra departures around those of People so it could skim off more of the extra traffic generated by the low fares. Not long after that, People decamped from Northwest's stronghold.

But it was one thing to identify a case of predatory pricing; it was another to prove it. There was little public outcry, since customers benefited from fare cutting, at least in the short run. And there was rarely a "smoking gun" piece of evidence to corroborate such charges. As David Hinson, Midway's chairman, put it: "The only way you can prove it is to get the guy to stand up and say, 'You're damn right, I predatorily priced. I admit it.' "

Kahn had been unable to persuade Mike Levine and other deregulation allies that newcomers ought to have some extra protection against predatory actions by the big lines. Levine had argued that such handicapping interfered with true deregulation. However, he soon got a firsthand taste of the airlines' cutthroat tactics.

IN THE MIDDLE OF 1982, Mike Levine, in his new role as chairman of New York Air, journeyed one day to the Justice Department headquarters in Washington, carrying a strange tale of airline skulduggery.

After leaving the CAB in 1979, Levine had gone to work briefly for Eastern Airlines as a consultant, and then in the middle of 1981 he joined Continental Airlines in its marketing department. Continental was then fending off Frank Lorenzo's hostile overtures. While Levine later confessed to some reservations about working for Lorenzo after the bitter takeover, he continued on in his marketing job under the new owners at Continental. Lorenzo immediately took an interest in Levine and began searching for an even better job for his newest star. Within a few months, Levine was the chairman of New York Air. He was, at last, running an airline. However, he quickly ran into some problems he hadn't foreseen at the CAB.

He had charged down to Washington that day in 1982 to ask Assistant Attorney General William Baxter to intervene in what he believed was blatant computerized bullying by both American and United.

New York Air had launched service from La Guardia to Detroit in September 1981, with very low fares. The public had immediately responded, and planes were flying 65 percent full. Judging from the first three weeks, the new route was a success.

Then on the fourth week, the airline was shocked to see a sudden change. The planes to Detroit were suddenly taking off two-thirds empty. "The bookings just seemed to stop," Levine recalled.

The route quickly became unprofitable, and by January 1982, New York Air was forced to pull out of the New York–Detroit market.

The mysterious fall-off was due, it seemed, to a change in New York Air's place in the New York–Detroit flight schedules listed in American's Sabre computer reservations system. Suddenly the new service, which was nonstop and therefore belonged in listings with the most convenient flights, was bumped off the all-important first screen that most travel agents relied on to make airline reservations, and ended up in a sort of Siberia of the rankings with the least desirable services. "You just could not find them" in the computers, said Elliott Seiden, who looked into the incident for the antitrust division.

Levine claimed that these computerized tactics went beyond mere bias in the screen display. He told Lorenzo that some of the big airlines could use their computers to learn which travel agents were selling the upstarts' tickets. Then the larger lines would send their salesmen in to make sure those agents got the message: If they kept selling all those tickets on the upstarts, they wouldn't get any more bonus commissions from the big guys.

These complaints were taken seriously at the Justice Department, which had already begun its own investigation into charges of dirty tricks and manipulation in airline computers.

In 1981, American and United had provoked outrage when they started charging other airlines a processing fee for every booking that was routed through their reservations systems. The fees could vary according to the whims of the airline owners. While in most cases the fee would be only twenty-five to fifty cents per booking, American said it would charge Texas-based Muse Air, the new airline in its backyard, fees of two dollars per booking. People Express refused to pay a transaction fee to Apollo, and was dropped from United's computer listings. Most airlines felt compelled to pay the booking fees, for they were increasingly dependent on the big computer systems. Within a few years, most of the nation's midsized airlines were getting more than half their reservations through the Sabre and Apollo systems.

Then, in a perfect example of a "reform" that led to greater abuses, the CAB in 1984 ordered the airline owners to stop imposing booking fees on a discriminatory basis. American and United complied by simply jacking up the fees for everyone. The airlines that lacked their own systems found that their cost of obtaining bookings through Sabre or Apollo had tripled or quadrupled almost overnight. Chicago-based Midway Airlines, for instance, paid out nearly $150 million in booking fees over the twelve years of its existence.

Eleven of the have-not airlines later joined forces to file a billion-dollar antitrust suit against American and United, inspired in large part by the increases in fees that the two computer giants had imposed. Continental Airlines filed its own similar action against the two. But the wheels of justice grind slowly indeed where antitrust allegations are concerned; the suit dragged on for years, with various plaintiffs eventually dropping out because of merger, bankruptcy, or settlements. Ultimately, it was dismissed.

There were tales of electronic espionage, even sabotage. The computer, it appeared, might replace the old smoke-filled room as the forum for anticompetitive behavior. American and United could capitalize on the fact that they owned the biggest computer reservations systems, the primary distribution outlet for every airline's services. They could use their powerful systems to squeeze their competitors.

Spying on a rival was easier with a computer. The system owners could track patterns of bookings on all airlines from a particular market, giving them a strategic advantage in planning how many flights to schedule and at what times to schedule them. That large airlines could possess this superior knowledge and use it against a competitor was another instance of the kinds of advantage that had eluded the architects of deregulation.

As a rash of airlines went bankrupt in the mid-1980s, the charges of computerized dirty tricks in the industry flew faster. Northeastern International Airways, a Fort Lauderdale–based jet airline, closed down at the end of 1984, charging that computer systems had been rigged to show phony bookings for people who never showed up.

Computer reservations systems were by then in most travel agency offices, and American's Sabre was the undisputed market leader. (By then travel agencies booked about three-quarters of all the airline tickets sold in the United States—and most were either using Sabre or United's Apollo, with TWA's PARS a distant third.) In effect, this linked a supposedly neutral travel agency intermediary with a particular supplier, to the detriment of the other airlines. Eventually, the travel agents became not just strongly attached to their airline-owned computer systems, but downright dependent on them—especially after the airlines that owned the systems paid their agency customers a bonus commission for bookings onto their airline. Some observers began to refer to the agent's relationship to his system as a "golden handcuff."

On busy routes, the number of flights available on a given day could easily fill more than one "screen" on the computer. After deregulation, travel agents were becoming so overworked that they would usually—70 percent to 90 percent of the time, according to some studies—book the passenger onto one of the flights shown on the first "screen," on the first flight they saw that departed anywhere near the time the client wanted to go. If the only options the travel agent saw on the first "screen" belonged to the airline that owned the system, the benefits of owning a system and having it in as many travel agencies as possible were obvious.

Allegations also mounted that certain airlines were deliberately slow in adjusting their computers' databases to show how competitors had changed fares or schedules, which meant that a travel agent would often come up with erroneous information on those carriers. One of the worst abuses was suppressing information that the system was normally required to list. Every week the airlines received a computer tape from the Airline Tariff publishers, containing fare changes for virtually all airlines. This was supposed to be loaded immediately into reservations systems, without editing, so it would be available to anyone booking a flight.

American had developed a "shoppers fare quote" in Sabre listing discount fares by route, with the lowest price first. But in 1981 Continental Airlines filed low fares that American declined to match. Instead, American simply failed to list them in its "shoppers quote" for two months. An internal memo showed that American had "deliberately" suppressed this information, although Justice Department depositions of American officials revealed there had been much internal debate over the propriety of such an act.

The carrier owning the system would also give its travel agent subscribers "last-seat availability" on its flights—that is, even if there was only one empty seat left on a particular American Airlines departure, the local travel agent who used Sabre would be able to find it and book it for his client. And when airlines developed the ability to issue boarding passes through a travel agent's ticket printer, this was initially available only for flights on the airline that owned the system.

In some hub cities, this gave an airline virtual control over the distribution of its product. In Dallas, for example, 90 percent of the travel agents used Sabre, and American had rigged the systems to give its own flights the premium positions on the computer screen listings. This meant that agents would be more likely to book a customer on American than on a competitor, even if the flights and fares were the same. United and TWA were doing the same with their systems in their "hubs." In fact, the airlines readily admitted to the accusations of "display bias," saying they had to give their flights preference to recoup the millions that they had invested in the computer reservations systems. The Justice Department investigated and urged the government to crack down on this practice, and in 1984 the CAB ordered the airlines that owned the systems to list the flights of all carriers in a totally unbiased manner.

Critics dismissed the CAB's regulations as inadequate. Three years later, Frank Lorenzo charged that American's Sabre and United's Apollo still exerted a "fundamentally monopolistic" control of the nation's travel agencies. "There will always be a way for the computer to beat the regulator," Lorenzo said.

All this cemented an airline's grip on its hub cities' air travel market, thus thwarting the free entry the deregulation law encouraged. And there were other weapons as well. Many aspects of the computer systems could be used to browbeat a rival. After Frank Lorenzo gained control of Continental Airlines, Bob Crandall refused to sell Continental some Sabre software it had been promised before it changed ownership.

Crandall explained his action in a letter to a senior executive at Continental. It is a revealing look into the American boss's strategy.

Crandall began by noting that Lorenzo also owned New York Air and Texas International, "companies [that] have made price a primary marketing weapon and could fairly be classified as 'low fare' carriers. For all those reasons, we have elected to put Continental, Texas International and New York Air on the list of competitors to whom we do not wish to sell service related software. In effect we feel our ability to provide superior service is one of the few weapons which may be available to us in the ongoing and ever more costly price competition our industry seems determined to inflict upon itself."

Computer power had also made it possible for American to launch its frequent-flyer program in May of 1981, the same concept dismissed as far-fetched only five years before. In the interim, however, American had designed an advanced automated system that would track members' miles and send them regular statements, just like banks. United came out with a similar plan eleven days later. Millions of travelers had signed up with one or more plans within the first year.

By giving travelers a financial incentive to stick with one airline, the big carriers had found another way to neutralize the cost advantages of the smaller lines, which lacked the technology—but more important, the vast route networks—to make a plan like that pay off.

Rivals cried foul, arguing that it amounted to a kickback to consumers. Don Burr denounced the frequent-flyer programs as "white-collar crime." Since employers generally paid the fares that allowed flyers to collect their awards, the Internal Revenue Service began to talk about taxing the free travel awards as income. That did not slow the explosive growth of the programs, generally considered one of the most successful marketing gimmicks of recent times.

The computers and frequent-flyer freebies were in effect the glue that held an airline's hubs together and allowed it to dominate those markets. It had taken only a few years for the industry to start to resemble the oligopoly that skeptics such as Ralph Nader had warned about back in 1977.

THE ORIGINS OF THE FORTRESS hubs that emerged in the 1980s can be traced to a deal between the CAB and Delta Air Lines in 1940. The federal government, looking for ways to help develop the economy of the rural South, asked Delta to begin flying on a number of short routes out of Atlanta to smaller southern cities nearby. In return, the CAB gave Delta some longer, more profitable routes out of Atlanta as well.

All of these routes became the "spokes" leading into a Delta "hub" at Atlanta. With it came the compelling benefit of passenger retention. Most airlines before deregulation exchanged passengers freely at major airports, the familiar practice of "interlining." But in Atlanta, 90 percent of Delta's transit passengers continued their journey on another Delta flight.

Once deregulation gave carriers freedom to enter and exit markets, airlines saw that there was no longer any point in handing their passengers off to someone else if they could keep them on their own airplanes for the entire course of their journey. The most efficient way to do that was not to schedule nonstop flights between a lot of cities, but to schedule the maximum possible number of connections: A wave of inbound flights converges on a central point, passengers scurry from one plane to another, and the planes all take off again back to the cities they came from. The route maps of the major airlines, which had looked like complicated cat's-cradles, now resembled spider plants.

The economic logic of creating hub-and-spoke route systems was so inescapable that by the end of the 1980s about two-thirds of all domestic airline passengers would travel through a hub before arriving at their final destination. And more than eight out of ten passengers who changed flights would remain on the same airline.

The old traditions were crumbling in another way. Outside of the biggest five airlines, whose large size transcended regional boundaries, there was a host of other major airlines with strong ties to their home bases. Continental in Los Angeles, Delta in Atlanta, and Northwest in Minneapolis were long viewed as hometown airlines; their owners were civic boosters. Before American moved in right after deregulation, Braniff had considered Dallas its exclusive turf. The airline battle for Dallas was, in effect, the battle between the old and new orders.

Typical of the old order was Braniff chairman Harding Lawrence, who fancied himself the last of the airline buccaneers. It was a conceit some of his peers thought he carried too far. When Eastern chairman Frank Borman came calling in the late 1970s, he was startled when he arrived for lunch at Lawrence's ostentatious office, replete with polar bearskin rug, private swimming pool, and a valet and cook on call. The airline at the time was hemorrhaging money.

Lawrence and his wife, advertising executive Mary Wells, had built Braniff to a flamboyant presence in the airline world. Declaring "an end to the plain plane," they repainted Braniff's fleet of aircraft into a rainbow of loud colors, even commissioning renowned artist Alexander Calder to hand-paint one of the big jets with an original design. Interiors were decked out with leather seats. Lawrence hired Italian designer Emilio Pucci to create new flight attendants' uniforms, and began staging in-flight fashion shows, a passenger diversion he called the "air strip" (because flight attendants changed clothes during the flight).

The grab for attention worked, and Harding and Mary were sought-after guests in Dallas, and in Acapulco, where they hosted lavish parties at the Braniff corporate villa. When deregulation came, however, Lawrence viewed it simply as a blank check for willy-nilly expansion. He considered merging with another airline and talked with Frank Borman about combining Braniff and Eastern. But Lawrence insisted in all such discussions that Braniff would have to be the surviving entity, and he the surviving CEO. When he got no takers, he decided that Braniff could grow just as fast without a merger.

The first indication of trouble came in December 1978, when

Braniff, using the dormant routes it had snapped up from the CAB, started service to sixteen new U.S. cities on the same day—an amazing feat for an industry in which airlines had previously been accustomed to adding perhaps one new route a year, if they were lucky. Within a matter of weeks, Braniff was flying on forty-nine new routes. But Lawrence appeared to be adding them to enhance his route map. On many of the routes Braniff operated only one daily round-trip, ignoring the dogma that only frequent service attracts profitable business traffic.

"I believe that businessmen do not want to commit suicide and rush into markets," Alfred Kahn had said back in 1977, expressing what turned out to be unwarranted confidence that airlines wouldn't abuse their newfound freedoms under deregulation. Regulation, after all, had protected airlines from their owners' whims. But Lawrence sought to dominate not only the United States but the world. Braniff quickly grew into a globe-girdling behemoth with routes across the Pacific to Korea, Hong Kong, Guam, and Singapore, and new trans-atlantic service to London, Amsterdam, Brussels, Frankfurt, and Paris, thanks to the CAB's new willingness to dole out foreign routes. Lawrence belatedly loaded up on 747s just when other airlines were trying to get rid of their fuel-hungry jumbos. But when Braniff launched new 747 service from Portland and Seattle to Hawaii, the jets, on average, took off with only 14 out of 375 seats filled.

Lawrence frantically tried to retreat, as losses soared to $131 million in 1980. A few days before Christmas, a somber group of businessmen assembled at Braniff headquarters, including several of its outside directors and many bankers and insurance executives from the Northeast, who were the distressed airline's biggest lenders. Before the holiday season ended, the swank CEO's office at Braniff headquarters was looking for a new tenant. Lawrence was pressured to resign.

The lesson of Lawrence's spectacular fall had not been lost on his competitors. Crandall, for one, had been watching as Lawrence "took the hub apart" that Braniff had enjoyed as a regional line before deregulation—adding new routes all over the place instead of concentrating them into and out of Dallas. Crandall's theory was that Lawrence truly believed deregulation wouldn't last, and that he wanted to snap up as many glamorous routes as possible before the party ended. American's people thought Lawrence's strategy was wrong, and were ready to rush in and fill the vacuum left by Braniff's failure. They couldn't believe that Lawrence hadn't figured out what

Delta had known all along—a "fortress" hub could make local customers virtually dependent on your services.

Lawrence unwittingly gave Crandall a helping hand when he sold American fifteen of his fuel-efficient 727-200 airplanes in an eleventh-hour attempt to raise cash. That allowed American to add more spokes to the hub it planned at Dallas/Fort Worth. But Braniff wasn't dead yet: In January 1981, Braniff's directors replaced Harding Lawrence by promoting vice-chairman John Casey to chairman, president, and CEO. A longtime Braniff executive, John Casey was the older brother of American Airlines chairman Al Casey, who had just moved in down the road. A few months later, Putnam, who had been president of Southwest Airlines and before that was at United as a marketing executive under Dick Ferris, took over as president.

The excesses of the Lawrence years had left the company with a negative net worth and a lot of nervous lenders. Fuel prices were still going up and airline passenger traffic, feeling the brunt of the country's recession, was actually declining. In 1982, the airline repeatedly appealed to its jittery lenders to cut it just a bit more slack. It managed to eke out a little public-sympathy business from civic-minded Dallas residents; the airline even distributed T-shirts in Texas that said "Braniff—With the Help of God, the Banks and You, We Can Make It!"

Soon, stories started to circulate in Dallas that American wasn't playing fair. The two Dallas newspapers, embroiled in their own competitive battle, played up the war between American and Braniff and started to sniff out various stories hinting, among other things, that American was secretly leaning on Braniff's lenders to pull the plug; that American had dumped millions of dollars' worth of Braniff tickets into the airline industry's central clearinghouse for immediate collection, in an effort to drain its rival of cash; that American's pilots were blocking departing Braniff planes on the taxiways to prevent them from taking off on schedule.

In March 1982 the CAB confirmed that it had begun an investigation into the charges of American Airlines' "dirty tricks" campaign against Braniff. Braniff brought its own civil lawsuit making the same charges. The Justice Department empaneled a grand jury to probe "possible anticompetitive behavior" in airline activities at Dallas/Fort Worth. By then, it had the Crandall-Putnam phone call as the subject of a separate grand jury.

But it took nearly a year for Elliott Seiden and his team at Justice to formally file their charges against Crandall. They finally did so in

February 1983, with a civil antitrust suit against American and Crandall on the attempted monopolization charge. As a penalty, Justice proposed that Crandall be removed from American or any other airline management for two years. That would likely have ended Crandall's remarkable airline career in disgrace.

American angrily denied the charges. Crandall's suggestion to raise fares was an "off-the-cuff remark," it said, pointing out that no agreement had ever been made.

Charles Rule, another antitrust attorney at Justice at the time, admitted that the case was perplexing. "We seriously considered bringing a criminal case," he said. "But the circumstances were just so novel." A few years later, Rule did successfully prosecute criminal wire-fraud cases in circumstances remarkably similar to the Crandall-Putnam situation, he said, where one competitor used the phone to encourage another to fix prices.

Crandall's supporters argue that his remarks were simply born of frustration at Braniff's rampant fare cutting in the midst of a recession. "That's the way Crandall is," one colleague noted. "He hears it, and immediately, without thinking of the implications of what he was saying, he blurts it out." But he added: "You need to understand that Bob suffered terribly as a result of that event. I don't think there was much the government could have done that would have been worse than the personal anguish that Bob went through, and the public embarrassment."

Other American executives insist that Justice was after Crandall. "I remember I spent three hours in front of the Justice Department explaining a note I had put on a piece of paper—words to the effect of 'Let's go kick their ass in Oklahoma City'—and they wanted to know what I meant by that," recalled American's Bob Baker.

To outsiders, it may have seemed that Bob Crandall was the personification of the newly rough-and-tumble airline business. But while Dick Ferris may have kept a lower profile, United Airlines, according to Justice Department sleuths, was every bit as adept as American in the electronic battle for passengers.

In November of 1983, Seiden filed a voluminous catalog of airline dirty tricks with the CAB, a number of them involving United. One incident concerned a new airline in California, Jet America, which found that in order to list its flights in Apollo, it first had to submit its plans in writing to United. The newcomer also promised United that it would not be a "maverick" in the fare department.

In another instance, a malfunction in the Apollo system showed flights on Frontier Airlines to be full when instead they had plenty of empty seats. When Frontier flashed a message alerting Apollo users to the mistake, United removed the message before many agents had a chance to see it and ordered the carrier never to do that again.

While the Justice Department valiantly prepared dozens of investigations and cases, none was ever tried. The department either settled cases or turned over its recommendations to the CAB, which in turn did not go as far as critics of the abuses would have liked. In any case, prior to the CAB's regulation of computer reservations systems in 1984, American and United could correctly argue that they weren't violating any rules, since none existed. In a filing at the CAB, United dismissed the growing chorus of complaints as the mere whining of "a small cabal of failing and fledgling carriers who, due to misguided management decisions, have been unable to compete effectively in the marketplace."

Indeed, from the early 1980s through 1988, the Justice Department's antitrust division launched a number of grand jury investigations into allegations of anticompetitive activity by American and other major airlines. Some of these were never revealed publicly because no indictment was ever brought. Among the charges investigated were an allegation that American and Piedmont agreed to stay out of each other's routes, and a charge that a senior official at American had an "open phone line" to a counterpart at a direct competitor. In 1988, Crandall was investigated for talking to competitors about rebating of air fares. The investigation was closed after a year with no action taken.

Later the architects of deregulation would claim that the failure to prosecute antitrust cases sent the wrong signal to the airline industry. Alfred Kahn saw it as part of a broader philosophy espoused by the Reaganite right. "They confused economic deregulation with simple laissez-faire," he lamented.

In any event, the government did not fare well with its civil antitrust case against American. A federal judge in Dallas threw out the case against Crandall, noting that in spite of his remark, nothing happened to prices as a result. An appeals court reversed that decision. Ultimately, some years after the incident, American reached a settlement with the Justice Department, in which Crandall agreed to keep a written record of all his communications with other airline executives for two years. He also had to submit an affidavit every three months during the two years attesting that he was in fact complying with the terms of the agreement. However humiliating this may have been, many people thought Crandall had gotten off with little more than a slap on the wrist.

Crandall's ill-advised phone call notwithstanding, nothing could reverse Braniff's fate. In the spring of 1982, it continued desperation tactics, making a deal to lease its South American routes to Eastern Airlines. By early May, Braniff ran out of cash. In the evening of May 13, the airline called its planes back to Dallas from distant stations to prevent creditors from seizing them. That night, the airline filed for Chapter 11 reorganization. Braniff was the first major airline to fail after deregulation.

The bankruptcy caught the industry and the traveling public by surprise. It had been no secret that Braniff was in serious financial trouble, but an airline bankruptcy was unthinkable. Decades of regulation and government protection had left the public with the impression that airlines were invulnerable to economic troubles, that someone would always bail them out. The grounding and bankruptcy of Braniff left many consumers with worthless tickets; no airline would honor them.

The litigation over American's alleged "dirty tricks" against Braniff was settled out of court in July 1983, when American agreed to pay $20 million for some of the bankrupt company's leases at Dallas/Fort Worth Airport—as long as the charges against it were dropped. The Justice Department's antitrust division did not oppose the transfer but added a stern warning: It would "continue to monitor the competitive conditions at Dallas/Fort Worth." Some time later, Justice Department lawyers concluded, on the basis of the Dallas experience, that the airline business was "readily susceptible to monopolistic or joint monopolistic behavior if entry barriers exist in markets."

In 1983, American officially declared Dallas to be its principal hub—where it operated a number of daily banks of connecting flights—and its share of the market shot up to nearly 60 percent. After it snapped up Braniff's gates, American controlled fully one-half of the gates at DFW airport.

Three weeks after Braniff had stopped flying in 1982, American announced plans to raise its fares by 25 percent to 40 percent on hundreds of routes—most of them routes where it had been competing with Braniff. To the victor go the spoils. Bob Crandall got his fare increase after all.

9

BLUE-COLLAR BLUES

Deregulation is profoundly anti-labor . . . there has been a massive transfer of wealth from airline employees to airline passengers.
—BOB CRANDALL

Alfred Kahn was feeling defensive on September 27, 1983, in an ABC television studio in Chicago, when he found himself cast as champion of a cause that had cost thousands of workers their jobs.

During the past eighteen months, both Braniff and Freddie Laker's Skytrain had folded. Continental had just declared bankruptcy and its unionized workers were on strike.

"I find it hard to believe that in a Democratic administration you would have implemented laws that you regarded as antiunion, yet . . . it seems antiunion," said Ted Koppel of ABC's *Nightline*.

It was indeed difficult to explain in TV-speak the complexities of the economic experiment Kahn had midwifed. Deregulation is benefiting the consumer, he said, with lower fares. Yet, he admitted: "We're going through very difficult times. . . . It's causing considerable pain and distress, especially to those companies with high costs."

One person causing much of this pain and distress was the man for whom Kahn still worked as a director of New York Air. Three days earlier, on September 24, Frank Lorenzo had taken an ailing Continental Airlines under Chapter 11 of the U.S. bankruptcy code, voiding all its labor contracts and briefly shutting the airline down.

When it reopened for business a couple of days later, Lorenzo had shed about two-thirds of the airline's routes and more than half its workforce. Remaining employees were invited to work at half their previous salaries.

When Lorenzo declared bankruptcy, Continental was not technically out of cash. With the recent failure of Braniff as a cautionary example, he explained, he did not want to wait until he was literally insolvent. Although some Continental employees did come back to work, within a few weeks the unions officially called a strike. Ugly incidents followed. In one episode, two striking Continental pilots arrested for speeding on a highway near San Antonio, Texas, were discovered to be carrying the ingredients of a homemade pipe bomb, which they intended to use against fellow pilots who had crossed picket lines. Other seemingly random attacks on pilots—rock throwing, arson—continued over the following months.

For years, Continental Airlines had been a sentimental favorite in the airline business. Founded by Los Angeles society figure Robert Six, a former barnstorming biplane pilot, the airline pioneered routes through the West and across the Pacific. On its long-distance flights it offered passengers luxurious service at high fares, and it had a well-paid, overstaffed workforce. Although it had long been a stable, profitable airline, once prices began to fall under deregulation it was doomed.

While Continental's first attempt to merge with Western Air Lines had been rejected on antitrust grounds, a year later the two companies returned with a new proposal. They thought they had answered the CAB's concerns by proposing to spin off some of their overlapping routes. The new plan won the endorsement of a CAB law judge, and the two sides confidently awaited the full board's approval. It was too late. By early 1981, Frank Lorenzo had jumped into the fray.

When Lorenzo announced a tender offer to Continental shareholders at thirteen dollars a share, the company fought back with every available weapon. It filed numerous suits designed to block the unwanted bid. It accused Lorenzo of stock manipulation and violating federal securities laws. Lorenzo, undaunted, accumulated more and more shares and soon his stake approached 50 percent.

In a last-ditch effort to halt Lorenzo, the employees of Continental said they would try to raise enough money to match or beat his offer. The war of words intensified. Lorenzo struck back, attacking the employee plan as a thinly disguised scheme to protect management; he threatened to sue the company's officers if it went through.

On August 9, 1981, the battle came to a tragic end when Continental chief Al Feldman, at age fifty-three, shot himself to death in his office at Los Angeles International Airport. Most press reports noted that Feldman had been despondent for months over his wife's death. But the unsavory takeover left a bad taste.

When Lorenzo's takeover became final early the following year, not only was employee morale low, but the airline was in far worse shape than anyone imagined. The company was losing about $20 million a month, Lorenzo recalled. By the time the company filed for bankruptcy, Continental's losses since deregulation had reached $500 million.

IN 1982, LORENZO KEPT CONTINENTAL'S headquarters in Los Angeles (although he would later move it to Houston), naming Phil Bakes executive vice-president. Lorenzo realized he needed someone who had experience dealing with labor unions to sell the employees on the unpalatable choice of reduced wages or unemployment. That December, he turned to Stephen Wolf, a forty-year-old senior vice-president at Pan Am, and offered him the job of Continental president. Bakes had wanted the job himself, but Wolf had the advantage of years of hands-on experience in airline operations. Perhaps more pertinent, he also had years of tutelage under Bob Crandall. Lorenzo was said to admire Crandall's toughness and financial acumen, and reportedly tried to hire Crandall for a top job. Wolf would be a good second choice.

Raised in a rough neighborhood in East Oakland, California, Wolf was not the typical Ivy League Lorenzo recruit. In high school he had worked in San Francisco loading trucks, and he later got part-time work in air freight while earning a degree in sociology at San Francisco State. He'd planned to go to law school and took a job in American Airlines' cargo department to save for tuition. But he excelled in the management program and won a supervisor's job after three months, instead of the usual year. He decided to stay in the airline business.

The first thing people noticed about Wolf was his six-foot-six-inch stature. Yet he came across as soft-spoken and unassuming, as if trying to compensate for the intimidating effect of his giant physique, a kind of reverse Napoleon complex. His workaholic habits also attracted attention and he was soon made director of American's Cleveland cargo office.

One day, Crandall arrived in the Cleveland outpost on one of his frequent trips to the field and noticed this young, ambitious manager. Soon, Wolf moved to a job at American's New York headquarters, starting in the unglamorous freight marketing division. To advance further he'd need to move out of cargo, so when the post of Kennedy Airport manager opened up, Wolf went for it. There he dealt with labor negotiations and operational problems. Within a year he had been named vice-president of American for the West Coast.

While Wolf may have been driven, he also "played as hard as he worked," said an old friend. A bachelor, Wolf liked to party late into the night—a lifestyle that set him apart from his mostly married peers in the top ranks of airline management. But as Wolf grew more ambitious, he saw less of his drinking buddies. "He outgrew us," one said.

After he had been in Los Angeles awhile, Wolf began to get impatient. Turned down for a top job at American's Dallas headquarters in 1981, he decided to join Pan Am under its new chairman, Ed Acker. There, too, he was frustrated when he missed out on a promotion. When Lorenzo came calling with the president's title he'd sought, he accepted.

Wolf's first task at Continental was to negotiate low-cost labor agreements. "It was a very tough year for Steve" at Continental, said Phil Bakes. The company's losses were mounting and labor negotiations had hit a stalemate.

Many of Lorenzo's lieutenants had only recently left jobs in government. Wolf stood out with his intimate knowledge of airline operations. "He knew things like the average time a passenger would wait in line and that kind of thing. And he spent an inordinate amount of time on things like carpeting and flight attendants' uniforms. He micromanaged the minutiae," said Bakes.

Wolf, however, did not get the labor agreements Lorenzo sought. In July, the company lost $8 million. In August the machinists union went out on strike after Continental rejected its demand for a 36 percent wage increase with no work-rule concessions. Continental managed to fly through the strike with only a few flights grounded and was back up to full capacity by the end of the month. But the company lost $17 million that month. Wolf's main goal, to bring down labor costs, was eluding him.

At the same time, Lorenzo was seeking to bring down the wages of pilots and flight attendants by some $100 million a year. In return, he offered to donate four million shares of stock to an employee stock ownership fund and to create a permanent profit-sharing plan. The proposal was turned down by all the unions, except the Transport Workers Union, which represented only several dozen flight dispatchers, and the company's nonunion personnel, who voted overwhelmingly in favor.

Sometime in the middle of September, Wolf stepped into Lorenzo's office for a private meeting. According to one account, it was brief. Wolf apparently disagreed with some of Lorenzo's ideas and told him so, at which point Lorenzo said something on the order of "maybe you better leave because I'm going to keep on doing things my way."

On September 21, he resigned, just three days before Lorenzo's Chapter 11 filing. "Steve was really devastated after that," said Bakes. "He'd never been fired from a job in his life and he felt he'd been fired from that job." After Wolf's departure, Lorenzo added the job of president to his own titles of chairman and CEO. But within six months, the president's job went to Bakes, after all.

Lorenzo's Chapter 11 erased a long-held conviction in the industry: that customers would avoid a bankrupt airline since, under competition, they'd have plenty of solvent lines to choose from. Right after the Chapter 11 filing, Continental immediately lowered its fares to forty-nine dollars one way anywhere in the country. Passengers quickly forgot the stigma of bankruptcy in their rush to snap up the cheap tickets.

Solidarity among the unions also eroded. Eventually enough Continental pilots returned—even at much lower wages—to get more than 50 percent of the airline's jets in the air by January 1984. Mechanics and flight attendants could be easily replaced, as Lorenzo discovered, and at much lower salaries. Labor costs, 35 percent of Continental's operating expenses before the bankruptcy, fell to 20 percent after the filing.

IN 1983, MORE THAN TWENTY THOUSAND U.S. corporations filed for bankruptcy, the greatest wave of business failures or reorganizations since the Great Depression. There were many culprits: recession, Reagan laissez-faire capitalism, competition from abroad. But it took a major airline to focus the public's attention on another reason behind the stampede to bankruptcy court.

During the 1980s, Chapter 11 became a "popular kind of corporate reincarnation," as Mary Graham wrote in the *New Republic*. Chapter 11 bankruptcy, a uniquely American phenomenon, allowing a company protection from creditors while the company is reorganized, is based on a lesson drawn from the Depression. Continuing a company as a going concern and saving jobs was deemed a greater value than the creditors' need for their money. Reorganization became much more widely used after a major revision of the law in 1978 made it even simpler.

This may have emboldened Lorenzo to shield himself from the liability of high labor costs. One of the biggest single expense items on an airline's ledgers was payroll, and deregulation had put enormous pressure on the companies to reduce the tab. Wages at major airlines consumed, on average, more than a third of all expenditures; they could go as low as 14 percent at some of the upstarts. Before deregulation, airline labor unions would ratchet up their wages and scale back their hours and work rules with each successive round of contract talks from one carrier to the next.

Management had simply passed along the higher labor costs to passengers. When deregulation severed the link between wage increases and fare hikes, it threatened the security of thousands of workers. Kahn and the other deregulators knew that but believed that the airline business would grow so much under deregulation that overall, employment would increase even though average wages might fall.

In 1978, the year airline deregulation was passed, the airlines did so well financially that union opposition was blunted. But the first few years of deregulation confirmed the fears of unionized airline workers. The recession of 1980 and 1981 killed business travel, and major airlines furloughed some twenty thousand employees between 1978 and 1981. Those laid off faced an unpalatable choice: Get a job with a new nonunion, low-wage airline, or find another line of work. The law's labor protection provisions were virtually useless. Workers displaced by deregulation were supposed to get the first right to be hired at other airlines, or be compensated if they didn't find work elsewhere, but Congress failed to appropriate the necessary funds. "We had people affected all over the place who never received one plug nickel," said William Scheri of the machinists union.

Those who stayed on the job with the major airlines faced a new economic reality. Their employers—some of whom were losing fistfuls of money—had to get their costs down in order to compete against the upstart airlines. Sometimes, they would run into a union or an individual who was willing to put up a fight.

One such individual was Charles Bryan, the head of the machinists local at Eastern Airlines. If Frank Lorenzo would come to personify the labor-bashing boss, then Bryan would be a symbol of union intransigence. The two men would ultimately collide in a match that Alfred Kahn described as "two scorpions in a bottle."

As it happened, Bryan was also a guest on the *Nightline* show that night in 1983 with Alfred Kahn, taking the diametrically opposed view, of course. Even the unflappable Ted Koppel was alarmed by some of Bryan's remarks that night, which seemed to suggest that passengers ought to be scared to fly on an airline that was seeking wage cuts from its contract workers. "Are you genuinely telling the . . . public they're in danger when they go up?" Koppel asked. Bryan suggested that yes, a workforce composed of unhappy or incompetent workers could bring down aircraft safety. Bryan would return to this theme often in his career.

In March 1983, Bryan was the central character in a contretemps that ultimately did as much to reshape relations between management and labor in the airline business as did Lorenzo's Chapter 11 filing.

Bryan, a stocky man of fifty, had by then achieved a certain notoriety in the airline world. He'd raised himself out of youthful poverty by working odd jobs, later living alone beneath the screen of a drive-in movie theater where he worked while finishing school. He studied aeronautical engineering at Ohio State University, learned the airline mechanic trade, and eventually joined Eastern.

In the 1970s, Bryan was elected general chairman for the International Association of Machinists, Local District 100 in Miami. Bryan and the other machinists were initially cheered when Frank Borman, who had joined Eastern in 1970, was made president in 1975. Borman's astronaut exploits made him a genuine hero. That could only help the airline, which still suffered from years of mismanagement. At first the two were on cordial terms; Bryan was even occasionally a guest at Borman's home.

Borman was regarded by many of his peers as the last of the flyboys, a sort of paternalistic version of Eddie Rickenbacker. To boost morale at the nation's fourth largest airline, he did away with a host of executive perks, such as a corporate jet, and drove to work in a beat-up car as an added fillip.

In 1977 Borman had crafted a solution to the airline's age-old fiscal troubles: a five-year plan that allowed employees to share in profits or receive warrants to purchase Eastern stock at a fixed price, in exchange for putting aside 3.5 percent of their pay as insurance. Workers got their withheld wages back if the company's earnings topped 2 percent of sales, and they shared in profits over that amount. But if earnings fell short of the goal, employees lost their contributions. At first the plan paid off, but by the early 1980s, workers had lost so much money that Bryan was able to use the resulting discontent to rise to leadership of the machinists local.

As Borman continued to attack Eastern's labor costs, relations with Bryan grew increasingly hostile. In one notable incident, Bryan actually ran out to the runway to block a departing jet in order to protest a new "powerback" technique Borman had invented, which entailed using a plane's own engines to push back from the gate. The idea was to save labor costs—Eastern, thanks to an arcane work rule, was the only major airline that used three mechanics to guide a plane back from a gate. Other airlines used two lower-paid baggage handlers who "walked" the plane back while one mechanic drove the truck. As Bryan refused to budge from behind the jet's wheels, Borman ordered the pilot to push back anyway, and Bryan, who fled to safety, complained bitterly about the episode for years.

Bryan, for all his intransigence, was doing the job for which he'd been chosen. The IAM had a long history of fighting to preserve its members' benefits and was proud it had never given back anything it had won. As Eastern's executives caved in over the years, the ante was simply upped for the next go-round. Borman, while he found Bryan impossible, had to confess some backhanded admiration for the total support Bryan enjoyed among his members.

In 1983, as Eastern suffered some of its worst losses in years, pilots and flight attendants agreed to pay cuts of roughly 20 percent, but Bryan wouldn't budge. When the deadline for negotiating passed, Bryan set a strike date and Eastern managers started training to take over machinists' duties.

However, on the eve of the strike, Eastern's bankers refused to extend the cash-strapped company's line of credit. The airline simply did not have the funds to weather a strike. With the Mutual Aid Pact no longer in place, it couldn't count on support from friendly competitors. Borman considered filing for bankruptcy, but his directors warned that unless he could avoid a walkout, the company could quickly go from a Chapter 11 reorganization into a Chapter 7 liquidation. Borman reluctantly agreed to give in to Bryan's demand for a 32.2 percent wage hike over the next three years. Later, Borman admitted this was his greatest mistake at Eastern. "I lost credibility to an incalculable extent," he said.

The deal with Bryan brought temporary relief but by late 1983, Eastern was again in deep trouble. It had racked up losses of $129 million and the banks froze the company's credit. Speculation about Eastern's imminent demise spread to the media, scaring away passengers and sparking a vicious circle, as passenger defections only pushed the company closer to failure.

Then Borman mustered some of the creativity he'd shown back in the late 1970s. The company's three unions agreed to buy 25 percent of Eastern's stock in exchange for giving up 18 percent of their 1984 salary (pilots gave up 20 percent). The unions' new ownership stake also gave them the right to name four members to the company's board of directors.

On its face, it was a far-sighted, almost visionary arrangement, perhaps heralding the opening of a new era in labor-management conciliation. The pilots named two outsiders to represent them on the board—Arthur Taylor, a former president of CBS, and Thomas Boggs, a powerful Washington lawyer and lobbyist. But when the machinists reached their own accord with Borman, Bryan insisted that he be their representative on the board. Robert Callahan of the Transport Workers Union also claimed the right to represent the flight attendants.

Suddenly Bryan became a company insider, a peer of the executives he'd been bedeviling. He joined assorted tycoons and civic leaders who sat on the board, such as Roswell Gilpatric, a patrician lawyer from New York law firm Cravath, Swaine & Moore and a former official in John F. Kennedy's administration. Bryan rarely spoke up at meetings and often sat there without reacting visibly to any of the actions being taken. He did not seem to be troubled by his dual role of labor leader and board member.

Bryan reportedly was most in awe of fellow board member Laurance Rockefeller, Eastern's largest shareholder for decades. Gilpatric recalled that Rockefeller spent an inordinate amount of time on Bryan. "He would take not just five or ten minutes but hours . . . to get Charlie to understand the economics of the airline business." Bryan's grasp of the situation was rather naive. Asked about the effects of deregulation, he usually responded that fares were way too low and a law ought to be passed requiring the airlines to jack up rates.

AT AMERICAN, Bob Crandall had faced a similar threat from his mechanics when he tried to sell American's entire workforce on lower wage scales. But Crandall had $1 billion in liquid assets to withstand a strike, and he was dealing with the Transport Workers Union, not the hard-line IAM.

In early 1983, Crandall gathered American managers in one of his typical marathon sessions. He told his staff: Identify the enemy and figure out how to duplicate his advantages. The opposition here was clearly the low-fare upstarts, who paid their employees about half what they'd earn at American. In fact, People Express employees enjoyed making fun of Crandall's predicament. Burr recalled, "We used to joke that Bob Crandall had a big bat with the name Don Burr on it. He'd take it to his employees and say—'Here's what'll happen to you unless you help me get costs down.' " Crandall gave his staff a proposition: Imagine they were starting a new airline the way Burr and Lorenzo did. Take People's costs—which were an amazingly low five cents a seat mile. Then if they "merged" the new airline into the existing company and averaged the old costs with the new ones, they'd have a viable cost structure.

The key was that employees on the payroll would not suffer any pay cuts but all new employees after a certain date would earn significantly lower starting rates. Only much later would the new employees reach the higher pay levels of the earlier employees.

The unions, naturally, distrusted any plan based on lower wages. But their objections to the "B-scale" concept were outweighed by management's offer: a promise not to cut their wages or benefits, a guarantee of job security, a pledge to rehire recently laid off union workers, a new profit-sharing plan, and the likelihood of faster promotions.

The pilots and flight attendants readily agreed to the plan, but when the mechanics balked, Crandall, in effect, dared them to strike. American's three unions all approved Crandall's new A and B wage scales by the fall of 1983.

American was poised to increase enormously in size, and it had a strong incentive to do so. The more it expanded, the more workers it would hire—all at the lower B scale wages—and the more its average costs would drop. In the next few years American would indeed expand rapidly, almost insatiably snapping up new routes and planes, doubling its staff and stretching its route network all over the map. Crandall did not use existing American planes for his hidden, lower-wage "airline" and instead ordered hundreds of new jets. Crandall and American finance executive Jack Pope went to McDonnell Douglas, which at the time was struggling to compete in the passenger airplane market, and arranged an unprecedented order for hundreds of the company's new Super 80 planes—a derivative of the DC-9— at an unusually low price.

Sometime in 1983, People Express finance executive Bob McAdoo encountered Don Carty, his opposite number at American. McAdoo recalls Carty expounding on the airline's grand plan. It was, essentially, to strategically place hubs across the country, from coast to coast and in between. "Someone would be able to get from any point in America to any other point in America without having to think of anyone except American Airlines." With their new B-scale workforce, Crandall and his team pursued that plan with singular intensity for the next few years, avoiding, for the most part, the disastrous mergers of their competitors. Crandall stood to at last regain the advantage over his archrival, United, that American had lost back in 1961. For in 1984 United was experiencing the very labor strife Crandall had managed to avoid.

For Crandall and a number of other airline chiefs, the deregulation law made a convenient whipping boy. After all, Congress had thrown out the high fares–high pay formula that had given airline employees unparalleled prosperity. Daniel May, head of Republic Airlines, was also fond of calling deregulation "antilabor." In early 1984, he faced a problem similar to Crandall's, and brought in Crandall's old protégé, Steve Wolf, to solve it.

Wolf arrived in Minneapolis just months after his unhappy departure from Continental Airlines. Republic was a true hybrid—combining North Central Airlines and Southern Airways in 1979, and expanding to the West with the purchase of Hughes Airwest in 1980. It also was a mess, with a disorganized executive team, a disaffected workforce, and a patchwork route system. "Bankruptcy was only a phone call away," said Sky Magary, a former Pan Am executive Wolf hired as one of his senior aides. The staff was still polarized into an Air West camp, a North Central camp, and a Southern Airways camp. The unions consented to so-called "partnership agreements," a concessions-for-stock deal that would save Republic $100 million a year. The deal had been nailed down in principle before Wolf arrived, according to Brian Freeman, a financial adviser to the unions, but Wolf set about winning rank-and-file support for the new regime.

Just as his former boss, Bob Crandall, had done, Wolf started traveling around Republic's system, making presentations to employees and spending hours at each stop answering their questions. He made videotapes with president's messages to reach employees he didn't personally visit. Wolf "had a very fixed picture of how the airline should operate," said Magary, "which was largely a result of the days he had spent at American."

Wolf soon won the title of president, and the airline experienced a $155 million improvement in its financial results within one year. Wolf earned the reputation as the industry's golden boy that was to stick to him thereafter.

Lorenzo's image as a darling of deregulation was badly tarnished by his record at Continental, however. The combination of a hostile takeover with a union-busting bankruptcy filing made some of his supporters, such as Alfred Kahn, uneasy. Several of his talented recruits had bolted—not only Wolf, but also Neal Meehan, who had been insulted when Mike Levine was installed above him at New

York Air. Meehan, who'd given up a good job with People Express to run New York Air, quit and sued Texas Air for breach of contract.

Levine was not to be happy at New York Air for long, either, although he'd done well at first. He moved the airline away from the straightforward concept of low costs and low fares to a more upscale product. He introduced in-flight "Nosh Bags" of snacks for passengers, heralded by a tongue-in-cheek ad campaign pointing out that Eastern passengers got only an airsickness bag.

In 1983 New York Air turned a profit of just over $4 million. But Levine began to run into problems with Lorenzo, who did not entirely agree with the move to a more upscale, more expensive product. "It was a conflict between two strong-willed people," said Alfred Kahn, who observed them as a director.

In early 1984, Levine abruptly quit. He continued to earn $180,000 a year as a consultant to Texas Air and refused to publicly discuss his resignation. Years later, however, he told an interviewer, with a sour look on his face, "I simply decided I did not want to work for Frank Lorenzo." "He couldn't work for Frank Lorenzo," said Alfred Kahn. "Mike's a strong person, and he wanted to run things his way. It was predictable that they wouldn't get along." Levine went back to teaching at the University of Southern California and later was made dean of Yale's School of Organization and Management.

THE CLEAR ANTIUNION SIGNALS FROM Washington, and Reagan's response to the PATCO strike, had emboldened managers around the country. Lorenzo had seen that the CAB did nothing when unions protested New York Air. Alfred Kahn confessed that he was disturbed by the labor unrest in the industry he'd done so much to reshape.

Not long after Mike Levine stepped down, Alfred Kahn resigned from New York Air's board. He told Lorenzo, with characteristic modesty, that "I'm much better at doing things for which I have responsibility than coming once every few months and presuming to advise people." But later, Kahn confessed that he had grown uncomfortable with Lorenzo's union bashing.

"He was so strongly antiunion," said Kahn a number of years later, when Lorenzo was embroiled in one of the worst labor disputes in memory. "And in a way I hoped he would succeed, because I knew he truly hated to raise fares.

"But the fact is, his confrontational methods failed."

10

THE BIG DEAL

Even if we got every break in the world, it would have taken us maybe forty years to get what we got in one day.
—DICK FERRIS

W hen the aviation elite journeyed to Charlie Gates's A Bar A Ranch in Wyoming during September 1984, it appeared the Conquistadores had managed to stand deregulation on its head. Nobody believed any more that a small and efficient airline could compete. Airlines had converted to a new religion, the belief that they had to attain a certain size not just to make a profit, but to survive.

The group that year mingled the retiring old guard, like American's Al Casey, and the newer flyboys who were by then running the airlines, including Frank Lorenzo, Dick Ferris, Bob Crandall, Don Burr, and Steve Wolf. In the quiet of their mountain hideout they huddled with Donald Douglas and T. Wilson of Boeing, who were turning out scores of new jets. Together they would chase the same goal: to amass the largest airlines the United States had ever seen.

Don Burr and Frank Lorenzo had finally transcended their outsider status. Their vastly different philosophies had led to the same result: large nonunion airlines with low costs that could offer consumers low fares. Burr had even been quoted as saying, "We think bigger is better," vexing those who'd assumed he would be content to run an East Coast version of Southwest. People Express was at the time the fastest-growing company in American history; in four years it had gone from 250 workers and three planes to 4,000 employees and a fleet of seventy-two jets. Its stock had reached fifty dollars a share at one point, giving Burr a paper fortune of more than $35 million. While Frank Lorenzo would win no popularity contests, Burr's natural charm and boyish good looks made him a media favorite. Colleagues intimated that he'd even considered running for president.

Dick Ferris was in the unfamiliar position of watching his next-biggest rival, American, embark on a growth plan that would allow it to overtake United. Ferris, however, had been quietly talking with another Conquistador for the past three years about a plan that would make his airline so much larger that American wouldn't have a chance. He would make United indisputably the largest airline in the world outside the Soviet Union.

MEMBERSHIP IN THE WORLD'S MOST exclusive aviation club had generally been closed to two groups: government officials and women. By 1984, the individual with the most influence over the airlines was both.

Elizabeth Dole succeeded Drew Lewis as transportation secretary in early 1983. On its face her appointment was a cynical move by Republicans to close the "gender gap" that threatened to cost them the women's vote in the next election. Yet editorial writers around the country applauded Dole's nomination. Her résumé equaled that of any mover and shaker in the capital.

Born Elizabeth Hanford in Salisbury, North Carolina, she had been both Phi Beta Kappa and beauty queen at Duke University. She picked up law and graduate degrees from Harvard, and arrived in Washington in 1968 to join President Lyndon Johnson's committee on consumer interests, later joining the Nixon White House in the same role.

In 1972 she met recently divorced Kansas senator Bob Dole during a visit to his office. When she married him three years later, she had risen to prominence as a federal trade commissioner. She later resigned to work on her husband's ill-fated presidential campaign.

As transportation secretary, Dole at first drew praise for her hard work. Soon, however, airline executives began to resent what they viewed as her aggressively political approach to their business. "She couldn't take a phone call without evaluating the political implications of taking the phone call. Every issue was assessing the political risk," complained a man who was chief executive at two major airlines during Dole's tenure.

One instance came in the fall of 1984, when Dole informed the airlines she was planning a public demonstration of "anti-misting kerosene"—a specially treated aviation fuel that was supposed to be significantly less flammable in accidents, and therefore could save lives in the event of a crash. To get maximum publicity, she arranged to deliberately crash a commercial passenger jet using the new fuel, inviting the networks to tape the event for the evening news.

Airline executives tried to talk her out of this stunt, pointing out that experts had cautioned that more research was needed. But Dole went ahead. On December 1, the aircraft with the nonflammable fuel erupted into a ball of fire upon impact. The television correspondents who'd dutifully responded to Dole's call gleefully aired the videotape of the charred jet on that night's evening news.

Dole, like other Cabinet members, was reluctant to take steps that would run counter to the president's budget-cutting goals. Consumer advocates criticized her for failing to add aviation inspectors, whose ranks had actually slipped during the first few years of the 1980s despite a sizable increase in the number of planes in the air.

At the end of 1984, Dole inherited jurisdiction over airline matters as the Civil Aeronautics Board prepared to close down for good. Dole had an even wider role than was originally intended. The Justice Department was supposed to get the authority to approve airline agreements such as mergers after the CAB closed down. Consumer protection was supposed to be transferred to the Federal Trade Commission. But the airline industry—as represented by the Air Transport Association—didn't like this scenario at all. The FTC and Justice's antitrust division had made many enemies in the business world, and Justice in particular had shown that it still cared about the antitrust laws. The airlines figured that they would never get approval from Justice for any agreements they might want to make among themselves. So the airlines banded together and convinced Congress to rewrite the law, handing over virtually all the remaining CAB powers to Transportation. Dole was suddenly an aviation czarina, with control over virtually all government functions affecting the airlines. Despite their sniping at Dole, a number of airline chiefs would find nothing to criticize in her department's handling of mergers.

• • •

IN EARLY 1985, DICK FERRIS called Ed Acker in an annual ritual that he had begun not long after Acker joined Pan Am in late 1981. He had quickly let Acker know that he would like to buy Pan Am's crown jewel, the Pacific routes that Juan Trippe had opened with his China Clipper nearly fifty years before. Acker politely rebuffed him, but Ferris kept up his entreaties, calling year after year.

United had been trying to expand into the Pacific for years without much success, winning its first route to the Orient, from Seattle to Tokyo, only in 1978. Few such opportunities ever became available through normal channels, since foreign rights were dependent on the United States negotiating more favorable aviation treaties with Asian nations. Trippe had long ago snapped up the best routes to the Orient, and Pan Am's only U.S. competition on the Pacific routes was from Northwest and, to a lesser degree, Continental.

United had actually passed up a rare chance to acquire the routes in 1979. General Seawell had hired the prestigious consulting firm of McKinsey & Company to suggest ways to restructure Pan Am's operations. The McKinsey team concluded that Pan Am should get rid of the Pacific division, not because it would fetch a high price, but because the McKinsey team didn't think the routes had much value. The consultants concocted the extraordinary theory that the Pacific flights didn't have enough business executives on them, because they were too full of Japanese and Australian tourists. "It was an incredibly hokum theory," was how one Seawell aide described it, but Pan Am went ahead and approached American and United. The two carriers demurred, since they were too busy coping with the immediate aftereffects of deregulation.

Ferris regretted United didn't grab the routes back then, but he was sure the ailing Pan Am would have to put them on the block again. In 1982, he convinced Acker to meet him at a hotel near Kennedy Airport. Ferris offered $50 million for Pan Am's Japanese routes, but the talks bogged down.

In early 1985, Acker was still loath to yield the Pacific. But Ferris sensed this time he might change his mind. For all Acker had accomplished, Pan Am remained the basket case of the industry.

Acker, a tall, mild-mannered Texan, had at first seemed a promising candidate to turn Pan Am around, for by 1980 he had accomplished the unusual feat of making a personal fortune in the airline business. After working in finance jobs, he became president of Braniff in 1970. He left that post in 1975 and soon afterward spotted an investment opportunity in an intrastate puddle-jumper called Air Florida. Figuring that the airline could profit from National's and Eastern's decision to cut back on flights within Florida, Acker bought several hundred thousand dollars' worth of stock in the carrier. Other Wall Street investors took notice and the stock price shot up sixfold. Suddenly, Acker's initial investment was worth a few million dollars. He moved to Miami and took over management of the company as CEO in 1977. When deregulation came the next year, Air Florida expanded rapidly, and by 1981 its fleet had gone from three airplanes to forty, and its profits were in the millions.

Acker's success with the rapidly growing carrier did not go unnoticed in airline circles. In 1981, he got a call from a headhunter asking if he would be interested in running Pan Am. Acker had a head start. At Conquistadores meetings, Acker had come to know Jack Parker, a Pan Am board member and vice-chairman of General Electric, a major supplier of jet engines. Soon after he'd accepted the Pan Am job, Acker joked that "I've always wanted to be captain of the *Titanic*."

Although the company was virtually bankrupt, the Pan Am board offered the already wealthy Acker a handsome package: a $250,000 lump-sum payment, a base salary of $350,000, a minimum annual bonus of $100,000, and options on a million shares of stock. A rent-free apartment at the luxurious Westbury Hotel on Manhattan's Upper East Side was thrown in.

The $500 million that Seawell had negotiated for the sale of Pan Am's Inter-Continental Hotels unit had been used to pay off jittery banks and to reduce corporate debt. Once the banks got paid off, they were reluctant to loan any more money to the struggling airline. Some of the first meetings Acker held after moving into the forty-sixth floor of the Pan Am Building were with bankruptcy lawyers. "We seriously considered it very early on," Acker said, but finally decided against it, largely because the disastrous Braniff bankruptcy was still on everyone's minds.

At first Acker appeared to justify his princely income. Two years after he arrived the company's stock price, which had been hovering just over two dollars when Seawell left, had nearly tripled. Acker trimmed some of the money-losing trophy routes Trippe had acquired and shifted planes into more profitable markets. He also cut down on the airline's bloated bureaucracy and hired bright young executives away from other lines, luring Gerry Gitner from People Express and Steve Wolf from American.

The company's five labor unions at first cooperated with the new regime and agreed to a 10 percent pay cut and a wage freeze for several years. But union leaders were wary, and the chairman's public image did not help. Acker and his young second wife, Sandy, enjoyed a lifestyle commensurate with their wealth, mingling with celebrities and jetting from one home to another, including a sprawling mansion they had bought on Bermuda.

By the end of 1984, Pan Am's labor contracts were coming due for renewal. And the union leaders, aware of the company's rising stock price and bullish reviews from Wall Street, wanted to get back some of what they had given up. Acker, however, felt the company couldn't take an increase in its payroll. Pan Am still had long-term debt of $1.2 billion, and many of the financial solutions applied by his new team were, like the labor agreements, short-term fixes. The airline's pension costs had quadrupled after the National merger. The company had also repeatedly deferred pension contributions— more than $130 million from 1980 to 1984. When that happens, a company has to amortize it and "that was killing us," Acker later conceded. Acker belatedly tried to sell the employees on a two-tier wage scale like American's and on work-rule changes that would improve productivity. But Acker's popularity with the rank and file had slid. The upshot was that the unions flatly refused to consider his proposals.

ON MARCH 1, 1985, THE fifty-seven hundred Pan Am mechanics and ground workers belonging to the Transport Workers Union walked off the job, shutting down most of Pan Am's operations. The strike lasted twenty-seven days. Acker was shocked when he reviewed Pan Am's balance sheet after it was over. He'd built up Pan Am's cash reserve from virtually nothing in 1981 to $300 million just before the strike. In just a few weeks, the cushion had dwindled to half that amount. "Business went to nothing," he said. With its revenues cut off, Pan Am needed some quick cash. Now it was his turn to pick up the phone and talk to Dick Ferris.

Within a week, Ferris and Acker, in a suite at the Plaza Hotel in New York, agreed in principle on what the deal would include: not only Pan Am's routes from the United States to Japan, but the whole vast Pacific network, stretching from the Philippines to Australia, from Korea to Singapore and Thailand. Also included were all the jets required to fly the routes (including eleven 747-SPs, "special performance" jumbos that could fly nonstop farther than a normal 747) and all of Pan Am's stations and equipment in the Pacific. This was fully one-quarter of Pan Am's airline business, and the Pacific division was also a profit-maker, earning $55 million in 1984, a year in which the company as a whole lost $95 million.

A few days later, Ferris and Acker settled on a price—$750 million for the entire Pacific division—and Ferris agreed to hire nearly three thousand Pan Am employees. Pan Am's directors, who'd selected Acker to restore Pan Am's glory as America's carrier to the world, were totally unaware that a big chunk of this hard-won empire was about to be parceled off.

Acker knew he'd sustain criticism for selling such a prize. But he also knew the airline couldn't afford to maintain it. To buy the expensive new long-range 747s that his rivals were ordering, and to build up West Coast hubs to feed the Pacific routes, he'd need to spend at least $3.5 billion, a sum Pan Am had no hope of getting.

Ferris was ecstatic over the deal, even though he knew it would give United many things it didn't want or need, such as a fleet of old clunkers. United mechanics inspected Pan Am's 747-SPs using red markers to circle "dings in the nacelles"—small dents in the engine covers. "When they got done with one of them, the plane looked like it had the measles," Ferris said. Before the purchase, United had figured it would cost about $35 million to rehabilitate the Pan Am airplanes, he said. It ended up spending more than twice that amount. Ferris recalled that on a visit to one Pan Am station in the Pacific, "I found a typewriter out there that must have come over with the first Clipper. And they were still using it."

Just before Pan Am and United dropped their bombshell, rumors started flying. Down in Dallas, Jack Pope, who was then Bob Crandall's chief financial officer, remembered hearing on a Friday afternoon about a major Pan Am asset sale to American's archrival.

"We at American never really got to participate," he said, and they certainly would have liked to. "I know that some calls were made over the weekend—they were trying to get Acker's attention." But they didn't. American never got a chance to bid on what was at that point the biggest deal in the history of the airline industry.

Crandall had no idea that Pan Am wanted to sell the Pacific routes, he later admitted. Pan Am insiders said that Acker dealt solely with Ferris because he was convinced that he would never get a better deal from anyone else, especially Crandall, who Acker reportedly believed would try to bargain him to death.

Shortly after the deal was announced, Jack Pope ran an analysis through American's computers and walked into Crandall's office with his evaluation of the transaction. "Well, they got a wonderful asset," he told Crandall, "but they paid way too much for it." His analysis, Pope recalled, indicated that by American's standards, the Pan Am Pacific division wasn't worth more than $575 million, tops. And besides the $750 million cash price, American estimated that with the assumed debt, the cost of rehabilitating the planes, and taking on all the Pan Am employees, United's true cost would be more than $1 billion.

Pope later admitted that "I was totally, completely wrong. It was probably the most brilliant airline acquisition of the century." Just a few years later, United's Pacific system would be valued at around $3 billion.

FERRIS AND ACKER WENT BACK to their boards for approval of the deal. They met in Washington for the closing, signing the contract the morning of April 22, 1985. Five minutes later, they were in Elizabeth Dole's office to seek her blessing, Acker recalled. The two then went out to call on anyone else in Washington who might be of help—on Capitol Hill, in the White House, at the departments of Treasury and State. "We really got a lot of support, and we got it early," Acker gushed.

Ferris made the curious, if not disingenuous, argument that the deal actually advanced deregulation. In a speech to a Washington aviation group, he claimed that his purchase of the Pacific routes "is proof that deregulation is working." But it is instructive to remember why United had broken ranks with the industry and pushed for deregulation in the first place. It wanted to get bigger and couldn't under the entry constraints imposed by regulation. So, as it had almost twenty-five years before when it merged with Capital, it grew by acquiring another airline—or at least a huge chunk of one.

Although many such deals at the time piled huge amounts of debt on the acquirer, Ferris did not let United fall into that trap. The company could well afford the purchase by tapping its existing sources of financing. Even though its revenue stream was suddenly interrupted around this time by a pilots' strike, which grounded the airline for a month, the airline had a substantial cash cushion.

Dole must have understood that her decision in the case would have grave consequences, and would set an important precedent for the industry. "It was literally turning over one-half of our [airline] activity in the Pacific to a new entrant in that market," said Matt Scocozza, who, as Dole's assistant secretary for policy and international affairs, reviewed most of the airline merger cases that came before the department. "It had lots of policy ramifications in terms of 'Should we transfer?' or 'Should we just chop it all up and let everybody have a little piece?' " The latter course, he admitted, was not considered an option.

The still perilous financial condition of debt-ridden Pan Am was in the deal's favor. The CAB had a longstanding policy known as the "Failing Carrier" doctrine, which held that if the only way to keep a struggling airline alive was to allow it to merge, then the merger should be approved. No previous administration had wanted the responsibility of a Pan Am failure on its hands.

The Justice Department came down on the opposite side from the politicians advocating the deal. Antitrust lawyers for Justice said that the deal could hurt competition in the Pacific, especially if United was allowed to keep the Seattle-Tokyo route it had won in 1978. Northwest Airlines, the only other U.S. airline with substantial transpacific routes, questioned whether one airline even had the right to sell government-awarded international route authority to another. And the airline labor unions insisted that DOT should require United to guarantee that it would protect the jobs of all Pan Am employees.

The arguments by Ferris's competitors ultimately concerned the implications for the future structure of the airline industry. Was it right that the nation's biggest carrier—indeed, the biggest airline in the Free World, as United sometimes called itself—should be allowed to get so much bigger all at once?

In November 1985, Secretary Dole responded, Why not? If a weak competitor was replaced with a strong one, competition in the Pacific would be improved, not lessened, she argued. Dole also dismissed the concern of some airlines that United's computer reservations system would give it an unfair advantage. "United's computer reservations dominance does not translate into economic power in these markets," she insisted in her approval of the sale. However, to appease not only the Justice Department but also her department's own general counsel, Dole agreed to begin a separate proceeding to decide whether United's Seattle-Tokyo route should be awarded to someone else.

Soon Washington was buzzing with the word that Dole's handling of the airline matters she inherited was highly political. "Carriers have become less discreet in their attempts to influence the department and Elizabeth Dole," reported the trade publication *Aviation Daily*. Part of the difference was procedural: Dole and other cabinet secretaries conducted much of their business in private, while the CAB's five members had been required to thrash out their decisions in public meetings. Still, the CAB, much as it had been maligned in the past, was now being cited in some quarters as a paragon of good government compared to the new regime at Transportation.

Any transportation secretary might have been perceived as more political than the bipartisan board of an independent agency. Yet Dole was by background and inclination a politician, and she was married to one. Unsurprisingly, she clearly seemed to be tilting in favor of the larger airlines. Many Washington insiders said that United's purchase of Pan Am's Pacific routes would never have gone through virtually intact if the CAB were still around.

The United Airlines purchase of Pan Am's Pacific division was to set off a domino effect. Many airlines were alarmed at the new competitor they faced, especially Northwest, which objected to the nation's largest airline's moving onto its Pacific turf. Dole's argument that the deal would put a much stronger competitor in the Pacific— one with a huge domestic route network that could feed passengers into its international flights—was not good news for United's rivals. In order to protect itself against this threat, Northwest knew it would need a substantially bigger domestic network of its own, and the fastest way to get one would be through a merger.

Soon it was clear that the government would not stand in the way of Northwest's pursuit of its own merger to offset the United deal's effect. The Twin Cities–based airline at first lodged strong protests with the Transportation Department to the United deal, along with other airlines. But as Transportation Department officials were reviewing the Pan Am–United route sale that summer, Northwest chairman Steven Rothmeier met with Stephen Wolf—then president of Republic Airlines—in a St. Paul steakhouse, where he listened to Wolf's proposal for a Northwest-Republic combination. Rothmeier stalled Wolf for a few months as he sought out a deal with a bigger partner, Delta. But those talks fell through, and Wolf and Rothmeier returned to the bargaining table.

A prominent aviation attorney in Washington insists that there was some communication from government sources to Northwest officials that they would indeed "get their own merger." Transportation officials deny that there was any such agreement, written or unwritten, and Wolf denied knowledge of such an understanding. However, at the end of July 1986, exactly nine months after Elizabeth Dole formally approved the Pan Am–United deal, the Transportation Department also approved the acquisition of Republic Airlines by Northwest for $880 million—brushing aside the vehement objections of the Justice Department's antitrust division. Justice said that the merger would be anticompetitive because the two carriers' systems overlapped in too many places, and would give the new airline a near-monopoly at Minneapolis and Detroit. It was that overlap, of course, that drew the two together in the first place, for they could cut costs by eliminating duplication and much of their competition all in one step.

With the Transportation Department now in charge, each new merger approval provided the airline industry with another reason to believe that no proposed acquisition would be blocked—and another reason for airline companies to seek out such partnerships, in order to better protect themselves against the larger competitors that had been created by the mergers already approved.

11

ICAHN THE TERRIBLE

*Maybe it's sex appeal, but
there's something about an
airplane that drives investors
crazy.*
—ALFRED KAHN

United's purchase of Pan Am's Asian routes had been a friendly transaction. But the generous price tag and the apparent promise of government consent caused excitement in the investment community. Only a few airline buffs and politicians still clung to the notion that an international airline was a national treasure and somehow immune from a raid. High visibility and the tenuous connection to foreign policy would make an airline an especially tempting target.

Trans World Airlines was undoubtedly the most inviting prize after the Pan Am route deal closed. Although it had lost more than $100 million since deregulation, TWA was still one of the best-known corporate names in the world. It flew to dozens of prime overseas destinations and its image, while tarnished, still had enormous value. Unlike Pan Am, it possessed a sizable domestic route network as well as the third-largest airline computer reservations system.

For the past decade, TWA had been headed by Carl Edwin Meyer, a colorless fifty-seven-year-old former accountant who had been the first chief executive to be promoted from within the company in forty years. Meyer's surprising ascent did not compensate for his singular ineptitude at dealing with the deregulated world, however. Tall and balding, Meyer had a distant and abrupt manner. He felt any proposals ought to come to him via proper channels. But little was bubbling up through the channels that could save TWA.

Meyer was not entirely to blame. He had to endure comparisons with a host of strong-willed predecessors, each of whom had made a mark on the company. The airline had been led out of the Howard Hughes era by Charles Tillinghast, a Wall Street lawyer and former Bendix Corporation executive. Tillinghast bought the jet aircraft Hughes had rejected and oversaw the construction of the distinctive Eero Saarinen–designed TWA terminal building at Kennedy Airport. The early 1960s—when Frank Lorenzo and Bob Crandall got their first jobs in the airline's finance department—were boom years for TWA. The airline made the highest profits in the industry in 1965, and Tillinghast became the first airline executive to make the cover of *Time* magazine. He groomed a successor, Ed Smart, a Harvard-trained lawyer and by all accounts a capable businessman. Then, in 1976, Ed Meyer was picked as president.

TWA was not prepared for deregulation. Its long-distance trans-continental and transatlantic route system endowed it with a fleet of large airplanes. Even on its domestic routes, it often used 707s and L-1011s after deregulation when smaller airplanes would have been much more efficient. Although it built up its St. Louis hub, it failed to create a second hub at Pittsburgh, again because it lacked the right airplanes.

An assault in the early 1980s by some Wall Street raiders set TWA up as a takeover target. A group called Odyssey Partners, created by former executives of Oppenheimer and Company, zeroed in on the airline as a drag on the fortunes of its parent company, TW Corporation, which also owned the Hilton International Hotels chain and other profitable subsidiaries, such as Canteen Corporation and the Century 21 real estate business. Odyssey Partners included a seasoned airline analyst named Bert Fingerhut, who argued that TW Corporation was worth much more broken up than it was whole.

Sizing up a company's breakup value was a popular pastime in the 1980s heyday of takeovers. With only 1 percent of TW Corporations stock, Odyssey mounted a proxy battle at the company's April 1983 annual meeting, urging fellow shareholders to "request" dismantling the company and selling off the parts—a maneuver they said would be worth a windfall of seventy dollars a share. They also estimated that an independent TWA might fetch some $800 million on the market.

Although the move was defeated, Odyssey claimed it had won

35 percent of the vote and vowed to continue the fight. That fall, TW Corporation, no doubt alarmed at TWA's worsening losses, did just what Odyssey had urged: It spun off TWA into a separate corporation.

Meyer tried to put the best face on it. But TWA, minus the protective embrace of its parent, was even more subject to the ups and downs of the airline business. Its stock traded at a pathetic eight dollars a share, while its book value was easily three to four times that, given its planes, airport facilities, foreign route rights, and other assets.

However, Meyer was doing little about the critical problem of the company's high labor costs. Several rounds of negotiations had failed to produce the employee concessions that TWA said were needed to bring its balance sheet into the black.

Talks between the machinists and management broke down in November 1984 and the union, along with the pilots, seriously doubted the company could turn itself around. Brian Freeman, an adviser to the machinists union international in Washington, had tried to talk to Meyer about brokering a peace. Not only had Freeman worked on the Republic Airlines labor agreements, he had also been involved in Eastern Airlines' equity-concessions swap. That was not a factor in his favor in Meyer's eyes.

"They were really upset at the Eastern deal, they were totally opposed to the employees having a say in the company," recalled Freeman.

With John Peterpaul, a senior official of the machinists union international in Washington, Freeman crafted a plan that included concessions and a greater voice for employees in company matters. It was immediately rebuffed by Meyer.

"Meyer just wanted concessions for free—with nothing for the employees in return. We said you just couldn't do that—just give concessions and subsidize bad management."

A few months later, at Shearson's annual transportation conference in Florida, Meyer had an unscheduled brush with his labor adversaries. Peterpaul and Freeman showed up to give a presentation extolling what they termed "concession capital," the notion that a good faith effort to solve problems must accompany any wage concessions. Meyer "just ignored us," recalled Freeman. Meanwhile, TWA's performance plummeted: it lost $29.4 million in the fourth quarter of 1984.

•   •   •

MEYER MIGHT NOT HAVE RESISTED union entreaties so strenuously had he known that for nearly a year, one of the more notorious corporate raiders in the country had been quietly eyeing a takeover of TWA.

It had begun in early 1984. Sanford Rederer, a Washington consultant who had worked for Alfred Kahn at the CAB, was studying a proposed takeover of Frontier Airlines by a group of investors. As Rederer scouted possible investors in the Frontier deal, an acquaintance at Wertheim & Company, a New York investment house, mentioned that one of his partners knew Carl Icahn and offered to introduce them. Sometime that summer Rederer sat down with the redoubtable financier and his longtime aide-de-camp, a rumpled numbers-crunching type named Alfred Kingsley.

Icahn almost immediately made it clear he was not interested in Frontier, but he was more than mildly interested in airlines, Rederer recalled, and the two chatted about the industry in general. Rederer was surprised when Icahn suddenly started listing possible acquisitions, expressing particular interest in TWA as an attractive takeover target. Icahn had obviously been following the events at TW Corporation. In fact, there was some speculation that the Odyssey group had approached Icahn about investing. By the end of the session, Rederer had been hired as a consultant by Icahn to draw up some analyses on TWA.

Over the next few months, Rederer prepared numbers and detailed reports, covering everything from TWA's operating costs and cash flow to its asset value and flight operations. Especially intriguing was TWA's profit-and-loss breakdown: The airline was losing $122 million a year on domestic operations but made more than $150 million on international flights. As Rederer continued to work with Icahn and Kingsley, they concocted strategies for improving TWA's cash flow. They focused on disposing of assets and cutting money-losing domestic routes—ideas that would cause a riot if the unions found out.

That September, Icahn and his assorted investment companies (mainly limited partnerships with quirky names like Excalibur) began quietly buying up shares of TWA common stock, which were then trading at around ten dollars. Initially they stayed below the 5 percent mark that would trigger filing requirements at the SEC under the Williams Act. At the same time, Icahn had developed a detailed plan for "fixing" TWA that included selling up to $500 million worth of assets and closing the airline's huge Kansas City overhaul and maintenance base, which employed thousands of workers. Among the assets on the block would be dozens of jets and facilities at such choice airports as O'Hare and La Guardia. All flights not operated through the airline's chief hubs at Kennedy or in St. Louis would be eliminated.

It was a curious plan. There was an old saw in the business that "you can't shrink an airline into profitability" given the need to develop enough critical mass to feed passengers from one flight to another. This strategy, however, was familiar territory to Icahn. A few years back he had acquired ACF, a St. Louis–based manufacturer of rail cars and other heavy industrial products. After buying the company, Icahn immediately sold off some divisions for a handsome profit, leaving the core rail business as a leaner and ultimately money-making company.

But the airline business had little in common with manufacturing, as Icahn would soon discover. A raid on a prestigious international airline with more than thirty thousand workers, whose planes touched down daily in such places as Paris, Tel Aviv, and Bombay, would be another matter. Icahn also had virtually no management experience. The airline takeover, however, would display Icahn's predatory instincts at their sharpest, temporarily masking his unsuitability for the job of actually managing his prey.

A DEVELOPMENT OUTSIDE THE AIRLINE business became increasingly important to the airlines in the next two years. Investment bankers were eager to broker a deal, to tap the largesse of an Icahn or a Lorenzo. As Brian Freeman put it, "Drexel was really hustling Lorenzo for deals." Drexel junk bond king Michael Milken actually got to know Lorenzo fairly well and occasionally proffered advice. Even though Milken and his junk bond obsession may have helped build Lorenzo's empire, Milken later repeatedly urged the Texas Air chief to get out of the business.

But in early 1985, Wall Street was hailing Frank Lorenzo as a hero. He had proved that an airline could be taken into bankruptcy and survive, indeed prosper.

Continental, in the two years after its Chapter 11 filing, confounded critics who had warned that passengers would desert a bankrupt airline. The airline had in 1985 posted the highest third-quarter operating and net profit in its history, admittedly with help of Chapter 11, which exempted the company from some debt payments. Its planes were flying two-thirds full. Its workforce had more than doubled, from the skeletal staff of forty-five hundred right after the strike to nearly ten thousand.

The company was still technically in bankruptcy and the court kept slowing Lorenzo's efforts to build Continental into a powerhouse. When Lorenzo tried to acquire eighteen new aircraft and launch new services to a score of cities, the judge overseeing the case questioned the company's eagerness to expand at a time when it had yet to work out a final deal with its creditors. At this rate, it would never rival United or American.

Continental's bankruptcy did not slow Lorenzo's acquisitiveness. Lorenzo simply used Continental's parent company, Texas Air Corporation, which was not in bankruptcy, as a fund-raising vehicle.

Lorenzo's tough stand against organized labor was an asset in raising money to finance expansion. Many Wall Street analysts issued bullish assessments of Lorenzo's ability to create a truly low-cost airline giant. Through several public offerings Lorenzo amassed a war chest of some $150 million.

Soon a target came his way, ailing Frontier Airlines, which was based in Denver, also a big stronghold of Continental's. This middling regional airline would not do much for Lorenzo's grand ambitions to create a huge international company, but it would take care of a nagging problem closer to home. Both Frontier and Continental were having a hard time competing with United at Denver, where the three carriers were engaged in a turf war reminiscent of the brawl among American, Braniff, and Delta at Dallas a few years before. Denver was not a big enough market to support all three companies and it was just a matter of time before one of the rivals was forced to fold. United had the might to simply wait out the bloodbath. Lorenzo's response was to try to buy his competition.

Frontier management had been looking for a cash-rich suitor to acquire the company. Employees, however, had their own ideas about how to rescue the crumbling company. Union leaders had formed a coalition to explore an employee buyout, and workers had already committed themselves to wage cuts as part of the plan. If it succeeded, Frontier would become the first employee-owned airline. The employee group entered into negotiations with RKO Corporation, which held the biggest chunk (40 percent) of Frontier's stock, and a deal looked feasible by the time Lorenzo declared his interest. Employees were sickened at the prospect of having to work for Lorenzo instead.

Organized labor would not forget how Lorenzo had gutted labor contracts at Continental back in 1983. Airline unions subsequently lobbied for a change in federal law that would prevent Chapter 11 from being used as a tool to break labor contracts. This amendment was passed by Congress in 1984. Labor leaders were convinced that the Continental experience had hardened Lorenzo irrevocably. William Scheri, an official of the International Association of Machinists who had dealt with Lorenzo at Texas International in the 1970s, recalled that "he was a changed man" after he took over Continental, even refusing to meet personally with union representatives.

Right after the Chapter 11 filing in 1983, "Continental shrank down to a small core of people who formed a circle around Frank," one former Continental officer remarked. "And they fought the battles with the pilots, and with the pipe bombs, and the violence and ugliness that came of the Continental bankruptcy. That forged a bond between Frank and this circle, and the circle stayed together all through the Continental regrowth. It became a siege mentality."

Early in April 1985, Lorenzo made an offer for Frontier, but it was laughed off as a lowball bid, just a typical effort by a raider to stir up the pot. "Bids were made on everything," said a close associate of Lorenzo's. "You throw in a bid to find out what's happening, maybe learn a little more about your competitor through due diligence" (gathering information on the target company). However, Lorenzo was soon distracted by a much more alluring target, the airline he most coveted—TWA.

BY THE TIME ICAHN HAD turned his sights on TWA, his net worth was estimated at $100 million. He had started out some twenty-four years before with little more than a few thousand dollars in poker winnings.

Icahn was raised an only child in the middle-class New York neighborhood of Bayswater, Queens. His mother, Bella, taught school; his father, Michael, was a lawyer and a frustrated opera singer who was a cantor in a nearby synagogue.

As a child, Carl Icahn excelled in chess. He became state champion at the game in college, and considered becoming a professional player. He attended Princeton University on scholarship and graduated in 1957. Princeton, however, was also Icahn's first exposure to the WASP establishment. He told friends later of the subtle anti-Semitism he experienced. Icahn did not mingle with the scions of old family fortunes—students like John Danforth, heir to the Ralston Purina fortune, who typified the old Princeton. Danforth did not know Icahn at Princeton, where they were one year apart, but years later, as a Republican senator from Missouri, he would become Icahn's chief nemesis on Capitol Hill.

After college, Icahn bent to his mother's wishes and attended medical school at New York University for two miserable years. After a stint in the Army, where he won several thousand dollars playing poker, he headed for Wall Street and with help from his uncle, wealthy businessman Elliott Schnall, got a job as a trainee stockbroker with Dreyfus and Company. In his first year at Dreyfus he made fifty thousand dollars but lost it all in one bad week in 1962. The shock of that setback convinced him to never again play the market with his own money.

Icahn soon found his niche in options, then a relatively obscure Wall Street field. He did well at several firms and then in 1968 he borrowed four hundred thousand dollars from his uncle Elliott to buy a seat on the New York Stock Exchange and to found Icahn & Company. Initially trading stocks and convertible bonds, he moved into options and risk arbitrage, another relatively undiscovered field, where stocks and options are traded to take advantage of slight differences in price on various markets. "Arbs" would also sink huge amounts into a rumored takeover target and then reap huge profits by selling out before the rumors were dispelled.

Alfred Kingsley joined Icahn then, and while the two split up for a time, Kingsley always returned, although Icahn refused to make him a partner until years later. Icahn did not really want any partners, and most of his other associates would eventually leave out of frustration. But Icahn and Kinsgley together played the oddballs in the starchy Wall Street crowd.

Icahn's first takeover bid, for Tappan Company, manufacturer of kitchen stoves, reaped him $2.7 million. From there, Icahn launched takeover attempts for Gulf & Western, American Can, Phillips Petroleum, and Hammermill Paper Company. Icahn would identify a company whose stock was undervalued, quietly buy shares, threaten to take it over and fire its management, then back off with a substantial payment from the target's managers or from a "White Knight" called in by the company to fight off Icahn.

This "greenmail," as it was soon dubbed, put Icahn in the company of such predators as Ivan Boesky and Saul Steinberg. Of the group, Icahn tried hardest to justify his actions. He portrayed himself as a champion of shareholders trying to oust incompetent management. He always claimed a genuine interest in acquiring his prey and operating it more efficiently. But since he had usually avoided ending up in the executive suite, his railing at bad managers seemed a thinly veiled rationalization for his plunder.

IN 1985, ED MEYER WAS one of the bad managers on Icahn's hit list. Near the end of March, TWA got a hint of impending trouble during Drexel's annual Predators Ball, or junk bond conference, in Los Angeles. Icahn showed up at a seminar given by TWA and began lobbing questions at Richard Peiser, a senior financial officer at the airline. Peiser was discomfited by Icahn's interest.

Brian Freeman, who had also attended the Predators Ball, sensed that something might be up, and he made a few efforts to contact Meyer on behalf of Peterpaul. By chance he ran into Meyer down in Washington—he found the TWA chief wandering, befuddled, around the corridors of a congressional office building, looking for a committee hearing. As Freeman guided Meyer to his destination, he again broached the subject of a meeting with the machinists, noting that rumors of a possible takeover attempt were circulating on Wall Street.

"Look, Ed, we can work with you and give you concessions that could block a takeover," Freeman said. Meyer hit the roof. "I don't need you to deal with my employees," he snapped. "I can deal with them myself. And there are not going to be any quid pro quos."

Freeman was appalled.

ON APRIL 29, ICAHN CROSSED the 5 percent line of ownership of TWA's common stock. He prepared to make the necessary 13D filing with the SEC within ten days, publicly declaring his intentions. Icahn would finally have to come out in the open with his plan to break up much of TWA.

Drexel was in a difficult position because it counted both Icahn and TWA among its clients. For Drexel to have even unwittingly aided one client in making a hostile raid on another was, to say the least, bad form, if not an outright conflict of interest. Once news of Icahn's holdings was out, Drexel tried to appease TWA's outraged managers by bringing the two sides together for a meeting on May 3. It was Icahn's first meeting with Meyer and other top TWA officials.

Icahn tried to sell the TWA team on his breakup plan, saying he favored it because it would let him acquire the airline without liquidating the entire company afterward. He also said he wanted an airline because he thought the industry was generally undervalued. TWA's managers were shocked. Here was this coarse outsider who talked about an airline as if it were a collection of spare parts. After the session, the feeling at TWA was that it would be impossible to talk business with Icahn. Meyer described him as "the greediest man on earth."

Soon after, on May 10, 1985, TWA declared war on Icahn. In full-page newspaper ads, TWA told the world what it thought was the truth about Icahn—his record of greenmail, his intention to dismantle a venerable company. It was a strategy based on the belief of TWA management that their case, much like a political campaign, could be won on character. Senator John Danforth, concerned about TWA employees in St. Louis, was only too happy to participate. One day, at a Senate aviation subcommittee hearing on the arcane matter of limits on international route certificates, Danforth popped up just as Ed Meyer arrived to testify on behalf of the Air Transport Association. The two men quickly steered the hearing to the subject of the struggle for control of TWA, and engaged in a colloquy about Icahn's unfitness to run an airline. The exchange struck some observers as rehearsed and somewhat forced, as if Danforth were dutifully toeing the line without having looked much further into the situation.

The TWA executives thought that they had one important recourse. The "fitness" test requiring an applicant to prove he is "fit, willing, and able" to provide air service had never been repealed. It was, after all, rooted in the basic interests of protecting safety—the idea being that if an airline were to come under the control of a thug, passengers' lives could be jeopardized. Anyone with a criminal record or apparent connections with known felons was not permitted to own an airline. TWA's strategy was to make Icahn look like a crook.

"God, we tried everything," recalls Jon Ash, then TWA's head lobbyist in Washington. TWA's management ran to the Transportation Department, asking the agency to investigate Icahn's fitness and his Byzantine financial dealings. It went to Congress and got a bill introduced squarely aimed at blocking his advances. It went to the state legislature in Missouri. In Washington, it hired high-priced lobbying talent, such as former White House aide Michael Deaver. TWA also called in Jack Valenti, the Washington pro and Motion Pictures Association chief, who was on the TWA board. Other TWA directors, such as World Bank president Robert McNamara, Los

Angeles Olympics chairman Peter Ueberroth, and former transportation secretary Brock Adams, began mobilizing to use their clout on Capitol Hill.

"We knew from the start we had little chance of success. The stock had been at eight or ten dollars and now it's going up to nearly twenty dollars. And the investors, the pension funds, they see that . . . nothing will stop that kind of thing, nothing. He [Icahn] had almost 20 percent by the time we realized what was happening," said Ash.

TWA then asked its investment banker, Salomon Brothers, to locate a more desirable buyer. TWA also went to federal court in New York seeking an injunction to block Icahn from buying more stock. On May 21, Icahn made his formal merger proposal to TWA, offering to buy up the 75 percent of the common stock he didn't own for eighteen dollars a share, a handsome premium for shares that were then trading for about ten dollars. But while waiting for the decision of the judge to come down, Icahn said he would not buy any more stock for ten days. That gave TWA management the reprieve it needed. On May 24, Frank Lorenzo flew up to New York from Houston and met with Ed Meyer and James Freund, his attorney from Skadden Arps.

Lorenzo was hardly TWA's ideal White Knight. But Salomon had gone to nearly every other airline in the country, and to other related industries, and had managed to scare up only two suitors: Texas Air Corporation and Resorts International, owner of casinos and hotels. Lorenzo was willing to top Icahn's bid and offer twenty dollars a share.

At first, TWA's advisers were concerned about Continental's lingering bankruptcy status and Lorenzo's unsavory reputation as a union-buster. But Lorenzo surprised the TWA team by his polite, soft-spoken demeanor and his insistence that he only wanted to be involved at the company's invitation. Lorenzo was obviously quite interested. As he inevitably did when pursuing a merger, he said TWA and Continental would be a "terrific fit." More to the point, it would make his Texas Air Corporation second only to United in size. Unlike his brash foray at TWA six years before, this time it was Lorenzo who was courted. Lorenzo had already amassed a stake of just under 5 percent of TWA stock in the past few months.

"The thinking was, at least Frank Lorenzo's an airline man," recalled one TWA executive. "We knew that he would come in here to run this as an airline, and not just use it as a spare parts department—sell bits and pieces and walk away from it."

Just weeks before he began hearings on airline industry competition in 1974, Senator Edward Kennedy (with then-wife Joan at his side) announced he would not seek the presidency in 1976.
AP/WIDE WORLD PHOTOS

Now a federal appellate judge, Stephen Breyer in 1974 was an aide to Senator Kennedy—and the one who got him interested in airline deregulation. TWIN LENS PHOTO

Cornell University economics professor Alfred Kahn, drafted by the Carter administration to run the Civil Aeronautics Board in 1977, became known as "the father of deregulation."

Drafted from academia to help Alfred Kahn run the CAB, Mike Levine later joined Frank Lorenzo's growing Texas Air empire.

Legendary flyer (and Pan Am consultant) Charles Lindbergh chats with Pan Am founder and chairman Juan Trippe.

In the pre-jet era, TWA was "the airline to the stars," run by the enigmatic Howard Hughes (left), and Jack Frye—who also founded the ultrasecretive airline executives' club, Conquistadores del Cielo.

TWA

The A Bar A Ranch in Encampment, Wyoming, site of the annual meeting of the Conquistadores.

Starting in 1958, the U.S. airline industry got a shot in the arm thanks to the commercial use of the jet engine, shown here on an American Airlines Boeing 707. AMERICAN AIRLINES

Long based in New York City, American Airlines abandoned Manhattan for Dallas in 1979—just one part of a corporate exodus from New York that included several major airlines. AMERICAN AIRLINES

Onboard passenger service got its start in the 1930s with the introduction of "hostesses," like this group from Pan Am.   PAN AMERICAN WORLD AIRWAYS

With Senator Kennedy looking on, President Jimmy Carter signed the Airline Deregulation Act into law on October 24, 1978. Looking over his other shoulder, front row, is Senator Howard Cannon, the Nevada Democrat and one-time Kennedy foe who later became one of deregulation's staunchest supporters. To the immediate right of Cannon is Congressman Elliott Levitas, the "Deltacrat" who almost derailed deregulation.   JIMMY CARTER LIBRARY

The deregulation experiment was sidetracked in 1981 when U.S. air traffic controllers walked off the job and were immediately fired by President Ronald Reagan.   AP/WIDE WORLD PHOTOS

Many new airlines that sprang up after deregulation tried to follow the successful model of low-cost Southwest Airlines and its irrepressible chairman, Herb Kelleher. Here, in a typical stunt, he dispenses peanuts to passengers aboard one of his 737 jets—the only type of aircraft in Southwest's fleet.

SOUTHWEST AIRLINES

Taking advantage of deregulation, Eastern in the early 1980s jumped into the transcontinental market in competition with American, United, and TWA, and also set up a hub at Kansas City. Both moves were short-lived.   BILL CANCELLARE

United Airlines' charismatic chairman, Dick Ferris, broke ranks with his peers in supporting deregulation and led the nation's largest airline through the first decade of the new competition. UNITED AIRLINES

At an April 1985 press conference in Washington, Pan Am chairman Ed Acker announced the sale of Pan Am's Pacific routes to Dick Ferris's United Airlines. AP/WIDE WORLD PHOTOS

Computer power: American Airlines chairman Al Casey and then-president Bob Crandall used computer power to American's advantage in creating "yield-management" pricing strategies, the first frequent-flyer program, and a loyal travel agency sales force.

American Airlines' Bob Crandall, praised as a management genius and feared as a ruthless competitor, turned American into the nation's largest carrier.

The new "Big Three": American chief Bob Crandall, Delta chairman Ron Allen, and United chairman Stephen Wolf huddle at a Washington conference in 1992. AMERICAN AIRLINES

United chairman Stephen Wolf (left) hobnobs with Chicago mayor Richard M. Daley and Suzanne Pelton, whose Chicago school won a grant from the "City in a Garden" charitable fund chaired by Wolf. Wolf was the highest-paid airline executive in the late 1980s, taking in $18 million in salary and stock options in one year alone. UNITED AIRLINES

Organized labor in the airline industry took some major blows as a result of deregulation. Among labor's leaders in the 1980s were, from left, International Association of Machinists and Aerospace Workers' chief John Peterpaul; Association of Flight Attendants leader Diane Robertson; AFL-CIO president Lane Kirkland; and Frederick Dubinsky, who headed the Master Executive Council of the Air Line Pilots Association at United Airlines.   EARL DOTTER

As Frank Lorenzo moved to take over Continental Airlines, his opponents were Continental president Alvin Feldman and longtime chairman Robert F. Six. This photo was taken just months before Feldman took his own life in August 1981, as Lorenzo neared victory.   GLEN MARTIN/DENVER POST

By 1979, Texas International chairman Frank Lorenzo was using the new freedoms of deregulation to plot his creation of a massive airline empire.   UPI/BETTMAN ARCHIVE

Don Burr abandoned friend and partner Frank Lorenzo in 1980, moving to Newark to create nonunion, low-fare carrier People Express along the lines of his own peculiar vision.
PEOPLE EXPRESS

Don Burr teaching a class of new recruits in 1983. Burr's religious training came in handy as he converted thousands of young college grads to his unusual management theories, using worker ownership to "create a better world." Many felt betrayed when a nearly insolvent People Express was sold to Frank Lorenzo in 1986. J. R. PRODUCTIONS

At a crowded Miami press conference in February 1986, former astronaut Frank Borman turned over the reins of Eastern Airlines to new owner Frank Lorenzo.   GERALD DAVIS

Setting his sights on the airline industry, Wall Street raider Carl Icahn edged out Frank Lorenzo in a bitter takeover battle for control of TWA in 1985.   J. A. GIORDANO/SABA

A Washington insider with plenty of political savvy, Elizabeth Dole reflected the Reagan administration's laissez-faire policies toward business as secretary of transportation in the mid-1980s.   AP/WIDE WORLD PHOTOS

Deregulation's low fares spurred big increases in the number of airline passengers, overwhelming the capacity of some airports and related infrastructure.

AIRLINE PASSENGERS OF AMERICA/
BLACK STAR/ANTHONY SUAU

On the eve of the disastrous merger of People Express and Continental in early 1987, Frank Lorenzo (far left) christened his new acquisition with a round of fare cuts, renting for a news conference millions in closely guarded bills—claiming that was what he would save consumers. Fingering the bills with Lorenzo are, from left, People's founder Don Burr, New York Air president Doug Birdsall, and Tom Plaskett, the American executive Lorenzo hired away from Crandall. © JODI BUREN

Former pilot and longtime Pan Am executive Martin Shugrue took his turn—along with several others—as one of Lorenzo's revolving-door presidents of Continental Airlines in the 1980s. Later he won vindication, of sorts, when a bankruptcy judge in 1990 tapped Shugrue to replace Lorenzo at the controls of Eastern as trustee.   CONTINENTAL AIRLINES

One-time Kennedy aide Phil Bakes went on to an airline management career with Frank Lorenzo and wound up telling Eastern Airlines employees in 1987 that their wages would have to be cut.   TRAVEL WEEKLY FILE PHOTO

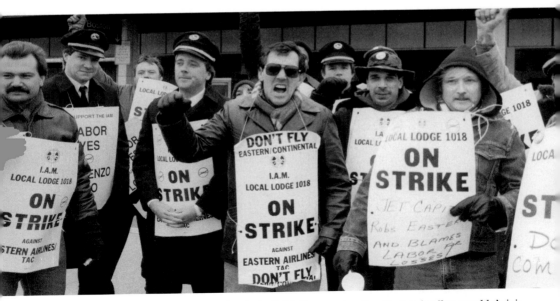

When Eastern machinists struck on March 4, 1989, Lorenzo bet that Eastern's pilots wouldn't join their walkout. He was wrong, and in two years Eastern was in liquidation.   AP/WIDE WORLD PHOTOS

By the late 1980s, some U.S. airlines had forged partnerships with foreign carriers to create huge global alliances, as Continental did with Scandinavian Airlines System and its visionary chief, Jan Carizon. SAS

To ease the congestion of recent years, like that shown here at New York's La Guardia in the mid-1980s, many airports have launched major expansion projects. J. GLAB

As his airline expanded quickly at its Newark hub in the 1980s, Don Burr's People Express didn't bother with some of the more traditional amenities—like jetways for passengers. J. GLAB

American Airlines controls dozens of boarding gates in two terminals at Dallas/Fort Worth Airport—a typical hub complex for connecting passengers. J. GLAB

Meyer and Icahn made one more attempt to talk, this time one on one. On an afternoon in late May, as Icahn's self-restraint on buying more stock was about to end, he sat down with Meyer in a bar at the Waldorf-Astoria Hotel on Park Avenue. It was a brief and chilly encounter.

"All you want is a fast buck," Meyer snapped. "All you've ever done in these raids is go for the fast buck."

"Why don't you admit that what you really care about is your job, and you're afraid I'm going to take it away from you?" Icahn retorted.

Icahn had long ago decided that Meyer would be one of the first to go if he took over TWA. After that day, the two realized there was no point in continuing discussions. Meyer, discouraged by having to put his airline up for sale, would soon announce his intention to resign and move to the top job at TW Corporation's Hilton International Hotels by the end of the year.

ICAHN, MEANWHILE, WAS STRIVING TO convince people that in this instance he was not after a quick profit. In a hearing in Manhattan federal court in mid-May, Icahn said he no longer wanted to break up the company, crediting his change of heart to his recent meetings with TWA and Drexel. "I don't want to get the image of a liquidator," Icahn said, suggesting that his newfound respect for TWA had reformed him. A few people noted that Icahn had been quoted only months before in an article in TWA's own in-flight magazine as saying he had no interest in running companies. His main fear, he said, was that Congress would take all the fun out of corporate buyouts. "Once they take the risk and terror out of it, the game's over. Me, I'll be doing something else." In any event, he somehow managed to persuade the judge that his intentions were benign, although TWA and its allies were still convinced that Icahn would back off if he were paid handsomely enough.

On May 28, the judge refused to bar Icahn from buying more stock. A few weeks later, Icahn owned a third of the company. He had already invested more than $100 million. Then another airline executive unexpectedly jumped into the fray—Frank Borman, whose unorthodox accord with his unions at Eastern Airlines had contributed to TWA's paralysis in its labor relations.

Soon a team of Eastern advisers appeared at TWA headquarters at 605 Third Avenue attempting to put together a bid. Just as he had during the battle for National, Borman woke up late in the game.

The TWA executives, however, were cool to this last-minute show of interest. They thought that with both Lorenzo and Resorts International lined up, it was a waste of time to talk to Eastern.

Borman, however, had long believed that TWA and Eastern would be an ideal merger; he'd referred to it as a marriage made in heaven. The two carriers had held merger talks back in the early 1970s, when Bob Crandall, then at TWA, strongly favored the idea. The union not only would create the country's largest airline but would combine Eastern's seasonal north-south routes with TWA's coast-to-coast network and feed them all into the latter airline's lucrative international flights.

Eastern had also been faring much better lately. Although it had come close to filing for bankruptcy in February 1985, it was now turning a profit, thanks in part to the strikes at Pan Am and United.

Early in June 1985, TWA won several victories in its battle against Icahn. A Missouri judge issued a temporary restraining order prohibiting the financier from making further stock purchases. Congressmen wrote to the Transportation Department urging the agency to investigate Icahn. Icahn bombarded Congress with his own missives, arguing that under deregulation the government had no business interfering in his transaction.

But the Transportation Department, which already had the proposed United–Pan Am Pacific routes deal before it, played down the TWA situation. At a congressional hearing mobbed with TWA employees wearing giant "Stop Icahn" buttons, Assistant Transportation Secretary Matthew Scocozza sent a clear message that the Reagan administration opposed a pending bill that would do just that. To TWA and its supporters in Congress, it was as if the department had endorsed Icahn by saying, in effect, that it would not interfere.

TWA realized that absent a forceful response from the Reagan administration, taking the high road was not getting anywhere. So it deployed a second strategy: Using its clout in Congress, which was certainly considerable compared with Icahn's, it would arrange to have a piece of special-interest legislation slipped through in the middle of the night that would stop Icahn before he knew what was happening.

Jon Ash recalled how the skids were greased. Danforth, a popular senator who carried enormous weight with his colleagues, would take the lead. "They were ready to go along," said Ash.

After eleven o'clock one night, with only a few senators on the floor, an amendment that would have blocked Icahn from owning an airline was taken up. But Senator Ernest Hollings, a Democrat from

South Carolina, jumped to his feet and cried foul. The Senate should have a full debate on something this important, he said. Veteran TWA hands could not figure out what had gone wrong. "Hollings, well, he's an independent man," shrugged Ash.

TWA was attempting to revive the old "airlines are different" argument that had been used, for the most part successfully, in the pre-deregulation days by Juan Trippe and his ilk. "You're not just talking about someone making a raid on a supermarket chain," said Ash. Yet to the Reagan White House, it was no different from, say, Ron Perelman going after Revlon or T. Boone Pickens going after an oil company. Icahn would simply hire trained professionals to run the airline for him—what did it matter who owned it? The Wall Street juggernaut was churning out billions in fees for the companies brokering these deals, and the Reagan administration could hardly have been expected to intervene.

TWA had failed to sense the great sea change in Washington and New York. Airlines were now just companies, no longer an extension of the U.S. government. Their book value was more important than any lingering value as a national symbol. Again TWA had failed to adapt to a new environment. Icahn had been right that it was a good time to snap up an airline at a bargain price. And it would be an even better deal if he could turn around and immediately shed it for a profit.

On the night of June 12, advisers to Lorenzo and Icahn gathered at the New York offices of Wachtell, Lipton, Rosen & Katz, the law firm representing Lorenzo. After a brief stay, Lorenzo left at around nine o'clock to go to his Upper East Side apartment. Icahn, as he often did, stayed up all night.

By the next morning, it looked as if Icahn and Lorenzo had a deal. For a payment of $16 million, amounting to "expenses" and a price support for some of his shares, Icahn would agree to stand aside and let Lorenzo acquire TWA. Icahn, who'd acquired much of his stock at under ten dollars a share, would be selling out to Lorenzo for twenty-three dollars a share, reaping perhaps his biggest killing ever—a total of $95 million, with the "standstill" fee, his reward for backing off.

Both Icahn's advisers and Lorenzo's later agreed on one thing: They believed that Lorenzo's team had his consent to negotiate a deal. Yet when Lorenzo's lawyers phoned him early the next morning to inform him of their night's work, they were stunned when Lorenzo rejected the deal. He reportedly expressed doubts about whether Icahn really had any serious intention to run an airline, and then offered $8 million instead of the $16 million he had offered earlier. Icahn, meanwhile, had had second thoughts about giving Lorenzo a "billion-dollar gift," as he liked to call the airline almost no one else wanted. He rejected Lorenzo's counteroffer.

Lorenzo seemed confident he would win TWA. He even set up his own personnel and labor relations specialist, John Adams, in an office at TWA's New York headquarters to begin figuring out who should fill which positions after the takeover. "He was sticking his nose into everybody's business," a former TWA manager said of Adams, "and this was even before there was a merger agreement. That's how close everybody thought this thing was to happening."

Meanwhile, the federal judge in Missouri who had barred Icahn from buying stock quickly lifted his order when informed that TWA had been shopping itself to other buyers. On June 13, 1985, TWA and Texas Air announced a $793 million merger agreement, creating, it said, the largest airline in the country. Lorenzo was hailed as a visionary in newspaper accounts of the purchase. Icahn even responded somewhat graciously by saying that he would not be a spoiler. But now, freed by the judge to add to his 33 percent stake in the company, Icahn could not be ignored.

The folly of Lorenzo's obstinacy in negotiating with Icahn soon became apparent. When news of the merger pact came out, TWA's unions were outraged. They had had no inkling that a deal with Lorenzo was imminent; management, instead, had been hinting that Resorts might actually be the favored merger partner.

"To management, he [Lorenzo] was the lesser of two evils," compared with Icahn, one former TWA manager said, "but to labor, he was evil incarnate. . . . The unions would have embraced the devil himself rather than work with Frank Lorenzo."

It was another stupendous bit of bad judgment to have underestimated the effect of a pact with Lorenzo on the labor unions. Ever since word of Icahn's stake had leaked out in April, the pilots had been trying to come up with their own employee buyout plan. Selling to Lorenzo was like waving a red flag. The pilots were particularly angry, and their leader, Harry Hoglander, said his union would never come to terms with Lorenzo, alleging that his actions at Continental proved he could not be trusted.

Up until then, the pilots had tried to stop Icahn so they could do their own deal. Now they started regarding the raider differently.

Over the next two weeks, Hoglander and other pilot leaders met with Icahn, and the usual platoons of lawyers and investment bankers, to disrupt the merger with Lorenzo. Many of these sessions would begin at odd hours; 11:30 P.M. seemed to be Icahn's preferred starting time. When Lorenzo's advisers learned of these meetings, they again tried to get Icahn to accept a standstill agreement. Lorenzo on one occasion went to Icahn's apartment at midnight and some time later agreed to Icahn's demand for a $25 million payment. But the handshake agreement unraveled all over again the next day, as Lorenzo wanted to change the terms he'd just negotiated. This time he wanted a pledge that he could buy Icahn's shares, or he would lower his price. Icahn refused, in part because he'd been advised by his lawyers that such a condition would cause problems for him under Securities and Exchange Commission rules.

By July, Icahn and the pilots had reached what became known as the twenty-twenty agreement—employees would get 20 percent of the airline while giving Icahn 20 percent wage cuts, assuming he took control of TWA. Lorenzo had again let Icahn slide through his grasp.

Meanwhile, the airline itself was suffering the worst crisis in its fifty-year history. On June 14, 1985, TWA's Flight 847 had been hijacked out of Athens by unidentified terrorists, setting off a seventeen-day ordeal. One passenger was murdered before the siege finally ended on the tarmac at Beirut. The airline's management holed up in a crisis room at TWA headquarters. Every day, it seemed, some new aspect of the incident made the headlines. A grisly photo of hooded terrorists peering out of the cockpit of the TWA jet, holding a pistol to the pilot's head, was flashed again and again around the world. Frightening tales circulated of hostage passengers' passports being scrutinized to identify Jews, and of beatings and harassment of other passengers.

While the TWA pilot and head purser were later commended for their courage, the post-mortems about how the hijacking had taken place highlighted the poor security at distant airports such as Athens, places that TWA, along with Pan Am, had made their specialty. The longer-term effect of the incident was to put a serious damper on Americans' plans to travel to Europe that summer. The outlook worsened when President Reagan made comments that seemed to hint at the possibility of further attacks on Americans. It was almost as if Reagan had told citizens to stay home, and many did. TWA, which had been expecting a strong summer for transatlantic travel, experienced an unprecedented rash of cancellations and its third quarter, when it usually made the bulk of its profits, was ruined.

In the first week of July, the crew and passengers of flight 847 arrived back in the United States after their ordeal. The hostage crisis had hardly attracted notice from Icahn and Lorenzo, who were still acting like two dogs tussling over a bone. It was as if nothing was more important than beating each other out on a minor point in a deal worth more than three-quarters of a billion dollars. At this point, the pace of their chess game picked up. Lorenzo spent $20 million to buy nearly one million shares and ended up with a 21 percent stake, and then he requested that the TWA board—which had, after all, invited him in—grant him lockups (a guarantee to sell him specific assets) and other provisions that would make it harder for Icahn to gain control.

A dark horse had not been ruled out. In mid-July, Eastern's unions sent emissaries to meet with their counterparts at TWA. Frank Borman even talked to Icahn on the phone, but Icahn, Borman recalled, insulted the Eastern chief with his standard palaver about bad management.

Eastern and TWA officials met one more time on the weekend of July 13, 1985, but everyone was struck by the magnitude of the problems facing them in the event of a merger—the need for pay concessions from both sides and the complexities of combining union seniority lists of two of the oldest companies in the business. That Monday, Eastern said it did not have enough time to prepare a serious merger proposal.

By August 5, Icahn's stake had reached 40.6 percent and the machinists had joined the pilots in agreeing to give Icahn—and only Icahn—the concessions needed to turn the company around. Some of TWA's old guard found considerable irony in the unions' willingness to give Icahn the pay cuts he wanted. "As it turned out, they gave Icahn more than the old management was asking of them," one former manager recalled. A former TWA vice-president agreed, noting that if the unions had made those same concessions to Ed Meyer in the first place, "Icahn might not have made the run on us."

Lorenzo's response to the unions' cozying up to Icahn was to insist on the lockups from the board. On August 13, Texas Air general counsel Charles Goolsbee appealed to TWA's directors to "take all steps necessary to accomplish this transaction." Lorenzo, he noted, had just offered to raise his bid to twenty-six dollars a share.

Texas Air wanted TWA, among other things, to allow it an option to buy TWA's transatlantic routes and its PARS reservations system, in the belief that without those assets TWA would be so unattractive that Icahn would drop his bid. But the prospect of more choice airline assets coming on the market so soon after the Pan Am Pacific sale was exciting interest from other airline chiefs. Strangely, one of them was Pan Am's Ed Acker, who fired off a letter to Meyer on August 15 expressing his "very serious immediate interest" in those assets, especially Europe and PARS. The only way that cash-strapped Pan Am could afford those assets would be to use the $750 million it had just made by selling off its own Pacific assets. American Airlines ran to the Transportation Department and cried foul, saying that Acker's interest in the TWA assets raised questions about his previous statements that he would use the proceeds from the United sale to turn Pan Am around financially. Pan Am then abandoned its show of interest.

Icahn refused to raise his bid above twenty-four dollars. Nevertheless, on August 21, TWA directors voted against giving Lorenzo lockups. That effectively assured victory for Icahn.

The following day, Icahn pledged to oust the very directors who'd just handed him the company, and to install his own people, dismissing the likes of Robert McNamara for such cronies as his uncle Elliott. The TWA board was just the kind of institution that rankled Icahn, symbolized by the "Golden Passes"—the right of directors and their families to fly first class, free, anywhere in the world. Not only were these privileges granted on a lifetime basis for board members but they were even passed on to their spouses if a director died. Most people regarded the passes as an innocuous perk; to Icahn, they epitomized what was wrong with corporate America.

In the days after Icahn's victory, the unions savored their defeat of Lorenzo. That Icahn's obsessiveness with such trivia as the passes might spread to other, larger issues was not even considered. Somehow, in a mere five months, Icahn had gone from greenmailer to seeming visionary, a creative solver of labor-management problems. The only flaw in this picture was the assumption that Icahn had done anything more than simply negotiate the best deal possible. Frank Lorenzo had indeed handed Icahn the "billion-dollar gift" that he'd had in his hand more than twice.

Lorenzo, in typical fashion, had not really lost at all. He still owned nearly a quarter of TWA, and by the time he agreed to renounce his merger bid in early September, he'd negotiated a package that would give him a $50 million profit. Lorenzo had pulled off another National-style coup, and with his cash hoard now approaching $200 million, he began quickly looking for new targets.

SOMETIME EARLY THAT FALL, BRIAN FREEMAN got a call from a man who identified himself as an aide to Ivan Boesky, one of Icahn's competitors in the field of arbitrage. Would Freeman come over for a chat? the man asked. Boesky, he said, was very interested in what had transpired at TWA and wanted to explore the possibility of launching a takeover of another airline.

When Freeman arrived at Boesky's offices, he learned what had prompted this inquiry. Boesky was envious because Icahn had an airline and "he's going to get respectable," Freeman was told. Meanwhile, Boesky was itching to catch up. If Freeman could try to work out a deal with the unions similar to Icahn's at another major line, say at Pan Am or United, Boesky would definitely be interested, his staff informed Freeman.

While the Boesky team seemed enthralled by the idea of snaring an airline with the enormous prestige of Pan Am, they knew nothing about the vagaries of the airline business. Their ardor cooled somewhat when Freeman explained to them why the industry was one of the least stable of investments and why Icahn would not have won TWA if he'd persisted with his plans to sell off much of the company's assets.

Freeman broke off contact with the group later on when he decided he couldn't work with them. But the point had been made. Icahn, at least temporarily, had been ennobled by his acquisition of an airline.

12

EMPIRE
BUILDERS

All empires die of indigestion.
—NAPOLEON BONAPARTE

Don Burr had always said emphatically that he would never merge People Express with another airline, because he didn't want to risk crushing its unique culture. Yet even he was drawn into the merger madness that gripped the airline industry. The man who personified deregulation more than any other individual would go back on all he had preached.

It had all started on the morning of January 18, 1985, when Bob Crandall dropped a bombshell on the air travel market. One out of every three seats on American would be marketed at fire sale prices—matching People Express fares on routes all over the country.

Bob Crandall's secret weapon was a new low fare, the Ultimate Super Saver, which had to be bought thirty days ahead of time and had all sorts of other purchase restrictions. The price was the same as—in some cases even lower than—the fares People Express, Midway, and other upstarts were charging for the same trip. In one step, he had eliminated People's whole reason for being: its price advantage. And unlike People, American didn't have to offer all its seats at the same low price; on each flight it could juggle the number of seats offered at various price levels, depending on demand. It was the "black art" of yield management at work.

Mike Derchin, who was then an airline analyst at First Boston, was one of the first on Wall Street to figure out what was going on. As an executive at American in the mid-1970s, he'd sat through many of Crandall's strategy sessions where they plumbed the possibilities of using computer power to make sure that no passenger paid any less than exactly what it would take to get him on the plane. Now, almost ten years later, Crandall had finally unleashed the potential that his programmers, pricers, and marketing experts had been quietly developing. "God, he's finally done it," Derchin mused.

Crandall had found an efficient and perfectly legal way to fight his low-cost rivals and possibly drive them out of business.

This was going to destroy People Express, Derchin thought. The prices were aimed directly at the passengers who'd been Burr's most loyal customers. Now they would defect to American, or United, or Delta, since all would quickly follow suit. Passengers would get a free beverage and a meal, baggage check-in, frequent-flyer miles, and all the other amenities People didn't offer.

Derchin picked up the phone and called Burr's office. He expected to find the People Express founder dejected, or even angry. Instead, Burr was surprisingly nonchalant, almost cheerful. No, this was not a problem, he said. He even thought that maybe it was a good thing, that these low fares would just make the market bigger for everyone. Derchin could not believe that someone who had been in the airline business as long as Burr had could be so naive.

A few days later, Burr arrived at a private club in New York to talk to several dozen airline analysts from all the leading Wall Street investment houses. He and his top financial officer, Bob McAdoo, came in with the same upbeat message. "Hey, things are great," he said, and on the surface they were. The airline was growing. Its annual revenues topped $2 billion, catapulting it into the leagues of the top ten airlines in the country. It was growing, but that was in fact the heart of the problem.

In the summer of 1984, People had launched several flights a day on both the Newark–Chicago and New Orleans–Los Angeles routes, essentially throwing down the gauntlet to American and United. People was now a contender and one that Crandall could no longer ignore. Burr later said the import of Crandall's pricing move finally dawned on him when his own mother announced she'd bought a ticket on American rather than fly on her son's airline.

Burr had finally gotten his comeuppance from what he used to laughingly call the "bull elephants." As one airline analyst said at the time: "If you whack an elephant with a baseball bat, he's going to turn around—and he did."

Burr realized, belatedly, that his brash personality had worked against him. "The guys in the industry that were hated the most were me, and then Lorenzo," he said.

Still, morale at People was high. Employees regularly filed into a company auditorium for Burr's pep rallies. "We couldn't wait to hear where we'd be going next," said Stephanie Owens, who worked as a flight attendant and recruiter. For employees who had started out with the prospect of flying to Buffalo or Cleveland, the idea of working for a glamorous airline that went to Europe and California was intoxicating.

Ever the evangelist, at staff meetings Burr read aloud from a religious tract called "The Greatest Thing in the World" by nineteenth-century Scotsman Henry Drummond, containing homilies about love and God. A manual distributed to new employees directed workers to "Be a MAGIC inspirational leader." He also channeled his evangelism into stock pitches. "You've got to buy more stock, show your support for the company," he would say. He promised the stock would keep on rising—which it had until 1985, even splitting at one point. Management took to posting the company's stock price every day, which added to the bull market atmosphere. Many of People's employees took Burr seriously and paid out a substantial chunk of their modest salaries to buy People's shares, sometimes at a discount, sometimes at market rates.

But as People grew exponentially, its operation was afflicted by record delays and overbooking. It soon earned the nickname "People's Distress." The airline simply couldn't manage its burgeoning inventory.

Still, Burr exuded self-confidence. "Ten years from now, there are only going to be three or four airlines left—and People Express is going to be one of them," Burr was fond of saying. But Lorenzo was racing toward the same goal, and would inevitably pounce on the next target that came his way.

IN AUGUST 1985 A COALITION of Frontier employees announced a proposal to buy 80 percent of the company's stock for $210 million, or about seventeen dollars per share. News of the imminent employee buyout got Lorenzo's attention. It was just days after he had signed off on his agreement with Icahn not to muddy the TWA deal. He had never quite called off his pursuit of Frontier, and he quickly sprang into action, proposing a tender offer for Frontier at twenty dollars per share and setting an October 18 deadline on the offer.

The ensuing imbroglio mirrored events at TWA. The unions were aghast at the idea of a Lorenzo acquisition and began a search for a White Knight. The employee coalition complained to the Transportation Department, accusing Lorenzo of "high-handed tactics" in his proposed takeover. The agency, consistent with its record, refused to stand in Lorenzo's way and soon signaled that it would allow Texas Air to buy stock in Frontier and place it in a voting trust.

When attorneys for Frontier tried to scare up another suitor, Burr got wind of the activity; he contacted Frontier to say he too would be interested in making a bid.

"We knew that by that time we were in deep shit, and we knew we were being underpriced everywhere. We knew we had to do something," Burr said. He actually had been attending to one crucial matter, development of a computer reservations system that would finally permit People to dabble in yield management, juggling its fares to meet demand. But the airline was years behind in this endeavor, in part because of an unfortunate deal it had signed with NCR. The computer company had spent virtually two years on the project and had come up empty-handed. People now turned to a West Coast software company, which had promised to produce a real reservations system by 1987. However, Burr was starting to doubt that People could survive independently until then.

After Burr's call to Frontier, Morgan Stanley entered the scene as People's investment banker. Now they had to convince People's board that the transaction made sense. Burr made a compelling pitch to his directors. "Here we've got this merger, and it gives us everything we've got to have: a frequent-flyer program, access to Denver, San Francisco, Los Angeles, and all the major airports in the West, because we wanted to fly there but there aren't any slots . . . and guess who has all that, plus a beautiful hub in Denver, a sales force, a computerized reservations system? We don't have time to invent all that."

Meanwhile, Frontier's board had scheduled a meeting for early October to consider Lorenzo's bid in New York City, where Burr was by then operating from a hotel, working furiously on the deal with his investment bankers. Late one night he went out and bought a copy of the next day's *New York Times*. When he opened the paper to the business section, he knew he had to act fast. A story reported that Lorenzo had suddenly sweetened his offer for Frontier to twenty-two dollars a share. The next day, Burr got in touch with the coalition of Frontier unions and offered them an appealing proposition: Give me concessions, and I'll rescue you from Lorenzo. Burr and the employees quickly put together a concessions-ownership swap to present to the Frontier board.

When the directors met as planned, Burr came in with an offer of twenty-four dollars a share plus the firm support of the unions for the deal. The board was speechless. Burr had been expected only to match Lorenzo's price. Now he was offering about $300 million for the airline, with about $100 million from People, the rest from the money already raised by the labor coalition. "That's a remarkable offer," said Gerald O'Neil, a Frontier director and the company's largest shareholder. "It's the deal of a lifetime," Burr gushed.

The deal that had been designed to save People would, however, destroy it. Burr had committed some cardinal sins in his rush to grab Frontier from Lorenzo. He'd garnered the support of Frontier's unions, in part, by guaranteeing jobs for up to four years at current Frontier wages. These pledges were not extended to Burr's own workers at People, who were predictably upset at their inferior treatment. And taking on a competitor like United at Denver was pure hubris. "God, even Lorenzo didn't realize it, but United owned every travel agent in that town," Burr remarked later.

When Burr actually got down to trying to merge the two companies, he committed another blunder in trying to spread People's no-frills service to Frontier. The results were disastrous. "It was more of a culture shock for the passengers than for anyone else," a former People employee recalled. "On Frontier, they were used to assigned seats, meals, a ticket counter . . . here at People, you'd get a piece of paper that looks like a grocery receipt. Passengers would charge onto the plane and take any seat they wanted. It was not for everyone, that's for sure."

Several weeks after the transaction, one of Burr's top financial officers, going over the figures on Frontier's operations, became increasingly distressed at what he kept seeing. Burr walked by, saw the odd look on the man's face, and demanded to know what was wrong.

"This Frontier thing is going to kill us," the executive reported. "It could very well eat up $100 million in cash in losses over the next few months, and we can't generate enough excess cash from our own operations to meet those needs."

Burr's response, according to the executive, was to say: "I don't want to hear about this! Don't come out of your office until you're ready to put a smile on your face. People will think you've got something to be worried about."

Burr had made the classic merger mistake of jumping into an essentially unknown situation. People had been breaking even, even managing to make a little money; Frontier was bleeding. Every week, according to People insiders, millions of dollars went from People's coffers just to pay Frontier's payroll and fuel bills.

BY MID-DECEMBER 1985, ICAHN also had begun to wonder if he had rushed precipitately into an airline acquisition. TWA was performing much worse than expected as a result of continuing terrorist attacks on American travelers overseas. In mid-December, gunmen had entered terminals at airports in Rome and Vienna and fired into crowds of passengers at check-in counters, reviving the memory of the recent TWA hijacking. The airline's loss for the year was approaching $200 million.

Icahn was sitting uncomfortably atop an airline that only six months before had seemed a choice collection of undervalued assets— assets that he had subsequently pledged not to sell off. He simply had not recognized the cyclical nature of the airline business, and how quickly fortunes could turn. Icahn, who prided himself on his poker-playing ability, might have been outbluffed after all.

A week before Christmas, Frank Lorenzo conveniently reappeared. He contacted TWA's board, saying his offer to buy the airline was still good. Despite TWA's downward slide, Lorenzo said he would offer twenty-two dollars a share in cash. Icahn, meanwhile, had come up with a new offer to exchange twenty-four dollars in TWA preferred stock for each share of common stock that he did not already own. Icahn's earlier proposal had included $19.50 in cash and $4.50 in preferred stock for each share of common stock. Several analysts noted that Lorenzo's all-cash offer might be the better deal.

However, Icahn had second thoughts about giving up too easily, especially since TWA's value might shoot up once the current crisis was past. Although Lorenzo was offering him a way out, Icahn made his peace with the TWA board and convinced them his offer was preferable. By January 8, Icahn was able to send a letter to TWA employees as their new boss.

"I believe TWA will emerge as one of the financially strongest airlines in the world," he boasted, claiming that his legendary skills as an investor would benefit his workers. "Like most of you, I did not have wealthy parents and have worked extremely hard for what I have earned. I take my investments very seriously and spend a great part of each day thinking and worrying about them. Since the Icahn Group has $360 million invested in TWA, I promise you will all have my undivided attention!"

Icahn also mentioned that Drexel Burnham financing had given TWA a cash cushion of between $750 million and $1 billion to weather the disastrous fall-off in transatlantic travel brought on by fear of terrorism. Even so, his optimistic letter did not assuage the concerns of all the TWA employees. Rumors continued to spread that Icahn would sell TWA as soon as he could reap a nice profit. And just a few weeks later, he was already busy confirming these fears, talking publicly about selling off one of TWA's more attractive assets, its PARS reservations system. No one was especially surprised. According to investment banker Brian Freeman, TWA's unions had always viewed Icahn as a short-term owner, someone whose primary function was to rescue them from Lorenzo.

LORENZO HAD SUFFERED TWO HUMILIATING defeats, and each time because an airline's unionized employees shifted the advantage to a challenger rather than having to work for him. But with Wall Street's merger-and-buyout fever reaching its peak, it wasn't long before another target moved into his sights.

One day in December 1985, Lorenzo strolled into the office of Phil Bakes at Continental's Houston headquarters. Lorenzo said he had just met with Eastern CEO Frank Borman to discuss a possible joint computer reservations venture and that Borman had surprised him by inviting him to consider buying all of Eastern. "What do you think?" he asked Bakes.

Bakes felt uneasy that it was Eastern, not TWA or Frontier. The two continued discussing the idea the following day when they went running together in Memorial Park. By then Bakes had become convinced that an Eastern merger would be a disaster and told Lorenzo so. Lorenzo's high profile as a labor foe would exacerbate an already hostile situation at Eastern, he said, and a true merger of the two companies would be unthinkable, because Continental was still largely nonunion. Bakes referred to Eastern as a "swamp" from which the company would "never return."

Lorenzo appeared to brush off Bakes's worries. Eastern's best point was its net asset value, he said, about three times that of Continental. Those assets included more than two hundred planes, valuable South American routes, and the profitable East Coast shuttle. Eastern also had an up-to-date computer reservations system, while Continental's was practically in the dark ages. Despite its labor woes Eastern had actually made money for several quarters in 1985. If Lorenzo won Eastern, he would control the biggest airline company in the world outside of Soviet-run Aeroflot, easily topping American or United. He would also get even with Don Burr for having snatched Frontier from him.

MANY OF THE MID-1980S AIRLINE mergers had some clear rationale: combining complementary route structures, giving one partner access to lucrative markets or foreign routes, or some other logical motive. The Eastern-Continental mixture would have no apparent reason beyond the laundry list of choice assets touted by Lorenzo. That led to one conclusion: To realize that value, the airline would have to be broken up or "cherry-picked," in the common parlance of the era.

Lorenzo was being advised to do just that by Gerry Gitner, who had rejoined his old employer as president of Texas Air after quitting Pan Am. Gitner delivered a coldly shrewd assessment: Eastern's assets were so valuable that it made sense to buy the package and then try to shed as much of it as possible.

Charlie Bryan apparently was not factored into the asset tally. But if Lorenzo and Gitner had bothered to follow closely the events at Eastern, they might have reassessed the value they lusted after. In late 1985, Bryan had announced that he was exploring the possibility of the employees' buying a controlling interest in the company. One tactic he used to stir up support was to make a far-fetched comparison between Borman and Lorenzo, calling the concessions Borman sought "Continental-type wages and conditions." Bryan was now stridently demanding Borman's resignation. While many managers dismissed Bryan's ideas as the "inmates trying to run the asylum," the IAM leader's position as a company director gave his plan more credibility with the media than it might have otherwise.

Lorenzo did not have time to look deeply into the situation. On Valentine's Day, 1986, Eastern banker Merrill Lynch gave him a deadline of the following weekend to make a bid, depriving him of time to gather adequate information on Eastern. Bakes and others warned Lorenzo that Borman was just using him to squeeze the unions.

Even Borman admitted that he had no desire to sell the airline. He had listed the options for Eastern as "fix it, sell it, or tank it," the last being the bankruptcy filing that he'd long dreaded. However, as option one had foundered, he was forced to beat the bushes for suitors. He shopped the airline to other airlines, naturally, and had some talks with Northwest. But other industry chiefs balked at the magnitude of Eastern's problems. Borman also sought out nonairline partners, such as Marriott Hotels. Roswell Gilpatric approached Texaco, where he had connections. Again, the response was that Eastern was a basket case and could not be fixed. Only Lorenzo, it seemed, had such an overweening need to own a huge airline that he could either overlook, or think he could overcome, Eastern's enormous liabilities.

February 28 was the deadline for Eastern to reach agreement for concessions from its unions or risk defaulting on its bank loans and thus entering bankruptcy. As the date approached, Lorenzo became increasingly nervous about Borman's motives, and that he would end up with another embarrassing defeat on his hands. One day, an angry Lorenzo phoned Borman to complain that the rumor mill was churning out reports that Eastern might be entertaining bids from other suitors, such as Pan Am. Borman assured him that he was first in line if the company decided to sell, although he reiterated that he hoped to reach an agreement with the unions on deadline.

However, that was not what Borman was telling his managers, his bankers, or the employees. Borman was doing exactly what Lorenzo feared—using the Texas Air chief as a bogeyman to scare the unions. Borman told associates that a sale to Lorenzo was highly unlikely and extremely distasteful.

Brian Freeman, who had represented the machinists union during the past three years, spoke to Borman as the deadline approached. Freeman was following the situation, although he had recently severed his relationship with the IAM because he disagreed with Bryan's strategy.

"Frank, you are only using Lorenzo to scare the employees," Freeman recalls saying to Borman. "You don't really intend to sell to him, you don't like the guy, and in fact you think he's a bad guy and he's going to screw these people. You've been paternalistic and decent to these people, whatever they think.

"And Borman replied, 'I'm never going to sell to Lorenzo.' And I said, 'That is a promise, isn't it? Because I'm going to rely on it.' And he said: 'It is.' "

Freeman got the same response from William Usery, the former labor secretary who had been brought in by Eastern to try to bring the sides together.

"He'll never sell," Usery told Freeman.

Freeman was concerned enough to book flights to Miami leaving every hour over the coming weekend. Then he called John Peterpaul, leader at the IAM's Washington headquarters. The two agreed that the safest course was for the machinists to put something on the table—some concessions—to avoid a takeover. Details could be worked out later. Bryan's call for Borman's head was an absurd demand that the board would never approve, Peterpaul and Freeman agreed. Surely Borman would step down soon enough anyway, if he were given a graceful way out. Peterpaul said he'd urge Bryan to stall Borman and wait until the following Tuesday when they could all meet in Miami.

By Friday, February 21, many Eastern employees had grown extremely nervous about the possibility of a Lorenzo buyout. Top management took great pains to assure the company that a sale was a remote possibility. Bankruptcy was increasingly an option and the public relations department quietly prepared an eight-page press release announcing that Eastern had filed for Chapter 11. Several pages of the document were devoted to fingering the culprits: not only the intransigent IAM but People Express and all the other low-fare upstarts unleashed by deregulation.

Even on that Sunday, when the board assembled to bring the drama to a conclusion, top management still believed that a compromise would save Eastern from Lorenzo's clutches. One vice-president, Bill Lush, remembered attending a meeting that afternoon with six colleagues, presided over by a senior vice-president. "He told us that there was no way Borman would sell the airline to Lorenzo, and that night Borman and Bryan would reach an accord—and that therefore the whole sale to Lorenzo was almost a nonissue."

But that night, Lush was awakened by the harsh ring of his telephone at 3:00 A.M. His wife answered the phone; it was his boss. Lush took the receiver and said, "Well, we're all speaking Texan now, aren't we?" And his boss replied: "Yep."

As the word spread Monday that the company had been sold, the employees reacted with disbelief, which grew as the details began to leak out. During a marathon board meeting that had begun the day before, various Eastern executives had shuttled back and forth to union leaders to negotiate new pacts. By late that night, the company had reached agreement with two of its three unions—the pilots and flight attendants—for wage concessions of about 20 percent. But Bryan held out for no more than a 15 percent cut for his machinists union, and he did hold a few cards—the IAM contract was not open, and he had less incentive than the others to reopen it only to give up 20 percent of his workers' pay. Bryan said, however, that he'd agree to 15 percent because the remaining 5 percent Borman was seeking could be made up in productivity gains.

In the end, Bryan gave the board an ultimatum—he'd agree to

the wage cuts only if Borman left the airline. It was exactly that demand that Bryan's superiors in the machinists union had feared, because they knew no board could accept it. By 2:00 A.M., the situation was getting desperate and Lorenzo, while he'd agreed to a brief postponement, would not wait much longer. The board simply decided that the best course at that moment was to sell to Lorenzo, who offered some $615 million—although more than half of that would come from preferred stock to be issued by Eastern, or money to be borrowed by Eastern, saddling the carrier with hundreds of millions of dollars of additional debt.

More details emerged at a news conference held the next day by Borman and Lorenzo. The Texas Air chief pledged to keep Eastern management in place and more or less leave the airline alone. But according to Lorenzo associates, that was never the plan. "After all," said one aide, "Borman had just lost his airline." Borman later said that he always assumed he would be leaving.

The Eastern unions, despite their 20 percent ownership in the company, had failed to block the sale. Bryan himself had given away some of his leverage—voiding a poison pill clause in the 1983 accords with management that would have given the employees veto power over any major transaction.

But right after the sale, Bryan tried to put a positive face on it, boldly proclaiming that "we can work with Lorenzo." Few of his fellow workers agreed, and their suspicions seemed to be confirmed when Lorenzo ignored a telegram from Bryan right after the sale, welcoming the opportunity to work with him. The transaction was still not final, since it required approval from both the government and the shareholders. Eastern pilots immediately began assembling a list of buyers who might be willing to take Eastern off Lorenzo's hands, including Jay Pritzker, the Chicago hotel magnate who'd bought an interest in Braniff Airlines.

But although Lorenzo had won Eastern for an outrageously low price, few of the corporate executives who possessed the means would dare go near the company. From the middle of 1986 through 1989, the ailing carrier would be shopped to a veritable Who's Who of corporate titans, practically the entire Forbes 400 list of wealthiest Americans. The list of erstwhile suitors would ultimately include Chrysler chairman Lee Iacocca, New Jersey trucking and real estate magnate Arthur Imperatore, Peter Ueberroth and, on repeated occasions, Carl Icahn.

When asked years later why he bought Eastern despite its glaring defects, Lorenzo continued to defend his action. "It was a very, very sensible acquisition—under normal laws. Eastern had substantial assets—financial, marketing, and route assets—and it was one of the original trunk airlines. It was a massive resource, and it was selling in the marketplace for nothing," he said.

Lorenzo's argument has several curious sides to it. The fact that Eastern was one of the original Big Four really had no value except nostalgia. And the airline was selling for nothing because its labor problems had scared off everyone else. Lorenzo claims that he believed he could, "with time," sort them out, a grandiose claim, given his track record. That was the reason aides had warned him to stay away—Lorenzo, of all the possible buyers, was arguably the worst suited to the task.

BURR SOON HAD CAUSE TO regret he hadn't let Lorenzo grab Frontier from him. He too had been tempted by an airline's apparent asset value, only to find it to be an illusion.

"Yeah, so we got a computer," he said later. "It was an old computer that didn't do much, but we got one. And we got a frequent-flyer program, but it wasn't United's, and it was pretty useless. And we got relationships with travel agents who said, 'Sure, we'll talk to you, but just remember that all those Apollo machines of United's get our first attention.' And of course, United and Continental, who'd been quite prepared to allow us to exist in Newark and had given us a lot of room there, were not prepared to have us in their hub at Denver." At one point Continental slashed fares to Colorado Springs to nine dollars one-way.

Doubts about Burr slowly started to bubble up among his loyal troops. Some of the pilots started calling their boss "Guyana Jones," after the People's Temple founder Jim Jones, who had led his followers into mass suicide in a South American jungle. Vendors and others who did business with the company weren't getting paid. "I'd start getting angry calls saying, 'Where's my money?' " recounts Sheryl Martin, who had been opening new stations for People and dealing with outside suppliers. Inside the company, she recalled, "Employees were in a state of denial. They kept on saying, 'Don will fix it.' "

Burr clearly saw himself as a guru, a self-anointed prophet of industry who would miraculously convert the misguided union employees of Frontier to his touchy-feely philosophy. But his top officers increasingly viewed him as remote and autocratic. Burr's increasing openness about his close relationship with his long-time assistant, Melrose Dawsey, was also casting doubts on his judgment, according to former associates. She held an officer title and a substantial share of company stock.

Burr's apparent refusal to face reality alarmed top officers. One instance involved the half-dozen 747s Burr had ordered in an expansive moment, cramming 450 seats onto each of the planes. "People like to fly on 747s," he said, but the traffic numbers showed that was true on only one route, Newark-London—elsewhere, the airline was losing as much as a quarter of a million dollars per flight with the 747s. A group of People officers went to Boeing and convinced the manufacturer to take back five of the six planes and replace them with 250-seat 757s, but Burr rejected the move, reasoning that since passengers liked the 747, it must make sense.

"He would just go chasing out after something; you couldn't rein him in even if you could show him numbers that proved his new ideas wouldn't work. . . . He couldn't admit he had made a mistake. He was running the company into the ground because he wouldn't listen to us," said one officer.

In January 1986 *Time* magazine hailed Burr's success on its cover. By July, *Newsweek* was calling him a "fallen hero." Later, Burr would confess to feeling "amazed" at how quickly a company could run out of cash. In nine months, People Express went from a profitable enterprise to flat broke. Burr's own board of directors was now regarding him much more critically. Several times, Bill Hambrecht, the banker most responsible for People's startup, was deputized by the directors to go to Burr and ask for his resignation. "Come on, Don, I think it might be best for you to step down," Hambrecht would say. But Burr was determined to stay on and fix the company. He finally started listening to his board's advice to make People more like a traditional company; it had clearly grown way too large for the sorts of job-sharing and vague job descriptions that had been its hallmark. Burr had considered bringing in more professional managers to run things, but his unconventional style had worked against him. Top officers at People Express made less than one hundred thousand dollars a year and did without secretaries and expense accounts.

Meanwhile, as these deliberations were going on, Burr was heading toward bankruptcy court. In June 1986, under pressure from his board, he put out a press release saying, in effect, that he was ready to sell any part or all of his airline.

United Airlines appeared as an unlikely savior, offering to take Frontier off Burr's hands for $146 million—less than half what Burr had paid for it a year earlier. News of the deal provoked an instinctive response from Lorenzo, who was understandably distressed to learn that United might soon be in a position to destroy Continental at Denver.

It was from a position of strength that Lorenzo went to his old friend and tried to help him out. He had finally achieved his critical mass by buying Eastern, but the transaction was not due to be finished for another six months while the government ruled on the merger. And while Lorenzo's lunge at Eastern had been as hasty as Burr's purchase of Frontier, the folly of the former would not be evident until much later.

Burr was touched, he said, by Lorenzo's interest.

"The other airlines just wanted us to collapse, so they could buy the planes. They didn't think our people systems were worth anything," said Burr. "But there is a piece of Frank that kind of respected what we do. And he was very enamored of Newark Airport.

"Look, don't do that United deal," Burr recalls Lorenzo saying. "We'll buy People Express and it will be a great deal. You can be president of Texas Air and I'll be chairman, and you can do all your 'people' things. The company will be about an $8 billion outfit and it should be big enough for both of us."

The two started spending time together, meeting at Burr's summer home on Martha's Vineyard or at Lorenzo's Nantucket house. Lorenzo agreed to make a bid for People.

Burr took Lorenzo's proposal to his board. However, there was some dispute over exactly how much Lorenzo's offer was worth. It was a cash and stock offering that a Morgan Stanley adviser valued at $7 or $7.50 a share. A Drexel analyst came up with a $9-a-share figure. And Lorenzo said it was more in the $10 to $11 range. But to sweeten the package, Lorenzo also threw in "an especially good deal" for the officers, Burr recalls.

"I thought this Texas Air deal was the best thing for us at the time," said Burr. "But goddammit, this Morgan guy comes in at 5:00 A.M. when we'd been up all night meeting on the offer. And he says he can't provide a fairness opinion on this one, because you can't trust Frank Lorenzo."

Burr was, as he admitted, "highly compromised" with the board at the time. The gap between him and his directors had widened to the point that the board had hired its own external legal counsel to protect themselves in their dealings with him. Then Burr got the rug pulled out from under him by another player. When Burr was asked what People's cash situation was, he gave the board one figure, but executive vice-president for finance McAdoo contradicted him and said it was about half that. So the board said it would back the United offer for Frontier and reject Lorenzo. To make matters worse, the message was delivered to Lorenzo in the vein of "go to hell," Burr felt. McAdoo left the airline soon after.

The United deal soon collapsed, too. Dick Ferris had second thoughts as he got a better picture of just how badly Frontier was bleeding. Ferris could pick up some of the assets he wanted, like Frontier's 737s, without assuming the burden of the entire company.

By late August, the pilots union had made up Ferris's mind for him. For the deal to be palatable to United, Frontier's unions would have to agree to substantial wage cuts for several years, but the proposed pilot contract, and the subsequent merging of seniority lists, was subject to approval by United's pilots. Still stewing over their own strike against United the previous year, the pilots rejected the deal.

Burr was right back where he had started, with Frontier still attached to People and still bleeding like an open wound, draining millions from his cash flow.

On August 24, Frontier Airlines ceased operations. On August 28, People Express announced that its Frontier Airlines subsidiary had filed in a Denver court for protection from creditors under Chapter 11 of the bankruptcy code. Burr angrily attacked what he called the "rigid and unrealistic" United pilots for torpedoing the deal that might have saved the airline.

Sometime that August, Burr got a long-distance call from Lorenzo, who was vacationing in the south of France with his family. "I guess you are having a little trouble with Frontier," Lorenzo said. "Why don't you come over to France and we'll talk about it."

Burr was grateful for the opening and he immediately said he'd be right over. As he was getting ready to leave, he got another call from Lorenzo, who said he was decamping from his rented house in Provence, where huge fires had been raging. But he was even more promising this time, almost nostalgically talking about the early days of his and Burr's partnership. "You and I are a great team," he said. "We'll get together as soon as I get back."

Weeks later, the two had hammered out a pact. It was, of course, much less generous than even the lowest estimate of what Lorenzo had offered in June. Now, Lorenzo was offering somewhere between four and five dollars a share. But it was an extremely good offer compared with what anyone else would have forked over. People then was barely solvent; analysts were regularly quoted in the press as saying that it should just be allowed to die, and that the big airlines would simply pick up the pieces.

Lorenzo was extremely covetous of Newark, so it was not an act of charity to buy People at a bargain basement price, although the purchase would conveniently spare Burr an ignominious end. Phil Bakes recalled the discussions down in Houston about a People acquisition. "We really needed that East Coast hub and we did not want anyone else to get their hands on it."

On the afternoon of September 15, 1986, hundreds of People employees filed into the huge amphitheater at People's reservations center near Newark Airport. On the stage were an uncharacteristically morose Don Burr and a smiling Frank Lorenzo. They gave the assembled People staffers the news: Soon they would be working for Texas Air. Despite the fact that Lorenzo was rescuing an operation no one else would touch, Burr, for perhaps the first time, was not delivering his standard upbeat message to his troops. Some hollow assurances were uttered about preserving the People Express culture, but the audience was skeptical. "Don would not even look at Frank," said Sheryl Martin. "I'll never forget it. It was awful. He looked shell-shocked."

Coincidentally, on that very day the fancy computer system that Burr had been after for five years, the one that would let Burr compete with Bob Crandall and all the other yield management wizards out there, the one that would let him launch a true frequent-flyer program and a travel agent program, was finally declared ready by the technocrats who'd been toiling for nearly three years. Too late.

NOW LORENZO TRULY SAT ATOP the largest airline empire the United States had ever seen. He commanded a fleet of six hundred planes, a workforce of sixty-two thousand people, and a truly nationwide route system, serving two hundred airports.

He also oversaw a chaotic assortment of clashing cultures, like a salad, as one observer put it, with the disparate parts still recognizable. To meld it into one seamless whole was an almost unimaginable task. Lorenzo had amassed a staggering amount of debt in his quest— twelve times equity, according to one assessment. Wall Street analysts started questioning his strategy, with one describing Texas Air's debt load as "horrendous."

Lorenzo had to reassign his lieutenants, and he was especially concerned about whom to put into the sensitive spot at Eastern. He had good reason to be worried, for in the five to six months since his middle-of-the-night purchase of Eastern, the airline's union leaders had seemingly spent all their time trying to undo the deal. After running through various suitors, all of whom cooled off over time, Charlie Bryan had teamed up with some investors to try to form a company called Mergerco that would be the vehicle for an employee buyout of the company. The group had even contacted Steve Wolf to see if he'd agree to run the airline if they succeeded. Anyone going into Miami from Lorenzo's camp would be as welcome as the general of a victorious army going into a conquered country.

So one day Lorenzo asked Phil Bakes, who by then had been president of Continental for almost three years, to give him a list of candidates for the job of Eastern president. Bakes prepared a short list of candidates, including Steve and one of his colleagues from the CAB, Darius Gaskins, who'd gone on to head the Federal Trade Commission and run a railroad. "I definitely didn't put myself on it," said Bakes, who still held to the beliefs he'd expressed back in February about the dangers of the Eastern situation.

In mid-September, after the People announcement, Lorenzo asked Bakes to dine with him at the Four Seasons hotel in Houston. He came straight to the point: Bakes had to agree to be president of Eastern. Lorenzo was all charm, telling Bakes he was clearly the only one for the job, that he'd saved Continental and no one else was even being considered. But he also did not leave him much choice. He'd already picked Bakes's replacement at Continental. It was Tom Plaskett, Crandall's longtime lieutenant and a possible successor to the top spot at American. Hiring Plaskett away from Crandall would be seen as a coup for Lorenzo, signaling his intention to mold the jumble of companies he'd acquired into a smoothly running machine. Lorenzo told Bakes that he'd like him to spend some time with Plaskett that coming weekend.

Bakes had another reason to take over the Eastern job. All his net worth was tied into Texas Air stock. He had become convinced that they had to make Eastern work; otherwise, he'd risk losing everything. If Eastern failed, it might drag Continental down with it.

Bakes was already the highest-paid executive at Texas Air after Lorenzo, with his 1985 income of $320,530 shooting up 25 percent for 1986, the highest bump of any of the Texas Air officers. (Lorenzo gave himself a 3 percent raise during the same year, to $473,994.) Earlier in 1986 Bakes also had been given options to buy fifty thousand shares of Texas Air common stock at thirteen dollars; by early 1987, shares were trading at around thirty-five dollars. The company had generously advanced some $462,000 to Bakes in the form of loans that carried annual interest rates ranging from 3 percent to 9 percent, most of which was used to exercise stock options, according to a Texas Air proxy statement filed with the Securities and Exchange Commission in early 1987. So Bakes felt he had little choice. He later referred to his decision to accept the job as "the dumbest thing I ever did." And buying Eastern possibly was the single biggest blunder of Lorenzo's career. For it would defeat much of what he had spent his life achieving.

13

THE MERGER
MESS

C arl Icahn celebrated his fiftieth birthday in February 1986 by blowing out the candles on a cake shaped like a TWA plane. But he clearly did not want to spend many more birthdays as an airline chairman. When invited to join the Conquistadores as a guest, he declined. Icahn did not even like flying. Alone among major airline executives, he acquired a private jet, sparing himself the experience his customers were getting.

Icahn's ascent, in short, signified the end of the era of romance and glamour that had pervaded the airline business. To Icahn, an airline was something to buy or sell.

Word quickly circulated around TWA's Third Avenue headquarters that Icahn was getting the airline in shape in order to shed it. It was a rumor his new employees were eager to believe. For while Icahn had rescued them from Lorenzo, the idea of this novice running a huge international airline was disconcerting.

Richard Pearson, a longtime airline man who'd taken over from Ed Meyer as interim president of TWA, accepted Icahn's offer to stay on but he didn't believe it would last.

"It was clear he wasn't going to be a day-to-day guy," Pearson recalled. "His ownership was clearly going to be short-term. He was going to get the books in shape and try to do a merger."

Pearson soon started dining every night with Icahn and his cronies, including Joe Corr, a soft-spoken man who'd worked for Icahn-owned ACF Industries in St. Louis. "We were trying to teach Icahn about the airlines," Pearson said. "But any time we talked about long-term stuff, he wasn't interested, and he seemed to have a short attention span. He would go from one thing another. It was really chaotic.

"He had his old pals, relatives in there. The board meetings were more like family get-togethers," he said.

One of the strangest transformations in airline history had begun—a stodgy but venerable company was suddenly under the thumb of a mercurial wheeler-dealer. Icahn's handling of his new acquisition was a perfect metaphor for the airlines under deregulation. Like Harding Lawrence and other airline chiefs who had trouble adjusting, Icahn apparently had no idea how to proceed in his new role at the helm of a complex organization in the wildly unpredictable airline business. He lurched from one idea to the next, with little regard for their eventual impact on the company. Under regulation, Icahn might have been saved from himself. But a regulated airline would have held no interest for the likes of Icahn.

Longtime TWA executive Peter McHugh had been following the rapid changes at his employer from London, where he'd been running the airline's European division. Rumors were rife that Icahn was about to do some wholesale housecleaning. Early in 1986, McHugh flew back to New York and requested a meeting with Icahn. "There was all this angst about what he was going to do," he said. "That he had a long list of people he was going to fire as soon as he took over. I, of course, wanted to know if I was on the list." On February 9, Icahn invited McHugh to dinner at the Pen & Pencil restaurant near TWA's Third Avenue headquarters. When McHugh arrived, he found Icahn seated with his uncle, Elliott Schnall, who was often at Icahn's side during these first few months. Schnall was one of the first directors Icahn installed after he purged Robert McNamara, Jack Valenti, and the other blue-chip "names" from the TWA board.

"Icahn would constantly turn to Elliott and say, 'What do you think?' " McHugh recalled. "Carl looked to Elliott. If someone wanted things from Carl, Elliott would sometimes say, 'I don't trust this guy, this guy's a jerk.' He was a sounding board." One of the things they did apparently agree on was that scores of longtime TWA executives, whom they considered overpaid hacks, had to go. "It was a corporate welfare state there," Icahn said later. The new boss never quite settled in to his office at TWA, preferring to remain in his own nondescript quarters on Sixth Avenue and Fifty-fifth Street, from which he had managed his wheeling and dealing for years. He'd been used to a bare bones office; now he was suddenly confronted with legions of vice-presidents and field directors.

Icahn later wove all this into amusing anecdotes. One of his favorites was a story about a TWA vice-president who always seemed to be writing speeches. "I said to him, 'What do you write speeches about—how to lose $400 million?' " Icahn cracked. So many seasoned executives were axed, or quit, that one Wall Street analyst commented, "It wasn't just fat they cut, but muscle, too."

McHugh, however, came away from his dinner that night with a promise of a job at headquarters but also with the impression that Icahn was uninterested in the nuts and bolts of running an airline. At first he was encouraged, however briefly, by his encounter with the notorious greenmailer. "All I'd heard was how he was this terrible person. My first impression was that he was actually unpretentious, casual, and quite smart, of course. But he'd be cordial, talk to you about football, or whatever you were interested in." Soon McHugh would see another side. Although Icahn courted a few longtime airline men—after all, he knew little about the business he'd just entered—in time, they would all resign in disgust.

An example of an old-timer who got the ax was Stewart Long, a veteran airline marketing man. Long was a colorful character with a background in the theater, who ate lunch at "21" every day and was conspicuous in his enjoyment of the expense account life. Yet according to his associates, he was a consummate salesman.

Soon after Icahn's arrival, TWA held a presentation for travel agency subscribers to its PARS reservations system. Stew Long rose to regale the audience with his usual stand-up act. Then Icahn stumbled through his usual diatribe about bad management, ending by saying: "If you want a friend, buy a dog." There was a stunned silence, until Long, with impeccable timing, returned to the microphone to deliver this riposte: "All I can say is 'woof woof.' " The audience went wild.

Long was gone from TWA by the following Monday.

Icahn brought in a few professionals, such as Mort Ehrlich, a longtime Eastern executive who'd quit after a bitter dispute with Frank Borman; and another Eastern veteran, respected pricing specialist Bob Cozzi. They tried to convince Icahn he needed a marketing plan. But as one former Icahn manager recalled, Icahn resisted the idea, protesting that "it'll make people think I'm hanging on to the airline." Icahn, the former aide said, was obsessed with "keeping people guessing" about his intentions, as if managing an airline were a poker game.

Icahn did appreciate the value of TWA's worldwide name recognition; he came up with some ways to exploit it that horrified his more conventional associates. The idea was to slap the TWA name on an ordinary product and, like a fashion designer putting his name on a pair of jeans, mark up the price accordingly.

While airline deregulation had unleashed some clever if not brilliant marketing ideas from the staffs of Bob Crandall and Frank Lorenzo, Icahn's gimmicks revealed an abject ignorance of the business he was in. Unlike the frequent-flyer programs and similar inventions, they had no relation to buying air travel. His aides succeeded in talking him out of a few of the wackier ones, such as a scheme proposed by one of his cronies to open a chain of "TWA Ice Cream Shops." The thinking was that an inexpensive brand of ice cream stamped with the TWA logo could be passed off as a gourmet treat.

Icahn especially liked the notion of selling merchandise to TWA passengers in-flight—not duty-free goods that passengers could buy at a discount, but regular consumer merchandise at somewhat inflated prices. Icahn became convinced that airline passengers were a captive clientele waiting to be exploited. On TWA's domestic flights he launched a line of "Ambassador Boutiques," in which flight attendants hawked scarves, costume jewelry, and other overpriced trinkets from a rolling cart. Employees quickly dubbed it "Junk from a Cart," and "Carl-Mart," and it lost money from the day it began. It took more than three years of losses to persuade Icahn to give it up.

Also during 1986 Icahn decided to use TWA to catapult himself into the television business. He had, in fact, long nursed an ambition to move into motion pictures. With an old partner and friend, Stanley Nortman, he had explored the possibility of producing movies but nothing came of it. Now, with TWA he could become a Howard Hughes in reverse—his airline providing the entree to the more enticing world of entertainment.

Icahn created a subsidiary of TWA called the Travel Channel, a twenty-four-hour cable TV operation with a variety of travel-related programming, some of it blatantly promotional. Naturally, Icahn allotted this ambitious venture only a shoestring budget, producing a parade of amateurish features, and often insisting that producers of the channel's travel films be paid not with money, but with barter tickets to use on his airline—frequently on a space-available basis. Icahn admitted that the Travel Channel lost money, although no public financial statements were ever issued. Even so, he was able to sell it several years later to the same company that produces the Weather Channel.

Just weeks after he'd won his airline, he set about doing two things—selling part of it, and acquiring another one.

EVEN BEFORE HE OFFICIALLY TOOK control of TWA, Icahn had decided the time was right to spin off TWA's PARS computer reservation system. Icahn had correctly seized upon that as a choice asset that could easily be spun off—TWA had the biggest system after American's Sabre and United's Apollo. It wasn't like international routes or other airline pieces, whose sale would upset his accord with the pilots; and besides, it was profitable.

So he rounded up Dick Pearson and some other top executives to put on a road show to sell junk bonds in the new TWA. His proposal assigned PARS a fair market value of $75 million, and he proposed that it be given to the Icahn Group in the form of a dividend. The Icahn Group would then lease PARS back to TWA for ten years for an amount that would cover costs and guarantee an annual profit of $25 million. The overall aim of the offering, however, was to allow Icahn to retain control of TWA while getting all his cash out—a type of financial legerdemain that *Fortune* labeled "the creed of the lever-aged-buyout honor society." But it bombed with the investors. One prospective buyer of the junk bonds was quoted in the press as saying, "Why should I risk anything in this loser if Icahn won't?"

Then Icahn was virtually handed a merger, his legendary negotiating tactics almost superfluous for once. For the previous year or so, Dick Pearson and Ed Meyer had been talking about a merger with their counterparts at the airline's chief rival in St. Louis, Ozark Air Lines. While Ozark was hardly a glamorous prize, it would give TWA a monopoly at its biggest hub and greatly enhance its domestic route map. While a deal had been close, negotiations bogged down, especially when the ownership of TWA itself was in doubt. Icahn, sensing he'd never get another chance this good, pulled it off quickly. On March 6, 1986, TWA offered a cash bid of nineteen dollars per share, or $239 million for the whole airline.

Immediately a cry went up from critics of the airline merger wave. It was bad enough, they said, that Northwest was taking over its biggest competitor, Republic, with the result that passengers in Minneapolis and Detroit would have virtually no choice of airlines. The merger of TWA and Ozark seemed even more clearly anticompetitive. The deal would give TWA three-quarters of all the gates at

St. Louis's Lambert Field Airport, a formidable presence that would discourage all but the most foolhardy challengers.

The Justice Department's antitrust lawyers were soon on the case. They told TWA they would oppose the purchase unless the combined company divested some of its St. Louis gates to open the field to new entrants. But the airlines refused, perhaps encouraged by the friendly reception that the other airline buyouts were getting from Elizabeth Dole's Transportation Department. Finally, in July, the Justice Department formally declared its opposition to the Ozark merger, saying it would bring higher fares and reduced service to customers unless new competition was allowed in St. Louis.

Three weeks later, a law judge in the Transportation Department brushed aside Justice's objections, recommending that Dole unconditionally approve the merger. Judge John Vittone reasoned that the merger wouldn't have much effect on competition nationwide, since St. Louis was only one market out of many.

Yet the TWA and Ozark combination would later be cited as one of the most egregious of all the airline deals that went through in the 1980s. It gave TWA a virtual lock on St. Louis. In a year or two, nearly nine out of ten passengers at the hub would be flying on TWA. So strong was TWA's hold on the St. Louis hub that it was able to raise fares with impunity—contestability theory notwithstanding. By mid-1987, TWA's lowest one-way fare from St. Louis to New York—where it alone offered nonstop service—was $310. On another monopoly route of about the same distance, St. Louis–Tampa, TWA's lowest fare was $330. But on the St. Louis–Denver route, with the same flying time as the other two but with competing nonstop service offered by Continental and United, TWA's lowest fare was $160. TWA's domination of St. Louis was ultimately such that Icahn refused to advertise in the local papers. "We own St. Louis," one employee heard him remark.

While Elizabeth Dole did indeed bless Icahn's Ozark deal in September, without strings attached, she ignored the fact that the law judge had at least raised one troubling concern. Vittone was incredulous that the managements of both airlines had spent so little time studying the effects of the deal on the company's employees. He warned that the deal would affect thousands of employees who "are important assets of substantial elements of the carrier's costs." However, even while expressing sympathy, he rejected the union's request for special labor protection provisions, arguing that they could protect themselves from the consequences of the merger through collective bargaining.

By spring of 1986, however, it was clear that Icahn did not view employees as "assets" at all but as fungible commodities. Although he'd gained control of the airline only through the support of the pilots union, the appearance of labor-management harmony did not last long. The flight attendants, unlike the pilots, had made no agreement with Icahn during the takeover. Their contract was up for renewal as he assumed the reins in the early part of 1986. This presented Icahn with his first real test as a manager of people and a negotiator with unions—dealings in which his tendency to go for an opponent's weakness, honed by years of financial gambling, would have unforeseen consequences.

First there was the issue of gender. Icahn had demanded that the mostly female flight attendants take bigger pay cuts than the mostly male pilots or machinists. The flight attendants accused him of saying that they weren't "breadwinners," and therefore should accept lower wages. "He told us that we were secondary incomes, that we were not the main wage-earners in our families, and that we should accept bigger cuts than the pilots or mechanics," on the order of more than 20 percent, reported union leader Vickie Frankovitch. Icahn strenuously denied that claim, but he wouldn't back down. The union went out on strike March 7.

When nearly all of his seasoned flight attendants walked off the job, Icahn hired replacements, most of whom were in their early twenties. They were hustled into the planes after only superficial training, and were paid about ten thousand dollars a year. Icahn seemed unconcerned about whether the quality of his airline's passenger service would suffer as a crop of newcomers bumbled their way through their onboard duties. What mattered more to him was the money he was saving. However, the airline was investigated shortly thereafter over a series of incidents that suggested new employees were being rushed onto the planes without adequate training.

Striking flight attendants had started regularly camping out and picketing in front of Icahn's mansion in the wealthy Westchester community of Bedford. Occasionally their pleas to meet with the boss were answered. Icahn would stroll down his long driveway and address the crowd gathered in front of the imposing stone walls and iron gates of his estate (which he had named Foxfield in honor of his greenmail of Chicago retailer Marshall Field).

Inevitably, Icahn gave the assembled troops his "If I hadn't come along, this airline would have gone under" diatribe. One afternoon, a TWA executive who was inside the mansion during the picketing witnessed an exchange between Icahn and his daughter, then about five years old.

"Daddy, why are all those people outside?" she asked.

"They think I don't pay them enough money," said Icahn.

"Why don't you pay them more money, then?" said the child.

"Because if I give them more money, I won't be able to give you any more dolls," her father replied, laughing.

The story became part of the Icahn lore around TWA headquarters, just one of many anecdotes that contributed to the boss's loopy image.

A few months later the flight attendants ended their strike but Icahn refused to hire most of them back, saying it would be unfair to their replacements. He was within his rights to do so, since there was no contract in force between him and the flight attendants. As positions gradually opened up, the original flight attendants were allowed to return—but only at the new reduced pay levels they had rejected a few months before.

Icahn viewed it as total victory. By hiring replacements at rock-bottom salaries and slashing the pay of the returnees, he had shaved millions of dollars from his payroll. Combined with the cuts he had won from pilots and mechanics, the total savings amounted to more than $320 million a year. However, he had also earned the continuing enmity of those strikers who had been left out in the cold. They did not let him forget it, continuing their picketing and loud public denunciations of Icahn at every opportunity. More than a year later, when the news came out that Pope John Paul II had joined TWA's frequent-flyer plan, the still-unemployed union flight attendants launched their own public relations barrage, protesting the pope's action on the grounds that TWA's labor practices went against the social teachings of the Church.

FEW IMAGINED THAT ICAHN CARED about his public image. Indeed, one of his first cost-cutting moves was to eliminate TWA's public relations department. But he again had failed to appreciate that the high profile of the airline industry had a downside.

The spring and summer months had been horrific for TWA. Terrorists had struck the airline again in April; a bomb placed on a Rome-Athens flight exploded in midflight, sucking some passengers out of the plane to their deaths. That tragedy was followed by the United States bombing of Libya and the nuclear accident at Chernobyl, all of which conspired to keep U.S. travelers away from Europe during the peak summer season.

Travelers in particular avoided TWA and Pan Am, believing U.S.-flag airlines to be more vulnerable to terrorist attacks than their European counterparts. The mobility of planes, though, saved TWA from a total debacle. Mort Ehrlich and the other experienced airline people on the staff swiftly executed a plan to shift many of TWA's jets back to routes in the United States.

But Icahn also saw the trouble overseas as a way to cut costs even further. He turned to the people who only months before had given him handsome concessions in exchange for his vow not to carve up the airline. According to a senior pilot with the airline, Icahn told the airline pilots' leaders that TWA was doing much worse than he'd anticipated. He wanted, he said, to "remind" them that he had the right to liquidate the carrier by selling any and all assets, from international routes to airplanes and ground equipment.

It was true that the pilots' agreement permitted Icahn to unload assets if the airline's losses surpassed a certain threshold. The threat had the desired effect. The pilots agreed to extend their contract to 1992 and to forfeit an earlier agreement that their wages would "snap back" to 1985 levels in just three years. Pilots would later brand that move a "tragic mistake." For only a few months later, Icahn got up before the TWA shareholders' meeting and announced that he had turned the airline around. "I believe you can now see how good we really are and how much we have improved," he crowed.

In a short time, he'd pulled off a string of coups. Soon after he gained control of Ozark in September 1986, he sold that airline's fleet of fifty jets and immediately leased them back. It was a classic Icahn maneuver: In one step, he had recouped the entire $240 million cost of acquiring Ozark. He then saved another $25 million by terminating Ozark's pension plan and submerging all of the airline into TWA.

Then he completed the PARS deal he'd been after. In November, Icahn sold 50 percent of the giant reservations system to Northwest Airlines, which had never bothered to develop its own, reaping another $140 million.

Icahn's PARS transaction was a fresh reminder of how the computer reservations systems had, in ten years, become cash cows for the airlines that had had the foresight to develop them. In 1986 alone, the five reservations systems generated $600 million in booking fees for their airline owners, much of that amounting to a transfer of wealth from airlines that didn't own reservations systems to those that did. The return on investment for system owners was estimated to be as high as 160 percent. And so vital was their grip on travel agencies that Sabre, Apollo, and other res system owners in 1986 paid nearly $200 million in cash and noncash benefits (such as free travel) to travel agents to either induce them to switch to their systems or to prevent them from jumping to a competitor.

American's Sabre by this time was literally an impregnable fortress—in 1987 Bob Crandall cut the ribbon on a $34 million facility in Tulsa that houses the mainframe for the mammoth computer system, still the largest in the industry. The underground computer center is earthquake-proof and capable of operating without external food, water, or power supplies for up to three days.

Icahn, however, had no interest in such long-term investments— he wanted the short-term lift of a deal. In December, Icahn felt confident enough of his cash position to state bluntly before an industry audience at the Wings Club: "TWA must acquire another airline." He had already approached a few airlines that might make a good fit, he said, but had been rebuffed. Rumors had already started circulating, however, that Icahn was eyeing USAir and Piedmont, two airlines that had managed to escape the merger binge. Although Icahn refused to comment publicly, he was in fact quietly buying stock in his intended prey.

"THE REAGAN ADMINISTRATION NEVER MET a merger it didn't like," complained Alfred Kahn. The mergers-and-acquisitions fever that was spreading among Wall Street's hungry investment bankers was in part inspired by the Reagan administration's attitude toward antitrust enforcement. Like many federal agencies, the Justice Department's antitrust division had been hit with staff cuts, and enforcement activity was directed more against anticompetitive practices, such as price-fixing (as Bob Crandall had learned) and less against challenging mergers. The Reagan Justice Department had dropped previously instituted antitrust cases against IBM and against the gasoline and breakfast cereal industries. William Baxter, the head of the Justice Department's antitrust division, also had promulgated new merger guidelines in 1982 that allowed significantly greater concentration of market power within merged companies than under the previous guidelines.

Just as an odd confluence of events lent deregulation a certain inevitability in the 1970s, the airline merger wave of the 1980s attained an unmistakable momentum. In the space of just six months in 1986,

Elizabeth Dole's Transportation Department approved, on average, one big airline deal a month. The total price tag of these acquisitions alone added up to almost $3 billion, much of it borrowed money that loaded the purchaser with a substantial debt burden. By the end of Reagan's second term, Transportation had received 24 applications for airline mergers or acquisitions. It approved every one of them.

Even with the more generous guidelines, the Justice Department strenuously objected to a number of the airline mergers. However, it failed to take legal action that could have changed the outcome. Justice could have gone to court, as it had in the past, to challenge the actions of another department, but in airline mergers, it generally bowed to the wishes of the political appointees in charge of the Transportation Department. "When the [Justice Department's] antitrust division signaled that it would not go to court to back up its objections, it was all over," said former Justice Department lawyer Donald Farmer, who went into private law practice in the capital. The industry got the message. "The guys in the antitrust department had gone to sleep," said Gerry Gitner. "Justice could make a lot of noise, but the fact was that the government would have let anything happen."

The two dozen airline deals included not only the megamergers of 1986—Texas Air–Eastern, Northwest-Republic, TWA-Ozark— but many less spectacular ones, such as Midway Airlines' acquisition of Air Florida, Southwest Airlines' buyout of Muse Air (which had been formed by Lamar Muse to get even with Southwest), and the merger of California airline Jet America with Alaska Airlines.

Even Bob Crandall got caught up in the merger mania. The way he went about it, however, contrasted sharply with the styles of Lorenzo and Icahn. And ultimately this difference would play as great a role as the chiefs' differing approaches to labor in determining which airlines would survive the deregulation wars.

At first, American executives had publicly scoffed at their rivals' acquisitiveness, boasting that American would grow much bigger without all the indigestion a buyout would bring. But Crandall did not sit by and simply watch the action. In the spring of 1986, he cut a deal with Ed Acker that would allow Pan Am to use American's Sabre system as its own reservations system, and to become a partner in American's frequent-flyer plan. This led to speculation on Wall Street that Crandall might be laying the groundwork for eventually folding the long-suffering Pan Am into his own rapidly growing operation.

Less than a year later, the reservations deal collapsed, and Pan Am and American ended up suing each other. Executives at Pan Am suspected that Crandall was using the deal simply to get a closer look at the inner workings of Pan Am. In fact, Jack Pope, American's chief financial officer, had pressed Crandall to go ahead with a Pan Am merger proposal.

Crandall and Acker did discuss a merger of their two companies in late 1986 and early 1987, when they were working out their computerization and frequent-flyer partnership. "I was thinking in those terms, he was thinking in those terms," Acker remembered, but in early 1987, "Bob decided he didn't want to pursue that. . . . He felt that he could cherry-pick—or at least he wanted to cherry-pick," by buying only certain Pan Am assets that interested him, rather than the whole airline.

Crandall was right. He did not have to buy Pan Am and take on all its problems to fly overseas. With modern aircraft, there was no longer any good reason why international flights had to depart from New York or Los Angeles; they could make transoceanic trips just as easily from the United States interior, where American had its hubs. Many of these inland markets—Dallas, Raleigh-Durham, and other places where American was growing—could not provide enough passengers to fill 747s, so Crandall bought some smaller 767 airplanes from Boeing. This allowed Crandall to cut out much of the feed upon which Pan Am and TWA had depended to support their international service, and was yet another blow to those two airlines' fortunes.

Crandall wanted to expand, and indeed he had to if he wanted to keep American's costs down by hiring more people at the lower "B" scale wages. At any opportunity he would snap up assets or new route authorities—controlling his growth in a way that Lorenzo, with his disparate collection of troubled airlines, could never imagine. Finally, in early 1987, Crandall approved a merger of American with West Coast airline AirCal, a $225 million purchase. This was by any standards a modest transaction. AirCal was a midsize regional airline, and there were no anticompetitive issues and few labor problems.

American by 1987 was definitely on a roll. It had posted record profits every year since 1982, and its financial performance overshadowed by far the rest of the big five airlines that had so dominated air travel before deregulation.

ALTHOUGH AMERICAN WAS AT THE top of the heap financially, Crandall was concerned about the growing threat he perceived from Frank Lorenzo's Texas Air empire. If Eastern's labor costs were brought into line with Continental's, Lorenzo would have the lowest costs in the industry as well as the largest fleet. This threat continued to influence the decisions made by other airline chiefs. And it was to vault Atlanta-based Delta Air Lines from a sleepy company among the top ten to its place today among the Big Three.

The paternalistic, tradition-minded Delta was more fortunate than most airlines: It enjoyed a strong presence at Atlanta, where its pioneering of the hub-and-spoke concept had given it an early competitive edge. It had a long history of profitability and encountered almost no competition from any of the low-cost upstarts that started to chip away at the established airlines' markets in the years immediately after deregulation. It had an equally long history of benign relationships with its workers—of whom only the pilots were unionized—not only because it paid highly competitive wages, but also because it instilled a sense of family among its employees and had never laid off anyone. So devoted were Delta's workers that they once chipped in and bought a new airliner for the company, at their own initiative.

At Delta, it was virtually unheard of for an executive to be hired from another airline; they all worked their way up from within. David Garrett, Jr., who was then Delta's chairman, had gone to work for the airline just after World War II as a reservations agent. So hidebound were Delta's ways of doing things that its annual meeting was always held in the same place—not Atlanta or New York, but the little town of Monroe, Louisiana, where the airline had its origin as a crop-dusting service.

But by mid-1986, Delta could no longer be assured that Eastern Airlines, its traditionally complacent foe at Atlanta, would remain a toothless rival. If Frank Lorenzo succeeded in adding Eastern to his Texas Air low-fare empire and in bringing its contentious unions to heel, it could lead to open warfare at Atlanta and in the Florida markets Delta served. At the same time, American and United were moving into some of Delta's East Coast markets through new hubs at Raleigh-Durham and Washington Dulles, respectively. Delta's profits had already started to fall in 1986, when Garrett huddled with executives of Western Air Lines and quickly cut a deal. In September of 1986, Delta stunned the industry when it announced it was going to acquire Western Air Lines for $860 million.

The proposed combination of Delta and Western would send the surviving Delta leapfrogging over the merged Northwest-Republic into the number-four spot among the nation's largest airlines. It would also give Delta a coast-to-coast route network with new hubs at Los

Angeles and Salt Lake City. Failure to make such a deal, Garrett and his people knew, could leave Delta in the dust as the industry consolidation wave swept past it. The deal was made, and the Transportation Department readily approved it.

BY EARLY 1987, ICAHN WAS so anxious to negotiate a deal that he began to drop hints whenever he could about another airline merger, adopting the airline chiefs' mantra, "critical mass," as his own. Not that he truly believed in it; many of his associates were convinced that he just wanted to pull off the old arbitrager's trick of stirring up interest in a property so he could sell at a higher profit.

Icahn naturally had noticed that the only airlines of any size left standing were Piedmont in North Carolina and USAir in northern Virginia, which had both originated as dinky local service airlines. USAir had changed its name from Allegheny in an attempt to erase its dowdy image.

Nearly 20 percent of Piedmont was owned by Norfolk Southern Railroad. In January, the railroad said it might seek to acquire the rest of the stock, and it followed through a few weeks later with a bid of sixty-five dollars a share.

That prompted a retaliatory bid from USAir, which had also picked up a case of merger fever, buying Pacific Southwest Airlines on the West Coast and an East Coast commuter, Suburban Airways. USAir's chairman, Edwin Colodny, offered an average of seventy-two dollars a share for Piedmont, half in stock and half in cash, or $1.65 billion. Norfolk Southern withdrew its bid. USAir and Piedmont covered the same general region of the country and were direct competitors on a number of routes, but by this time that was hardly a concern in airline merger planning.

The USAir-Piedmont deal was a concern to Carl Icahn, though. Shortly after USAir made its bid, Colodny got a phone call from Icahn. He told Colodny a combination of Piedmont with USAir would put TWA "in a difficult position," and that he couldn't just sit by and watch it happen.

He didn't. Piedmont's directors had met in Winston-Salem on March 4 fully expecting to give their formal approval to USAir's offer, when they got a news bulletin that put their vote on hold: Carl Icahn had just bid $1.6 billion to buy USAir, or fifty-two dollars a share— a premium of more than 18 percent above its price at the time. Icahn had started buying USAir stock through a TWA subsidiary set up for that purpose, with the name Swan Management.

As far as Colodny was concerned, however, this swan was the ultimate ugly duckling. He didn't know what was worse—having the Piedmont acquisition killed by Icahn's move, or facing the threat of losing his own company to this airline industry interloper. Some Wall Streeters saw a more devious purpose to Icahn's bid. They speculated that Icahn was hoping USAir would forget about Piedmont, and instead turn around and offer to take TWA off his hands. To add to the confusion, Icahn even hinted that a three-way combination of TWA, USAir, and Piedmont into one airline might be the best solution for all concerned.

Colodny immediately went to work to block Icahn's move, and he got a lucky break. On the same day that Icahn announced he was bidding for USAir, the Securities and Exchange Commission announced that it was investigating Icahn's investment activities as part of its broader probe of insider trading. That may have distracted him long enough for Colodny to renegotiate with Piedmont. Piedmont's directors said they now wanted an all-cash deal, which meant Colodny had to convince USAir's principal lender, Manufacturers Hanover, to ante up another $800 million. The night after Icahn made his bid, the bank came through, and the following day, both USAir's and Piedmont's boards approved their merger plan, forcing Icahn to back off.

But the merger still needed regulatory approval. Although that might have been a mere formality in 1986, it had become a major political issue by the second half of 1987, when the Transportation Department took up the two carriers' merger application. The department was in a difficult position on this case, since it was coming at the tail end of a series of sometimes questionable merger approvals. The anticompetitive implications were obvious, since the two airlines were such direct competitors in the eastern United States. But if DOT turned it down, critics would charge that the agency was merely caving in to political pressure late in the game, to the disadvantage of these two companies.

Indeed, *The Wall Street Journal* editorialized that for the government to block this merger after it had rubber-stamped so many others would be "the antitrust equivalent of musical chairs. When the music stops, all of the big carriers that gained market share through recent mergers will be able to make competitive squeeze plays against the two smaller carriers that aren't allowed to combine." But some members of Congress, as they watched DOT approve merger after merger, became increasingly concerned about the impact on competition, since each merger removed another competitor from the industry.

Even one of the law judges at Transportation recommended that the merger be rejected. Then, on October 1, Elizabeth Dole left the secretary's job to work for her husband's presidential campaign, and Reagan nominated Deputy Secretary James Burnley to replace her. With Burnley facing a possible confirmation fight as the deadline for action approached, the decision on the merger fell to Dole's assistant secretary, Matthew Scocozza.

"I did that one all by myself," Scocozza later boasted. Curiously, he seemed especially proud that his entire staff at Transportation fought him on it the whole way. The analysts inside the agency, he said, "just thought this was a terrible merger, bad for competition. But they could not prove it." So Scocozza, true to his and Dole's earlier record, approved the merger.

When all the merger dust had settled, the United States aviation landscape had irrevocably changed—and the resulting consolidation of the industry led to some serious sniping, in hindsight, at Dole's handling of the situation.

Later the General Accounting Office issued a harshly critical report on the mergers, taking Dole and Scocozza to task for failing to consider critical industry changes in the analyses of the mergers' impact on competition. As a result, the airline business became "more concentrated than it was when the government regulated entry, exit and fares," the report concluded. In just two years, by the end of 1988, the nation's five largest airlines would control three-quarters of the air travel market, while the market share of the post-deregulation new entrants would shrink to 3 percent.

Even Scocozza later admitted that he recommended approval of some deals that he regarded as stupid. But under deregulation, he argued, the government had no right to intervene in business decisions to save companies from the mistakes of their owners. "These are not deregulation problems," he said, "they're management problems."

And of all the management decisions, the worst was Lorenzo's decision to buy Eastern. "I don't know where the boards of directors were on a lot of these," Scocozza said. "But to allow Texas Air to merge with People Express, and to throw Eastern into that pot, along with Continental, it would have taken a miracle to make that work."

"I think there was very little choice," said American's Crandall. "If you're going to have a deregulated industry, you're inevitably going to have a small number of large carriers. If those mergers had not been approved, I think it would have inevitably led to the failure of the small carriers."

14

THE BIG BANG

Although some Washington bureaucrats privately thought it insane, Frank Lorenzo's Byzantine airline empire was a hit on Wall Street. The price of Texas Air shares soared to $50, and financial columnists raved about how Lorenzo had, in just six years, transformed a Texas puddle-jumper into the largest airline company in the Western world. Unlike Icahn, Lorenzo seemed to have a clear vision of what he wanted it to be: a low cost mega-airline that would be the industry's price leader, challenging the more sedately managed American, United, and Delta. It was the way in which Lorenzo pursued this goal that was ultimately his undoing.

At Eastern's shareholders meeting on November 25, 1986, Lorenzo was labeled "merger mad" by the various gadflies in attendance. Lorenzo did not attend the meeting himself. By the time the Transportation Department gave its blessing to his purchase of Eastern in October 1986 the question of control was moot; Lorenzo had amassed a stake of 51 percent of the company. Lorenzo had also been warned by Eastern managers that the public meeting would be a "circus" with Charlie Bryan as ringmaster. The meeting, held in New York City, did in fact degenerate into a shouting match between the Bryan and Eastern management factions. When Bryan ran over his allotted time for speaking, the directors declared the session over and turned out the lights. Bryan continued his monologue, alone, in the dark.

Lorenzo by then was enjoying the trappings of success. He owned a large house in River Oaks, an exclusive Houston neighborhood, homes in Nantucket, Aspen, and the Upper East Side in New York City.

But Lorenzo liked to affect the pose of a humble self-made man and took to driving a modest Volkswagen on occasions when the press was out in force. Lorenzo had inherited the auto from the old Continental, where it was an executive perk. "When we moved [Continental] to Houston we took it along, and would sometimes trot it out for public appearances," said one Lorenzo confidante. Lorenzo aides nicknamed the vehicle the "press conference car," for their boss in fact drove a very expensive BMW.

At first, Lorenzo had approached the veteran Eastern executives cordially. He visited Miami during the summer after the sale and invited many of the top managers out for intimate dinners. Eastern was, after all, different from Continental, Frontier, People, or any of the other airlines in his collection. Lorenzo respected the trimmings of its distinguished past, such as its blue-chip board and the suite of offices it still occupied at Rockefeller Center. Lorenzo seemed to like the fact that he was now rubbing elbows with Laurance Rockefeller; he asked Roswell Gilpatric to sponsor him for membership in the exclusive River Club on New York's East Side. But Lorenzo immediately signaled his displeasure with Charlie Bryan's presence in this august company. The machinists leader was dislodged from the board in the fall.

When Texas Air started sending over senior managers from Continental to Eastern that fall, the inevitable culture clash began. The first of Lorenzo's lieutenants to arrive were John Adams, senior vice-president of human resources, and Mickey Foret, a finance executive. Adams was the architect of many of Lorenzo's labor policies at Texas International and later at Continental, and his appointment was read as a sign—if any was needed—that Lorenzo intended to be much tougher on the unions than his predecessor had. Lorenzo wasted no time publicly adopting a get-tough stance toward the machinists. He labeled their contract "absurd" and pledged he'd bring it into line with "reality"—a euphemism for seeking big wage cuts. And all this was being done before Lorenzo had approval from the government or the shareholders to take control.

When Phil Bakes first set foot in Eastern's Miami headquarters, he was struck by its dilapidated condition, which reflected the company's general decay. The empty fountain in the courtyard, with its tarnished plaque of Eddie Rickenbacker, symbolized all that had gone wrong; it had been turned off to save energy in one of the carrier's frequent cash crunches. One of Bakes's first acts after arriving at his new job as president was to order the fountain turned back on.

Lorenzo soon started pressing for ways to slash Eastern's labor costs. Bakes at first tried to get Lorenzo to move slowly in this incendiary situation. Just as Steve Wolf had done so effectively at Republic, Bakes traveled around the Eastern system, visiting as many stations as he could and answering the inevitable questions about Lorenzo's—and his own—labor-bashing history.

But early in 1987, not many weeks after ending his road show, Bakes told thousands of Eastern employees at an auditorium in Miami that Eastern wanted $490 million a year in wage cuts. Much of it would come out of the machinists' paychecks, he said, which had been expected. But the pilots and flight attendants would also have to accept big pay cuts. To soften the effect of this devastating news, Eastern promised it would pay to retrain unskilled baggage handlers for higher-paid skilled jobs, either within the airline or outside, if necessary.

The unions reacted as would be expected. The machinists didn't have to open their contract for another year and they had a well-documented history of never giving up anything they'd won. The pilots and the flight attendants, on the other hand, had already agreed to 20 percent wage cuts on the eve of the sale to Lorenzo and felt they should receive some recognition for their cooperation, not demands for additional cuts.

The new confrontational atmosphere seemed to pervade all parts of Eastern. Soon after Bakes's speech, employees started noticing that the company's employee newspaper, instead of concentrating on the usual fluff about promotions and anniversaries, was printing items about employee theft, absenteeism, and pilots' drinking on the job. "It was clear that they wanted to break the unions; otherwise what they were doing didn't make any sense," said Richard Magurno, who stayed on as an Eastern executive after the Lorenzo sale.

Unlike the other airlines in Lorenzo's group, Eastern could not be merged into the whole. Its strong unions and long history of labor-management hostilities meant that Eastern would have to remain separate from the nonunion companies Lorenzo had smashed together as Continental. The reasons behind almost every other airline merger of the period—to create daunting mass, to eliminate overlap and duplication, to wield more power in certain markets where merged airlines joined—would be defeated. The critical mass that Lorenzo appeared to have gained was illusory.

When Lorenzo bought Eastern it was one instance when he did not describe an airline acquisition as a "perfect fit." Instead, while Lorenzo was slapping People and Continental together, the public was treated to the odd spectacle of Eastern and Continental working at cross-purposes despite their common ownership.

And Lorenzo seemed to verify the worst fears of Eastern's unions—that he would gradually shift the airline's assets over to his nonunion operation—when he sold six of Eastern's wide-bodied Airbus planes to Continental soon after the takeover. There were other instances: On several occasions Eastern exited a route only to see Continental come right in. Technically there was no reason Lorenzo could not do that—he owned both companies—except when it involved a transaction so large that it would invoke a provision in Eastern union contracts. But union leaders argued that virtually all of these transfers—which would later include Eastern jewels like its System One reservations system—ate into Eastern's revenues.

In early 1987 Lorenzo seemed less interested in Eastern than in the pressing matter of cementing his presence at Newark, which was, after all, the reason he had bought such a motley assortment of airlines to begin with. Insiders would later refer to the operation as the Big Bang. The thankless task of pulling it off had fallen to a man who'd just left a secure job at American Airlines to gamble his future on the proposition that Lorenzo's grand plan would succeed.

TOM PLASKETT ARRIVED IN HOUSTON on November 1, 1986, for his first day of work as president at Continental Airlines' utilitarian headquarters. It was a sharp contrast to the atmosphere of American's campuslike domain 250 miles to the north. Lorenzo was still surrounded by his "guerrilla managers," longtime aides who'd thrived on the adrenaline highs of running from one crisis to another. Lorenzo had once confessed that his managers, accustomed as they were to the "blood-rushing" business of stalking prey, might not settle so easily into managing the companies that they had bagged. Plaskett seemed just the sort who would tame them.

But Plaskett's habits, like leaving the office at four on Friday afternoon to play golf, quickly drew ridicule from the Continental managers who reported to him. Plaskett was the type, recalled one Lorenzo aide derisively, who "wanted four in-baskets and multiple-choice action memos. He was an administrator, and God knows, Continental did not need an administrator." At Continental, a successful executive ran marathons, pulled all-nighters, and eschewed country clubs, meetings, and memos.

"He would sit there and say things like 'carry on,' " said one former Continental manager. "Well, what the hell does that mean?"

Plaskett was not the first executive to be perplexed by the Continental organization. General counsel Charles Goolsbee, a lawyer and former banking executive who joined Lorenzo in 1980, called the company "the least institutionalized organization I've worked for. It's a hard environment to get used to, both because you have to work so hard and because you have to reorient your thinking to the risk-taking aspect."

That Plaskett would experience culture shock at Continental was no surprise. He had worked his entire life at General Motors and American Airlines, smooth-running machines. He was used to management organization charts, memos, and meeting agendas. Continental managers reveled in their unorthodoxy and were outspoken in their contempt for conventional companies. Instead of learning from Plaskett the key to American's success, they were arrogantly dismissing him—defeating Lorenzo's purpose in hiring him.

Marketing vice-president Douglas Birdsall even bragged about the lack of formality to a Harvard Business School professor who visited Continental headquarters to study its operation. "Nobody's much of a stickler for procedures. . . . We don't care much about whether the budget information presented in the meetings does or does not conform to accounting standards or a rigid format, just as long as you convey what you need to . . . and we have no time to track decisions that require no tracks, like the latest personnel procedure or the addition of 10 computer mnemonics from our system. American would have not one but two memos on these subjects," he said.

Meetings would begin at all hours and last until everyone was too tired or hungry to go on. Plaskett, however, seemed to adhere to a prearranged schedule, drawing more snide remarks. Some of this sniping finally came out into the open. One time, when Texas Air gathered some senior executives from its subsidiaries, Dick Magurno was shocked at the cavalier treatment Plaskett got from his underlings. "There is a certain kind of deference you pay to a guy who is president, a certain level of respect. Plaskett was totally abused by the people who worked for him," Magurno said.

Said a senior executive at Continental: "Early on people basically began to regard Plaskett as a short-timer. One of the things people never seemed to understand was that Frank effectively functioned as an owner. The lack of respect paid to Tom was a function of that. There was a very hardened and cynical group of top management people who had been through a lot at Continental . . . everyone who came in sooner or later would leave."

Lorenzo tacitly went along with this loosely defined situation. After all, it was working to his benefit. Plaskett would find, as did others who held the same job, that certain officers junior to him had direct lines to Lorenzo, in effect doing an end run around the president's office. Decisions that in most companies would require the president's approval were being made without Plaskett's knowledge. Once Plaskett discovered Continental suddenly had started operating some new flights of which he was totally unaware. In other cases, studies were ordered without his approval—all because Lorenzo would simply pick up the phone and call someone else.

It was in this atmosphere that the company was approaching a momentous decision about what it would ultimately become, with no clear idea of how to arrive there. Rather than turn Continental into an American, it looked as if Plaskett might end up with just the opposite—with the decentralized and at times chaotic organization of Don Burr's People Express.

Plaskett got into a debate with Frank Lorenzo about how to handle the People acquisition. Lorenzo's close ties to Burr complicated matters further. Lorenzo now seemed willing to experiment with Burr's "people ideas" he'd insultingly rejected years before.

The culture clash brewing within the suddenly enlarged Continental was a reflection of the larger strategic divide in the deregulated industry almost a decade after the law had been passed. On one side of that divide was the cautious, internal growth approach taken by Bob Crandall and on the other, the wild expansion-through-acquisition binge of Lorenzo.

The bigger question facing Lorenzo at the moment was whether it made sense to smash his new airlines together in one day, or to combine the disparate companies gradually. The folly of the former approach had already been amply demonstrated on October 1, when Northwest had hastily absorbed merger partner Republic, with disastrous results. Horror stories abounded: On one Northwest flight, the baggage never got loaded; on another, there was no food because someone forgot to put it on the plane; on another, the departure was delayed while the flight crew tried to figure out which airplane they were supposed to use. During the first week of October, about three of every four Northwest flights were late. Northwest at one point had to take over an entire hotel at Minneapolis to accommodate stranded customers.

In Detroit, where Northwest brought in new baggage handlers at wages higher than those of Republic employees, Republic baggage handlers were so outraged that some of them rebelled, sabotaging equipment, cutting wires, and tearing the destination tags off passengers' luggage, until the airline found itself with a warehouse full of lost bags at Detroit. "Northwest is an embarrassment to the American business community," went one typical complaint that arrived on the desk of harried Northwest president John Horn. "This cannot continue. Get your act together because the public will not put up with this insanity forever." Northwest Airlines thereafter acquired a long-term reputation for indifference to passengers.

Airlines that rushed into mergers during the mid-1980s gambled that the public's memory of their growing pains would quickly fade, in time for them to reap the benefits of larger size. Yet the airlines were different from other industries that were experiencing similar waves of consolidation. The high visibility of air travel, the very factor that had launched deregulation of airlines ahead of other industries, would now prove the bane of the airline managers who were clumsily squeezing together their acquisitions. It was one thing for record companies or textile manufacturers to merge; while causing much disruption within the companies, the results were often invisible to the consumer. The emerging mega-airlines were roiled both by internal strife and by very public service problems, and this would make the airlines for a time among the most reviled industries in the United States.

TEXAS AIR SHAREHOLDERS APPROVED THE merger of Continental and People Express on December 31, 1986. Lorenzo told his surprised staff he wanted the merger completed almost immediately. His haste was aimed at stemming People's losses, which were continuing at the rate of some $1 million a day. Continental managers said it was impossible to complete such a complex operation that fast. Lorenzo insisted, but he finally acceded to a brief postponement. The combination was set back to February 1.

Workers started repainting the brown-and-tan planes of People Express in Continental's red and gold; the two-letter PE code was expunged from computer reservations systems and replaced with the CO identifier of its new owner.

This operation was infinitely more complex than even Northwest and Republic; it would crush many disparate companies into one—not only People Express and its subsidiary Frontier, but also New York Air, which Lorenzo had decided to absorb into the mass, since it seemed unlikely to survive on its own. There were several smaller commuter lines that were also part of the overall merger—Rocky Mountain Airways in Colorado, which had been bought by Continental; Provincetown Boston Airways and Britt Airways, two commuter lines snapped up in a feverish expansion binge by Don Burr; and Bar Harbor Airways. In all, it was a mish-mash. Alfred Kahn himself could not have dreamed up such an incompatible collection of airlines uniting as a result of the deregulation battles.

Nothing was alike at any of these airlines. Each had different types of aircraft with different cabin configurations. People Express, because of its unique no-frills service, didn't even have galleys in its planes. "We had something like thirty-two different types of equipment coming together under one umbrella," said a Continental worker.

One camp argued for putting People into Chapter 11 bankruptcy. Phil Bakes, for one, liked to describe Burr's company as a "black hole," an airline with almost no infrastructure and an anarchic operation that would eat up and destroy anything else that came within its orbit. Texas Air didn't want another bankruptcy but Bakes and others felt that this was a different case; People had already been written off and was being treated in the media as if it had already gone bankrupt. Its subsidiary Frontier, in fact, was already in Chapter 11.

Some people also suspected that Lorenzo decided not to throw People into bankruptcy in order to save Don Burr's personal fortune. In bankruptcy, his shares in the company would have been worth little or nothing, but thanks to the merger agreement he'd worked out with Lorenzo, Burr reportedly would get about $5 million to $10 million—as well as a top job at Texas Air to help smooth the transition.

Burr claimed later that Lorenzo had promised him the president's post at Texas Air but reneged, just as he had years before when he had first joined Texas International. This time, Lorenzo threw him a bone in the form of a vague title, naming him executive vice-president of the Texas Air holding company. In any event, it didn't matter much what his title was, since his job responsibilities were unclear.

When he arrived at Texas Air early in 1987 as People's ambassador without discernible portfolio, Burr merely irritated the longtime Lorenzo associates who reported to him. A Continental executive recalled that Burr was "always out screwing something up. His nose was always under the tent. He was always at Newark. He was acting like he was the boss and he wasn't." Burr still clung to the hope that he would be able to preserve some of People's unusual culture.

To promote the merger in the New York area, Continental officials cooked up a wild scheme to pass out to the public hundreds of thousands of free tickets, but the promotion had to be abandoned. Not only did Madison Square Garden and the huge Meadowlands sports complex across the river in New Jersey turn down Continental's request for a place to hold the giveaway, but New York City police frowned on the whole idea, fearing that up to a quarter of a million people would turn out for the freebies, creating a near riot.

Even if Continental couldn't hand out free tickets, it went ahead with the merger plan. But no one was clearly in charge, and somehow the event took on an ominous inevitability that no one could stop. Continental was far from prepared.

Lorenzo also decided that this was the time to launch some new fares he'd been working on, MaxSavers, which were billed as the deepest discounts ever—slashing 40 percent off coach fares. The thinking was that the fare cuts would be just the thing to introduce the "new" Continental to the public. "It was a typical Texas International stunt," said one employee. And it would succeed, but not in the way Lorenzo had intended. The last thing that Continental needed was to overwhelm its already overworked reservation agents. By compounding the merger problems, the MaxSavers simply brought forth lots of negative publicity.

Elliott Seiden had only recently left the Justice Department to join Texas Air as assistant general counsel. As he sat down at Continental's Houston headquarters he viewed D-Day with increasing alarm. Three years after it had shut down and shrunk to one-third its former size, Continental was just emerging from bankruptcy proceedings. It was simply unprepared for a huge increase in size—from 100 to 315 planes, and double the number of employees.

Continental even handled its crew scheduling manually—a team of clerks sat in an office and wrote out the schedules for pilots, engineers, and flight attendants. The airline had just bought an automated scheduling system that "would bring us into the twentieth century," but it wouldn't be ready until the eve of the merger. "That first day it was so overwhelmed that it became irrelevant," said Seiden.

"Here Continental barely had the systems to take care of itself and all of a sudden you were just laying on this enormous operation. . . . It was chaos. Literally overnight the whole airline almost melted down. I've never seen anything so awful."

As Continental managers arrived at Newark to look things over, they were shocked. People's aircraft maintenance records were so disorganized that no one knew when a particular aircraft might need a mandatory maintenance inspection required by the FAA. No one seemed to have any idea where any of People's seventy-five-odd planes were in terms of their maintenance cycles. Continental had no choice but to perform the new checks on each plane so they'd at least have a benchmark. This was an extremely costly proposition, running into millions of dollars, not only for the expense of performing the checks but also because each jet had to be taken out of service for days.

Meanwhile, poking around in a closet up at Newark headquarters, Continental people came across a stack of unmarked cardboard boxes filled with thousands of passenger refund requests that had simply been forgotten in the confusion at People's headquarters.

Continental's people were livid. Ignoring refund requests violated not only a Federal Reserve Board rule but also a Federal Aviation Act requirement that a company process a credit card refund in seven days and a cash refund in twenty-one days or face steep fines.

Some of the refund requests in the boxes were a year old. The Transportation Department could fine the company one thousand dollars for each day that each refund was overdue. Continental had only a dozen people to handle this area, and until D-Day they'd managed to stay current. The company quickly hired more people to try to dig out before the federal authorities caught on.

An unprecedented number of complaints started pouring into the Transportation Department about the new, larger Continental in the weeks after the merger. The airline was becoming the ultimate realization of Murphy's Law.

People Express had never had much of a baggage operation, since it actively discouraged customers from checking luggage. "So you had all these people at Newark who had never learned the codes for airports," said Seiden, and who now had to select the correct coded baggage tag for each piece. "These people were putting bags on any plane they wanted; they didn't know where they were going and they didn't care. Bags were going everywhere but their destination."

The Continental baggage operation was losing five hundred to one thousand bags a day, ten times the number an airline can typically handle. Storehouses at airports were full. Managers at such crowded stations as Chicago, for example, would phone their counterparts in less traveled airports, such as Syracuse, and ask them if they had any space in their storerooms. If they did, the manager would load one hundred errant bags onto a plane and send them off just to store them somewhere.

"We even had professional thieves move in and steal bags," recalled a Continental executive. "It was easy . . . because customers were going to assume that Continental had lost their luggage."

The damage from this type of service problem is impossible to measure. In a very short time Continental alienated much of its bread-and butter business, the frequent travelers on whom any airline must depend for profits. The airline, which had just emerged from Chapter 11 a few months before with a promising future, was dealt a crippling blow.

Continental's employees found themselves in a system that didn't work, and the strain started to show. Every day they confronted justifiably angry passengers, and many of them dreaded going to work. It was another vicious cycle. Pretty soon the word spread that Continental wouldn't just lose your bag or delay your flight, they'd be surly about it as well.

Continental's people were struggling to adjust to People's flight scheduling, which was often managed by its pilots. Flights that could have fed passengers to each other were scheduled to misconnect by a couple of minutes, losing the carrier thousands of dollars in revenue. A flight from Syracuse with passengers bound for Atlanta would arrive at Newark, say, three minutes after the Atlanta flight had left. Those headed for Atlanta would simply go to another airline. And the airline's on-time performance was suffering so much that it would not have mattered even if the illogical scheduling had been straightened out. During the month of February, almost half of all the flights operated by the new, enlarged Continental arrived late.

Former People employees were also unhappy, angry, and feeling betrayed. Burr had contributed to those feelings by portraying Lorenzo as a cardboard villain in the year before the sale, calling the Texas Air chief "Darth Vader." Burr had made his intemperate remarks before a sale to Lorenzo was even a possibility to distinguish People's style from Lorenzo's colder approach, as part of his overall morale-building enterprise. But his remarks were to backfire, as his employees went into Continental feeling that they'd been made prisoners of war. Many of them quit. But those who stayed on to become Continental employees were equally disillusioned. "I feel like one of General Lee's men at Appomattox," said one of the People Express pilots.

The chaos of the merger of Continental and People was also

affecting Eastern. At Newark, Eastern lost more than half of its gates to make way for the expansion of Continental. Eastern's official explanation was that Continental, now the New York area's biggest airline, would use the facilities "more efficiently."

Employees of Eastern, which had served Newark since 1930, were incensed. A *New York Times* reporter who went out to Newark Airport one day found Eastern workers demoralized and angry, especially as they dealt with the service problems brought on by the rushed merger: public address systems that did not work, a shortage of in-flight meals, and more seriously, an apparent disregard for passengers. In one instance, a worker said that ticket agents were being ordered to close the plane door and depart even as passengers were still checking in at a counter a few yards away.

What was worse than any spillover into Eastern's operations was the effect of the Continental merger on the reputation of Texas Air. "It took away the credibility of Texas Air, and therefore the credibility and ownership of Eastern," said Phil Bakes several years later. "And it gave the unions a drum to beat, and a fairly big one at that. They could say, 'Here they can't even manage an airline, and they're a nonunion company and they're screwing up passengers and delivering lousy service.' The media was awful; it should have been. It was awful and there was no excuse for it."

Lorenzo apparently agreed. He fired Plaskett in July of 1987 and effectively forced Don Burr to resign, signaling his ultimate rejection of Burr's humanist philosophy of business. This brought the saga of Don Burr and Frank Lorenzo full circle. Burr had been brought back in only to be callously pushed out. For a time he withdrew to write a book about his philosophy and experience with People Express, a project he was still working on six years later. He could not get the airline business out of his system, however, and religiously attended Conquistadores meetings. A year after his resignation, in a curious turn of events, Burr seriously considered buying Eastern when approached by a consortium of union-backed investors. Burr was intrigued by the prospect of testing his unorthodox ideas on the distressed airline, although disinterested observers thought it would be crazy to even attempt it. That quixotic plan was to be his last foray into the business for some time.

Finally, three months into the Continental–People Express–New York Air merger, the level of consumer complaints about Continental to the Transportation Department had tripled. Elizabeth Dole knew something had to be done, even if it was after the fact. So Dole charged Continental with violating various consumer protection laws.

The airline paid a quarter of a million dollars to settle the claim.

If Congress or the media cranked up the pressure, then Dole would take some highly visible action—levying a steep fine or the like—and the critics would be silenced, for a time. But little was done about underlying causes of the airlines' problems—the understaffing of the air traffic control system and the failure to fund adequate airport and runway expansion, as well as the rush to merge. There was another aspect that seemed to draw little attention from Dole's department: The merging companies were loading up so much debt that their ability to maintain equipment in safe condition could be called into question.

By year-end, Secretary Dole was under intense pressure from the public, the media, and Congress to do something about the disastrous condition of air travel. According to former associates and several published reports, Dole around this time started to panic. The presidential campaign season would soon be under way and any further disruption of air service would be extremely embarrassing to the administration. And for all her outward composure, Dole was said to be highly sensitive to what was written about her performance. It was the delays, the scenes of crowded airport departure lounges, that had gotten Dole worried, not the anticompetitive implications of the mergers themselves.

Among all the problems facing Elizabeth Dole none seemed to grab more attention from politicians or the press than airline delays. Senator John Danforth told reporters he had experienced so many flight delays himself that he coined a new verb, "to tarmac," which he defined as sitting on a plane after it leaves the gate but before it takes off.

Horror stories abounded. Eastern captain Ray Davidson, a fifty-nine-year-old veteran pilot, pulled his plane off a long takeoff line at Atlanta one day in 1986 and told stunned passengers over the intercom: "I'm fed up with it. I'm sick and tired of the delays, tired of the waiting. I'm hanging it up. You can have it. This flight will be my last." He took the plane back to the terminal, walked off, and never returned to the cockpit.

The syndicated columnist George Will wrote with typical acidity in a late 1986 article: "Deregulation has been good for the masses. And the masses are making flying a mess. The masses are so very, well, numerous." But it wasn't necessarily deregulation that was causing the problem. It was the government's failure to administer what regulation remained. Airports and airspace hadn't been deregulated, and that was where much of the problem began. The air traffic control system had remained woefully understaffed since Reagan fired the controllers in 1981. With the advent of giant hub-and-spoke route systems, delays tended to multiply more rapidly, as one late flight could set off a chain reaction, delaying dozens of other connecting flights.

Late in January 1987, Dole signaled that she would be receptive to giving airlines antitrust immunity once again so they could hold scheduling discussions to ease delays, which had increased to a frightening number the year before—367,000 flights were late in 1986, 75,000 more than the year before.

At Dole's behest, airlines formed a "scheduling committee" free from antitrust prosecution just like the old days. Over the next few weeks, airline representatives did realign their schedules somewhat to ease delays, often by the simple expedient of padding their scheduled flight times.

Airlines themselves were responsible for many of the delays through deceptive scheduling practices. Airline reservations computers listed airline schedules by departure time, and carriers competing in a given market all tried to schedule departures for the time most likely to be requested. If a businessman asked his travel agent for a 9:00 A.M. flight, for instance, it would be booked before a 9:05 A.M. departure. It was not unusual to see six flights at an airport listed for the same departure time.

If flights had the same scheduled departure time, the one with the earliest arrival would be listed higher on the screen, so airlines tended to underestimate the actual travel time in a bid for a better listing. But after the scheduling talks, many of the delays were eliminated simply by extending the estimated travel times in the computers to more realistic levels. Later, the airlines agreed to drop elapsed flight time as a factor in ordering schedule displays, and eventually, the Transportation Department instituted a mandatory reporting system for airlines' on-time performance, with the results disseminated to the media every month.

Ironically, the solution that worked the best to cure the delay problem so embarrassing to the Reagan administration harked back to the old days of government interference. Allowing competitors to agree on schedules under antitrust immunity was hardly what the deregulators had envisioned, and the Justice Department, predictably, opposed the idea as anticompetitive.

The airlines, for their part, blamed the government for not attending to the matters that were still under its control. The federal ticket tax paid by airline passengers went into a fund that was supposed to be used exclusively for airport and airways expansion and improvements, the airlines pointed out, and yet billions of dollars were sitting unused in that fund because Congress hadn't approved their disbursement for such projects. The airline industry mounted a public lobbying effort against this, charging that the huge surplus was unspent simply as a cynical bookkeeping trick to make the burgeoning federal deficit under the Reagan administration look a little smaller than it really was.

15

ALLEGIS

It was not surprising that Dick Ferris, who had set off the merger frenzy when he bought Pan Am's Pacific routes for United, had never acquired another airline outright. After all, United was so big at the outset that it virtually set the "critical mass" standard to which its smaller competitors aspired. Not that Ferris was not as much of an empire-builder as the next airline CEO. While his peers labored with their misbegotten mergers, Ferris was assembling an empire unique in the airline industry, because it went far beyond the business of flying planes. Just as he had been the only airline chief to break ranks with his fellow Conquistadores by supporting deregulation in the mid-1970s, Ferris was once again following a different path in the merger-and-growth binge of the 80s.

On April 30, 1987, Dick Ferris asked the shareholders of the UAL corporation to approve the name he had chosen for his ambitious venture—Allegis, a combination of Latin words meant to signify customer loyalty and protection. The odd-sounding moniker drew snickers from the public. Ferris brushed aside the ridicule, for the name was the last piece in an endeavor that had consumed his energies for nearly two years. He had gone on a buying binge that had startled his peers in the industry, adding Hertz Corporation and Hilton International to the corporate family of United Airlines and Westin

Hotels. The UAL corporation now had a value of some $9 billion, and was surely the largest travel conglomerate ever assembled.

The point of Ferris's strategy was not merely to create mass. He had come up with the novel idea that having related companies under a single umbrella would nurture each division. Ferris sincerely believed that a United Airlines passenger, for instance, could be induced to book a Hertz car and stay in a Hilton. The passenger would be his not only for the flight but during the entire trip.

Even so, the shareholders at the 1987 annual meeting peppered him with nearly four hours of questions about why their stock wasn't worth as much as it should be, considering the alleged value of its various assets. Ferris sought to reassure them that in time—say two or three years—the value of the combined Allegis empire would indeed be more than the sum of the parts.

While Icahn, Lorenzo, and others had been expanding their airline companies horizontally, Ferris had been expanding UAL vertically. And while UAL expanded, he and his advisers had spent much of the previous two years devising tactics to protect UAL from outside predators, for the breakup value of Ferris's empire was too tempting for any raider to ignore.

WHILE HE WAS BUSY ASSEMBLING the superstructure of Allegis, Ferris failed to notice a soft spot in the foundation.

That soft spot had already grown into a crack that Ferris had been trying to patch in the days before the shareholders convened. About three weeks before the annual meeting, United Airlines' pilots had put forward a plan to buy the airline for $4.5 billion and separate it from Ferris's travel empire. The UAL (now Allegis) board had dutifully weighed and quickly rejected the pilots' offer as inconsistent with the company's long-range plans. Nonetheless, Ferris—sounding a conciliatory note unusual for such a strong-willed executive—said he was now open to working out some kind of partial equity participation in the company for United's employees.

Ferris hoped he finally had some breathing room from the circling Wall Street vultures and the United pilots, who were led by an uncompromising, blunt-spoken man named Frederick "Rick" Dubinsky. But he wasn't sure.

DUBINSKY AND FERRIS FIRST MET in 1978, not long after the young Cleveland-based copilot was elected to the Master Executive Council

(MEC) of the United Airlines branch of the Air Line Pilots Association. The MEC, an elected group of more than two dozen pilots, had the authority to make virtually all the major decisions for United's six-thousand-plus unionized pilots.

With deregulation facing the industry, Ferris had appeared before the pilots' leadership to broach the subject of possible wage concessions and productivity increases. Most of the pilots present were sympathetic to Ferris; they had even broken with the national leadership of their union and helped Ferris to push the concept of deregulation before Congress.

"I stood up and told him that I fully understood that employees sometimes have to take reductions," Dubinsky recalled later. But Dubinsky said he also told Ferris that "if the pilots give up anything, they ought to get fair value back, other than just the right to come to work in the morning. I said if he came to me when I was on the MEC and talked in terms of concessions, he better come with a fistful of stock certificates. And he just looked at me and said, 'Over my dead body.' " Ferris's remark deeply disturbed Dubinsky. As the years passed, it echoed in his mind and grew into a personal challenge.

Nevertheless, in the early years of deregulation, Ferris and the leadership of the MEC grew closer. The outspoken Dubinsky became branded by the union's leaders as a troublemaker, and was "exiled," as he put it, from the mainstream of ALPA activity for years. "The leadership [of the pilots] at that time was very taken in by Ferris," he said.

Ferris went out of his way to court the pilots. Not only had he taken the time to earn his own pilot's license, but he often personally appeared before the pilots' MEC to discuss company issues, an unusual step for a CEO. He even hobnobbed with the pilots at company gatherings. "He was more at ease with them" than with other employees, one former United executive recalled. "After all, these guys make a lot of money, they're in the stock market, they play golf . . . mechanics don't play golf."

So when Ferris, faced with rising competition from low-cost, nonunion airlines in the early 1980s, approached the pilots for their help and cooperation, they were willing to give it. In 1981, the pilots voluntarily made work-rule concessions under a "Blue Skies" agreement. They put in more flying time, gave up certain bonus pay provisions, and agreed to use a crew of two rather than three in the cockpits of certain aircraft. This cut the company's costs by 15 percent. In exchange, the pilots got a basic wage increase, protection against layoffs, and a pledge by Ferris that the company wouldn't try to create a nonunion subsidiary as Lorenzo had done with New York Air.

The pilots were so responsive to the perils of United's competitive situation under deregulation that they sometimes went beyond the terms of their contracts to help Ferris and the company. When United experimented with its low-cost Friendship Express 737 flights on routes where People Express was moving in, "the pilots kind of ignored their work rules to be able to chase People Express out. That was all caught up in that Blue Skies era," Dubinsky said. And when Frank Lorenzo put the pilots union out of business at Continental Airlines in 1983 and cut workers' pay in half, Dubinsky claimed, United's pilots told Ferris that on routes where United was competing against Continental, they were willing to fly for nothing.

Ferris did not take up their offer. "His response to us was, 'You guys fly the airplanes, I'll manage the company,' " Dubinsky said. Pilots were upset by Ferris's brushoff. They were also deeply troubled by what Lorenzo had accomplished at Continental, one of United's biggest competitors, since both airlines had major hubs at Denver. "I think Ferris and a lot of the management welcomed the circumstances at Continental," Dubinsky said, "because it was going to be the benchmark they would try and shoot for in terms of labor costs. The rest of us clearly understood the threat that Continental posed."

THE PILOTS WEREN'T THE ONLY ones troubled by the changes at Continental in 1983. Ferris was looking closely not only at Lorenzo's Chapter 11 tactics, but also at Bob Crandall's efforts that same year to sell the new A- and B-scale wage structure to American Airlines' unions, with lower rates of pay for new employees. In both cases, Ferris saw United's two major competitors gaining a big cost advantage that he couldn't ignore.

Ferris and his team had cut United's costs through large-scale layoffs and by more efficient use of aircraft. But that wasn't enough: Once Crandall had pushed through an A- and B-scale wage structure with his unions, Ferris knew he would have to do the same. "We had to," Ferris said. "It was very simple: You can't let your major competitor find a way to a lower cost base. We had to match them." United's labor costs, amounting to about 40 percent of its revenues, were among the highest in the industry. United's pilots were earning average salaries of $85,000 to $90,000 a year; a senior 747 captain would make more than $150,000.

Ferris got a break in 1984 when the machinists agreed to a new contract that provided for a two-tier wage scale. The union, representing fourteen thousand United employees, including baggage handlers and other ground employees as well as mechanics, would get a raise for incumbent workers, but new employees' pay rates would drop dramatically. The IAM pact put even more pressure on the pilots to go along with a similar deal.

However, Crandall, with his A- and B-scale wage system already in place, was plowing the money saved into new airplanes and routes, steadily chipping away at United's market share.

"We were falling behind American and others who were very aggressive in re-equipping during that time period," one United official recalled. Ferris wanted to buy more airplanes too, but his hands were tied in making that kind of capital commitment until he was sure he could count on a more modest pilots' payroll in the future.

Rank-and-file pilots had been watching their leadership cozying up to Ferris for several years, and with management now demanding more concessions, the union membership lost confidence in its executive council. "The rank-and-file pilots revolted," Dubinsky said. "They felt betrayed, and they basically turned on the leadership, threw them out and replaced them with a new MEC."

Chaired by a pilot named Roger Hall, the new Master Executive Council took a harder line with Ferris, although not a radical one. As realists, they recognized that a two-tier wage scale was inevitable. But they wanted one that would allow B-scale employees to climb their way into the A-scale pay levels within seven years. Ferris agreed that new employees should reach parity with earlier employees—but he wanted to stretch the schedule out to twenty years. Ferris refused to negotiate a compromise, sticking to a demand that the pilots felt was unreasonable.

United's pilots went out on strike on May 17, 1985, just three weeks after Ferris had announced his plan to buy Pan Am's Pacific division. The airline's operations were shattered. Almost 90 percent of United's flights were canceled, and thousands of passengers were stranded. Ferris's advisers had assured him that even if ALPA called a strike, most United pilots would report for work, but they didn't. Even five hundred new pilots who had been in training as strike replacements defied Ferris and refused to come to work.

As their final revenge, the United pilots called in Ferris's old nemesis, Dubinsky, as their field general for the job action. He was adept at organizing and pioneered new strike tactics. He set up national teleconferences with pilots, and held strike-support meetings with pilots' families. United's executives noticed the rabid intensity with which Dubinsky directed the pilots' strike, and tagged him with the nickname "Mad Dog." Dubinsky had a personal score to settle. His ultimate goal was not just to run a successful strike, but also to bring down the chairman.

Eventually management and the pilots did come to terms, agreeing to a two-tier wage scale but leaving the duration of the B scale to be determined later. Thorny back-to-work issues complicated the already acrimonious negotiations, and the strike dragged on for nearly a month before the pilots agreed to go back into the cockpits.

FERRIS HAD A LOT MORE on his mind during the strike than just a new labor contract. After Icahn purchased his stake in TWA, speculation ran rampant about other corporate raiders turning their sights on the airlines. Even before his buying binge, Ferris knew he was sitting on top of a prime target. United's stock was considered undervalued, and the company had some prime assets that canny raiders could smell a mile away: a big fleet of jet airliners, prime downtown real estate in its Westin Hotels unit, and employee pension accounts that, in management's estimate, were overfunded by nearly a billion dollars.

In the middle of the pilots' strike, published reports hinted that UAL might be the target of Wall Street predator and Icahn acquaintance Ivan Boesky, or Hyatt Hotels billionaire-owner Jay Pritzker, or both of them working in tandem. The biggest fear of UAL's management was that someone of that ilk would buy up the company's stock, and once they had won the prize, use the excess pension funding and the proceeds from selling off a few prime hotels to pay down their acquisition debt, giving them the airline for almost nothing.

Ferris, however, was crafting a plan that would not only shield the company from outside attack, but make United into such a fearsome competitor that Crandall, for all his apparent labor peace, would not have a chance. Ferris already had one piece of his puzzle in place after the deal with Ed Acker to buy Pan Am's Pacific routes. And while his negotiators were nailing down a new contract with the pilots, his financial planners went to work on the next phase. Ferris's main adviser was Eric Gleacher, a tough, commanding investment banker from Morgan Stanley who acquaintances say was the mirror image of the United chief in personal style.

First, Ferris announced that UAL was going to sell certain hotels in the Westin chain to new real estate partnerships being created for that purpose, although Westin would retain management contracts for the hotels. Each such deal was expected to bring in several hundred million dollars in cash. A week later, UAL said it was taking $962 million from the overfunded pension plans and putting it into a trust exclusively for corporate expansion. Management also won shareholder authorization to increase the amount of UAL common stock from 50 million to 125 million shares, if it deemed such new issues necessary to fight takeover attempts.

With the cash generated by these plans, and the savings from the new pilots' contract being ironed out, Ferris began his shopping spree. He paid a call on his old friend Frank Olson, chairman of Hertz Corporation, who set up a meeting between Ferris and Thornton Bradshaw, chairman of Hertz's parent company, RCA. Ferris knew RCA had been thinking about shedding Hertz for some time, and since he was so eager to add it to UAL, there was little haggling. "It was pretty straightforward," Ferris recalled. "We wanted to buy, he decided he wanted to sell." They settled on a price of $587 million, and Ferris asked Olson to stay on as Hertz chairman.

Bob Crandall did a double-take when he learned of UAL's plan to purchase Hertz. Within a matter of weeks, his own financial advisers were sniffing around the edges of the nation's number-two rental car operation. American looked "very carefully" at Avis, Crandall said, but decided against making a bid. Crandall said he thought that Ferris was making a big mistake in trying to amass his travel empire. Both American and Pan Am had sold off hotel chains years earlier to concentrate on their airline operations, and the conventional wisdom was simply against Ferris.

But now, Ferris had his hands around the nation's biggest airline, a chain of fifty-four deluxe Westin hotels, and the world's largest car rental company. He was betting that by packaging the three businesses, United could offer business customers an attractive proposition: One-stop shopping for all their travel needs, all linked by the company's state-of-the-art reservations and pricing computers. If United Airlines could use its size—its frequent-flyer program, hub dominance, computer reservations system deployment, and so on— to its advantage, why not apply the same concept to the overall travel market, especially the higher-paying business travelers who would be frequent buyers of Hertz rentals and deluxe hotel rooms?

His basic concept, Ferris said, was to create something that would make United, by virtue of the combination with its partners, superior to other airlines in the eyes of the customer, and to achieve the same for Hertz and Westin in their business spheres. "It's very hard to differentiate your product in the airline business," Ferris noted, since all offered basically the same thing: "In the airline business, everybody's got a silver tube," and competitors rarely allow one another to maintain a pricing advantage.

Some of Ferris's own lieutenants and a few board members, including UAL corporate treasurer John Cowan, had initially suggested that Ferris buy a company that was not travel-related, as a hedge against downturns in the business cycle. During recessions, when airline traffic falls off, so do car rentals and hotel stays; the three are inextricably linked to the ups and downs of the economy.

Ferris, however, ever the convincing pitchman, made the concept sound so good to his directors that they readily gave their assent to his purchases and his concept. Some of them would have preferred more detail. "Dick was a very broad thinker," said one board source. As for the specific details of implementing his strategy, "those were things Dick considered to be 'execution' issues that would work themselves out one way or another. He would leave that to the operating segment of the business."

THE PILOTS' 1985 STRIKE COST United tens of millions of dollars in lost revenue and devastated the airline's bottom line that year. Even after it was settled, a lingering bitterness remained between ALPA and United's management that manifested itself in a wave of poststrike litigation.

In the fall of 1985, United finally followed through on its overdue plans for fleet renewal, placing a massive order with Boeing for up to 116 new jet aircraft, including 747s to replace the aging Pan Am planes on the Pacific, and 737s for domestic routes. Ferris's corporate buying spree continued. At the end of 1986, he went after Hilton International, whose eighty-eight hotels were scattered around the globe, nicely complementing Westin's North American presence. Hilton's parent, Trans World Corporation, which had spun off TWA in 1984, was again the target of a takeover threat in 1986 and decided to sell off various units. After a deal to sell Hilton International to Dutch airline KLM fell through, Ferris was waiting in the wings with $980 million in cash, debentures, and UAL stock. Hilton International was his. The empire was now complete. The total price tag was more than $3 billion. All it needed was a new name.

LATE IN 1986, IT WAS time for United's pilots to cast their votes once again for the leaders who would sit on their Master Executive Council.

Roger Hall, who had chaired the union through its bitter strike, was stepping down, and the pilots chose a new MEC chairman—someone who had earned their respect through the leadership he demonstrated in orchestrating the strike; someone who they knew would have the nerve to stand up to the ever-more-powerful Ferris. They elected Mad Dog Dubinsky.

From Ferris's point of view, they couldn't have made a more unpalatable choice. During the pilots' strike, "Dubinsky made Ferris the enemy, the individual who was trying to create a B scale, the fellow who was buying other businesses instead of new aircraft, which would have given everybody [in the union] a chance to move up into the left seat [that is, be promoted to full captain and earn top wages]," said UAL board member Frank Olson. "Ferris went from being the most loved airline chief executive to the most hated, all because of these union activities. It's the same tactic the machinists used against Borman," he noted. "They didn't focus on Eastern as a company, they focused on Frank Borman. It's easy to dislike a person; it's hard to dislike the company you work for."

When Dubinsky took over the chairmanship of the United pilots union in December, Roger Hall turned over to him a batch of documents related to union business. Among them was a thick file labeled "ESOP."

Dubinsky was stunned. He sat quietly as Hall explained that during the late summer of 1985, he and two other leaders of the MEC had secretly put together the groundwork for an Employee Stock Ownership Plan by which they intended to buy the airline. The general scheme was to finance such a deal with pension funds, union concessions, and borrowed money. When the other two unions at United showed no interest in participating, however, Hall had put the idea on the shelf. Dubinsky, remembering how eight years earlier Ferris had dismissed out of hand any prospect of employee equity, was deeply interested.

The new pilots' chairman made no secret of the fact that he didn't trust Ferris, and his skepticism grew as he watched the UAL chairman's corporate buying spree. "By mid-January of '87," Dubinsky said, "I had concluded that we were in a fight to the death with this guy: It was either him or us, and we had to do something to take him out."

At that point, Dubinsky placed a phone call to another pilot, who was married to a United flight attendant. But this pilot wasn't an employee of the airline: he flew his own plane on business. His name was F. Lee Bailey.

Dubinsky had retained the famous lawyer as counsel during the strike. Bailey had experience representing the striking air traffic controllers who had been fired by Reagan. Dubinsky remembered that during one of the pilots' teleconferences, Bailey had suggested that "the best way to prevent these things from happening ever again was for the employees in the industry to pool their money and take over these companies." The concept had already been set into motion by ALPA, and Dubinsky was determined to see it through.

Dubinsky sensed an ominous parallel between Ferris's expansion and Frank Lorenzo's actions at Texas Air and Continental. He asked ALPA headquarters in Washington to conduct an analysis of what tends to happen when airlines form holding company structures and diversify. The union concluded that the airline becomes a cash cow, Dubinsky said. "They attach all these parasites to it, they suck it dry and leave an empty shell with a whole bunch of debt. . . . And that's what he was doing: The airline was feeding obscene amounts of cash into these other businesses."

Just as Lorenzo had done at Texas Air, Ferris was also separating certain divisions, such as fuel purchasing and the computer reservations system, from the airline into independent subsidiaries of the holding company. These divisions were servicing the airline on a cost-plus basis, above what the airline had been charging itself. Unions alleged that this practice just meant more cash flowing out of the airline and into the holding company. The airline, in effect, had to buy its own services back.

In January 1987, Dubinsky and F. Lee Bailey started planning an ESOP for United. Bailey located a potential takeover ally for the pilots in T. Boone Pickens, whose investment group proposed a hostile takeover of the entire corporation, to be followed by the sale of the airline unit to the pilots. But the pilots, fearful of legal repercussions and worried that Pickens's true motive might be greenmail, shied away from this partnership. Instead, at the urging of the national ALPA leadership, they hired Lazard Freres to help them plot a friendly takeover plan.

Ferris, meanwhile, met with financial analysts in late February 1987, spelling out his vision for a huge travel conglomerate with all the segments fueling each other's growth through marketing synergies. Wall Street's reaction was less than enthusiastic. In the days following his briefings, Ferris watched UAL's share price drop three dollars.

The analysts who responded to Ferris's plans by suggesting the sell-off of UAL shares may not have been motivated strictly by economic considerations. Many of them simply didn't like Ferris. Indeed, Ferris had had a running battle with the analysts for years. While other airline CEOs recognized the political necessity of periodically traveling to New York's investment houses, Ferris had steadfastly resisted such pilgrimages. Instead, he would send an underling or no one at all. The analysts' meeting he addressed in February 1987 was said to be the first one ever sponsored by UAL.

The following month, word leaked out that real estate mogul Donald Trump had quietly bought up almost 5 percent of UAL's stock. Ferris's response was to use the authority he had obtained earlier from his stockholders to issue another five million shares, diluting the value of Trump's stake.

News of Trump's buying set Wall Street abuzz with rumors of a UAL takeover, and the stock price started to rise. Dubinsky and his advisers, seeing the cost of their own takeover plan getting bigger by the day, rushed to put the final touches on the pilots' bid for the airline, which was announced in the first week of April. UAL was definitely in play.

Trump's intentions were unclear, but the publicity-hungry New Yorker didn't hesitate to sound off about how UAL should be run. Trump took a swipe at the new corporate name, for instance, telling reporters he thought Allegis sounded like a "world-class disease." But Trump's interest combined with the pilots' buyout plan boosted the price of Allegis shares in just a few days from fifty-seven to seventy-one dollars. Trump cashed in shortly thereafter and walked off with profits in the tens of millions.

The pace of events quickened that spring. The financial press jumped on the possibility of a UAL takeover in the weeks before the April shareholders' meeting, pondering the significance of every little move. When Donald Trump lunched at Manhattan's Côte Basque restaurant with Felix Rohatyn, managing director of the pilots' financial advisers, Lazard Freres, it set off more frenzied speculation.

Questions arose about whether the pilots' plan would pile too much debt on United—that is, if banks would even lend them the money. The doubts intensified when the International Association of Machinists at United declined to join the pilots' proposed union buyout. Instead, the IAM proposed its own plan, for the parent company to spin off part of its nonairline assets, giving the machinists partial equity in the airline in exchange for employee wage concessions. This plan also went nowhere.

While Ferris had been busy building his empire, the company's core airline business had lost more than $80 million in 1985 and again in 1986. And the outlook for 1987 was no brighter, thanks in large part to Lorenzo's new MaxSaver discount fares. In mid-April, rumors circulated that Ferris's job was in peril and that some of his outside directors had lost confidence in him.

When the rumors ended up on the front page of *The Wall Street Journal*, Charles F. Luce, the retired chairman of New York power company Consolidated Edison and UAL's senior outside director, struck back. In a letter to the editor, Luce said he was "appalled at the inaccuracies and anti-management bias" in the *Journal* article and insisted that the UAL board was "four-square behind Mr. Ferris, his management team and his long-range strategy." It was true, he conceded, that directors were disappointed in the airline's earnings, but he blamed the low earnings on "fare wars begun by non-union competitors," not on mismanagement.

Four days later, the board rejected the pilots' buyout proposal. Ferris had reason to feel more confident than he had in a while when he faced the shareholders at the end of April and won their approval for the new Allegis name. To further reassure Ferris and his team about the persistent takeover threats, the board had also granted them golden parachutes. If Ferris were to lose his job without cause or due to a change in control, he would be guaranteed his current salary for the next five years. In 1986, Ferris's compensation totaled nearly $580,000.

However, at the same time Ferris was extolling the Allegis concept to his shareholders in Manhattan on April 30, Dubinsky was a few blocks away, meeting with Chicago billionaire Jay Pritzker. The pilots wanted someone like Pritzker to acquire the entire Allegis corporation, after which the partner would sell them the airline portion and do what he wanted with the rest. The pilots had even lined up a potential buyer for Hilton International. But the deal with Pritzker fell apart over a disagreement on the terms of a partnership.

Then in late May the most serious threat to date emerged. A New York investment firm called Coniston Partners revealed that it had accumulated 13 percent of Allegis's outstanding shares, and said in an SEC filing that it planned to seek the consent of other shareholders to replace the existing board and totally restructure the corporation, splitting it up and selling off the pieces. Coniston also filed a lawsuit in Delaware, asking the court to declare illegal a special financing deal Ferris had arranged with his friends at Boeing by which the manufacturer could have controlled up to 16 percent of Allegis's common stock. Coniston argued the transaction was merely a ruse designed to entrench the current management and what Coniston saw as its faulty business strategy. Now Ferris had good reason to worry.

"Trump was never a serious player," recalled Hertz Corporation chairman Olson. "Trump's name in '87 was strong in the market, and there was plenty of money around for anybody to buy stock and then make announcements, run up the stock, and sell out. But Coniston had investors that were serious, and they easily could have raised the money. The question was, what would the pilots do? And remember, back then we had lost most of our institutional investors because the arbs started to buy the stock."

As arbitragers moved in on Allegis, Ferris and his advisers became alarmed. "I think at one point, the estimate was that more than 50 percent of our stock was held by arbs," Ferris recalled. "And you knew they were going to sell their mother for an eighth of a point. There wasn't any long-term shareholder value in their minds—it was a question of 'What can I get right now?' "

Ferris considered his alternatives. In order to save his hard-won travel empire, he had to give the increasingly impatient shareholders some kind of immediate return; failing that, he could swallow his pride and try to cut a deal with the pilots, to forestall them from forming an alliance with the takeover crowd. At this point, employee equity was becoming a more acceptable alternative to Ferris.

Coniston had moved in when the stock was in the seventy-dollar range; most analysts put the break-up value of the company at somewhere between $120 and $150 per share. The low market value of the stock was largely a reflection of the disappointing airline earnings record as a result of the continuing fare wars in the industry.

Ferris convinced the board that they should placate shareholders with a special one-time dividend of sixty dollars a share. The Allegis buying spree and the aircraft order had depleted the corporation's resources and line of credit; to finance the payout, the company would have to borrow $3 billion, which would more than double Allegis's long-term debt. And it was unlikely that enough banks wanted to lend it.

Then Dubinsky and his pilots suddenly came up with a new offer to buy an 80 percent stake in United for $5 billion, with shareholders getting a dividend of seventy dollars a share. The pilots threatened to team up with Coniston if the board rejected their offer. All this activity led to a rush of buy orders on Wall Street, pushing Allegis's stock price up to $90.

● ● ●

IN THE FIRST WEEK OF JUNE, Ferris picked up the phone, gritted his teeth, and dialed Mad Dog Dubinsky's number. The board of directors was going to meet in New York the following week to decide what to do with the company. Ferris traveled to Ohio, where Dubinsky lived, for a weekend meeting. The two then flew together in a Lear jet to New York for consultations with their investment bankers. Ferris was at the controls, and at one point he even asked Dubinsky to try his hand at steering the little jet. But the brief show of friendliness went nowhere. The two could not agree on how much of the airline should be owned by employees and their unions, and how much by management. They also disagreed on whether Allegis should be broken up or somehow kept together.

Dubinsky claims Ferris backed away from a tentative joint ownership deal they had discussed. "I wouldn't trust him as far as I could throw him," Dubinsky said of his old boss. "He's a sideshow barker."

"I had nothing against an employee-owned airline," Ferris said, "as long as it was an airline owned by all the employees so there would be equal representation. The pilots wanted inordinate control, in my opinion."

Ferris had little to offer to save Allegis immediately. It might be possible to finance the special dividend, but it was becoming more obvious that whatever strategy prevailed, some of the company's recently purchased nonairline subsidiaries might have to be sold. "I think Dick had reached that conclusion in the end," said Frank Olson. "As difficult as it was for him to swallow, I think he would have. But I don't think it got to the point where he had a chance to."

A FULL BOARD MEETING WAS called for June 9. While Ferris and Dubinsky had been holding their futile talks, another small gathering had been taking place in New York. The outside directors had assembled to talk about the desperate Allegis situation on their own, away from the persuasive Ferris and his executive allies on the board. Leading this secret meeting was none other than the author of that stern rebuttal to *The Wall Street Journal* just six weeks earlier, Charles F. Luce.

Before the board convened, Frank Olson—who, as the chairman of Allegis's Hertz subsidiary, was an inside director and thus not at the secret meeting—was visited by Luce, who told him about the outside directors' session.

"Chuck came to me and told me the board [that is, the outside directors, who held a majority] had decided to remove Dick, and asked me to take his place," Olson remembered. "I told him I thought that was a mistake. I said I thought Dick was being unfairly judged here, and that he could accept the sale of nonairline assets. As a matter of fact, Dick and I had talked about it." After Luce left, Olson picked up the phone and tried to persuade some of the other outside directors to keep Ferris. But the next day, Luce told him that nothing had changed, and asked again if Olson would take on the chairmanship.

Olson tried to beg off, saying that he would prefer not to; Ferris was his friend, and he didn't want to do that to him. Moreover, Olson didn't want to leave his own company, Hertz.

But Luce was unmoved. "He told me they were going to sell Hertz, and that I would be in a better position to protect my own company if I did this than if I didn't do it," Olson said. "And he said that if I didn't take the job, they were going to appoint one of the other directors to it—one of the outside directors."

Olson reluctantly agreed to replace Ferris as the new chairman of Allegis. Just before the directors convened their meeting in the Morgan Stanley boardroom, Olson went up to Ferris, who had sensed something was up. "I think the board's going to ask for your resignation," Olson told him, explaining the scenario that Luce had spelled out for him.

A minute later, Luce came up and asked Ferris and the other inside directors to wait outside for a while. Soon a small group of the outside directors emerged, came up to Ferris, and said they wanted his resignation. Ferris returned to his hotel, where his wife and youngest son were waiting. He picked them up, flew back to Chicago, "and that was it," he remembered. "I didn't even go back to the office; the staff emptied everything out."

To keep United Airlines whole, the board proceeded with a decision to sell Hertz, Westin, and Hilton International and share the proceeds with stockholders. Olson, as he had planned, stayed with Hertz and resigned the holding company's chairmanship after a brief interim period. The following year, the board belatedly dropped the corporation's useless Allegis name and changed it back to UAL. United Airlines was on its own once again.

Dick Ferris had been thirty-eight years old when he became president of United. He was fifty when he left UAL/Allegis. Ferris later admitted that he should have taken the possibility of a takeover more seriously. "We had a raider's dream," he said later. "Perhaps in another decade it would have worked."

Even without airline deregulation, Ferris said later, "I think in time there would have been an Allegis strategy. Whether it would have come as soon, I don't know." Certainly the tenor of the times on Wall Street—the mad dash to acquire, to merge—helped Allegis along as Ferris and Morgan Stanley assembled its pieces.

But the brevity of Allegis's life could be attributed not only to the greed of the arbitragers, but also to deregulation: If Frank Lorenzo's Texas Air had not plunged the industry into a round of costly fare wars with his MaxSaver discounts, United's earnings might have been healthier and UAL's share price might never have dropped enough to attract the quick-buck artists in the first place.

When it was all over, Ferris said, his son put forward his own theory about why his father's global travel empire had collapsed: "He said, 'Dad, the reason they busted it all up was that it had a terrible name.' "

JUST MONTHS AFTER FERRIS'S SACKING by the UAL board, Ed Acker was in similar straits. Pan Am's fortunes had soured since Acker had sold Ferris the Pacific routes two years earlier. The causes could not have been foreseen, but Ferris's coup was, in hindsight, Acker's worst mistake.

Acker had planned to use the proceeds from the Pacific sale to build up Pan Am's presence on the transatlantic routes to Europe and the Soviet Union. But like TWA, Pan Am was badly hurt by the effects of a wave of terrorist attacks on transatlantic travel. Pan Am lost nearly $463 million in 1986 and when it hemorrhaged another $94 million in the first quarter of 1987, Acker came under increasing pressure. A loose coalition of unhappy shareholders began to agitate for a voice in running the company, and the unions joined the growing chorus. That February the Pan Am unions—which were organized under a single labor council—declared their intention to look for another airline to buy Pan Am and pledged to give such a buyer a cost-saving package from labor as an enticement.

Acker and his team also searched for someone who could put some serious cash into Pan Am, in exchange for partial or total equity. Some prospective saviors even met separately with management and with the labor leaders as this odd parallel pursuit of wealthy investors continued. Even though both sides were pursuing the same goal, the unions' council—which at the time had come strongly under the sway of William Genoese, the head of Pan Am's large and powerful Teamsters Union—would have no part of a joint effort with Acker's management and its banker, Drexel Burnham.

A series of suitors made their way to Drexel or to the Pan Am building to look over the merchandise. They included British financier Sir James Goldsmith, MGM magnate Kirk Kerkorian, Hyatt Hotels and Braniff owner Jay Pritzker, and a little-known but publicity-hungry investment outfit called Towers Financial, run by Steve Hoffenberg, who later gained notoriety in a failed bid for the *New York Post*.

Kerkorian emerged as a strong possibility, according to Acker, especially after he met with both management and the labor side. However, the discussions collapsed when it became clear that Kerkorian was not ready to make a proposal for attacking the airline's daunting problems.

Eventually, Braniff owner Jay Pritzker emerged as the clear front-runner among the potential suitors. The Pan Am unions tentatively agreed to work out a program of wage concessions with him, and he moved ahead with a formal plan to acquire Pan Am. In December, the plan fizzled almost as fast as it had burst forth: Pritzker would not go ahead unless he could get a fantastic $800 million in concessions from the workers.

The unions had failed to come to terms with Pritzker. But they could claim one victory that December: They got Acker's head.

Labor leaders told the Pan Am board that they refused to negotiate with Acker or his representatives. "The unions, particularly the Teamsters, absolutely hated Acker, and were constantly running diatribes against him in their own publications," one Pan Am board member recalled. "At the very end, the board didn't think that Acker was giving them the straight dope on what he had been negotiating with the various unions. Morale and labor relations were a terrible problem in the company at the time."

At a meeting around Christmas, Pan Am's directors concluded that Acker could no longer lead the company. The continuing losses were causing alarm among shareholders, and the impasse that had developed between management and labor was just too intractable.

Acker, like Ferris, had been given a strong shove out the door by labor and shareholders. While United would reap the benefits of the sale of choice assets bought by Dick Ferris, Pan Am could not sell any of its assets without seriously crippling its core business. It had long ago sold off its Pan Am Building and hotels—although Acker did add one valuable piece, an East Coast shuttle. Now it would have to dismantle more of the golden route networks Trippe had built up around the world.

16

THE
RELUCTANT
FLYBOYS

It was not Carl Icahn who took over TWA, but TWA that took over Icahn.
—NEWSWEEK

By early 1988, Carl Icahn claimed he had turned TWA around financially. He was hailed in the business press as the savior of a treasured airline, and article after article described him as the "new" Icahn, the greenmailer turned manager who had proven corporate streamlining could work.

But this picture was false. The "recovery" was largely an illusion, the result of a confluence of unusual events. TWA's profits were fueled by its labor concessions, many of which were scheduled to "snap back" to their previous levels. TWA also reaped an unexpected windfall, the $50 million settlement of a decades-old lawsuit the airline had brought against Howard Hughes for failing his fiduciary duty by refusing to buy new jets. Strangely, Icahn would repeat Hughes's mistakes, leaving TWA with the oldest fleet in the industry.

That Icahn would not only relive the Hughes days but be rewarded for them was just one of the ironies that characterized the airlines as they moved into the next phase of the deregulation wars. TWA and Eastern had traditionally been the worst-managed of the Big Four, having to pay for the whims of their owners. Now, with Icahn at TWA and Frank Lorenzo at the head of Eastern, the pattern was being repeated at both companies.

For a while, Icahn had been content to leave TWA's operations to his professional managers. Instead of managing the airline, he was using it as a vehicle for hostile raids on other companies, such as USX and Texaco. But by the summer of 1988, his executives started to worry as Icahn turned all his attention to the airline during a break from his Wall Street activities.

He had never learned the peculiarities of the airline business, such arcane matters as the techniques of yield management and the psychological importance of fleet modernization to the flying public at a time of growing concern about the safety of aging aircraft. Instead, Icahn's renewed interest in running his airline expressed itself in a new round of penny-pinching. He tended to disbelieve the data TWA's number-crunchers showed him, if it was at odds with his own perception of how things were going. And he often shrugged off advice from senior officers.

Icahn did express some interest in management philosophy, and he referred to a book on Japanese management that he had picked up. His staff claimed, however, that he had read only half the book. Icahn started holding what he called "Japanese-style meetings," assembling forty managers at a time for what Sandy Rederer described as a "painful" attempt to bring Icahn's loose management style into focus.

One person who began to appear more often in TWA's offices around this time was Shelly Kravitz, a rotund advertising man from New York who was advising Icahn. Kravitz was an old friend of Icahn's and also acted as Icahn's bookie, placing bets on football, basketball, and other sporting events, an activity that neither tried to hide from the rest of the TWA management team. Icahn and Kravitz often enlivened staff meetings at TWA with discussions of the previous night's wagers. Icahn took his gambling seriously, and one executive remembered hearing him yell more than once at Kravitz: "Goddamnit, I lost forty thousand dollars last night because of you!" Kravitz's growing role at TWA cast further doubt on Icahn's judgment.

Several of Icahn's top executives discovered an unsavory episode in Kravitz's past—something that would bar him from an officer-level job at TWA or any other airline. Years before, Kravitz had been a criminal trial lawyer in New York City. On November 16, 1963, he was disbarred.

After Kravitz's exit from the legal trade, he went into advertising, working for a succession of small and mid-sized agencies. He won a reputation for battling what he called the "creative types," in favor of a meat-axe approach to getting the job done as cheaply as possible.

Icahn called on him to secure a reduction in billings from Young & Rubicam, the nation's largest ad agency, which had handled the TWA account for years.

A profile in *Adweek* referred to Kravitz as "the advertising account guy from hell," a description he seemed to take to heart. He convinced Icahn that Young & Rubicam was wasting his money, and they themselves should take charge of producing TWA's television commercials. Kravitz argued that there was no reason network television commercials for TWA—which normally involved production costs in the $100,000 to $200,000 range—couldn't be produced for a mere ten thousand dollars. Why shoot all that expensive color? Kravitz asked.

His low-budget black-and-white commercials soon became the laughingstock of the advertising world. The dickering over production costs even came down to such essentials as the soundtrack. At one lengthy meeting, Icahn and Kravitz got increasingly huffy, demanding to know if the commercials' cost couldn't be reduced by eliminating the accompanying musical track. A witness remembers thinking, "Here they were—ready to launch a six-million-dollar ad campaign, and they didn't want to spend two thousand dollars to put in the sound!" Y&R later took the unprecedented step of resigning the TWA account when Icahn demanded they reduce their agency fee from $6 million to $4 million for handling the airline's $45 million account.

Icahn's constant fretting over costs was only the most obvious manifestation of a darker side of his psyche. He had apparently become convinced not only that employees were overspending but that they were literally stealing from the company. As head pilot Kent Scott put it: "He had a rather broad definition of stealing. He thinks sick leave is stealing."

Icahn hired a large staff of internal auditors to peruse purchases and expense reports searching for surreptitious employee ripoffs of company funds. In mid-1988, Icahn moved TWA's headquarters to Mt. Kisco, a suburb an hour north of the city, to an office complex a few miles from his home.

Soon TWA employees started noticing the presence of several people whom Icahn apparently had asked to "investigate" alleged theft and fraud. One day, Mort Ehrlich was sitting in his office when an Icahn crony paid him an unannounced visit.

The talk turned to the free travel that Ehrlich, as head of TWA's sizable sales force, was authorized to dispense to top-producing travel agents or other valuable business contacts whom he wanted to indulge. Ehrlich's own salespeople also had considerable discretion to upgrade certain passengers to a higher class of service. These were the basic tools of the airline trade, used by all carriers to stroke their most valued customers and distributors. But Icahn's investigator alleged that such practices amounted to theft of TWA property.

Ehrlich, a respected veteran executive in the airline industry, was stunned that Icahn's ignorance of the business would lead to such a bizarre conclusion. "Get the hell out of here!" he yelled at his tormentor. "And tell Carl I don't want to see you in my office again."

Icahn's obsession with saving money had impaired his ability to make the kind of major spending decisions that running an airline like TWA required. He spent time dithering over such picayune matters as the cost of hotel accommodations for flight crews during their layovers, in one instance ordering flight attendants to vacate a hotel on Miami Beach and move to a cheaper motel inland.

Meanwhile, TWA's long-term prospects remained uncertain. At a packed luncheon of the New York Society of Security Analysts on Wall Street in May 1988, Icahn told the assembled brokerage executives that he was going to either sell the airline or try to buy another one to merge with TWA. "We're going to see more consolidation in the airline industry," he said, giving many the impression that he was eager to advance that process. This sort of talk was an elixir to the crowd, many of whom stood to rake in hefty fees for brokering just such a deal.

Icahn was at it again, hinting at a buyout. He apparently enjoyed it so much that he began regularly making such statements, in magazine interviews, at financial institutions, and in speeches. His loose talk not only damaged employee morale; in the minds of some senior executives, it also scared off many of the airline's best customers— the high-fare-paying business travelers, who were notoriously squeamish about booking seats on an airline with an uncertain future.

The wave of airline mergers and acquisitions had peaked the year after Icahn bought TWA and Ozark. Now, he wanted to stir up the pot again—to make that final, ultimate deal that would determine which airlines would be on top when the bloodbath was over.

While Icahn kept everyone guessing about the airline's future, the looming problem of aging aircraft was still being ignored at TWA. By 1988, this had become a major public concern after metal fatigue contributed to two highly publicized aircraft accidents. Even though other airlines were acquiring the best new airplanes available, TWA's geriatric fleet was becoming an embarrassment.

Since his takeover two and a half years earlier, Icahn had demonstrated little interest in aircraft, except for his habit of giving model

747s as gifts to retiring executives or friends. He had trouble dealing with real ones, however, because of the giant prices they commanded. Icahn tried to claim that he had fulfilled his pledge to the pilots to buy "new" planes when he acquired Ozark and its fleet of fifty planes. That was not what the pilots had in mind. If TWA didn't enter the next decade with the fuel-efficient, state-of-the-art jets that American, Delta, and other stronger lines were flying, it could be doomed.

The unpalatable task of persuading Icahn to make a very costly purchase, one he would not immediately be able to turn around and sell at a profit, fell to Joe Corr, the tall, imposing midwesterner brought in by Icahn as TWA's new president. Corr was not an airline industry insider, but unlike his new boss, he had managed a large company—the ACF rail-car company that Icahn had acquired in 1984.

Like other airline executives before him, Corr started taking flying lessons. Icahn was ultimately to regret hiring Corr, who succumbed to the airline mystique that Icahn so abhorred.

Icahn disdained Corr's efforts to sell him on the latest equipment. Corr had been persuaded by the pilots' arguments that TWA couldn't fly its way to success without better airplanes, but Icahn would not listen. "Show me the numbers," he would say.

Corr set out on his big-ticket shopping trips with relish, dashing around the country to meet the heads of major manufacturers—men like Sandy McDonnell at McDonnell Douglas in his old hometown of St. Louis and Jean Pierson of Airbus Industrie, the big European aircraft consortium that was treading on the U.S. manufacturers' turf. This was heady stuff for someone accustomed to poking around midwestern rail yards. The airplane makers were consummate salesmen and expert at wining and dining potential customers—not surprising in a business where even the smaller products cost more than $25 million apiece. An airline executive with a checkbook was often invited to spend a weekend at a chateau in France or golfing at a castle in Ireland.

In August 1988, Corr was confident that an agreement was near. On one of his cross-country trips to nail down a deal, he stopped at an airport pay phone to call a reporter who'd been following the story. "I think we're really getting close," he said excitedly.

He was looking at an order for sixty single-aisle jets, including firm orders for at least twenty and options on the rest. (Manufacturers always allow airlines to hedge on their total orders until specified future dates, when they must decide whether to turn optional orders into firm ones.) Corr worried about Icahn's reaction to the $1 billion price tag of his shopping spree, but he thought the chairman would approve, especially since manufacturers usually gave buyers a long time to pay.

But Corr was wrong. Icahn had become distracted by the prospect of yet another deal.

THE NEW DEAL WAS A merger with Eastern, a marriage that would unite the two weak sisters of the old Big Four. Two of Icahn's most trusted executives at the time, Sandy Rederer and Mort Ehrlich (himself an Eastern alumnus), were excited about the prospect. TWA's route map had the cream of the European capitals, profitable transcontinental service, and an east-west route network funneled through St. Louis. Eastern's routes showed virtually no overlap with TWA's, since they were mainly north-south in the eastern half of the country and continued south into the Caribbean and Latin America.

"This could be a world-class airline—what with their size and their routes, we'd be in a league with American and United," Rederer told Icahn. This optimism typified the unreality of the planning behind the airline mergers of the eighties. Combining the unionized workforces of TWA and Eastern would be a horrendous job, worse even than the Pan Am and National debacle earlier in the decade. Just attempting to merge the seniority lists of TWA's and Eastern's pilots would be a nightmare. Moreover, Eastern had lost almost $650 million from 1986 through 1988. Still, it was worth trying to bring Icahn and Lorenzo together to discuss it, Rederer thought.

Lorenzo and Icahn were both at a point where they might negotiate, not because of the practicality of the deal but because they were both growing more disillusioned with the constant aggravations of the airline business. Lorenzo was eager to remove the thorn in his side that Eastern had become, and Icahn almost reflexively jumped at any chance to make a deal.

Icahn was anxious to get back the cash he had put into TWA when he bought his majority stake. During 1988, in fact, he was putting the final touches on a plan to take the company private in such a way as to win back all of his original $486 million investment.

As developments continued to unfold, a grand scheme began to take shape: If Icahn could pick up Eastern at a good price, maybe he could turn around and unload both TWA and Eastern. Joe Corr had already launched an attempt to buy the airline along with McDonnell Douglas, which had hoped to get TWA as a customer for its new planes. Let them suffer through the firestorm of labor problems that would surely follow any merger, Icahn surely thought.

So it happened that Icahn and Lorenzo began talking again—by phone at first, and always tentatively.

One day that summer, Lorenzo traveled to Mount Kisco, where he and Icahn had a private chat over dinner at a modest Italian restaurant. No deal was struck that night, but they agreed to have dinner again. Lorenzo came to call a few more times, but they couldn't make any solid progress beyond stating their mutual desire to sell their companies.

The stewardship of Lorenzo and Icahn at two of the country's oldest and largest airlines all but guaranteed those companies' continued decline. The two men paid little attention to service, which was closely tied to employee morale. To doomsayers, this appeared to confirm the dangers of opening up the airlines to competition, although to Alfred Kahn and other deregulators, that was part of the "painful" process of adjusting to a free market.

On September 7, 1988, TWA shareholders met for the last time at the Grand Hyatt Hotel in Manhattan. Icahn had convened the special meeting to vote on his plan to take the company private. TWA pilots had converged from all over the country to attend, buttonholing anyone who crossed their paths with a plea to stop Icahn. The pilots claimed that Icahn was looting TWA for his own personal gain by loading the airline with debt so he could get his initial investment out. They planned to file a lawsuit against him that very day, charging Icahn with violating their 1985 agreement that had effectively handed Icahn the company.

But the shareholders, predictably, had already indicated their approval of the plan, for it would give them more money for their shares than they could ever get on the market. Icahn himself would get $469 million for his own shares, winning back nearly all the cash he originally invested—and even better, gaining control of 90 percent of the company. He also gave himself preferred shares that would be worth $415 million five years hence.

To do that, he would leave TWA burdened with $2.8 billion in debt, with an annual interest payout of $466 million. The airline even admitted in a filing with the Securities and Exchange Commission that it was unlikely TWA's cash flow could ever cover its debt payments. And even though Icahn liked to point out that the airline had $1.3 billion in cash and marketable securities, unions were worried about what would happen to that money, since most of it was in the form of USX and Texaco stock.

A few minutes before 11:00 A.M., Icahn strode onto the podium.

TWA captain Thomas Ashwood jumped up and handed him the court papers. Icahn feigned surprise—"What's this?" he said, laughing. He had been expecting the summons and brushed it off as a mere irritant.

Later, the dispirited pilots held a news conference and almost no reporters showed up. Their battle was lost. Icahn had taken TWA private, and now was legally accountable to no one but himself. He no longer had to make any public filings with government authorities; he didn't even have to report TWA's financial results to anyone if he chose not to. "That day, TWA ceased to exist," said pilots' leader Kent Scott.

During September Icahn continued his merger talks with Lorenzo, and it appeared that the two notorious hagglers might finally be getting close to a deal. They were getting down to numbers by then and had made a tentative pact calling for Icahn to buy Eastern for $350 million if Lorenzo threw in System One, Texas Air's computer reservations system. But there were still several bones of contention.

In a manner reminiscent of their previous dickering over TWA in 1985, the two got bogged down in details that were minor given the overall size of the proposed deal. Finally, recalled Sandy Rederer, "It fell apart over price . . . a couple of items that Lorenzo wanted Icahn to pay for. They were really small items, given the fact that with all the debt and assets involved, we were really looking at a multibillion-dollar transaction."

Icahn tried talking to Lorenzo's nemesis, Charlie Bryan. He invited the truculent machinists' leader to be his houseguest at Foxfield the weekend of October 15. A claque of lawyers, labor advisers, and TWA managers arrived late Friday night, and the often spirited talks continued late into the following night. Almost all the union people in attendance went away with the impression that they had something resembling a deal with Icahn, having agreed to make more wage concessions in return for ousting Lorenzo from Eastern.

On Monday, October 17, Icahn put out an announcement: He no longer wanted to buy Eastern. (Lorenzo had already announced the sale of the prized Eastern Shuttle to Donald Trump for an inflated $365 million, but that would have been scrapped if a deal were struck with Icahn.) Those who had been at Icahn's home over the weekend were shocked. "We were screwed," said one labor leader. "Icahn was just using us."

Joe Corr, too, had been feeling used. A contract for the long-awaited purchase of new jets had been sitting unsigned on Icahn's desk for months. Icahn barely talked to him anymore.

Mort Ehrlich had quit soon after the going-private plan was approved, and he stood to reap a nice sum from the sale of his own TWA stock. Other executives, seeing no future for the company, were tempted to follow Ehrlich out the door. Corr was tired of fighting with Icahn.

One day in mid-November 1988, Icahn sat down with his top managers in TWA's conference room for their regular meeting. The meeting quickly degenerated into a shouting match between Icahn and Corr. "They were yelling so loudly that people could hear them all the way down the hall," said an executive present at the session. Icahn, it seemed, was displeased with the latest monthly financial results that showed TWA trailing behind industry basket case Pan Am. TWA couldn't afford to buy any new planes, he told Corr.

Corr was soon gone from the company.

Icahn continued to defend his refusal to buy jets. Indeed, his competitors had a lot of empty seats on their hands when the recession caused a massive falloff in traffic a year later. But Corr and his allies claimed that their aim was not to expand TWA's fleet but to replace the older fuel-guzzling models with more efficient aircraft. They presented Icahn with figures showing that each new jet could save the company up to $1 million annually by lowering operating and maintenance costs. Icahn responded that the airline just did not have the money to purchase the planes.

On December 15, Corr accepted an offer from Frank Lorenzo to become chairman and CEO of Continental Airlines in Houston.

BY THEN, LORENZO'S COMPANY HAD, like TWA, come to symbolize all that had gone wrong with deregulation. What with massive service problems, severe labor strife, and hemorrhaging finances, Texas Air seemed to encapsulate everyone's worst fears.

It had been ten years, in fact, since Eastern president Phil Bakes had helped to write the deregulation law. Now he had little reason to celebrate. The tenth anniversary brought forth a barrage of criticism of the airline business and various calls to reregulate.

During the spring of 1988, Bakes had been spending a lot of time in Washington on a frustrating mission, trying to persuade the National Mediation Board to release Eastern from negotiations with the machinists in order to trigger the thirty-day cooling-off period that would precede a strike. That might just turn Eastern's fortunes, for it would allow Lorenzo to impose his terms on the machinists union. Bakes's efforts had not paid off. In fact the chairman of the mediation board, Walter Wallace, said publicly that he believed Bakes and Lorenzo were not serious about negotiating in good faith, just as the unions had been saying all along.

A host of other problems brought lawsuits against Texas Air that year. Early in 1988, before it had even considered offering it to an outsider like Trump, the company announced a plan to spin off the profitable Eastern Shuttle and put it into a separate subsidiary of the parent company. The unions cried foul, ran to court, and won a temporary restraining order to block the transfer. It was yet another move that incited the unions' suspicion that Lorenzo simply wanted to push the company into bankruptcy and then "cherry-pick" the remains. Lorenzo had made other similar moves on Eastern's assets. He had moved the airline's reservations system into a new subsidiary and paid for it, not with cash, but with a twenty-year note. But the shuttle transfer was perhaps the most damaging act, at least in terms of employee relations. According to many observers, it was the one action that succeeded in finally uniting the normally fractious unions at Eastern into one determined bloc against Lorenzo. It had also made the federal government interested enough in the unions' charges to launch a highly publicized safety investigation of Texas Air that only succeeded in scaring off passengers.

Against this backdrop, Bakes arrived at a Washington hotel one evening in the middle of 1988 for a dinner hosted by the Democratic Congressional Campaign Committee. Democratic presidential candidate Michael Dukakis had been bashing Lorenzo's record in some of his campaign speeches, and the unions' animosity toward Lorenzo was causing some politicians to stay at arm's length. Bakes thought the low had been reached when Dukakis arrived in Miami on a flight with Congressman Claude Pepper. The two debarked, held a brief news conference denouncing Eastern, and immediately took off again. "That's really something when they come into your hometown just to throw dirt at you," he said. Others eagerly joined in. Congressman Doug Bosco, a California Democrat, quipped that "Frank Lorenzo is the neutron bomb of the airline industry—he kills all the workers and leaves the planes."

During the dinner, Bakes spotted Ted Kennedy across the room. He had not had much contact with his old mentor since he'd helped manage Kennedy's ill-fated presidential campaign eight years earlier. However, Kennedy had not forgotten Bakes; the machinists reminded the senator on many occasions that he had set in motion the events that had put Bakes in his current position. Bakes had even heard that the machinists were telling their Democrat allies that he was a turn-coat, a "Nazi."

The machinists were especially upset because they'd always been such strong supporters of Kennedy. During the 1980 campaign, they'd given him hefty donations, and later, when the campaign hit hard times, they loaned the candidate their Lear jet. The deregulation effort that began back in 1974 as a way to make Kennedy seem worthy of the presidency was now—as deregulation seemed an utter disaster—getting him into trouble with one of the few constituencies that remained loyal to him.

Even so, Bakes had not seen Kennedy in a while and went over to say hello. But when he greeted Kennedy, the senator said in a loud voice: "This goddamn dereg . . . you know, Phil, you double-crossed me. You lied to me. You said the unions were going to support deregulation," Bakes recalled him saying.

People stopped eating to stare as Kennedy kept up his harangue. "You double-crossed me!" Senator Paul Simon, who'd been approaching the pair, turned on his heel and escaped the embarrassing scene. "He kept screaming about how I'd double-crossed him. He's talking about deregulation—ten years ago."

Bakes did not hear from Kennedy again.

LORENZO RESPONDED TO THE MACHINISTS' intransigence by launching a campaign to paint Walter Wallace as a shill for labor. Wallace, a Republican appointed by Eisenhower who had often sided with management in disputes, hardly seemed to fit the bill. Lorenzo hired some expensive lobbying talent in Washington, such as Democratic heavyweight Robert Strauss, in an attempt to persuade Congress to oust Wallace from his chairman's seat.

Texas Air researched the history and activities of the IAM, producing an eighty-page White Paper full of pithy asides that painted the IAM as a far-left fringe group, and its leader, William Winpisinger, as an "outrageous socialist" and a shameless self-promoter who was simply using his "Joe Lunchpail" members. However, the document also seemed to confirm the futility of trying to wring concessions from the machinists who, the report stressed, had never given back any gains.

Later in 1988, the National Mediation Board finally took the action Lorenzo had been waiting for. They declared an impasse in the long-drawn-out negotiations between Eastern and the IAM. This set the clock in motion for a cooling-off period, and a strike date was set for March 4, 1989.

Around this time Eastern launched an ad campaign that struck some observers as strange—for the spots featured none other than Frank Borman as the pitchman for the airline he had lost to Lorenzo. The strategy harked back to the days when Borman made a series of memorable television ads for Eastern, before the labor-management strife had turned poisonous. Now the beleaguered Eastern management appealed to Borman's sense of duty to help his old airline; after all, he was still on the Texas Air board. "He was the only one in the family that had any credibility," admitted Phil Bakes. "We wanted him in the ads for a variety of reasons. He was a public figure, and he no longer had any direct interest in Eastern. Yet he obviously knew the airline well."

Borman played the good soldier for a number of years after the sale, refusing to criticize Lorenzo's stewardship. But much later he commented tersely on the style of his successor. "We were on a course of trying to work with employees" before the sale, he said. "And they subverted that. But you have to remember that these guys had broken a strike at Continental and they had an idea they could win at Eastern."

Just after the New Year, Icahn and Lorenzo made yet another attempt to strike a deal. The two met and agreed on terms, and Icahn left with the impression he had a handshake deal. Yet Lorenzo's negotiating style had not changed much since 1985. The next day, Icahn went to a law office in New York City where he waited in vain for Lorenzo to arrive to sign off. Lorenzo never appeared, and he was finally tracked down at a ski resort. Icahn was livid. "He welched on the deal," Brian Freeman recalled him saying. It turned out that Lorenzo had discovered a new item he wanted added to the liabilities Icahn would assume if he acquired Eastern. At that point, Icahn gave up, convinced that Lorenzo did not really want to sell Eastern.

Lorenzo's ambivalence about selling suggested he still believed he could beat the unions. Even if the mechanics walked off the job, Lorenzo thought, most of the pilots would cross the picket lines. The airline would remain aloft, since most of the machinists could be quickly replaced. Thus, Eastern would rid itself of the troublesome IAM and stay in business. Lorenzo would get credit for turning around another airline.

However, Eastern's management underestimated the pilots' resentment. On the eve of the strike, a fifteen-minute video featuring Lorenzo being "interviewed" by a journalist was sent to all the pilots' homes. It showed Lorenzo giving the details of a new agreement that he was offering the pilots—a five-year contract that would provide pay increases, guarantees against sales of international routes, and a minimum number of captain's positions. Lorenzo signed the agreement before the camera and urged the union leaders to do the same.

On closer inspection, however, the agreement was deemed unacceptable by the pilots, who claimed that it would shave their benefits to the tune of $64 million. More disturbing was a warning from the pilots' lawyers that the agreement would be moot if Eastern declared bankruptcy.

A pilots' leader recalled the basic mistrust on both sides. "Lorenzo was counting on the basic greed of pilots," he said, the old divide-and-conquer approach, based on a belief that pilots would not risk their six-figure salaries for Joe Lunchpail.

"But our belief was that Lorenzo was going to destroy the airline anyway and the best chance we had was if we all stood together," he said. "Even dealing with a bankruptcy judge gave us a better chance than dealing with him. The majority of our people knew there was a serious risk the airline would not survive, but we all hoped that wouldn't happen, that he would finally see reason and sell it."

Meanwhile, extensive strike preparations were carried out at Miami. The company hired seventeen hundred guards to watch over idled aircraft, ground equipment, employee parking lots, and other places. More than two million maintenance records were duplicated. Manhole covers over phone lines between buildings were welded shut. A satellite communications system was installed for reservations and flight planning, just in case phone lines were cut.

The extent of Lorenzo's miscalculation became clear on March 5 when not only the mechanics but most of the pilots walked off the job. Joe Leonard, Eastern's president, gave several news conferences that day, and in each successive appearance his estimate of how many flights would continue to operate fell dramatically. The other Eastern managers joked that he was "Joe Isuzu Leonard." Only 85 of Eastern's 1,040 flights got off the ground the first day, and the number rose to just 125 the next day. Thousands of passengers were stranded, and shots of angry customers jamming ticket counters went out to television viewers around the country. It was reminiscent of the fiasco at Newark Airport two years earlier, with an added layer of union hostility. On March 9, with virtually no money coming in, Eastern filed for bankruptcy in New York City.

Pilots also believed someone would buy the airline from Lorenzo. A White Knight soon emerged: former baseball commissioner Peter

Ueberroth, who had a sterling reputation for turning difficult situations around. Union leaders were brought in—pilots' chief Jack Bavis, Charlie Bryan—and talk about concessions began.

By the end of March, the unions had agreed to give some $200 million in wage cuts or productivity increases to a group that Ueberroth had formed to take over Eastern. Drexel Burnham pledged to back the deal with junk bond financing. After several more weeks of difficult negotiations, in which Lorenzo managed again to walk away from handshake agreements, the two sides thought they had a deal. And for Lorenzo it would come none too soon. The strife at Eastern was taking a personal toll; pickets regularly appeared outside his home, his children were afraid, and he'd been made into such a world-famous villain that his name was even spray-painted on the Berlin Wall with the familiar slash drawn through it.

On April 6, Ueberroth and Lorenzo held a news conference to announce a deal that would give labor 30 percent of the airline, in exchange for the concessions they'd pledged. But arduous all-night negotiations continued for weeks, during which the details of transferring the airline to the new owners became the main sticking point. The unions insisted that a trustee be appointed for sixty days before Ueberroth's team finally got control. Former defense secretary Frank Carlucci agreed to take the post.

But when the scheme was presented to bankruptcy judge Burton Lifland, who had a reputation for siding with management in Chapter 11 cases, the idea was doomed. Lifland was concerned how it might appear if he handed Lorenzo's airline over to a trustee without a full examination of the matter, which could take months. Meanwhile, the situation rapidly degenerated as the two sides wrangled over minor amounts of money and who would be paid what if the deal fell through. An exhausted contingent of lawyers and executives finally appeared before reporters in mid-April and said that the deal had collapsed. Press accounts generally faulted the unions for insisting on a trustee, but the story was more complicated than that. The pilots union had tried to communicate to the judge that they would not object if Ueberroth ran the airline while Lorenzo was still technically in control. A greater problem was that Ueberroth and Lorenzo had started squabbling over who was to pay what to whom if the sale were aborted. Lorenzo never conceded any responsibility in the sorry affair. Years later, he still insisted that he sincerely wanted to sell the airline, "only the unions wanted me to turn it over to someone who would come right in off the street."

17

END
OF THE
LBO

I n early 1988, forty-seven-year-old Steve Wolf was chairman and CEO of United Airlines, putting him clearly in the same league as his old boss and mentor, Bob Crandall. Ever the workaholic, Wolf had a private gym installed next to his office so he could squeeze in two twenty-minute workouts a week without having to stray far from his desk. In style, however, Wolf was closer to Dick Ferris than to the combative Crandall. He wore natty red suspenders, and when he appeared before the public or the press he maintained a soft-spoken, dignified manner.

However, for the first time since its merger with Capital in 1961, United was no longer the largest airline in the country. By the fall of 1988, American not only had more planes in the sky than United, but had nosed past United in U.S. market share, making American the new number-one airline and giving Crandall his biggest victory since deregulation.

Crandall took this all very seriously. He would trot out the latest traffic results as if they were sports scores. On one occasion, Crandall even suggested that American might catch up with the humongous Aeroflot in size. Although Soviet secrecy kept the world from knowing the exact size of the state-run airline, Crandall clearly had a lot of catching up to do: Aeroflot by most estimates had more than twelve hundred jets—triple American's fleet.

Crandall kept American expanding with a vigor that reflected his intense "competitive anger," as it was known to his troops.

Wolf was to play Ferris's old role with Crandall, re-enacting the historical rivalry between C. R. Smith and Pat Patterson. But neither Smith nor Patterson had to deal with hostile takeovers or leveraged buyouts. They had taken care of truculent labor unions with their Mutual Aid Pact. The old flyboys perhaps could not have worked their way out of the predicaments that Wolf and Crandall faced.

When the UAL directors started looking for a new chairman and CEO after Ferris's forced departure, they reportedly sent out feelers to Crandall. But Crandall, who had been fighting most of his career to help number-two American catch up to number-one United, had no interest in joining the enemy camp now that he had won first place.

In January 1988, not long after the UAL team began searching for a chairman, the board of American Airlines parent AMR formally agreed to give Crandall 355,000 shares of restricted AMR stock— roughly eight times as much as he already held. It was restricted in that he wouldn't be fully vested in the award until eight years later, assuming he stayed with the company; the board told shareholders it wanted to make sure Crandall stayed with American "for the balance of his career." Crandall was already taking in roughly a million dollars a year in compensation—half in base salary and half from an incentive scheme that rewarded American's senior executives handsomely each year that the company's return on investment exceeded 8.6 percent.

United's board inevitably turned to Crandall's former protégé, Wolf, who had continued to demonstrate his skills as a turn-around artist. After he brought Republic Airlines back from near bankruptcy in the mid-1980s, Wolf had become chairman of Tiger International, parent of Los Angeles–based cargo carrier Flying Tiger Line. There he again won substantial wage and work-rule concessions from labor and returned a nearly bankrupt operation to health. But he did it by threatening to declare bankruptcy, a step one critic described as "a page out of Lorenzo's book."

Especially impressed with Wolf's performance at Tiger was mega-investor Saul Steinberg. His Reliance Group Holdings owned 13 percent of the company, bought at around twenty-one dollars a share, and he had watched his stock slide to five dollars before Wolf came on board. After Wolf left, Tiger's share price was on a sharp upward track; Federal Express bought the company in 1989 for twenty-one dollars a share.

United's directors were especially interested in finding someone who could bring their unions to heel. Even after Dick Ferris left the stage, Mad Dog Dubinsky and his pilots continued their efforts to put together an ESOP for the airline through 1987. The UAL board, which had already taken the corporation through incredible contortions with the Allegis collapse, was in no mood to deal with the pilots. Even if the board had been receptive, the stock market crash on October 19, 1987, would have made it difficult to finance a buyout.

Directors also wanted a new second-in-command—a financial sage who knew his way around capital markets, loan covenants, and huge aircraft purchase orders. It was an easy choice: If UAL couldn't attract Bob Crandall, it could at least steal his top financial adviser. It hired Jack Pope, who had come to American from General Motors and was regarded as Crandall's heir apparent. United, which had always gone its own way, was now being run by Crandall clones.

Wolf's spiritual predecessors, the scarf-and-goggles crowd, had reveled in a show of indifference to material gain. "The way to make a little money in the airline business is to start out with a lot," went an old adage. The aviation pioneers were well off, to be sure, but with the exception of Howard Hughes, who inherited his fortune, they did not live as ostentatiously as their counterparts in other industries. After all, they were running what amounted to public utilities, their unexceptional profit margins barely enough to buy them the planes they needed.

In a deregulated climate, airlines would enrich a fortunate few, for reasons that sometimes bore little relation to the performance of their airlines. Wolf, who twenty years before had been loading bags onto airplanes, would surpass Crandall in income many times over. He was already a millionaire, thanks to stock options from his earlier jobs. And United directors were so intent on snaring him that they agreed to protect the value of the stake in Tiger International that Wolf would forfeit, giving him a signing bonus worth anywhere from $6 million to $15 million on top of a first-year salary of $575,000 and options on 250,000 shares of UAL stock. Wolf also had a piece of personal business to settle as he agreed to take on the UAL job. He was going to get married, and that decision would cost Crandall still another executive: personnel resources vice-president Delores Wallace, whom Wolf had been seeing ever since he worked at American in the 1970s.

The pilots had considered Wolf as a candidate for their CEO-in-waiting when they were putting together their ESOP the previous year, but they rejected him. "The man had the reputation in the industry of not being really oriented toward the welfare of his employees if he could take advantage of them. He demonstrated that at Republic and Flying Tiger. We interviewed the pilots from those carriers extensively, and came away with a pretty bad feeling about Stephen Wolf," said pilots' union chief Dubinsky.

The pilots still wanted to buy their airline for $110 a share and were not pleased by the prospect of working for Wolf. "Basically, we had identified him as a public enemy; it was just a matter of time until we locked horns with him, and we were going to beat him up badly," Dubinsky said. "That was our goal."

IN STYLE, CERTAINLY, WOLF HARKED back to the old airline bosses as a true operating man, not a deal-maker. Wolf immediately set about reducing United's costs as much as possible and improving the quality of its passenger services. He eschewed the limelight as much as possible, rarely granting interviews to the press. He declined to be listed in *Who's Who*.

Wolf went over United's budget line item by line item, squeezing out whatever he could. He terminated the service that delivered flowers to his own office and got rid of the rented plants that decorated United's headquarters. He sold off some works of art owned by the company, trimmed the size of United's airline timetable to save on printing costs, and got rid of unused furniture in company offices. Following up on an employee's suggestion, he cut ninety-six hundred dollars from the budget by replacing a labor-intensive sculpted radish with pickled ginger in the salads on United's transpacific flights to Japan—an odd parallel to Crandall, who earlier had become celebrated for saving American some forty thousand dollars a year by eliminating the lone olive from its in-flight salads.

Like Crandall, Wolf made it a point to maintain lines of communication with United's thousands of workers. As soon as he joined the company, he set off on a road trip to meet as many of them as possible and began producing videotapes to be played to the rest, explaining the problems he and they had to tackle together: for example, that United's domestic market share was shrinking, that archrival American still had a cost advantage of around $600 million a year that had to be matched or overcome, and that passenger service had to improve. He also started a series of "chairman's lunches" with rank-and-file workers.

Wolf's attention to United's level of service also ranged from the big picture to the minutiae. Once, when waiting for a flight at O'Hare, he noticed that a men's room in United's terminal was dirty. He called the appropriate underling and ordered that it be cleaned up. He began weekly meetings at which his officers reported to him on various measures of quality control.

He also quietly started negotiating with Boeing to purchase up to 370 new planes for United's aging fleet. At the end of 1988, Delta had placed firm orders or options for 334 new planes, and American for 211, while United had only 136 aircraft on order. United was sitting on a cash hoard of more than a billion dollars, however, so Wolf quickly got to work upgrading United's fleet. He put in a massive order for 190 Boeing 737 and 757 jets, a deal potentially worth $15 billion.

As Wolf was putting United on what he hoped was a steady course, UAL's stock had jumped 60 percent in a year to $112 a share. Reliance Group Holdings chief Saul Steinberg accumulated a 5 percent stake in the company and kept buying more. But Steinberg wasn't the only raider with his eye on UAL stock.

In the summer of 1989, dealmaker and oilman Marvin Davis, who had just lost out in a three-way contest to negotiate a leveraged buyout of Northwest Airlines, made a sudden bid to buy United Airlines for $240 a share. If straight airline mergers were on the wane, a new wave of airline takeovers by outside investors with borrowed money seemed about to begin.

NORTHWEST WAS THE FIRST AIRLINE target. Although it had achieved "critical mass" by merging with Republic, Northwest carried a lot of baggage from its pre-deregulation days under Donald Nyrop. His successor, Steven Rothmeier, became CEO in 1985 and continued Nyrop's autocratic management methods, dictating employee hair styles, deciding what kind of jewelry flight attendants were permitted to wear, and generally maintaining a military discipline. Executives were expected to report to work by 8:00 A.M. and spend at least two Saturday mornings a month in the office; Rothmeier even insisted on approving the kinds of civic organizations his managers joined. Rothmeier's lifestyle contained elements of discipline as well: A bachelor, a Vietnam veteran, and a fitness enthusiast, he lived in a house outside Minneapolis that resembled a medieval castle.

Rothmeier's tight-fisted style had at least made the airline profitable to the tune of a record $135 million in 1988. That in turn brought forth a couple of takeover artists looking, as Icahn had, for a quick kill on an undervalued stock. In early 1989, Northwest said that an unnamed investor group had bought up 4.9 percent of its stock and wanted to discuss a takeover. The suitors were soon unmasked as a trio who had all once worked together at Marriott Hotels: Alfred Checchi, Gary Wilson, and Fred Malek. Checchi had moved on to become a Los Angeles–based private investment adviser, and Wilson, a former director of Northwest's parent company, NWA, was chief financial officer at Walt Disney Company. Malek, who had been president of Marriott Hotels, was a Washington-based financial consultant and Republican party insider who had gained some notoriety during George Bush's presidential campaign. He had resigned as deputy chairman of the Republican National Committee in the fall of 1988 after it was disclosed that in 1971, when he worked for the Nixon White House, Malek had conducted a headcount of how many Jews held high positions in the Bureau of Labor Statistics.

Only a few days after this triad's interest in arranging a leveraged buyout of Northwest became known, Marvin Davis announced he was planning a proxy fight to facilitate his own takeover of Northwest Airlines for $2.7 billion; Davis had accumulated a 3 percent stake and was offering ninety dollars a share.

Northwest was now in play, and its directors dithered about what to do. At first they fought back, filing suit against Davis with an allegation that he was interfering in its union negotiations. They also got some support from such politicians as Minnesota congressman James Oberstar, who demanded and received assurances from Davis that he wouldn't break up the airline. "I want to put some restraints on the financial buccaneering that is going on in the airline industry," Oberstar said at the time.

Nevertheless, by mid-April the NWA board had faced up to the reality of its situation and said it would consider selling the company. But Davis and the Checchi group weren't going to be the only bidders. Tom Plaskett believed a purchase of Northwest Airlines might solve all his problems—and Plaskett's problems were pressing.

PLASKETT WAS THE LATEST occupant of Juan Trippe's old office on the forty-sixth floor of the Pan Am Building. After he was fired by Frank Lorenzo following the Continental debacle, Plaskett had been at loose ends. Meanwhile, Pan Am directors were searching for Ed Acker's replacement. Plaskett was well known in the industry and soon he was offered the top job at Pan Am, at a salary of five hundred thousand dollars. He moved to New York at the beginning of 1988. That put Crandall and his protégés at the top of three of the five dominant airlines in the United States.

Acker had left Pan Am festering with labor discontent, and the Teamsters threatened to strike during Plaskett's first few months on the job, but backed down. The airline was wallowing in more than a billion dollars of debt. Its service had deteriorated to the point where Pan Am ranked dead last in domestic on-time arrivals.

Plaskett started spending money on a service improvement program and on hiring more employees, but some thought Plaskett reacted too slowly. Employees even made up a crack about the Tom Plaskett doll: Wind it up and it does nothing for a year. Some took him to task for spending too much time on the golf course. By the end of 1988, Pan Am was in such a bad cash position that it again had to resort to selling anything it could lay its hands on. The airline even sold its place in line to buy some Airbus jets.

In December 1988, Pan Am's situation turned desperate. On December 21, Americans watching the evening news were shocked to see pieces of a Pan Am 747 strewn across the Scottish countryside. Terrorists had blown Pan Am's Flight 103—full of Americans returning home for Christmas from London to New York—out of the skies over the village of Lockerbie, in alleged retaliation for the U.S. Navy's accidental shooting down of an Iranian airliner. All 259 on board the Pan Am plane died. The Pan Am name, once a valuable asset because it was so closely linked to the U.S. flag in the minds of the world, had become a deadly liability by making the airline a symbolic target.

The impact on Pan Am's transatlantic traffic was immediate and severe. In the first three months after the bombing—the first quarter of 1989—Pan Am lost $151 million, estimating that the Lockerbie incident had a direct cost of $55 million to $60 million in lost revenues. And bookings for the second quarter didn't look much better. Plaskett knew that this called for desperate measures.

"One-oh-three was absolutely devastating, in economic terms and human terms," Plaskett said. "It was a turning point. I think it was the point at which I really began to understand what the ultimate outcome of the situation was going to be. It was truly awful." Over the longer term, he estimated the impact of Lockerbie on Pan Am at $400 million to $450 million in lost revenues.

As investigations of the bombing went on, Pan Am was widely

criticized for inadequate security measures; this raised in the public's mind the grotesque possibility that the airline itself bore the responsibility for the tragedy.

In an early February 1989 speech to a Shearson Lehman Hutton investment conference in New York, Plaskett said that Pan Am could no longer survive on its own. The airline's track record in the merger department was lamentable, of course, and in large part its current problems had begun with the National acquisition. But now Plaskett suggested a curious course: The nearly bankrupt Pan Am would acquire another airline. He settled on Northwest as a suitable partner.

The idea of a Pan Am–Northwest combination had first been considered during Ed Acker's final years at Pan Am, when a computer analysis had identified Northwest as one of the best potential candidates for a merger. New studies ordered by Plaskett confirmed that such a marriage would produce additional revenues and savings for both partners, and Plaskett went to work on Pan Am's biggest problem: finding enough people to finance its planned bid of $110 a share. Prudential-Bache made a quick commitment to kick in $320 million and brought in another investment partnership called the Airlie Group, upping the ante to $400 million.

Northwest's board set May 30, 1989, as the deadline for bids. Plaskett set off on a whirlwind last-minute financing tour to meet with bankers in Hartford, Boston, Los Angeles, Minneapolis, San Francisco, and even Tokyo, flying most of the way on Northwest. His marathon paid off, as Plaskett brought back commitments from the money men to provide up to $2 billion. Pan Am's representatives put in their bid with Northwest's investment bankers at 2:00 P.M. on the day of the deadline. Plaskett had not slept during the previous fifty-two hours.

In the end, though, Pan Am lost, and so did Marvin Davis. The Checchi group bid $121 a share, and Plaskett only had financing to bid $115. The forty-year-old Checchi and his investment partners, including by that point the Dutch airline KLM, had won the contest, with a total bid of $3.65 billion. However, only $700 million of their financing was equity capital, and $400 million of that came from KLM. All the rest was borrowed money that would have to be paid back with interest.

WOLF AND HIS AIDE-DE-CAMP Jack Pope realized that if this phenomenon of buyouts continued, United would be next on the list. Wall Street thought so too: On June 19, the day Northwest announced that it was accepting the Checchi group's bid, shares in UAL went up by more than six dollars, to $128.50.

Perhaps it was sex appeal, as Alfred Kahn had suggested, that attracted the legions of deal-makers to the airlines. More likely, it was the irresistible lure of making a big profit off the rich assets of the target company. In a typical LBO the acquired company would be broken up and chunks sold off to pay down some of the huge debt. These tactics, pioneered by the likes of Henry Kravis and other LBO specialists, had just begun to provoke a belated outrage among disinterested observers. For the end result often was to enrich a few investors at the expense of thousands of employees, and to sacrifice the well-being of a company, whose choicest assets were often immediately parceled off after the deal was done. For United, that could be a devastating development, since it had already shed its nonairline subsidiaries in the Allegis bust-up.

Wolf's fears were realized in the first week of August 1989, when Marvin Davis made a bid to buy UAL for $5.4 billion, or $240 a share. When word got out on Monday, August 8, the company's stock ran up more than forty-six points, to $210. Some Wall Street analysts put the company's takeover value at $250 to $300 per share.

Wolf and Pope knew they were on dangerous ground, for the same reason Dick Ferris had been two years earlier. There was a provision in the UAL bylaws that allowed for a consent process, by which any shareholder could call for a vote to bring in a new slate of directors, just as Coniston Partners had done before Ferris's ouster. That would be inevitable once the arbitragers got into the act. To avoid having a Marvin Davis takeover forced on them by the arbs, Wolf and Pope quickly came to an uneasy truce with the pilots union. Davis would have to borrow huge sums to finance his proposed $5.4 billion acquisition, and he would certainly demand concessions from United's unions. If the unions were going to have to make wage concessions and productivity improvements, why shouldn't they get some equity in the company in return, instead of getting nothing?

Dubinsky was uncharacteristically eager to bury the hatchets his pilots union had been tossing at Wolf that summer. "When Davis showed up," he said, "we had a different kettle of fish—we had a common enemy. Management approached us and asked if we were interested in joining forces to put together an LBO to take the company over." Since Dubinsky had been fighting so long for an ESOP, he jumped at the chance to get some equity for his members.

The Davis raid brought about a harmony among the United factions that had not been seen since the days of Eddie Carlson. An

LBO coalition was formed among management, the pilots, and United's nonunion workers. "Because it was moving so fast, we concluded the best thing to do would be just to do it with management and the pilots, and later on, if the other labor unions [the machinists and the flight attendants] wanted to come in, they could," Pope explained. "We left room for that to happen." Meanwhile, the price kept going up. Davis had increased his earlier bid to $275 a share, so the union-management coalition raised the ante to $300, pushing the total price of the buyout to $6.75 billion.

That breathtaking amount had the industry agog. It was declared the biggest airline transaction ever, and the largest employee buyout, and plenty of other superlatives. The deal would dwarf all previous airline transactions. Observers were understandably interested in just how Wolf and Pope planned to fund their acquisition.

United's management immediately agreed that they would neither use junk bonds nor sell any assets. Thus encouraged, the pilots offered concessions worth $250 million and added a matching amount from their pension fund. For the rest, Wolf and Pope wanted to rely on bank debt and on a "strategic equity partner," as Pope put it. It didn't take them long to find the latter. They already had a link to an airline with deep pockets, having forged a marketing alliance with profitable British Airways two years earlier. British Airways agreed to chip in $750 million in return for a 15 percent stake in UAL and a seat on the board.

FOR BRITISH AIRWAYS, the United pact was the latest and by far the most substantial of a string of deals. The British line's chief executive, Colin Marshall, soon arrived in New York City to tout the plan before a throng of airline analysts. The normally reserved Marshall gushed: "It's an unparalleled opportunity." Certainly it was for Marshall, who like his peers in the United States had spent much of the 1980s building his own airline empire.

The fifty-five-year-old Briton had worked his way up from a purser's job at a shipping line to become the chief executive of Avis Rent a Car before joining British Air in 1983. BA's service was so terrible at the time that its passengers joked that its initials stood for "Bloody Awful." Marshall's mandate was to get the airline in shape so that Margaret Thatcher's government could sell the state-run line to private investors. After firing a lot of management deadwood and spending money to spiff up service, Marshall in 1987 snapped up his largest competitor, British Caledonian Airways, a merger that even the laissez-faire Reaganites might have questioned. He formed marketing alliances with foreign airlines, but most of these ties lacked the cement of an equity stake.

The United deal was different. BA's cash infusion promised to give Marshall enormous influence in Chicago. There was no question that United's vast domestic system and British Air's huge global network would be the perfect fit that other airline chiefs coveted. The two lines quickly began mapping out strategy, publicly talking about pooling resources and linking up at scores of cities around the world. Critics cracked that Marshall's real aim was to recreate the British Empire in the skies—as he was simultaneously pursuing deals in Australia and other former British colonies. But what was more intriguing was he was willing to plow an amazing three-quarters of a billion into United for a 15 percent stake. That led to speculation that British Air would gradually be permitted to increase its voting shares in its U.S. partner.

Other airlines predictably cried foul. But since the buyout plan included so much employee participation, pundits predicted it would easily sail through regulatory hurdles in Washington. "It's like Mom and apple pie," said Mike Derchin. "Any deal that includes that level of employee ownership would be hard to turn down."

But down in Washington, some changes had taken place that would have a profound impact on all this wheeling and dealing, as the federal government started to realize the toll that the previous decade's merger-and-LBO binge was taking on the economy. Some senior officials at the Transportation Department, in particular, began to question the effects of highly leveraged buyouts and foreign investment on the airline industry.

Two changes had occurred: Authority to rule on airline mergers had been transferred from DOJ to the Justice Department, and George Bush was in the White House. While the new regime was hardly inclined to reregulate the airlines, it was disturbed at the specter of the U.S. airline industry hobbling under a giant mound of debt. Bush's team worried that this could hurt the airlines' ability not only to compete in a global marketplace, but also to buy the state-of-the-art planes needed to carry them into the next century. They also sensed the growing public outrage over the costs to society of some of the more egregious takeovers and leveraged buyouts: the crippled companies, the lost jobs. Bush's people would have to deal with the wreckage of the takeover craze that the previous administration had done so much to encourage.

Bush appointed former Illinois U.S. attorney Sam Skinner as

transportation secretary. Skinner had a pilot's license and ingratiated himself with his airline constituents more easily than had Elizabeth Dole. He was also known for his tough record on crime, and he immediately turned his steady gaze on the airline business. Skinner was alarmed not only by the crushing debt the airlines had taken on but also by the threat of a wave of foreign takeovers. Both KLM's investment in Northwest and British Air's in United raised the larger question of whether the United States should allow a substantial part of the country's commercial airline fleet to come under foreign control. U.S. law, in fact, was clear on that point: It limited foreign investment in a U.S. airline to 25 percent of the voting stock and barred foreigners from exercising control of a U.S. airline for reasons of national security. (During wartime, the government depends on airlines to provide significant military airlift capacity.)

Skinner's department had some leeway in interpreting what constituted "control." Also, even though the Justice Department now had authority over airline mergers, Transportation still had the power to apply the traditional "fitness test" to an airline, that is, to judge whether any particular owner of an airline was financially fit to operate it competently and safely, and to award or withhold an operating certificate based on that determination. Could an LBO with its associated high debt levels and high interest payments be an indication of lack of financial fitness?

The new administration in Washington clearly believed it could. In late August, Jeffrey Shane, who had succeeded Matt Scocozza as assistant transportation secretary for policy and international affairs, put Wall Street and the airlines on notice—by way of a much-discussed interview in *The Wall Street Journal*—that they shouldn't "discount the possibility that the DOT will take active steps in response to the levels of debt and levels of foreign ownership being discussed" in airline LBO attempts.

Part of the government's concern about European airlines' buying into U.S. carriers had to do with the shifting political situation in Europe. With the European Community planning to unify into a single political entity in 1993, there was growing concern that a united Common Market might seek to end the privileges U.S. airlines had long enjoyed within Europe—the right to transport passengers between one European city and another—unless European airlines got equal rights inside the United States.

"The prospect of having European airlines enjoying the benefits of our market through investments in U.S. airlines is one we don't readily welcome," Shane said in the interview. Later, Shane said that

Skinner had instructed him to "get the word out that the administration would take a dim view of highly leveraged airline buyouts." The day after his remarks were published, he recalled, the Dow Jones transportation index dropped about twenty points.

The morning his interview was published in the *Journal*, Shane's phone started ringing. One of the callers was Frank Lorenzo.

"Do you know what happens to the market when you say something like this?" Lorenzo fumed.

"What kind of market is it, if that's how it reacts to this type of statement?" Shane retorted.

But Lorenzo was unmoved. "I thought that's why we elected a Republican administration, in order to avoid this kind of interference," he told Shane.

This was unpleasant news for United's management, pilots, and British Airways, who were planning their LBO. It was also a letdown for Lorenzo, Carl Icahn, and other deal-makers who expected that the Reagan laissez-faire philosophy would continue under Bush. Icahn later admitted that his ardor for airline mergers cooled after Skinner's warning.

Secretary Skinner himself repeated the warning against LBOs and excessive foreign ownership during a mid-September speech to an airline industry group in Washington. "I will not allow excessive debt in the airline industry to jeopardize the public interest, especially in the area of safety," Skinner said, reflecting the growing public concern—fostered by the massive anti-Lorenzo publicity campaign mounted by Eastern Airlines unions—that an airline losing money or heavily in debt would try to cut corners on maintenance and safety.

A week later, Northwest bowed to pressure from Skinner and agreed to drastically scale back KLM's equity investment in the Northwest buyout, from $400 million to $175 million. Even though the arrangement with KLM as originally structured had kept its formal voting power well below 25 percent in compliance with federal law, Skinner decided that the 25 percent rule should apply not just to voting power, but also to equity investment. Of the total $700 million in nonborrowed funds put up for the Northwest purchase, $400 million was just too much, Skinner believed. But $175 million came to 25 percent. KLM also had to give up its presence on the NWA board. This raised a serious question in the banking community about whether British Airways' $750 million contribution to the UAL deal's financing would be permitted.

Bush's administration was proving to be much more interventionist than the Reagan White House had been, where the airlines were concerned. In June 1989, for example, the Justice Department gave the airlines a clear signal that things had changed when it threatened to go to court to block a plan by then bankrupt Eastern Airlines to sell its Philadelphia airport gates to USAir, which already controlled more than half of all departures at that airport. Eastern had to sell the facilities to Midway Airlines instead, to meet Justice's insistence that some semblance of competition be maintained in the Philadelphia market. Alfred Kahn lamented that this was all too little too late: "They shut the barn door after letting the horses out."

The new attitude in Washington made some bankers wary about putting their resources behind a deal that might very well be torpedoed by the government. Still, Wolf and Pope proceeded with their plans for a management-led buyout of UAL. In forty-eight hours, Pope said, they had tied up commitments for $3 billion from Citibank and Chase Manhattan. The bankers also issued "highly confident" letters to cover the balance. Pope was especially proud that the deal was done without junk bonds.

However, as the month went on, Pope recalled, "There were beginning to be warning signals in the banking industry and in the takeover business that maybe we had hit the top and were on the way down. The banks were beginning to get a little skittish—the Japanese banks particularly."

In late September, another flap arose over how much money Wolf and Pope stood to gain personally from the transaction. A tender offer disclosed on September 22 indicated that if the deal was accomplished, Wolf stood to make $76 million from selling the UAL stock and options he was holding, and Pope could get nearly $38 million. But the amount that their management investors' group was committing to the buyout financing was only $15 million, in return for a 10 percent stake.

The unions were understandably outraged. As economist Robert Kuttner commented, "Wolf will realize a $76.7 million windfall from the buyout. The employees will realize pay concessions. Some partnership." The machinists union in particular made an issue of Wolf's and Pope's potential windfall. The effect was to stir up more uncertainty in the minds of Pope's likely financiers. Wolf, stung by the criticism, agreed not only to work for no salary the following year, but to work without an employment contract, eliminating his golden parachute benefits. The unions dismissed that as a token gesture.

In fact, the machinists were so incensed by Wolf's take in the deal that they called some Japanese bankers to warn them away from participating in the financing, saying that if it went through, they were going to demand substantial wage increases. The Japanese, who are known to be wary about getting involved with any company facing labor unrest, reacted with predictable alarm and soon backed off.

As the financing effort continued into October, the bandwagon effect that the Citibank and Chase commitments were meant to inspire never materialized. The syndication effort for the remaining $4.2 billion faltered. Pope said he had been assured by the lead bankers that the additional financing was imminent. But Citibank and Chase could well afford to be optimistic, since, whether the syndication succeeded or not, they would share $8 million in fees for their efforts.

The LBO deal, and the fragile coalition of factions it represented, began to unravel. Even two bank executives who sat on the UAL board failed to bring their institutions on board for the financing effort: Richard Cooley, CEO of Seattle First National Bank, and John McGillicuddy, CEO of Manufacturers Hanover. Some banks did commit to limited financing, to the tune of $1.4 billion, but no big lenders emerged to take the lead in the syndication.

IN EARLY OCTOBER, word spread on Wall Street about an unusual amount of trading going on in the shares of another airline company, AMR, American Airlines' parent. On Thursday, October 5, the news came out that Donald Trump was bidding $120 a share, or a total of more than $7.5 billion, to buy up American's stock, which had been selling the day before at $83.

It was perhaps inevitable that before the airline LBO craze ended, it would draw in the man who, to much of the country, personified the excesses of the 1980s. Trump couched his offer in such outlandish terms that it was hard to take seriously, even in the heady atmosphere of the time. Although he'd only owned the Eastern Shuttle for a couple of months—renaming it after himself, of course—he boasted that he had already picked up "substantial insight" into the airline business, insight from which American might profit. As American had racked up earnings of $1.5 billion over the previous five years, Trump's remarks simply seemed silly.

Crandall claimed later that he was never terribly worried about the Trump bid. However, it was one of the rare occasions when Crandall made a public announcement to all the employees at the airline's sprawling headquarters campus near Dallas/Fort Worth Airport. All of American's buildings there are wired into a central public address system, and Crandall had a microphone in his office. He used it only for general announcements to the workforce, such as telling them they could go home early when the weather was threatening. Since employees heard it so rarely, the disembodied voice of the chairman often startled them when it came rumbling through the PA system. "It's like hearing the voice of God," one former employee said.

On this occasion, Crandall, on the PA, informed his managers and employees about the Trump bid and, perhaps remembering his own loose-lips experience with Braniff president Putnam back in 1982, warned them all not to discuss it with anyone lest they run afoul of the SEC.

Wall Street settled down to watch the fight for AMR. *The Wall Street Journal* labeled it a "Battle of Titans." No one expected Bob Crandall to sit passively by while Donald Trump bought his airline and then told him how to run it. The day Trump made his announcement, AMR shares jumped only seventeen dollars, to ninety-nine dollars—well short of Trump's proposed price. Some arbitragers thought Trump's bid wasn't serious, that he was just trying to push up the price again before selling out; others doubted his ability to take over a company that Crandall didn't want taken over.

Besides, it had become clear that Trump had wildly overpaid for the Eastern Shuttle and his other trophy property, the Plaza Hotel in New York. Even though an upgrading of those two properties brought in more revenue, it was not enough to cover his expenses or interest payments. And the shuttle had some unforeseen problems.

"Lorenzo must have been laughing all the way to the bank," said a former Trump aide, John O'Donnell. Trump had praised his acquisition as a "diamond," but it turned out to be a fake—its fleet of over-twenty-year-old gas-guzzling jets needed a major overhaul. Trump lavished money on the old planes, going well beyond the required repairs and decking them out with opulent lavatories featuring faux marble sinks. Flight attendants got new uniforms and pearls, and the in-flight service was spruced up. But the competing Pan Am shuttle—which, ironically, Ed Acker had also purchased from Lorenzo's New York Air unit a few years before—had already gained market share during the bitter Eastern strike that preceded Trump's purchase, and it had offered similar amenities all along.

Trump soon showed he knew little about the business he had just entered. He made an unseemly effort to steal business from rival Pan Am's shuttle by implying that the airline's losses and debt load made it unsafe to fly. Even in the combative airline business, that was considered an extremely low blow. Airlines rarely accuse each other of poor safety practices, since that would simply stoke more general fears of flying. And when someone pointed out that his own planes had come from equally cash-strapped Texas Air, Trump had no retort.

It was ludicrous to imagine Trump in Bob Crandall's shoes. Yet Crandall and his team quickly put together a defensive strategy, including an immediate bid for legislative relief. Both the House and Senate aviation subcommittees were considering a bill that would give the Transportation Department specific authority to approve airline takeovers, and American's lobbyists sought to revise that bill to include a provision requiring DOT approval before a potential buyer could wage a proxy fight to dump an airline's board, something they feared Trump might try to do.

BY THEIR SELF-IMPOSED OCTOBER 12 deadline, United's management had failed to come up with anything near their financing goal. On Friday, October 13, Jack Pope remembered waking up with the sinking realization that "it clearly was not going to get done," he recalled. Wolf had just returned from a last-minute trip to Europe to make a personal pitch to bankers there. It failed.

The word of UAL's bad luck spread quickly in lower Manhattan: The biggest airline buyout attempt in history had itself just become history. But the failure of the UAL deal carried a message that went beyond the airline industry. It signaled to all the deal-makers and investment bankers on Wall Street that the day of the big score, the megadeal, might be over; the limits of debt accumulation might have been reached, in the minds of government officials, lenders, and shareholders. The Dow-Jones average responded with a drop of 190 points, a minicrash bigger than any since Black Tuesday in October 1987. Trading in both UAL and AMR stock was halted for the day, after UAL's announcement.

Some critics contended that the projections provided by United's management and by its advisers at First Boston for the airline's future operating performance—and thus its ability to pay off the interest and the debt from an LBO—were unrealistically optimistic and were perceived as such by many potential lenders. Pope leveled some of the blame at the Japanese financial community for not supporting the deal, but in the end, the root of all the potential lenders' reluctance was no doubt Washington's tough new stance on airline LBOs and foreign investment in U.S. carriers, including British Airways' proposed equity in United.

Meanwhile, in London, Colin Marshall got the news that his great global deal had unraveled. Marshall, it was said, was furious—

he apparently felt Pope and Wolf had kept him in the dark about their problems in securing financing. The two United officers also sustained criticism in the financial community. The buzz was that they had been defeated by their overconfident assumption that financing was theirs practically for the asking. "The fiasco of the decade" was how one financial magazine, *Euro Money*, described the botched deal.

The collapse of the United deal and the subsequent market sell-off also put an end to Donald Trump's bid to become Bob Crandall's new boss. Trump had lost interest anyway after a tragic helicopter crash on October 10 killed three close associates. On October 17, he surprised few onlookers when he withdrew his bid for AMR. When trading in the two airline companies reopened on October 16, AMR's share price dropped by twenty-two dollars and UAL's plunged by fifty-seven dollars.

Ten days after the collapse of its $300-a-share buyout, UAL stock was trading at $170. A large number of arbitragers had come on board and stood to lose fortunes if they bailed out; one estimate put their paper losses in the UAL and AMR buyouts at $500 million. These short-term investors exerted continuing pressure, especially on the UAL board, to do something to revive the value of their investments. Wolf's friend Saul Steinberg also saw the value of his 9.7 percent stake in UAL plummet, and Wolf and Pope watched their potential windfall shrink by tens of millions of dollars as the share price continued to drop.

There were some clear winners in the UAL debacle, however. Citibank and Chase Manhattan, for instance, walked away with their $8 million in fees; the law firm retained by the pilots union—Paul, Weiss, Rifkind, Wharton & Garrison—received $6.8 million in fees, and the union's financial advisers at Lazard Freres took home more than $8 million; UAL management's law firm of Skadden, Arps pocketed almost $5 million, and so on. Various estimates of the professional fees claimed by the small army of lawyers and investment bankers involved in the United LBO negotiations range from $58.7 million to $74 million.

UNITED'S PILOTS TRIED TO RESURRECT the buyout effort with Wolf almost immediately after the first one had failed, but absent the threat of an outside raider and unwilling to risk a second failure, management wanted no part of it this time. "We thought we had established a working relationship with the guy," Dubinsky said, "but it wasn't long-term. It was as if he had never met us before."

The pilots went ahead without Wolf. They put together another buyout effort in the spring of 1990, and they almost succeeded. This time they came in with a lower bid of two hundred dollars a share, and with the support and participation of the other unions.

The UAL board huddled for nearly twenty-four hours before deciding to move ahead with the buyout. "We ultimately came to the conclusion that we had no choice but again to sell the company to the employees," Pope said. "Partly because that's what the share-holders wanted, and partly because of this consent thing—if we wanted to stop it, we'd get thrown out and somebody else would do it anyway, through the consent process."

The shareholders Pope mentioned included a disproportionate number of arbitragers who had purchased their stock during the runup the previous fall. "A lot of these people owned the stock at two hundred or whatever, and they lost a lot of money on it, and so they were trying to make something happen to get their money back," he said. "So we agreed to sell it."

To the amazement of UAL's management, the pilots hired a stellar executive to run the airline after they bought it, Chrysler vice-chair-man Gerald Greenwald, the heir apparent to chairman Lee Iacocca. They also said that when they took over the company, they were going to fire Wolf and Pope.

This time, it seemed that the pilots would finally pull off their long-sought buyout. Wolf was convinced that he was about to be out of a job, so he decided to cash in some of his stock options. He ended up making $18 million from United in 1990, most of it from those options. This touched off yet another furor among employees, who thought Wolf was still out for personal profit at their expense.

The second week of August was set as the target date for the outside financing to be assembled for the employee buyout. "I think they had it pretty much pulled together," Pope said, "had it not been for the invasion of Kuwait."

On August 6, Saddam Hussein's paratroopers dropped into Ku-wait City. The resulting uncertainty in the world financial markets killed the deal as nervous lenders withdrew their commitments.

FOR FOUR YEARS, UNITED AIRLINES had been going through almost continuous internal turmoil, except for the relative calm of 1988,

Wolf's first year at the helm. By the time the 1990 buyout failed, pretty much everyone in the company, from top management on down, was sick of dealing with investment bankers and Wall Street lawyers. It was time to get back to running an airline. At American, Crandall was already well ahead of them in launching international routes to Europe, and he had just snapped up a trove of Latin American routes from bankrupt Eastern. Wolf and Pope sat down in front of United's route map and started looking abroad, wondering how they could get a leg up on the competition.

18

GOING GLOBAL

T he deregulators had long predicted that their ideas would migrate overseas. As the domestic air battles simmered down in the late 1980s, the megacarriers created in the United States were running out of places to expand at home. And a number of airlines were looking beyond U.S. borders for financial help.

The race to tap foreign sources of capital accelerated in 1988, even before British Air's aborted investment in UAL, with an unlikely long-distance courtship between Frank Lorenzo and Jan Carlzon, the suave forty-six-year-old president of Scandinavian Airlines System. The two men could not have had more contrasting personae. Lorenzo was crucified in the press almost daily, while Carlzon was celebrated in northern Europe for turning a lackluster state-run airline into a profitable business that consistently won passenger preference surveys. Carlzon, a strikingly handsome, silver-haired Swede, drew the intense publicity usually reserved for film stars or royalty. He was recognized wherever he went in his native country, and when his first marriage broke up his personal life became fodder for the tabloids.

Carlzon's success with SAS had led the European media to crown him the "Lee Iacocca of the aviation industry." He wrote about his experience in a book called *Moments of Truth*, which was a best-seller. His basic premise was that a service company's overall performance is the sum of countless interactions between customers and employees, moments that either bring a passenger back or send him to the competition. SAS's service had been suffering from low employee morale. Carlzon's solution was to "flatten the pyramid," removing layers of bureaucracy from the organization and giving all employees more power to make decisions.

After a few years at the helm, Carlzon had changed SAS from a traditionally run company into one where even airport ticket clerks could make split-second decisions, for example, on how much to compensate a bumped passenger or how long to hold a flight for connecting customers. That giving workers more autonomy would spur productivity was hardly a new idea, but Carlzon's masterful salesmanship ensured that he was widely quoted by the time he finally met Lorenzo, who would provide the key to the next stage of Carlzon's grand plan.

Carlzon's airline was still a niche player, hemmed in by the borders of Europe. With a small home base on the edge of the continent, SAS would never be in the same league as British Airways, Air France, or Lufthansa. Carlzon's intention to create a company with the critical mass to compete worldwide had been clear soon after he had joined SAS in 1980. But in the early 1980s, European aviation was essentially a network of state-run monopolies in which "flag carriers," propped up by bloated subsidies, brooked no threats to their turf. Carlzon's ambitions needed to find an outlet elsewhere.

MUCH OF WHAT TRANSPIRED among global airlines during the mid to late 1980s can be explained quite simply: A single country—the United States—produces nearly half the world's total airline passenger traffic. As they watched the free-for-all of deregulation unfold in the United States, the chief executives of many foreign airlines saw an opportunity to tap the richest market in the world. Moreover, they also saw that deregulation might soon reach their shores, making it even more imperative that they strengthen their market position abroad. The only sensible course was to pursue transborder alliances that would allow a foreign airline to pick up passengers all over the United States with the help of a U.S. partner, in exchange for which the American company would get more access to protected markets overseas, especially as the U.S. megalines found their ability to expand overseas blocked by the rigid treaties that still governed international air transport.

Just what shape these ties would take was another matter. A

straight merger was out of the question, thanks to the U.S. law restricting foreign ownership.

Despite these restrictions, an airline could still exert plenty of influence over a partner within legally allowable limits, and it was with this in mind that Carlzon began his campaign to get a U.S. deal locked up before his European neighbors started paying attention.

Although Carlzon often claims to have pioneered airline "globalization," it was no doubt on the minds of many of his rivals. Carlzon may simply have drawn attention with his youthful charm and sales skills—a rarity among European airline chiefs of the time, who, with the exception of Colin Marshall at British Airways, acted more like managers of public utilities.

Carlzon, by contrast, had started out in a marketing job at a Swedish tour operator and then headed Linjeflyg, the money-losing domestic Swedish arm of SAS. Carlzon did the unthinkable—cut fares—to boost that regional line's fortunes. When he joined SAS, it had been in the red for two years, but rather than lay off employees, Carlzon invested $25 million in service improvements. The airline made $75 million the following year. In short, Carlzon was already behaving like the head of a deregulated airline by the time he got around to talking with U.S. airline executives about a partnership.

First he sought out Frank Borman, whom he admired for his astronaut fame as well as his stewardship of Eastern. The plan they drew up in early 1985 was modest: Eastern and SAS would share the Eastern terminal at Kennedy Airport in New York, where SAS's transatlantic passengers would switch to Eastern flights for the domestic journey, and vice versa. Borman and Carlzon prepared to team up but their deal fell apart, mainly because of Borman's concern over costs, which were soaring after his jet-buying binge.

Carlzon then approached TWA, again with the idea of connecting at Kennedy. After meeting with Ed Meyer, a team of SAS executives prepared to make a presentation at TWA's next board meeting. But before Carlzon had a chance to give his sales pitch, Ed Meyer was gone and the carrier's board had given control of the airline to Carl Icahn.

At around the same time, Carlzon increasingly preached his gospel to the Europeans, arguing that as competition spread around the world, airlines had to combine to survive. He predicted that by the mid-1990s, there would be only four or five airlines left in the United States, four or five in Europe, and about the same in Asia. He hit upon a catchy slogan—"one of five in '95"—to sum up his goals for SAS. But he was politely brushed off by the European airline chiefs, who simply couldn't imagine the day when each nation wouldn't have its own flag carrier.

Having lost out with Eastern and TWA, Carlzon spotted another stateside opportunity that looked even better. He'd watched Continental tighten its grip on the Newark hub after its merger with People Express. It was clear SAS needed a connection in the New York area, and neither of the other biggest airlines, American or Delta, had much service there. So Carlzon called up Frank Lorenzo and delivered his patented sales pitch: Continental's vast domestic system and SAS's European network would make a perfect fit.

SAS would move from Kennedy to Newark, where its transatlantic passengers would connect to points all over the United States on Continental. The two would share a whole host of services—marketing, scheduling, promotions, frequent-flyer programs—thereby reducing costs. SAS would consider investing in Continental and lending it training know-how, but it wanted a seat on the board. As Carlzon recalled, Lorenzo listened, said he thought it was an interesting idea, but declined to go much further.

Within a few months, however, Lorenzo's Texas Air empire was reporting the worst losses in airline history for a single company and the Eastern situation was rapidly deteriorating. Continental had failed to rebuild its reputation after the disastrous overnight merger with People earlier in the year. Carlzon and Lorenzo resumed their talks at a Conquistadores meeting in Wyoming. The conquerors, too, were becoming more international. Carlzon was one of several foreign airline chiefs tapped by the group and had been quickly welcomed into the inner circle, winning a seat on the club's board. Sometime after their encounter at the Conquistadores, Lorenzo agreed to meet Jan Carlzon at the Waldorf Astoria in New York.

Lorenzo, as Carlzon remembers the encounter, presented his "brilliant idea" about a partnership, which was, in effect, the same concept Carlzon had pitched to him twice before with no results. "Where did you get that from?" asked Carlzon, laughing. The two began what must have been, for Lorenzo, among the friendliest negotiations of his deal-making career. "They were never real hard negotiations," said Carlzon.

One reason for this harmonious deal-making was that SAS was willing to put up a hefty amount of cash to back its position. Carlzon said he felt it imperative to take a financial stake to cement the partnership. "That was my interpretation of U.S. culture," he said. "To us it was obvious we should have some say. We wanted to have a seat on the board. We wanted to have money in there so it would be easier for our management to sit down with theirs."

In October 1988, SAS announced it had agreed to buy 9.9 percent of Texas Air's common stock for $50 million. In return, SAS got a seat on the company's board. That was just the beginning. The following year SAS plowed another $40 million into Texas Air and Continental to maintain the deal.

All this was happening at a time when the wrangling over Eastern's future had reached fever pitch. The SAS deal received relatively sparse U.S. media coverage amid all the excitement over the sale of the Eastern Shuttle to Donald Trump, Charlie Bryan's labor grandstanding, and the like.

But in Scandinavia, the deal was major news. European unions were alerted by their counterparts in the United States to the new ties between SAS and the union-busting Lorenzo, and trade union leaders in Scandinavia began beating the drum. The Europeans in general seemed to view deregulation as a dread disease, in part because of the kind of upheaval for which Lorenzo was so notorious. One European newspaper ran a cartoon showing Lorenzo and Carlzon in bed together, with the caption: "It's fine if you go to bed—just make sure you don't go to sleep."

With unintended irony, SAS landed its first flight at Continental's terminal at Newark on May Day, 1989. Scores of striking Eastern employees greeted Lorenzo's new partner with picket lines outside the celebratory party SAS had hosted nearby.

But the polished Carlzon eluded the unions' efforts to tar him with Lorenzo's image. Many industry watchers thought they saw some of Dick Ferris in Carlzon: a charismatic, charming visionary, even if a bit naive at times. He was, like Ferris, the first among his European peers to come out solidly for deregulation, but for very different reasons. United liked the idea because it was big, while SAS wanted deregulation because it was too small to survive on its own. Carlzon believed that open competition would benefit efficient companies like his over state-supported behemoths. Carlzon also resembled Ferris in one other way: He was pushing to turn SAS not only into a global airline, but also into a total travel service company that also included airline-owned hotels. Carlzon believed in the same kind of "synergies" as Ferris, and like Ferris he bought hotels for his passengers to stay in.

European airline managers hesitated even to use the word deregulation, preferring the more innocuous "liberalization." They were convinced the U.S. experience, especially the wave of bankruptcies, would be unpalatable in their system, which in the late 1980s was evolving from a network of state-controlled monopolies into something more competitive. Some governments, like that of the United Kingdom, were privatizing their airlines, and others promised to do so in the future.

Since most countries didn't have Chapter 11, the prospect of insolvent airlines, especially state-owned airlines, shutting down overnight was indeed troubling. European politicians were more sensitive to preserving jobs than a private-sector manager would ever be. European airline service resembled the U.S. system before deregulation: cheap charters for the masses and high-priced, half-empty scheduled service for business travelers, all overseen by protective government regulators.

But curiously, even the remote prospect of loosening up this system had the airlines leaping into mergers just as a number of U.S. carriers had on the eve of deregulation. In 1987, British Airways bought out British Caledonian, the only serious competition it had in Great Britain, and Air France did likewise with UTA French Airlines and French domestic carrier Air Inter in 1990.

THE NEXT MASSIVE WAVE of consolidation in the airline business was clearly going to take place internationally. Deregulation and the attendant merger mania had allowed U.S. airlines to reshape their route maps and solidify their hold on markets. Now airlines would have to buy their way into foreign markets, if not through direct acquisition, then by something close to it. International route licenses were scarce commodities and thus had incredible value to their owners, much in the same way the old domestic route licenses had been the lifeblood of the regulated airlines. Carlzon's snappy slogan said it all: To survive into the mid-1990s, an airline had to become a global mega-airline. And despite their huge size, American, Delta, and United were still primarily domestic lines.

Bob Crandall, naturally, was not happy that both United and Texas Air had found foreign dancing partners. Publicly, Crandall's posture was that these alliances were overhyped marketing gimmicks. Privately, however, he was worried about being passed by, just as he'd missed out on the Pan Am Pacific deal.

Crandall assigned Wes Kaldahl, the crusty airline planning man who'd been his most trusted aide for years, to scout for possibilities. Kaldahl studied a map and came to the conclusion that, with British

Air already taken, the Dutch airline KLM offered the best attributes for partnership. "We chose them for geography," he said, and their dominance of Schiphol Airport at Amsterdam, where KLM flights fanned out to destinations all over the globe.

So some time before KLM teamed up with Al Checchi and his partners in the Northwest takeover, Kaldahl and Crandall sat down at a private club in New York City with the senior management of the Dutch carrier. As with Texas Air and SAS, it was something of a culture clash. The Dutch airline was conservative and low profile; it eschewed the dominant personal leadership cult typical of U.S. airlines and was run instead by a committee of colorless managers.

Yet Kaldahl said later, "we felt they thought very much like American." Since 1980, American had made profits every year except one, and it had avoided the management turmoil of United. KLM was also a consistent moneymaker.

As Kaldahl remembered the encounter, the KLM people were somewhat taken aback when Crandall proposed an alliance. "We probably came on a wee bit strong," he said with a laugh. For what American wanted was ambitious—not just a transoceanic relationship but a deal that would connect the airlines wherever possible, feeding passengers at all of the U.S. line's hubs.

Over the next few months, American and KLM negotiated a deal. But at the last minute, the talks hit a snag over the seemingly minor detail of KLM's participation in American's frequent-flyer program. American had already welcomed some foreign partners—including KLM—into its program because it needed enticing foreign destinations to offer its members as rewards. But it had to pay these partners for the seats they reserved for American's flyers, and American was losing $5 million a year on the KLM tie-in alone. Crandall and Kaldahl thought that if American teamed up with KLM, it shouldn't have to subsidize the arrangement anymore. It offered KLM a face-saving option: It would be taken off the dole "gradually." But KLM's hidebound management insisted that the frequent-flyer fee still had to be charged to its U.S. division.

American had decided to hold a board meeting in Germany that year, where it was adding many new flights. Kaldahl and Crandall waited in a hotel room in Frankfurt for the call from Amsterdam that would let them know if the deal was on or off. When the phone rang, it brought the news that KLM had said no.

Kaldahl said later one of the KLM executives had told him confidentially that "he couldn't believe that they let it go." However, there was also speculation that KLM was worried about American's aggressiveness. Crandall's reputation as a tough bargainer had already hurt him, when Pan Am hadn't even bothered to sound him out about buying its Pacific routes.

IN MANY WAYS, the arcane world of international aviation mirrored the old regulated regime in the United States. It, too, was run by a club, the International Air Transport Association, which Alfred Kahn and others condemned as a "naked cartel." It did in fact fix prices and provided a forum for member airlines to make all sorts of anti-competitive agreements that even the old CAB would not have stomached. For example, in Europe, competing carriers would often "pool" flights, that is, agree on how many flights they'd offer between, say, Paris and London, and then divide the total sales among themselves. This eliminated any incentive to provide better service and lower prices to gain market share.

Flights between countries have traditionally been governed by bilateral treaties, making air rights a political tool to extract concessions from a negotiating partner in a wholly unrelated area. Once, an airline services agreement with Japan was linked to fishing rights, and the United States and Great Britain have often mixed politics with the business of flying airplanes between the two countries.

In 1944, the United States challenged this tired system when airlines from the allied countries got together in Chicago to agree on international aviation rules. The Chicago Convention created the system of the "five freedoms of the sky," spelling out when airlines are entitled to pick up and drop off passengers on transborder flights. The U.S. delegation had called for an "open skies" environment—essentially permitting any nation's airlines to serve any point in the world—and the conference soon deteriorated in political bickering.

Typically, Pan Am's Juan Trippe was maneuvering behind the scenes. Halfway through the conference, the leader of the American delegation, Assistant Secretary of State Adolf Berle, was replaced by Edward Stettinius—who just happened to be Trippe's brother-in-law and a close associate of President Roosevelt (he also served as secretary of state from 1944 and 1945). There was speculation that Trippe had gone to Roosevelt himself and asked him to replace Berle with Stettinius. Pan Am wanted to squelch the notion of open skies because it feared too much competition. Instead, it wanted to preserve the prewar system of bilateral aviation treaties negotiated between countries. Whether that would have been the outcome anyway—many diplomats were suspicious that the Americans were pushing free trade because of their clear superiority in commercial aviation—Pan Am's viewpoint carried the day. Nearly a half-century later, the United States would push aggressively for the very open skies regime that Trippe helped to torpedo.

THE CASH INFUSION THAT TEXAS Air got from Jan Carlzon's SAS couldn't solve the massive conglomerate's continuing problems of a huge debt load and an embittered workforce. Eastern Airlines remained Lorenzo's worst dilemma; even his sale of the carrier's Latin American routes to American for $330 million could not stop the company's downward spiral.

On April 18, 1990, the federal bankruptcy court in New York stripped Lorenzo of control of Eastern, little more than four years after his middle-of-the-night purchase. Phil Bakes and Frank Lorenzo had dinner the night before a trustee was named, at the Post House, an expensive steak house in midtown Manhattan. Both were aware the Texas Air–Eastern saga was nearing its end.

Lorenzo asked Bakes if he'd like to return to Houston and offered him the post of president of Texas Air, with the idea that Bakes would eventually return to his old job as president of Continental, the one he'd left reluctantly three and a half years before. Bakes demurred; he wanted to take a few months off, he said, and would get back to Lorenzo after that.

By the following evening it was over. Judge Burton Lifland issued a withering verdict on Lorenzo's stewardship of Eastern. Despite repeated infusions of cash, the airline had lost $1.2 billion since declaring bankruptcy, Lifland noted, and had completely lost the confidence of its creditors. "The time has come to replace the pilot to captain Eastern's crew," he said; Lorenzo "is not competent to reorganize this estate."

Lorenzo was not there in person. Bakes had the unpleasant task of informing him by phone late that night. Lorenzo, Bakes recalled, took the news calmly. At that point he realized that there was nothing he could do.

Martin Shugrue, who had served a brief stint as Continental's president a year earlier, before Lorenzo forced him out, was appointed Eastern's trustee; Bakes resigned his post as CEO of Eastern. Stripped of its Eastern unit, Lorenzo's Texas Air umbrella company reorganized into Continental Air Holdings.

At about the same time, the U.S. Attorney in the Eastern District of New York announced that he was investigating allegations of widespread safety violations at Eastern. A number of Eastern employees were indicted on criminal charges, the highest ranking of whom was maintenance vice-president Ed Upton. Eastern pleaded guilty and paid a $3.5 million fine. But although the indictments were handed down in 1991 and assigned to judge Leo Glasser, as of early 1994 no trial had been scheduled.

Lorenzo's humiliating tongue-lashing by Lifland was apparently soon forgotten. A mere four weeks later, Sharon Lorenzo threw a lavish fiftieth birthday party for her husband at their River Oaks mansion. Close associates said that Lorenzo had attended Saul Steinberg's fiftieth birthday celebration sometime before and had been quite impressed by the billionaire investor's extravangaza, which was said to cost more than $1 million, a fitting symbol of eighties' excess.

On Lorenzo's birthday, it was a beautiful day, one guest recalled, and a few hundred guests mingled outdoors. Everyone came dressed in Western wear, reminiscent somehow of Lorenzo's annual frolics with his fellow Conquistadores in Wyoming. A large tent was set up outside where an elaborate sit-down dinner was served.

The only odd note was the presence of newly appointed Eastern trustee Martin Shugrue, who, although invited, was not expected to actually show up, according to another guest. Guests were thus treated to the spectacle of Frank Lorenzo rising at one point and introducing to his guests Frank Borman and Phil Bakes, the two past presidents of Eastern, followed by Shugrue, their successor to the head of the company that had just been wrested from Lorenzo.

By the summer of 1990, Lorenzo finally recognized that his continued presence at Texas Air was the company's biggest single liability, given the continuing crusade that the unions were waging against him. Lorenzo still could not hold on to executives, either. Joe Corr had left abruptly after less than a year as Continental's chief executive. That August, just six months after his ouster from Eastern, Lorenzo sold his personal holdings in Continental to SAS for $50 million—three times the market price of the stock—admitting that his continued association with the airline had hurt it. It was a sorry admission, after nearly twenty years in the business, from someone who a few years earlier had been viewed as the personification of deregulation.

But Lorenzo was lucky once again. Just as he'd done with National Airlines in 1979, he'd cashed out at a premium. And his timing was impeccable. When Iraq invaded Kuwait just weeks later, the attendant rise in fuel prices fell disproportionately hard on such weakened airlines as Continental, which, unlike American and

United, didn't have the cash cushion to withstand the shock. In December 1990, Continental Airlines went into Chapter 11 for the second time. SAS's entire $100 million investment, representing a 20 percent stake in Continental Air Holdings, was suddenly worthless, as the value of Continental common stock was effectively wiped out. Although Carlzon thought he had an agreement from Lorenzo to step down from Continental's board, the bankruptcy also got Lorenzo off the hook on that one. The former Texas Air chief had agreed he'd make the change at the next shareholders meeting. After Chapter 11, there simply weren't any more such meetings. Lorenzo even tried unsuccessfully to remain on the powerful executive committee of the airline. The only remaining benefit to SAS for the $150 million it spent on Continental was the incremental transatlantic traffic it got from Continental at Newark Airport, but even that was called into question, as a reorganizing Continental later found a new transborder partner, Air Canada.

Meanwhile, deregulation in the United States had already entered its final phase: the transfer of wealth from the weak to the rich airlines.

19

THE VULTURES'
FEAST

On a frigid New York evening in February 1990, Kent Scott changed from his pilot's uniform into a dinner jacket and set out for the Waldorf-Astoria Hotel on Park Avenue. It was the night of TWA's annual Employee Achievement Awards Dinner, where department heads dispensed prizes to individuals nominated as the best performers of the year.

Scott was looking forward to the event. It was a rare occasion when he and other TWA employees could share a pleasant evening of socializing with management and set aside their acrimony for a few hours. As the head of the TWA pilots union, Scott was all too aware of the poor employee morale. Moreover, the illusion of TWA's "turnaround" was gone; the airline had lost almost $300 million the previous year.

As Scott entered the Starlight Ballroom, he spotted Carl Icahn next to his wife, Liba. Icahn had not prepared a speech and instead scrawled notes on his menu while the awards presenters droned on. By the time he stood up, the event had already dragged on for hours, but most of the people there were anxious to hear from the chief: Icahn had virtually no contact with the rank and file.

Squinting at his menu scribbles, drink in hand, he cleared his throat and began: "I'm the only guy who could've held this airline together. I saved this airline from disaster, and if I hadn't come along, you know, what with the hijacking, the bombs bursting over Libya, you all would have been out of a job."

So far it was the standard Icahn spiel, a self-congratulatory peroration familiar to anyone who had ever read an Icahn interview. Then his tone turned surly.

"If the people here don't do more . . . this airline is headed for trouble," Icahn warned, his eyes scanning the audience.

His listeners exchanged stunned looks.

"Yes, I've done everything I can do—now it's up to you, the employees, especially the union groups," Icahn continued, staring at the table where Scott sat with his colleagues from the flight attendants and the machinists.

Icahn told everyone to prepare for more pay cuts. Many of the people in the room had seen their salaries shrink in recent years.

As his audience paused to digest that unsavory piece of news, Icahn delivered his parting words: If more sacrifices weren't made, the airline would have to be shut down. A few guests had already stalked out of the room.

Microphones had been set up to give employees one of their rare opportunities to question Icahn, but no one moved.

The party was over. As Scott left the ballroom he surveyed the scene: "People were cursing him out, others were sobbing," he said.

A few women ran into the ladies' room to vent their anger out of Icahn's earshot, amid the flowered walls and gold-edged mirrors. A dark-haired woman emerged from one of the stalls: It was Liba Icahn. As an embarrassed silence settled over the room, one of the women stammered an apology. But to their shock, Liba Icahn said she completely agreed with them. She attempted to comfort her husband's employees, telling them not to take it too hard—that's just the way he was.

The disastrous celebration at the Waldorf was soon the talk of the company and came to symbolize for many the point of no return in the downward spiral of the airline's fortunes. It was not simply Icahn's intemperate remarks or his poor judgment that so distressed the employees, but that his performance confirmed what many had suspected: that he lacked the management skill to run TWA at a profit and was frustrated because his two-year effort to sell the airline or to merge it with Frank Lorenzo's bankrupt Eastern had led nowhere.

During the months following the Waldorf affair, Icahn saw many more of his top executives walk away from the company for good: Bob Cozzi, senior vice-president of marketing; even Sandy Rederer, one of his most trusted advisers, who had helped him win the takeover battle for TWA. There was only one way out. So began the Battle for Britain.

AS THE 1980S DREW TO A CLOSE, it was clear that the competition deregulation had unleashed, which had eliminated scores of independent airlines and created huge megalines in their wake, was shifting to the international skies. A new race had begun, to create not only an airline of such daunting size that it would blanket the entire United States, but one that would allow a traveler to go almost anywhere on the globe without changing airlines.

Mike Levine described it as a high-stakes game of musical chairs. "Airlines are pursuing a risky strategy to grow themselves into complete networks, available to all domestic travelers and as many international travelers as possible.

"These networks seek to cover the whole country and ultimately the whole world. The imperative to build these networks has been so strong that airlines have pursued it despite economic conditions and the stubborn parallel determination of competitors."

This, he says, produces a "concomitant terror of being left standing without a chair when the music stopped."

Competition was taking a heavy toll on TWA and Pan Am, still the nation's premier overseas airlines. The United States had been opening more and more of its airports to new service from foreign airlines. By 1988, British Airways in ten years had doubled the number of cities it served in the United States. The Transportation Department had also been granting more and more foreign routes to U.S. carriers that had been considered domestic operators. The impact on Pan Am's and TWA's transatlantic market share was unmistakable: Before deregulation, they had controlled just under half of the transatlantic passenger market. By 1988, they were down to a combined market share of 30 percent.

Bob Crandall had snatched every opportunity to extend American's route system into Europe. United might have beaten him to the Pacific, but Crandall wasn't going to let that happen across the Atlantic. Before 1982, when it took over the old Braniff route from Dallas to London's Gatwick Airport, American had no transatlantic service. By 1989, American was flying to more than a dozen European cities. Even such airlines as Delta, Continental, and USAir were expanding their route networks to Europe from their U.S. hubs. The only major U.S. carrier that didn't fly there was United.

For giant domestic carriers like United and American, which now dominated their home market, "there is a steadily diminishing opportunity for growth," Pan Am's Tom Plaskett said in September 1989. "However, their strategy for dealing with deregulation requires that their growth continue. . . . Therefore, with the domestic market firmly in hand, growth economics turn to international markets."

In most cases, it was a lot tougher for a U.S. airline to gain access to a new foreign market than to a new domestic one, because international air services were still tightly regulated by bilateral agreements between the United States and foreign governments. Many foreign airlines were government-owned, and the political leaders in most countries thought their national interest demanded that they protect their flag carriers from too much overseas competition. The United States had very liberal agreements with some nations, such as the Netherlands, but others, such as France, were loath to give up much of their market to the Americans and Uniteds of the world. To win immediate operating rights to a foreign country, a U.S. carrier had to buy the route authority from another U.S. airline.

A massive transfer of assets from the weak and failing airlines to their strong and growing competitors was now under way, and an international route authority was usually at the top of the buyers' shopping lists. Led by the big U.S. airlines, the worldwide airline industry was now heading for global consolidation; wherever governments permitted it to happen, the strong airlines were going to devour the weak—if not all at once, then piecemeal.

Pan Am and TWA had one advantage on the North Atlantic—their lock on service to London's Heathrow Airport, the busiest in Europe and the most heavily traveled transatlantic gateway for trips to and from the United States. The air services agreement between the United States and Great Britain specified that only two U.S. airlines could operate to that airport: Pan Am and TWA—or, if anything should happen to them, their "corporate successors." Any other U.S. airlines flying to London had to use the city's less convenient and less popular Gatwick Airport, which offered far fewer connecting flights.

To these troubled airlines, a presence at Heathrow was the last and perhaps the most precious asset they had left to sell. Yet it also posed a paradox. To survive, they needed the cash these sought-after rights would bring. But if they disposed of them, not just their viability abroad but their very existence might be at stake.

• • •

CRANDALL HAD LONG FUMED ABOUT being shut out of Heathrow. Although he had won much of what he wanted in transatlantic route awards, he had never been able to get satisfactory London service. For years, American's Washington staff had been pressuring the Transportation Department to reassign the Chicago-London route authority from TWA to American, arguing that American's big hub-and-spoke operation at O'Hare made it the logical best candidate to provide British Airways with some stiff competition. But the route still belonged to Carl Icahn.

Finally, though, as TWA's losses continued to mount, Icahn was eager to do a deal. He agreed to sell Crandall a number of gates, takeoff/landing slots at O'Hare Airport, and related facilities for $95 million, and the Chicago-London route authority for $110 million. The only catch was that because of the restriction in the U.S.-U.K. agreement, American would have to fly into London's Gatwick Airport instead of Heathrow.

If the London route deal was a coup for Crandall and a blow to United—since American had picked this plum from United's own back-yard at Chicago's O'Hare—it sent TWA's unions into a frenzy. Icahn cited TWA's continuing operating losses as the reason he decided to sell, adding that it was time for TWA to take a long look at some of its assets that thus far had been "untouched purely because of tradition," as he put it. To TWA's unions, Icahn's comments meant he was finally planning to dismantle the airline and sell it off, something they had warned about since Icahn took control four years earlier.

If Crandall's deal to buy the London route was upsetting to TWA's employees, his other December 1989 transaction—to take over all of Eastern's sprawling Latin American routes—was bad news for Tom Plaskett. American's announcement was not only a dramatic confirmation of Plaskett's predictions just three months earlier about the international juggernaut that American and United would come to represent, it was also a direct threat to Pan Am's survival, since Pan Am's profitable Latin American route network was the one bright spot on its balance sheets. Pan Am carried twice as many passengers in those markets as Eastern did, because Eastern had always been a weak competitor with no resources. Plaskett knew all too well from his thirteen years at Crandall's side just what kind of battle Pan Am would now be facing for Latin America.

AT UNITED'S HEADQUARTERS OUTSIDE CHICAGO, Steve Wolf knew he had to do something about Europe. All he had to do was to look at his airline's route map: The European continent was a gaping hole that had to be filled in.

Soon after Wolf joined the airline in early 1988, he had a long-distance chat with British Airways chief executive Colin Marshall about the two carriers' marketing partnership. As a colleague paraphrased it, Wolf's side of the discussion went: "Look, we think this is a wonderful relationship, but you've got to understand: United must fly to Europe, and we're going to do everything in our power to come to Europe, including the U.K."

So much for the much-ballyhooed "marketing marriage" the two lines had forged the year before. If United was to be a global player, it had to hold its own in London, the world's preeminent international gateway.

By 1989, Wolf was speaking publicly about his plans to extend United's routes to Europe. He placed an order with Boeing for fifteen 767-300 extended-range aircraft, taking options on fifteen more. He wanted that model, Wolf said, because it had sufficient range to fly nonstop from any point in the continental United States to Europe. Aside from his competition with Crandall, there was a pressing reason behind Wolf's impatience to get to Europe. If European unity came about on schedule in 1993, a new "fortress Europe" might be much more reluctant to grant American-flag airlines access to the continent's most lucrative markets.

On May 15, 1990, United landed its first planes in Europe, touching down in Frankfurt with a nonstop flight from Washington. Just weeks later, the airline began flying to Paris from Chicago. Still, Wolf could not assemble a global empire without a place in the British capital.

POPE AND WOLF SAT DOWN to talk about ways United could grow across the Atlantic. They still wanted London, but any new service would have to go into the less popular Gatwick Airport unless the bilateral U.S.-U.K. aviation agreement could be changed. Pan Am and TWA still had a lock on London's Heathrow Airport.

"I'll bet you if we go and talk to Plaskett, he'll sell us [Pan Am's routes from Washington] Dulles and San Francisco to London," Pope suggested.

"Well, if we're going to do that," Wolf replied, "why don't we go for the whole London authority from Pan Am?"

So they arranged a meeting with Tom Plaskett.

• • •

PROBLEMS CONTINUED TO PLAGUE PAN AM into 1990 in the wake of the Lockerbie bombing. Even though its passenger revenues started to show significant increases, its fuel costs shot up by a third in the first quarter. And on its domestic system, Pan Am suffered revenue declines, largely because it competed with Eastern Airlines on so many East Coast routes and had to match the last-gasp bargain fares that Eastern was offering that winter in a bid to stay alive. By March 31, 1990, Pan Am was down to its last $90 million in cash; only three months earlier, it had had nearly $204 million. Moreover, Plaskett faced increasing competition from American, which was taking over Eastern's Latin American routes and adding still more flights to Europe that summer.

Early in 1990, Plaskett said, he had Pan Am's attorneys secretly prepare for a bankruptcy filing. At that point, he recalled, "It was clear to us that ultimately we would probably have to do it. But we obviously didn't want a lot of public exposure that early."

Plaskett scrambled to stem Pan Am's losses. He arranged to defer $100 million in payments coming due to Airbus and United Technologies for new aircraft and engines; he sold and then leased back three 747s to pick up another $75 million; he requested more deferrals on the company's contributions to employee pension plans. In spite of all this, Pan Am Corporation's first-quarter 1990 net loss was more than $190 million—even worse than the winter quarter the year before, when the post-Lockerbie scare was at its peak. By the second quarter, Plaskett's mounting desperation could be inferred from Pan Am's decision to give first-class passengers only one hot towel instead of two, and to save five hundred thousand dollars a year by eliminating soup from the luncheon service on some of its shorter flights.

The long-term picture on Pan Am's balance sheet was most disturbing. During the ten years through the end of 1989, the company lost nearly $3 billion and sold off assets worth $1.2 billion. Its stock had dropped to less than two dollars a share, and the company had reached a point at which Plaskett could not reasonably expect any sane person to lend it more money; he could only continue to beg for more time from Pan Am's creditors and search its catalog of assets for something else to sell.

In May of 1990, the Pan Am shuttle went on the block. Pan Am also agreed to turn over its Berlin-based German route network to Lufthansa for $150 million, since the German carrier was now permitted to fly to the former German capital after reunification.

Plaskett also approached a potential buyer for the whole airline—

the same one Frank Lorenzo had turned to when he wanted to unload Eastern: Carl Icahn. Soon, Icahn began to envision a three-way deal shaping up, and he brought in a third party, Bob Crandall.

But Pan Am's situation was never so bad that it couldn't get worse, and in August of 1990, it did. Saddam Hussein's invasion of Kuwait created the possibility of renewed terrorist acts, especially against U.S. flag lines.

Plaskett was desperate for cash to keep Pan Am flying. He even had his Washington staff look into the chances of a federal bailout, perhaps hoping the traditional White House attitude toward Pan Am—that no president wanted to see the airline go down on his watch—might still apply. But there was no such luck in 1990.

"They had great sympathy," Plaskett said. "Every government official I talked to, from the White House all the way down to the bureaucrats at DOT, had great sympathy for Pan Am." But that was the most he could hope for from Washington. So when Wolf and Pope came calling, Plaskett agreed to talk.

Skinner agreed that sympathy was all he could dispense in a deregulated marketplace. "I tried everything I could," he insisted. "But short of an outright bailout, there wasn't much we could do."

When the Pan Am–United talks started shortly after the Kuwait invasion, "I thought he'd sell a few" London routes, Jack Pope said. "Wolf thought we should try for the whole thing, and he was right. For the right price, he was prepared to do the whole thing . . . within a three-week period we had a handshake deal."

However, the discussions were not quite as quick and simple as when Dick Ferris and Ed Acker had met in a Plaza Hotel suite in 1985 to arrange the sale of Pan Am's Pacific routes. "He doesn't negotiate on a one-to-one basis," said Plaskett of Wolf's style. Instead, he said, Wolf relied on consultations with his "brain trust" at Chicago headquarters. But the international wrangling was suddenly to take an acrimonious turn.

ON MONDAY, OCTOBER 15, THE Transportation Department doled out new routes to Japan that set off yet another fierce competition between Crandall and Wolf.

The biggest plum was an award for nonstop service between Tokyo and Chicago's O'Hare, the nation's busiest airport and, of course, the primary battleground between American and United.

Both Steve Wolf and Bob Crandall wanted that route so badly

they could taste it. United's financial experts had put the likely value of the route at $300 million a year in additional revenues. Both companies unleashed intense behind-the-scenes lobbying efforts in Washington, and each airline called on its home-state politicians to put their weight behind the effort as well.

Crandall had won the first round in June 1990, when the Transportation Department's public counsel recommended that Chicago-Tokyo should go to American. He had been confident of success, especially since United already had such a big presence in the Pacific. After all, the Bush Transportation Department had seemed more sensitive to competitive concerns than Reagan's under Elizabeth Dole.

But, to Crandall's shock, the route went to United. The American chief was beside himself. He immediately requested a hearing to review the decision, and Crandall vowed that this time, American's arguments would be made so cogently and forcefully that they could not be denied: He was, incredibly, going to make the presentation himself. Aides say Crandall stayed up most of the night before the hearing, sharpening his remarks and driving American's lawyers crazy. United's Wolf did not make a similar appearance across the table from his old boss, however: He left United's presentation at the hearing to a senior executive.

The Chicago route was worth, by Crandall's reckoning, a dollar a share to United, net, every year. This bounty would flow to United "forever—[from] that one route," he griped. "We really think that was a miscarriage of the judicial process."

Crandall's views did not prevail and United kept the route. Transportation officials said United would provide better service beyond Tokyo to other Asian destinations.

American's officials were furious. They pointed out that when Elizabeth Dole approved Pan Am's Pacific route sale to United in 1985, she stated that future transpacific awards should go to carriers other than incumbents United and Northwest, in the interests of competition. That was how American and Delta got their first Tokyo authority in 1986.

Insiders at American were convinced that Wolf's success with the Chicago-Tokyo route had more to do with politics than with service proposals. "We think the Illinois political delegation was unusually effective" in helping United win the route, one executive said, noting that Illinois is United's longtime home base. American executives voiced suspicions about the role of Transportation Secretary Sam Skinner in the award, since Skinner came from a politically sensitive regulatory job in Illinois, where he had worked for a Republican governor and for George Bush's presidential campaign. A former American lobbyist said that Crandall even hired a detective to investigate rumors that Skinner had somehow communicated to the relevant Transportation Department officials the importance of granting the route to United.

Skinner insisted that he made no effort to influence the outcome of the route awards. "I had no ex-parte communications with anyone on this case," he said, despite Crandall's suspicions to the contrary. But that didn't quell the rumors, since Skinner was widely expected to run for public office some day in Illinois.

On the other hand, some sources in Washington suggested that Crandall's abrasive manner of dealing with the Transportation Department—he and other American officials often criticized the agency for failure to win enough foreign route opportunities for U.S. carriers, particularly American—might have worked against him in the case.

"He hates Washington," one senior DOT source said of Crandall. "He cultivates Washington officials with a thin veil of contempt. . . . He really lacks an understanding of how Washington works; he has a cynical view of government." Moreover, the source added, "Crandall thinks United is always being favored" by DOT.

Patrick Murphy, the senior career official at Transportation who made the judgment that prevailed in the case, insisted that no outside influence was at work in the Chicago-Tokyo decision. "I make my decisions in a bubble—insulated," he insisted.

However, because DOT's international route award decisions are made behind closed doors, many in the airline industry suspected that the process might still be as political as in the days of Juan Trippe.

The Chicago-Tokyo route award turned the intense rivalry between American and United even more spiteful, at least on Crandall's side. Not only did his senior aides publicly badmouth the government and United during and after the Tokyo decision, but they started filing complaints with the Transportation Department against United on a variety of matters. Wolf did not respond with a counterattack, however. Instead, he turned the other cheek, telling all United employees that the lawsuits and "associated unsavory remarks" about United emanating from American's headquarters "are not to be responded to in kind. . . . All of us should refrain from responding at the level expressed by their executives."

Crandall got another shock on October 22, when Pan Am announced that it had ended its talks with Carl Icahn about a possible TWA–Pan Am merger. The following day, Pan Am and United announced tentative agreement on a $400 million deal that would give United a number of Pan Am's transatlantic routes—including several key routes into London's Heathrow Airport. A mid-November deadline was set for closing the sale.

Just as Dick Ferris had done in 1985, Wolf stunned Crandall by pulling off a coup that would give United not just a major presence in Europe, but a hub at the one European airport—Heathrow—that Crandall was desperate to move into. Wolf was assuming—incorrectly, as it turned out—that the British would raise no objections to United replacing Pan Am at Heathrow. Down in Dallas, Crandall knew this was something that could not be allowed to stand. He got on the phone to Icahn to ask if he might be interested in expanding their 1989 deal for TWA's Chicago-London route, which was still awaiting federal approval.

Icahn later claimed he had proposed to Plaskett during their merger talks that Pan Am and TWA combine operations and sell off their duplicate international routes, including routes into Heathrow; he even lined up Bob Crandall as the buyer. Icahn said Crandall was eager to buy virtually all the European route authority he could get and even offered to pay $450 million to $500 million for entree into Heathrow. But in the meantime, Plaskett had gone off and cut his own deal with United. Icahn claimed Plaskett didn't want to deal with Crandall because the two "had a feud going." Plaskett maintained he preferred the marketing partnership plan that Wolf was offering over American's proposal simply to buy the routes. United even agreed to protect Pan Am ticket holders up to $100 million if the airline shut down.

"Frankly, I do not recall your ever broaching the subject of a long-term marketing program in our discussions concerning American's interest in acquiring Pan Am route authorities," Crandall retorted in an October 26 letter to Plaskett. Crandall said that no mere marketing agreement could possibly be worth as much as American was willing to ante up, noting that the London routes alone were worth "in excess of $500 million" to American, and adding that American was willing to buy not only routes but also airport properties, airplanes, and other assets.

Crandall hinted that Plaskett owed it to Pan Am's shareholders to consider his offer. Icahn also made an eleventh-hour bid to block the sale, offering to buy all of Pan Am's stock, then trading around $1.50, for $1 a share in cash and $2 in face value of preferred stock or promissory notes, or a total of $450 million in cash and securities, but only if Plaskett would cancel the United transaction and keep those London routes for Pan Am.

But Plaskett wouldn't do it. His agreement with United was legally binding, he claimed. United's executives, for their part, thought Crandall was trying to block the United deal after the fact. Buying Pan Am's London route network, said Jack Pope, "was our idea— American had never even thought about buying it." But once it happened, he said, Crandall tried every tactic he could think of to stop the deal, first pressuring the government to withhold its approval, then offering to outbid Wolf. "When that didn't work," Pope said, "they [American] then concluded that they had no choice but to do the same sort of deal, and Icahn was sitting there licking his chops."

Some airline executives said Plaskett was ultimately hoping this deal with United would lead to an even closer relationship, perhaps even a full merger. They said Plaskett remembered from their days at American that Pope had been an advocate of a Pan Am acquisition, and he was hoping Pope still felt that way now that he had Wolf's ear.

But that was not in the cards. "I frequently say I've spent a good portion of my career trying not to buy Pan Am," Pope said. United seriously considered it two or three times, he said, but when Pope ran the numbers, it was never a workable deal.

Even so, Plaskett estimated that even a symbiotic relationship with United could generate $150 million to $200 million in annual revenues for Pan Am. The route sale went through as planned in mid-November, with one condition: It was subject to the British government's approval of Heathrow landing rights for United as Pan Am's "corporate successor."

WOLF'S FIRST HINT OF TROUBLE came within days of the Pan Am announcement, when British officials started to tell reporters that they didn't consider United to be Pan Am's "corporate successor." Pan Am was still around, they said; how could United be its successor? And if it wasn't, then United had no right to fly into Heathrow. It became obvious that the British were not going to turn over landing rights at Heathrow to a competitive powerhouse like United without getting something extremely valuable for their own airlines in return.

Meanwhile, Crandall put his acquisition team into overdrive that fall, eager to catch up with United's Heathrow presence. It didn't take him long. About a month after Wolf and Plaskett closed their deal, American announced three international route acquisitions. It bought the Seattle-Tokyo route for $150 million from Continental Airlines, which had just gone into Chapter 11 for the second time. It bought bankrupt Eastern Airlines' route authority from New York to Montreal and Ottawa for $10 million. But the main prize was a total of six more TWA routes into London—most of them into Heathrow—for $445 million. These included the choice New York, Boston, and Los Angeles rights.

The day after the TWA-American route sale was announced, Icahn once again made a bid to take over Pan Am, this time for $225 million in cash and $150 million in securities, using the money from his London route sale. So talks between the two ailing airlines started up once again and continued through Christmas of 1990. However, Plaskett and his team were becoming increasingly irritated at the seeming evanescence of the various terms and offers in Icahn's proposals, and Icahn seemed equally annoyed by what he considered mixed signals from Pan Am. Plaskett wanted some up-front money from TWA in the form of a bridge loan, but Icahn balked; Icahn wanted Pan Am to file bankruptcy and declare TWA debtor-in-possession, giving it first right to reclaim any funds it provided to Pan Am. Plaskett balked at that.

Icahn invited TWA pilots' leader Kent Scott and other union leaders to the Mount Kisco headquarters on a Sunday in December. As Scott recalled, Icahn broke the news about the London sale rather abruptly. "He tried to put a positive face on it, about all the cash he would be getting, how he would put it back into the airline," Scott said. The employee leaders were stunned. "We were in shock," he said. Finally he spoke up. "This is crazy," he said. "You are getting rid of the crème de la crème of the airline."

TWA's unions were growing increasingly agitated about the way their chairman was running things. If they had been upset in 1989 when he agreed to sell the Chicago-London route, they were outraged that he would take TWA out of London altogether. Just as they had predicted a year earlier, Icahn was continuing to sell off the airline's assets. Where would he stop?

The unions quickly won a powerful ally—Icahn's old Capitol Hill nemesis, Missouri senator John Danforth, who decided to make an issue out of the route sale. Danforth wrote to Attorney General Dick Thornburgh, charging that the TWA-American deal "inevitably will lead to a dramatic reduction in domestic airline competition."

Icahn and Plaskett continued their sparring as Christmas approached, and Plaskett said later that he had to doubt the seriousness of some of Icahn's merger proposals—particularly one that arrived at Pan Am's offices at eight o'clock on Christmas Eve 1990.

"I think there were some proposals where he was very serious," Plaskett said. "I think there were others where he really made the proposal to serve his own purposes with his employees—especially the one on Christmas Eve. Here he had just sold the Heathrow routes to American, and the [TWA] unions were telling their members that he was liquidating the airline. He needed to do something to say to the employees, 'Gee, that's not right.' So what he said was, 'I'm taking the money from American and I'm going to buy Pan Am, so I'm not really liquidating, I'm growing.' "

Icahn couldn't believe that Plaskett objected to his timing. Pan Am was about to go under, he said, and "Tom knew every offer I made was serious."

Things got worse after that. First Icahn wouldn't put his latest bid in writing; then he insisted on firing Plaskett as a condition to a deal, a proviso that understandably cooled Plaskett's interest.

Since neither the U.S. nor the U.K. governments had yet approved the transfer of Pan Am's London routes, Plaskett still hadn't received the bulk of United's payment for that transaction, and Pan Am's cash situation was getting critical.

Pan Am rang in the new year virtually out of cash. Its transatlantic planes were almost empty, thanks to Saddam Hussein. Plaskett was faced with the unhappy prospect of shutting down operations unless he could come up with some money, and fast. He turned to Bankers Trust and to United Airlines for a loan of $150 million to keep Pan Am flying until the London route sale could be approved. They were willing to give it to him, on one condition: Pan Am had to go into Chapter 11 so that the loan could be granted with "debtor-in-possession" status. Under bankruptcy law, that would give United and the bank the right to be repaid before any other Pan Am creditors.

On January 8, 1991, Pan Am's lawyers went into federal bankruptcy court and put the company under the protection of Chapter 11. It was an ignominious, although long-expected, fate for the airline Juan Trippe had built into a huge, globe-spanning empire that dominated international aviation for decades. While the man in the street may have looked upon this as just the latest in a growing number of corporate failures, Pan Am's 1991 bankruptcy filing was a portentous event indeed for the millions of people who worked in the airline, travel, and tourism industries, not just in the United States but all over the world. Pan Am had been more than a U.S. institution; it was a global institution. It was one thing for a brash regional airline like Braniff or Continental to go broke. It was quite another matter when it was Pan Am.

Ironically, on the same day Pan Am filed for bankruptcy, the Transportation Department tentatively approved the London route sale, noting that Pan Am obviously needed a cash infusion. But Pan Am wasn't out of the woods yet. At the rate it was losing money, $150 million wouldn't go very far.

That same month, Transportation Secretary Sam Skinner also eased up on his strict 1989 interpretation of the rules covering foreign investment in U.S. airlines. He said the United States would now permit foreigners to hold an equity stake of up to 49 percent, as long as their voting power didn't exceed the 25 percent mandated by law. It was too late for Pan Am or TWA to benefit from foreign saviors, but the policy change did permit KLM to put more money into Northwest, which was struggling to cope with the huge debt burden left over from its 1989 LBO.

Meanwhile, negotiations dragged on between the United States and Great Britain over the fate of U.S. carrier landing rights at Heathrow, and things were not going well for the Americans. They were working against a deadline of March 8, 1991, when Pan Am was expected to pay back its loan from Bankers Trust and was also due to pay a large airplane-leasing fee to Airbus Industrie. After the Gulf War began, the financial situation became much more serious not just for Pan Am but also for TWA, because international air travel dwindled to a mere trickle almost overnight, and so did their revenues.

In trying to cut a deal with his British counterparts that winter, "I recognized that Pan Am and TWA might not survive," said Secretary Skinner.

The U.S. side tried to open up a public relations front in the negotiations, hinting that if Pan Am went out of business, it would be on the conscience of the British transportation officials. The British simply didn't care. The fate of Pan Am was not their problem, they replied; they were in no great hurry to conclude an agreement. The American side gradually started giving in to the British demands, one by one. Skinner even resorted to the time-tested stratagem of getting his old friend President Bush involved. Bush brought up the subject with British prime minister John Major during a Washington visit. In February, when British Airways wanted to lower its fares in the United States in a bid to stir up some bookings from the dormant market, the Transportation Department denied the airline's request.

Skinner said that if Pan Am had been forced to stop flying as a result of the deadlock in talks, he had even been prepared to recommend to the White House that the United States cancel British Airways' landing rights and terminate the aviation agreement between the two nations.

The United States ultimately gave the British virtually everything they wanted—mainly better route rights and better treatment in U.S. reservations computers for British carriers—just before the deadline, and Pan Am again got a stay of execution as United paid up for its new London Heathrow routes.

But Bob Crandall got a nasty surprise a few days later. In mid-March 1991, the Transportation Department turned down the American-TWA deal. Crandall was shocked, especially because United's Pan Am route purchase had won federal approval. DOT said American should only be allowed to buy three of the six London routes from TWA (not counting the Chicago route, which was approved in a separate decision): New York, Boston, and Los Angeles. The route authority from Philadelphia and Baltimore to London ought to go to someone else, DOT said, and TWA should be forced to keep the St. Louis route for itself.

Some in the airline industry saw the hand of Icahn foe Senator John Danforth at work here. Danforth had been a vocal critic of Icahn ever since the 1985 takeover, and more recently had allied himself with a band of civic leaders in St. Louis who were in court trying to stop Icahn from shedding any more of TWA's assets.

"Skinner cut the three routes out in order to take care of Jack Danforth, to keep Jack happy," one industry executive remarked. "And then Carl [Icahn] was sitting there with a lot of cards."

Icahn, the old poker player, knew that Bob Crandall was going to be calling him about this unfortunate twist in their route sale agreement. He was determined not to budge an inch when Crandall insisted on reducing the purchase price because he was only going to get half of the routes they had agreed on. "I'm a good poker player," Icahn said. "I stuck with my guns. I wouldn't have backed down and let him get [the routes] any cheaper. After all, he got the routes he really wanted—we threw in the others to make a deal.

Icahn knew he had Crandall cornered. The American chairman would pay almost any price to get into Heathrow, especially since United was going to start flying there in a matter of days.

Crandall knew it, too. "We didn't expect to be successful," he said of his effort to renegotiate with Icahn. "The routes we got were clearly the routes that had the greatest strategic importance to us."

But he also lashed out at the Transportation Department's exclusion of Philadelphia and Baltimore from the deal. Icahn later sold those two London routes to USAir for $50 million.

TWA, like Pan Am, was in deep financial trouble in 1991, trouble that had been getting worse ever since Icahn took the company private in 1988. By March of 1991, TWA still faced a debt burden in the billions. And its losses were staggering: An operating loss of $162 million for all of 1990 ballooned to a deficit of $144 million just for the first quarter of 1991. Before DOT finally approved Icahn's route sales to American, TWA was falling behind on interest payments to noteholders and on other debts, and in March a group of noteholders went to court in an effort to take possession of some of TWA's aircraft and engines. Icahn now became the lightning rod for labor that Lorenzo had been. The TWA unions were working with such Missouri political leaders as Danforth and Representative Richard Gephardt to try to convince Los Angeles billionaire Kirk Kerkorian to make a bid for TWA. The unions agreed to give Kerkorian $137 million in concessions if he would move in—a parallel to what they had offered Icahn to get rid of Frank Lorenzo six years earlier.

Icahn needed to do something, and that summer, he saw an opportunity for one more big deal. As usual, it involved Pan Am.

Struggling for a strategy to bring Pan Am out of Chapter 11, Tom Plaskett came to terms with the industry's perennial dark horse, Delta Air Lines, on a plan to transfer Pan Am's remaining European operations to Delta for $260 million, keeping Pan Am in existence as a regional Miami-based airline operating into Latin America and the Caribbean. Just as he had done in his London route sale to United, Plaskett apparently was willing to do business with Delta without waiting for other bids. But this time, Carl Icahn and Bob Crandall weren't going to let him, and they found a well-placed ally for themselves in a lawyer named Leon Marcus, who headed the Pan Am creditors' committee and was anxious to see the bankrupt company bring in as much cash as possible for its assets.

Icahn cooked up a complicated $450 million bid for Pan Am's European operation and its Northeast corridor shuttle in a partnership with Crandall. Under Icahn's scheme, TWA would pay $310 million in cash, assume $30 million in ticket liabilities, and find outside investors to inject $140 million into the remaining Pan Am Latin American business. Since TWA's own funds were limited, to say the least, Icahn would be bankrolled largely by American, which would kick in $250 million of the $310 million cash portion. In return, American would get some choice European routes and the shuttle.

Some analysts speculated that Icahn was gambling once more, this time on the likelihood that he could stir up a bidding war for Pan Am assets on the premise that if Pan Am's assets could be valued at a higher price, so would TWA's if and when he decided to sell them off. Icahn's tactic worked. Delta immediately teamed up with United Airlines to make a joint bid for Pan Am with a total value of $495 million. The proposal would give Delta the European routes and the Pan Am Frankfurt hub, the Northeast shuttle, and a number of aircraft for $260 million; United would get the Latin American network and routes from Miami to London, Paris, and Frankfurt for $235 million.

By the beginning of August, even Secretary Skinner stuck his nose into the proceedings, after hearing complaints from various parties that Plaskett seemed willing only to do a deal with Delta. Skinner publicly urged Pan Am to consider all reasonable bids for its assets before making a firm deal. The following weekend was a swirl of shifting alliances and urgent meetings among airline executives, lawyers, and creditors, as the price tag hanging over Pan Am kept getting larger. The penultimate offer carried a total value of $1.3 billion from a tripartite alliance of TWA, American, and United, which would split up the assets among themselves.

The southerners who ran Delta may have been slow on the uptake in the race to buy up the assets of floundering airlines, but they knew a major acquisition from Pan Am was their best chance to vault themselves overnight from the ranks of domestic giant to global mega-carrier.

These megadeals had been orchestrated over a hot August weekend in New York. The TWA-American-United bid had been presented to creditors on a Sunday, and by 9:30 that night, Delta's team had come back with their own package, upping the ante by $400 million and blowing the TWA-led coalition out of the water.

But just as the creditors and their lawyers were exulting over the Delta bid that night, Carl Icahn approached creditors' coordinator Leon Marcus with one final offer: He said he would raise the bid to a flat $2 billion, but it would be payable in zero-coupon bonds maturing in the year 2500. Icahn loved a joke; that was his way of bowing out of the bidding.

THE TRANSFER OF ALL THESE international route rights into the hands of the three largest U.S. survivors of deregulation was one more step toward the creation of global megacarriers—a trend that was spreading to the world's other large airlines in the form of transborder investments between and among companies. It also led to more political battles over international market access.

Mike Levine, one of the original deregulators, observed in 1991 that too often during the previous decade, U.S. negotiators had failed to capitalize on opportunities to gain new access to foreign markets for American carriers. The U.S. diplomats "got commercially snookered over and over again," he remarked, because "we Americans weren't as good at horsetrading" as negotiators from other nations.

Yet some pundits were trying to put a positive face on the emerging global oligopoly in the airline business.

Alfred Kahn saw the eventual evolution of eight or ten global megacarriers as a good thing for competition, as long as they all had free access to the world's markets. He compared the aviation picture to the changes in the automobile industry.

"American consumers should not have slept well in the late 1970s, when they were served preponderantly by only three major U.S. automobile companies," Kahn told the House aviation subcommittee in 1991. "But today, eight or ten megamanufacturers, operating worldwide, supply us with ample competitive protection." He foresaw the same thing happening with aviation—if governments allowed market access. Cynics dismissed that as woolly-headed idealism, considering the difficulties other U.S. businesses had in competing on a level field in such countries as Japan.

U.S. airlines, which collectively lost a staggering $4 billion in 1990, were looking at another $2 billion loss in 1991. In those two years, the airline industry lost more money than it had earned in total profits since commercial aviation began in the 1920s. The casualties were everywhere. Eastern Airlines went into liquidation. Midway Airlines and America West Airlines, two of the best hopes of the post-deregulation optimists, both filed for Chapter 11 reorganization. Midway thought it had found a buyer that fall, when Northwest Airlines agreed to acquire the failing carrier, but after Northwest's financial people took a closer look at the books, they changed their minds. Midway Airlines stopped flying and went into liquidation.

Pan Am, diminished and battered but eager to start fresh from a new home in Florida, made ambitious plans for its smaller Latin American operation. Tom Plaskett was replaced by a new management team, the airline's labor unions agreed to a new round of money-saving concessions, and the new Pan Am kept flying—for a while. Delta obligingly wrote support checks for more than $100 million to keep its new little partner operating, but then its own number-crunchers took a detailed look at the business projection that they had accepted as part of their deal with Pan Am, and at the actual revenues that were being recorded in Pan Am's ledgers. The numbers didn't match. Delta concluded that it was pouring money down a black hole and decided to stop.

On Wednesday, December 4, 1991, Captain Mark Pyle piloted a Pan Am 727 named Clipper Goodwill on an early-morning departure from New York to Barbados, arriving on the island before noon. As he and his flight crew walked off the aircraft, they saw the local Pan Am station manager waiting for them with a message from headquarters: At nine o'clock that morning, while they were somewhere over the Atlantic, Pan Am had gone out of business. There was no cash left.

The flight attendants wept.

The station manager asked Pyle to fly the plane back to Miami for storage, and to return some waiting passengers to the United States, and he agreed. At 2:00 P.M., the plane took off again. As Pan Am Flight 436 approached Miami, a radio message came in. The dispatcher wanted Pyle to make a low pass over the airport, a symbolic gesture of sorts. As chance would have it, he told Pyle, Flight 436 was the last Pan Am aircraft returning to home base—the last Pan Am flight ever.

Pyle made the low pass, swung the aircraft around to a final approach, and landed. As he brought the plane up to the taxiway, airport vehicles were lined up in formation; TV crews with video cameras were scrambling for position. Many people on the ground saluted the aircraft as it rolled slowly past. Finally, a fire truck blasted a stream of water over the plane, and Pyle had to turn on the windshield wipers to bring the plane the last few yards to the gate.

Pan Am was history—and so, some said, was America's dominance in world aviation.

EPILOGUE

" **I** haven't had any fun for the last three years," Bob Crandall complained to a visiting reporter in the summer of 1993. His company had lost a breathtaking $1.2 billion since 1990, ending a long profitable streak. For his part, Steve Wolf was forced to tell shareholders at UAL Corporation's 1993 annual meeting that United Airlines and other industry giants were "in danger of becoming corporate dinosaurs" in the new environment.

By 1993, after three years of recession and slumping passenger business, American, United, and Delta—ostensibly the Big Three winners in deregulation's first decade of open competition—were all awash in red ink. They were routinely canceling orders for new aircraft, grounding planes, laying off hundreds of pilots and thousands of other employees, stopping service on many shorter routes and some transatlantic ones, and reducing flight operations at hub airports.

As one of its first acts, the new Clinton Administration had empaneled a blue-ribbon commission to study what had gone so wrong with the U.S. airline industry and what could be done to correct it. This high-minded mission was doomed from the start. With only three months to complete its report and with half its members having little background in the industry they were studying, the panel not surprisingly recommended only a few minor palliatives, such as alleviating the industry's tax burden. Yet a multitude of pundits and critics continued to claim that only a new era of federal regulation could save the industry and the flying public from further deterioration in airline service.

The call for a return to regulation of the airlines brought forth some strange remedies from the very people who had pushed for deregulation nearly two decades before. Ralph Nader in late 1993 outlined a detailed plan for what he termed "semi-regulation" of the airlines. In his book *Collision Course: The Truth About Airline Safety,* Nader advocated limited price regulation, using state regulation of the insurance industry as a model, to prevent price gouging and predatory pricing. "Semi" regulation of the airlines was ridiculed by critics in other quarters as akin to being partially pregnant. In truth, few disinterested observers gave the re-regulationists much chance of ever mustering the political support vital to pushing such a solution through Congress.

Instead, the buzz in airline management circles was that the critical-mass credo that governed their actions during much of the 1980s—bringing us the airlines' merger mania, fortress hubs, and the like—had been discredited. The model for successful airlines was again none other than Southwest Airlines, the same ideal that the original post-deregulation upstarts had tried so hard, and failed so miserably, to emulate. A Transportation Department study in 1993 even referred to the industry's primary force for change as the "Southwest Effect": a resurgence of low fares on short routes and a concurrent increase in prices on longer segments.

By late 1993, a new wave of upstarts like Kiwi International and Reno Air was on the scene to advance the Southwest Effect, helped along by the easy availability of veteran airline employees who had lost jobs in the earlier shakeout and by low lease rates for the hundreds of grounded airplanes on the market. Like their predecessors, they brought a significant cost advantage to the table, enabling them to undercut the major carriers' fares. Moreover, low-fare specialist Southwest was growing—ordering new airplanes and adding employees—while the giants were shrinking. And both Continental and TWA had emerged from Chapter 11 with lower costs as well, adding to the pressure on the Big Three. Continental even formed a low-fare airline within itself that would mimic Southwest along the East Coast. The plan, dubbed Continental Lite, was remarkably similar to United's short-lived Friendship Express experiment ten years before.

"Among consumers," Wolf told his shareholders, "price is becoming a sole criteria for choosing one carrier over another, especially for short trips." With their powerful yield-management software, of course, the giants could match the prices of the young, new airlines—but they had to be much more cautious about their competitive responses in the new era.

For one thing, predatory pricing was on everyone's mind. In the summer of 1993, Bob Crandall took the stand in a Galveston, Texas, courtroom to defend American, and himself, against a massive predatory pricing suit brought by Continental and Northwest over American's 1992 air fare strategies. At issue was a sweeping overhaul of American's fare structure that harked back to Crandall's 1985 "Ultimate Super Savers"—the same ones that Don Burr claimed drove People Express out of business. However, it is a lot easier to make such charges than it is to prove them, and the Texas jury took little more than two hours to return a verdict for American. Still, the issue of how far an airline should be allowed to go in underpricing its competitors remained on the table.

That same question was attracting careful scrutiny in the Clinton Administration, which sent some clear signals to the industry in its first six months. For example, Transportation Secretary Federico Pena warned Northwest to stop apparently predatory scheduling practices aimed at start-up carrier Reno Air in the western United States, unless it wanted to face Justice Department scrutiny. Similar charges had been brought to Justice's attention in the mid-1980s, but this time, the federal government was taking firm action.

Charges of price gouging were flying as well. The Justice Department investigated charges that the airlines had electronically fixed prices—signaling to each other through computers their intention to raise fares. The airlines vigorously denied this and criticized the government for failing to understand the airline pricing system.

BUT DID A MORE ACTIVE GOVERNMENT mean that the initial promises of deregulation might finally be fulfilled, that a whole new generation of challengers might take on the entrenched airlines?

The "dinosaurs" were again far from extinct. Even if they couldn't resort to the tactics that had served them so well during the Reagan years, they still knew a thing or two about cutting costs. Just as American and United had both done in the first years of deregulation, the Big Three each began an ambitious program of making themselves smaller, shedding airplanes, routes, and employees—and abandoning the previous decade's conventional wisdom that "you can't shrink an airline to profitability."

They also started examining the prospects for employee ownership once again in exchange for union concessions. TWA had emerged from Chapter 11 in part through just such a restructuring—its employees came away with a 45 percent stake in the airline, with the rest going to creditors. And Northwest in 1993 fashioned an employee equity-for-concessions package in a successful eleventh-hour bid to stay out of bankruptcy court. By year's end, even United's unions appeared to have their long-term goal of employee ownership within reach.

EVEN AS THE MAJOR AIRLINES struggled in the early nineties to adjust to the new competitors, economic reversals, and global deal-making, one aspect of their environment remained constant. Year after year the Conquistadores del Cielo made their annual Lear Jet migration to Charlie Gates's Wyoming ranch. In the fall of 1992, they hailed a new chief: Bob Crandall became president of the secret society, and around the same time, he also took over the chairmanship of the International Air Transport Association, the worldwide airline cartel.

As head Conquistador, Crandall apparently threw himself into organizing a posse of horseback riders that fall with his trademark intensity. His fellow riders were the usual suspects: Steve Wolf, Ron Allen of Delta, and Herb Kelleher. But there was also a surprising newcomer—deregulation prophet Mike Levine, who had just taken a top job at Northwest.

"It was déjà vu all over again," as Yogi Berra said. The industry shakeout that began with Ted Kennedy's presidential ambitions back in 1974 had come full circle.

In 1994, instead of a Big Four created by a helpful government official, there are a Big Three, a couple of contenders for the fourth slot, and a few weakened major lines rescued from untimely demise by Chapter 11 or infusions of foreign cash.

And just as regulated airlines in the past sought out mergers to acquire the valuable route certificates that they might never obtain on their own, emerging global carriers are seeking transborder alliances or near-mergers to gain prized international route rights that are as scarce as the carriers' old domestic licenses. Bob Crandall's rage at losing to United the lucrative Chicago-Tokyo route touched on a bigger issue: Despite deregulation, the future viability of a number of U.S. airlines depends in part on winning a franchise of enormous value from political appointees who make their decisions—as the CAB did under regulation—in private.

With international passenger traffic growing at a much faster pace than domestic, the major airlines have to plug themselves into an increasingly global network of foreign partnerships. British Airways had put the fear of God into United, American, and Delta when in 1993 it finally succeeded in finding a big U.S. partner. The British carrier made a $400 million investment in USAir, gaining access to hundreds of U.S. markets and starting a domino effect in the industry. Within months, Continental had forged a marketing agreement with Air France and United had crafted a wide-ranging tie-in with Lufthansa.

And the airlines' survival may also depend on their success in tapping the largesse of their counterparts abroad, companies that for the most part have been spared the depredations of deregulation.

TRYING TO EVALUATE THE OVERALL impact of deregulation on the industry and the marketplace is complicated by the abundance of scholarly and government research produced in its wake, with various studies—some of them funded by airlines—often coming down squarely on opposite sides of the same question.

THE CONTINUING CONTROVERSY CENTERS ON a couple of key areas:

Pricing. Today the vast majority of passengers travel on discount fares, at rates substantially below the full coach fare and substantially lower than they could have expected to pay without deregulation. At the same time, undiscounted fares—those paid by business travelers and others traveling on short notice—have gone up considerably. In addition, government studies have determined that passengers flying out of hub airports dominated by a single carrier pay fares more than 20 percent higher than they would pay for a trip of comparable distance out of a nonhub facility. By 1992, more than a dozen airports were considered to be such "fortress hubs," where one airline controlled more than 60 percent of the traffic.

Many complain about the crazy-quilt fares—how someone who paid four hundred dollars for his ticket can be sitting next to someone who paid one hundred dollars. The answer is simply that this is yield management at work, and why shouldn't airlines allocate their perishable product the same way other businesses do, by adjusting price to demand, cutting prices to move goods that might otherwise go unsold?

Several researchers have determined that after adjustments for inflation, the average price paid for U.S. air travel declined by 20 percent or more from 1978 through the end of the 1980s. Two respected economists affiliated with the Brookings Institution, Steven Morrison and Clifford Winston, concluded that consumers saved $6 billion in the first eight years of deregulation. However, critics of deregulation, such as the large airline union groups, cite a study by the Economic Policy Institute to claim that fares were already on a long-term downward trend before 1978, and that they "fell at a significantly slower rate—some 30 percent slower—after deregulation than before."

Key to the pricing debate is whether a reduction in the number of competitors has led to less competitive air fares. Some, like America West Airlines, insist that it has. But other studies, including those of the Transportation Department, have concluded that the consumer's airline choices have actually multiplied, on average, for a trip between any two cities, because of the dramatic growth of the surviving airlines and the proliferation of potential connections through their hub-and-spoke route networks.

Safety. A major concern of deregulation's critics was that opening the industry to free market economics would lead to less safe air travel, assuming that as airlines looked for ways to cut costs, they would cut corners on maintenance, training, spare parts, and other safety-related items.

There may have been a few instances of this kind of behavior— for example, in 1990, Eastern Airlines was hit with a sixty-count federal indictment charging it with improper maintenance practices—however, fatality statistics for the major carriers over the past decade and a half show no evidence that passengers were more likely to die in a plane crash after deregulation than before. It is easy to forget that safety regulation was specifically retained by the FAA when the government backed away from economic regulation. Airlines must still follow strict federal maintenance rules.

Nonetheless, a combination of factors during the second half of the 1980s left passengers seriously worried about air travel safety: more congestion in the skies as airlines expanded their operations; widespread publicity about an apparent increase in the number of "near-misses" (although this may have been a statistical blip caused by more stringent FAA record-keeping after 1985); stories about aging aircraft coming apart in the sky; and the relentless drumbeat of public relations blitzes by airline unions seeking to scare passengers away from Frank Lorenzo's Texas Air companies, charging Eastern and Continental with all sorts of safety lapses.

In 1989, a survey of passengers found that nearly two-thirds considered air travel less safe than five years earlier. As the industry settled down, however, safety became less of an issue. In a 1991 poll, passengers ranked safety concerns only in fifth place among the factors that influenced their choice of airline, after fares, departure times, and other more mundane concerns. Perception and reality are often at odds: The rate of fatalities in airline crashes in the United States remained more or less the same during the period, and the skies of North America during the 1980s were statistically the safest place in the world to fly.

The union campaign against Eastern's safety record was successful in scaring passengers off, even though the allegations were mostly unproven. Yet during the same period in 1987, Delta Air Lines was implicated in a dozen mishaps, ranging from the bizarre (a plane bound for Lexington, Kentucky, landed at Frankfurt, eighteen miles away, by mistake) to near-tragedy (a Delta plane almost plunged into the Pacific). But the press treated Delta kindly and passengers kept flying on it, because the airline had built up an enormous reserve of goodwill to withstand just this type of reversal.

Even if the fatality statistics don't show it, some critics allege passengers aren't as secure as they ought to be. A pilot at a major airline cites just one unpublicized example, telling of an aging wide-body airplane that limped into its destination with only one of its four engines still operating.

"It's nice to take comfort in the statistics," he said. "Statistically, the industry looks great. But you peel that skin off, and this thing is a rotten apple. . . . If you're looking for blood in the water to determine if things are safe, you are rolling dice you shouldn't be rolling."

During the Reagan years, the FAA's budget was chopped and the number of inspectors reduced at a time when the system was under increasing strain as passengers multiplied and air traffic controllers were cut. Unions argue that even if airlines meet what they call the FAA's "minimal" maintenance standards, they should be required to do more. Deregulation, by making management more beholden to bottom-line considerations, may have narrowed the margin of safety to less than comfortable levels. The solution is not to return to economic regulation but to beef up the Federal Aviation Administration's budget and to change the law to require more frequent inspections of aircraft.

Does ownership of a computer reservations system give some airlines an unfair competitive advantage over nonowners? A 1988 Transportation Department study concluded that the owners of reservations systems were imposing a difficult to justify 100 percent markup over their actual costs on the fees they charged competing airlines for bookings routed through their computer systems. A lengthy 1991 investigation of the industry by the Transportation Research Board stated flatly that these systems "provide the airlines that own them with considerable competitive advantages." And F. Warren McFarlan, a professor and director of research at the Harvard Business School, even referred to American's Sabre system as "the fulcrum that subverted the legitimate intent of U.S. airline deregulation, because it introduced huge economies of scale and consequent reconsolidation in what had promised to become a fragmented, highly cost-competitive industry."

On the other hand, a 1992 investigation by two researchers affiliated with George Washington University concluded that there was "no valid evidence of [computer reservations systems] contributing to the insolvency, bankruptcy and mergers" of any airlines in the 1980s.

New competition. In this respect, deregulation worked like a charm—initially. But after fifteen years of deregulation, the only original "new entrants" still around are America West, operating in Chapter 11, and Herb Kelleher's much-ballyhooed Southwest Airlines, which wasn't really a new entrant; it existed before deregulation as an intrastate airline, but grew substantially as a result of the law.

Southwest has also been careful in its expansion not to pose a direct challenge to any of its larger competitors, preferring to operate out of secondary airports and concentrating on the no-frills, price-sensitive market instead of going after the company-reimbursed business traveler.

And it is unlikely that any of the new Southwest wanna-bes will ever grow into another People Express. A number of economists argue that the airlines, given their enormous need for capital, will always naturally tend toward cartelization. The current fragmentation of the industry into a few behemoths that dominate the business, with lots of little ones nibbling at the edges, fits the characteristics of an industry with monopolistic tendencies. Moreover, the existing barriers to entry—scare airport space, computer reservations power, frequent-flyer plans—are likely to be as effective against any new entrants as they were during deregulation's first decade.

Protecting jobs. The labor protection provisions of the deregulation law were never seriously enforced, and in the early years of deregulation, thousands of jobs were cut, as they were again in the early 1990s because of the industry's pitiful financial performance. But over the longer term, the total workforce has grown, along with total passenger traffic and industry capacity: According to the Labor Department, total airline industry employment jumped by 50 percent during the 1980s, as opposed to a growth of 19 percent for other industries.

But the massive overhaul of labor agreements during the early to mid 1980s at some major airlines, and the management-imposed restructuring of wages and work rules at others, meant that the good old days of fat paychecks and slow-paced workdays were over. A 1992 study by two academics found that the inflation-adjusted average compensation per employee in the airline industry went from $42,928 in 1978 to $37,985 in 1988; and in the same period, employee productivity increased by 43 percent.

For some airline employees, the worst is yet to come: The airline industry was among the most serious offenders in failing to make adequate contributions to employee pension funds during the 1980s. At TWA, for instance, the biggest obstacle to Carl Icahn's effort to take his leave from the beleaguered company in late 1992 was that its employees' retirement accounts were underfunded by an estimated $1.2 billion and the Pension Benefit Guaranty Corporation was trying to hold him personally responsible for the shortfall. Likewise, the shortfall in company contributions to pension funds was estimated by the PBGC at $910 million for Pan Am, $700 million for Eastern, and $390 million for Continental.

WHY DID SOME OF THE big pre-deregulation airline companies prosper in the new environment while others failed? Two differences immediately come to mind: The successful carriers displayed the most creative approaches to dealing with labor and the most conservative approach to accumulating corporate debt.

Of the current Big Three airlines, Delta has always been a model of management-labor solidarity and cooperation, both before and after deregulation. At United and American, Steve Wolf and Bob Crandall both cultivated ties with their workforces in contrast to the adversarial relationships that emerged at such troubled competitors as Texas Air and TWA (although that did not guarantee labor peace, as a strike by American flight attendants demonstrated in late 1993).

Texas Air's Lorenzo and TWA's Icahn, on the other hand, tended to isolate themselves from labor, hiding within a circle of personal aides and advisers that grew tighter as their companies' fortunes waned. Moreover, Lorenzo changed top executives at his subsidiaries about as often as George Steinbrenner changed managers at the New York Yankees in the 1980s (one former Texas Air official remarked that the standing joke within the company was, "Lorenzo pays his executives well—not long, but well"). And Icahn's inner circle was formed not by professional airline management types—whose counsel he regularly ignored—but by personal friends and relatives from outside the industry.

Maintaining good relations with labor is a key to success in the airline industry primarily because it is a service business. An unhappy airline employee in a public contact job can, with each surly remark, drive a loyal customer into a rival company's planes for the rest of his life.

There was also a direct correlation between an airline's debt accumulation and the likelihood that it would wind up out of business or in bankruptcy court. The General Accounting Office, in a 1991 report to Congress, looked at airlines' long-term debt as a percentage of total capitalization, and found that during the 1980s, that figure at Eastern Airlines rose from 79 percent to 473 percent; at Pan Am, it went from 62 percent to 273 percent; at TWA, from 62 percent to 115 percent; and at Continental, from 62 percent to 96 percent. By contrast, American's debt-to-capitalization ratio actually declined during the period to 34 percent, while United and Delta held their ratios to under 60 percent.

Acquisition artists such as Icahn and Lorenzo, like the other Wall Street deal-makers of the 1980s, always seemed more concerned with making the next big deal than with figuring out how to pay for the previous one over the long term—something that is especially difficult in the cyclical airline business. And Steve Wolf and Jack Pope at United are probably lucky that the leveraged buyout they tried to arrange never found its financing, or the debt load might have precluded some of the company's subsequent strategic acquisitions.

As for Pan Am: In spite of some decisions by its post-deregulation management that seem, in retrospect, clearly questionable, the fate of Pan Am in the new environment was probably sealed even before the law was passed. The continuing refusal of the old CAB to grant

Pan Am any domestic route authority for thirty years, while the agency handed out an increasing number of international route rights to other U.S. and foreign carriers, put Pan Am at a strategic disadvantage that may have been insurmountable by 1978. It was much easier for the big "domestic" carriers to add foreign routes from their U.S. strongholds than it was for Pan Am to back into the domestic market from its web of worldwide flights. That strategic disadvantage, along with some incredible bad luck from international events, led Pan Am to a doom that may have been inevitable.

Carl Icahn finally bowed out of the airline business in January 1993, some nine months before his troubled airline finally emerged from Chapter 11 under new ownership of its employees and creditors. Based on his departure, it seemed unlikely that the crafty financier would ever venture back into the business. Icahn called TWA "the worst investment I ever made," and *The Wall Street Journal* estimated he lost more than $100 million on the airline.

And Frank Lorenzo, after selling out his interest in Continental Airlines Holdings in September 1990 and serving as a consultant to some small airlines for a few years, couldn't stay away either. By late 1993 Lorenzo was the primary investor in a new airline company called ATX that was seeking federal certification to begin low-cost, low-fare operations on the East Coast from a base at Baltimore/Washington Airport. Lorenzo assembled some of his old Continental cronies to help run the enterprise, but he faced a massive lobbying effort by airline unions to deny him an operating license based on his previous performance in the industry.

DID AIRLINE DEREGULATION WORK? To true believers in Adam Smith's invisible hand, the free market can do no wrong; whatever it does is, by definition, in the best interests of the largest number. To others, there will always be a need for government to protect its citizens from the greed of unfettered capitalists who heed no law but the bottom line and serve no masters but their shareholders. That is why Congress, when it deregulated the airlines, did so only on the economic side; it continued to impose federal controls on safety-related matters.

Given the government's experience before 1978, a return to a full-blown regulatory bureaucracy for the airline industry hardly seems wise. Instead, the government could improve the industry's situation largely within the framework of existing law. The FAA, for instance, could beef up safety enforcement, especially with attention to aging jets. The Justice Department has been getting more active—as seen in the pricing-signaling antitrust lawsuit it initiated at the end of 1992—and that kind of scrutiny is long overdue.

There is probably no way to eliminate politics from international aviation matters, but the United States could devote more attention to preserving a level playing field for U.S. carriers as it pushes for "open skies" with its trading partners. Given the disproportionate size and importance of the U.S. air travel market, foreign nations' airlines will almost always stand to gain more from such agreements than U.S. carriers will. The United States could use a liberalized foreign investment policy as an enticement to win favorable aviation agreements.

The often-suggested idea of forcing the big airlines to divest their computer reservations systems is probably impractical, given the size of the investment those carriers have poured into the systems. Besides, all are now owned by holding companies or airline partnerships, and all of them are becoming not only increasingly independent from their former single-airline owners, but so interconnected and global in scope that they will eventually reach some level of functional equivalency. They have progressed far beyond their original function of handling airline reservations and have mushroomed into worldwide travel information and booking systems for all types of services.

Perhaps the final evaluation of deregulation can never be made; perhaps the first "cycle" of deregulation—the proliferation of low-cost operators, followed by the industry's consolidation into a few powerful giants—will indeed be repeated again and again. The story is clearly continuing, and even some of the same characters who appeared on the scene in the early 1970s have emerged again.

Notes and Sources

Although we began the research for this book in 1991, both of us have been following the airline business as reporters for more than fifteen years. For this book alone we conducted nearly two hundred interviews. We also drew on previous interviews and materials we had gathered over the years.

Every person mentioned more than briefly was either interviewed by one or both of us or given a chance to comment. Nearly all of the personalities who figure prominently in our account talked with us, some at length, over the course of more than a year. There are several notable exceptions: Stephen Wolf and Elizabeth Dole both declined repeated requests for interviews. Two of the early proponents of airline deregulation, Senator Edward Kennedy and Ralph Nader, did not respond to requests for comments made through their staffs.

A few of our interviews were off the record and we acceded to the requests of some people not to be quoted by name. Several former employees of Frank Lorenzo and Carl Icahn were barred from speaking for attribution by clauses in severance agreements they had signed when leaving their jobs. In these cases, these sources are on deep background, and are not quoted directly or mentioned by name.

Interviews were our single most valuable primary source, but we also relied on federal government documents, some of them obtained through the Freedom of Information Act; written notes by several of our sources; and in some cases, intracompany memos and documents from airlines covered in our book.

Published sources that proved especially useful include studies by the Harvard Business School on People Express, Don Burr, Continental, and Eastern, among others, and specialized publications, such as *Travel Weekly, Travel Management Daily,* and *Aviation Daily.* Several books were also useful. *The Predators' Ball,* by Connie Bruck, covered Icahn's takover of TWA, and *Grounded,* by Aaron Bernstein, provided much detail on Lorenzo's tenure at Eastern.

CHAPTER 1: HOW DID IT COME TO THIS?

PAGE

14 *"Conquistadores del Cielo":* The description of the Conquistadores is drawn from several interviews with members, who requested anonymity. See also *Wall Street Journal,* September 17, 1985, front page of second section, and Anthony Sampson, *Empires of the Sky* (New York: Random House, 1984), p. 42.

CHAPTER 2: THE CLUB

PAGE

22 *From its beginnings:* See Carl Solberg, *Conquest of the Skies—A History of Commercial Aviation in America* (Boston: Little, Brown & Co., 1979), p. 63 ff.

23 *Brown showed his visitors:* Walter F. Brown's spoils conference is described in Frank Kingston Smith, *The Legacy of Wings— The Harold F. Pitcairn Story* (New York: Jason Aronson, 1981), pp. 228–31; and in Solberg, *Conquest of the Skies,* pp. 138–42.

24 *"Legalized murder!":* Solberg, *Conquest of the Skies,* p. 144.

26 *Few new agencies:* An account of the Senate hearings that led to passage of the Civil Aeronautics Act can be found in the *Civil Aeronautics Board Practices and Procedures—Report of the Subcommittee on Administrative Practice and Procedures of the Committee on the Judiciary of the U.S. Senate* (Washington, D.C.: U.S. Government Printing Office, 1975). See also Robert Burkhardt, *CAB—The Civil Aeronautics Board* (Dulles Airport, Va.: Green Hills Publishing Co., 1974), and Solberg, *Conquest of the Skies,* pp. 199–202.

27 *One came from former Air Force pilot:* See R. E. G. Davies, *Rebels and Reformers of the Airways* (Washington, D.C.: Smithsonian Institution Press, 1987), pp. 119–36.

28 *Charters proved that a wide:* See discussion of charter carriers in David Corbett, *Politics and the Airlines* (London: George Allen & Unwin Ltd., 1965), p. 295; John R. Meyer and Clinton V. Oster Jr., eds., *Airline Deregulation—The Early Experience* (Boston: Auburn House Publishing, 1981), pp. 22–24.

PAGE

28 *An outfit called North American Airlines:* Davies, *Rebels and Reformers of the Airways,* pp. 83–99.

29 *One of the worst was concocted:* The Mutual Aid Pact's creation is discussed in Burkhardt, *CAB,* pp. 23–24.

29 *By the 1970s:* Burkhardt, *CAB,* p. 65.

30 *Richard Nixon was president:* For account of Secor Browne/Bob Timm administrations at CAB, see Anthony Brown, *The Politics of Airline Deregulation* (Knoxville: University of Tennessee Press, 1987), pp. 99–102.

31 *Once, when Lyndon Johnson's confidant:* Account of the Murphy appointment from interview with M. Levine.

31 *Murphy's successor:* Quotation from Browne is from interview with his former aide, Monte Lazarus.

31 *Nader went after the airlines:* "Allegheny Air Loses Damage Suit for Bumping Ralph Nader," *Wall Street Journal,* October 19, 1973.

32 *Some had even printed up:* Account of bumper stickers is from interview with Patrick Murphy.

CHAPTER 3: THE TRIAL

PAGE

33 *At a few minutes past 11:00 A.M.:* Account of Brinegar meeting from interview with Stephen Breyer.

36 *"The biggest political television":* Stewart Alsop, *Newsweek,* October 2, 1973, p. 98.

36 *Columnist Tom Wicker: New York Times,* September 16, 1973.

36 *It turned out that Watergate burglar:* Howard Hunt's visit to Chappaquiddick and other connections between the two scandals covered in Leo Damore, *Senatorial Privilege* (Washington, D.C.: Regnery Gateway, 1988).

37 *"I want to see what I can really do": Washington Post,* September 27, 1974.

40 *The news made the front page: New York Times,* November 8, 1974.

42 *"Last Friday I learned that I am a fool":* Gingery's letter is printed in its entirety in *Oversight of Civil Aeronautics Board Practices and Procedures—Hearings Before the Subcommittee on Administrative Practice and Procedure of the Committee on the Judiciary, United States Senate* (Washington, D.C.: U.S. Government Printing Office, 1975), p. 2300.

44 *"An instrument of political blackmail": New York Times,* February 26, 1975.

PAGE

44 *"peculiarly susceptible":* Anthony Sampson, *Empires of the Sky* (New York: Random House, 1984), p. 134.

45 *Kennedy found numerous examples of:* The case of "Air Europe" is discussed in "Report of the Subcommittee on Administrative Practice," pp. 165–70.

48 *even that was called "controversial":* Travel Management Daily, June 26, 1975.

48 *"We are going to get the airline eggs":* Alfred Kahn's recollection of his comment in "Deregulation: Looking Backward and Looking Forward," 7 *Yale Journal on Regulation* 325 (Summer 1990), p. 331.

CHAPTER 4: THE UNITED FRONT CRUMBLES

PAGE

49 *"He looked up and said":* Account of Nyrop is from interview with Monte Lazarus.

49 *"You fucking academic":* Account of Crandall's rudeness is from interview with witness.

52 *Early on he showed:* Extensive personal profile of Crandall appeared in Dan Reed, "American's Ace," *Ft. Worth Star-Telegram*, October 8, 1989.

53 *Ferris grew up in:* Details of Ferris's background appeared in "Winning His Wings—United Airlines' Ferris Sets Expansion Plans, Alarms Carrier's Rivals," *Wall Street Journal*, March 2, 1979, p. 1.

54 *The idea first came up:* Anecdotes about Ferris's flying lessons are from interview with Ferris.

57 *His favorite illustration showed:* From interview with Mike Derchin.

58 *He convened a large meeting:* Following account is from interview with Crandall.

61 *a primitive "iron wheel":* Description is from interview with Chuck Novak, retired United executive.

62 *His motives became clear:* "United Offers Agency Automation; American and TWA Reluctantly Follow Suit," *Travel Management Daily*, January 29, 1976, p. 1.

63 *A few weeks later:* Account of Woodside Group meeting is from interview with former Woodside Group president Thornton Clark.

63 *"organized, hyperthyroid":* Nicholas von Hoffman, *Capitalist Fools* (New York: Doubleday, 1992), p. 54.

CHAPTER 5: THE NEW FLYBOYS

PAGE

67 *For them Lorenzo was an attractive:* Davies, *Rebels and Reformers,* p. 119.

67 *"This is ridiculous":* Account of Peanuts fares from interview with Frank Lorenzo.

69 *Lorenzo's eagerness got him:* Incident reported in *Columbia Daily Spectator,* May 1, 1959.

71 *What he did mention was nevertheless:* Lorenzo's testimony before Senate Commerce Committee subcommittee on aviation, May 1976.

78 *"I said I thought":* From interview with Mike Levine.

CHAPTER 6: MERGER FEVER

PAGE

79 *Lorenzo's bid for National:* See "Lorenzo the Presumptuous," *Forbes,* October 30, 1978, p. 115.

79 *He was unmoved:* "Texas International Air Files Bid to Acquire Control of National Air," *Wall Street Journal,* September 15, 1978.

80 *Pan Am was in much worse shape:* See "Plagued by Problems, Pan Am Fights Rivals as Well as Internal Ills," *Wall Street Journal,* January 10, 1979, p. 1.

81 *As early as 1973:* Pan Am internal study was disclosed by Sky Magary in interview.

82 *"Tall, wavy-haired and just good-looking enough":* Marylin Bender and Selig Altschul, *The Chosen Instrument* (New York: Simon and Schuster, 1982), p. 519.

84 *rules at the CAB were changing:* See "CAB Chairman Kahn Leads Agency Activists Spurring Competition," *Wall Street Journal,* July 3, 1978, p. 1; "Mr. Kahn's Cans and Can'ts," *The Economist,* September 2, 1978.

84 *"This is the last time":* Kahn quotation from "Airline Merger Moves May Snowball, Causing New Carrier Alliances," *Wall Street Journal,* August 28, 1978, p. 1.

85 *Seawell also turned to Lewis Carroll:* Ibid.

85 *The top antitrust official:* Shenefield quotation from "Justice Agency Says Merger Panic Grips Airline Industry; Intervention Is Slated," *Wall Street Journal,* September 5, 1978.

PAGE

86 *By Borman's account:* From Frank Borman and Robert Serling, *Countdown—An Autobiography* (New York: Silver Arrow/William Morrow, 1988), p. 357.

88 *Yet, despite all the urging:* "CAB Rules Either Pan Am or Texas International May Merge with National," *Travel Management Daily,* July 11, 1979, p. 1.

88 *A merger would subject:* "United's Competition Key Factor in CAB's Rejection of Continental-Western Merger," *Travel Management Daily,* July 24, 1979, p. 1.

89 *Two months before the CAB:* "Pan Am Acquires Texas Airline's Stake in National," *Wall Street Journal,* July 30, 1979.

90 *The labor contracts were merged:* See "Meshing Problems for Pan Am and National," *Business Week,* January 21, 1980, p. 56.

90 *For example, the rules:* Example is from interview with Sky Magary.

92 *In 1980, Pan Am agreed to sell:* "Why Pan Am Sold the Pan Am Building," *Business Week,* August 11, 1980, p. 25.

92 *Internecine warfare:* "Pan Am Turmoil Laid to Deficits, Shake-Ups and National Merger," *Wall Street Journal,* August 3, 1981.

93 *Pan Am, said an internal CAB study: The Consequences of Airline Mergers Since Deregulation—Report of the Civil Aeronautics Board and the Department of Transportation* (Washington, D.C., April 1982), p. 16.

94 *He turned his gaze on TWA:* Details in "Who Says Little TIA Can't Buy Big TWA? Many Believe It Will," *Wall Street Journal,* September 17, 1979, p. 1.

94 *Lorenzo's reputation as renegade:* "Texas International's Quiet Pilot," *Business Week,* August 30, 1979.

Other sources: Pan Am annual reports, 10-Ks.

CHAPTER 7: THE UPSTARTS

PAGE

95 *"You've got a big job":* S. Zuboff, *Don Burr,* Harvard Business School, Teaching Note (5-490-065), 1990.

97 *"A good new entrant can clean their":* *Business Week,* June 15, 1981.

100 *The officers by then included:* Information on the salaries of the officers and their stock shares is contained in Hambrecht and Quist's prospectus for 3 million shares of People Express common stock issued November 6, 1980.

PAGE

101 *For years Burr argued:* Account of rift between Lorenzo and Burr from interviews with Don Burr.

103 *"An upstart carrier called New York Air":* *Business Week,* September 22, 1980.

107 *Sometime later that day, President Reagan:* From interview with Dick Ferris.

107 *"Yes, perhaps they deserved to be fired":* From interview with Alfred Kahn.

CHAPTER 8: DIRTY TRICKS

PAGE

110 *"I think it's dumb as hell":* Transcripts of Crandall-Putnam phone call appeared in *Travel Management Daily,* February 24, 1983, p. 1; Justice Department complaint filed with U.S. District Court for the Northern District of Texas. Account of Justice's reaction from interview with Elliott Seiden.

110 *That morning, Crandall exploded:* Account of Crandall's reaction to ad is from interview with Tom Plaskett.

113 *Ferris, like Crandall, was struggling:* "Richard J. Ferris—Flying a Risky New Route for United," *Business Week,* August 18, 1980, p. 78.

113 *Among the first people to be tried:* Account of Patterson's antitrust activities in Nicholas von Hoffman, *Capitalist Fools* (New York: Doubleday, 1992), pp. 57–78.

114 *In 1980, Eastern started flying:* "Eastern Air Will Enter Two Big Markets, Joining New York–West Coast Routes War," *Wall Street Journal,* March 4, 1980.

114 *"Friendship Express":* "United Takes on the Upstarts," *Business Week,* October 19, 1981.

116 *These complaints were taken seriously:* See also comments and proposed rules of the Department of Justice, November 17, 1983, before the CAB, Docket 41686.

116 *The fees could vary:* "Airlines Fight Over Systems for Bookings," *Wall Street Journal,* January 18, 1982.

117 *Ultimately, it was dismissed:* UPI wire story April 6, 1992, "U.S. Supreme Court Lets Stand Victory for United, American."

117 *In effect, this linked:* For detailed accounts of the competitive uses of computer reservations systems in travel agencies, see David Wardwell, "Airline Reservations Systems in the USA," *Travel*

PAGE

& Tourism Analyst, January 1987; Joan Feldman, "CRS and Fair Airline Competition," *Travel & Tourism Analyst,* No. 2, 1988.

119 *and in 1984 the CAB:* "CAB Approves Rules for Eliminating Bias in Reservation Systems," *Wall Street Journal,* July 31, 1984.

120 *The origins of the fortress:* Account of Delta's hub creation in Atlanta is in Michael Jay Jedel, *Post Deregulation Strategic Employment Relations Response of the Successful, Surviving Major Domestic Airlines: A Story Not Fully Told* (Atlanta: Georgia State University: Institute of Personal and Employment Relations, 1990), p. 21.

121 *The economic logic:* Data on connecting traffic is from Air Transport Association reports.

121 *When Eastern chairman Frank Borman:* Account is from Frank Borman and Robert Serling, *Countdown—An Autobiography,* (New York: Silver Arrow/William Morrow, 1988), p. 358.

121 *Lawrence and his wife:* "Braniff Bucks the Headwinds," *Forbes,* October 15, 1975, p. 65.

121 *He considered merging:* Borman and Serling, *Countdown.*

122 *Lawrence frantically tried to retreat:* "Cash-Pinched Braniff Slashes into Its Fleet," *Business Week,* August 11, 1980.

122 *A few days before Christmas:* "How Braniff's Lenders Forced Chairman to Resign," *Wall Street Journal,* January 6, 1981, p. 1.

123 *Soon, stories started to circulate:* "American Airlines Gets a Bad-Guy Image in Dallas from Its Harsh Attacks on Braniff," *Wall Street Journal,* March 12, 1982.

123 *In March 1982:* "CAB Probes Charge American Air Helped to Create Braniff Crisis," *Wall Street Journal,* March 11, 1982.

123 *The Justice Department empaneled:* "U.S. Grand Jury Anticompetitive Probe Centers on Dallas/Ft. Worth Air Traffic," *Wall Street Journal,* April 22, 1982.

124 *That's the way Crandall is:* From interview with Tom Plaskett.

125 *Indeed, from the early 1980s:* Information on Justice Department investigations obtained through Freedom of Information Act request.

126 *an airline bankruptcy was unthinkable:* "Despite Bleak Outlook, Braniff Is Expected to Keep Flying," *Wall Street Journal,* January 20, 1982, p. 1.

126 *It would "continue to monitor the competitive conditions":* "U.S. Agency to Look for Antitrust Conflicts in Any American Air Bid for Braniff Fleet," *Wall Street Journal,* June 3, 1983.

PAGE
126 *Three weeks after:* "TWA, American to Raise Fares on Braniff Lines," *Wall Street Journal,* June 3, 1982.

CHAPTER 9: BLUE-COLLAR BLUES

PAGE
128 *Ugly incidents followed:* "Continental Air Workers Crossing Picket Lines Face Rising Hostility," *Wall Street Journal,* October 11, 1983.

129 *Raised in a rough neighborhood:* Stephen Wolf's background detailed in Mike Steere, "Up in the Air," *Chicago* magazine, May 1991; interviews with friends and acquaintances.

131 *Labor costs, 35 percent:* Analysis of Lorenzo's successful use of Chapter 11 at Continental was in Roy Rowan, "An Airline Boss Attacks Sky-High Wages," *Fortune,* January 9, 1984.

132 *This may have emboldened Lorenzo:* "Congress Wrote Continental's Ticket," *Wall Street Journal,* October 11, 1983.

132 *But Congress failed to appropriate:* For example, "Income Protection Bill Urged by Pilots Is Rejected by Senate," *Wall Street Journal,* August 13, 1982.

134 *Borman reluctantly agreed:* "Eastern Air Averts Machinists Strike with 3-Year Pact," *Wall Street Journal,* March 24, 1983.

136 *American was poised to increase:* See Kenneth Labich, "Bob Crandall Soars by Flying Solo," *Fortune,* September 29, 1986, p. 118.

137 *Wolf earned the reputation:* David L. Brown, "Republic's Stephen Wolf: The Right Man at the Right Time," *Airline Executive,* January 1985, p. 20; "Back on Course: Republic Airlines Succeeds with a Revamped Three-Hub Route Structure," *Barrons,* December 16, 1985.

General source: Michael Jay Jedel, *Post Deregulation Strategic Employment Relations Response of the Successful, Surviving Major Domestic Airlines: A Story Not Fully Told* (Atlanta: Georgia State University: Institute of Personnel and Employment Relations, 1990).

CHAPTER 10: THE BIG DEAL

PAGE
139 *When the aviation elite:* Account of fall 1984 Conquistadores meeting from not-for-attribution interview with guest at ranch.

PAGE

139 *People Express was at the time:* The Economist in 1984 named People Express the largest-growing corporation in U.S. history.

141 *One instance came: Frequent Flyer,* April 1985, p. 58, "The Fuel That Flamed," by David Martindale.

141 *At the end of 1984:* "The Contest over Who Will Inherit the CAB's Powers," *Business Week,* February 6, 1984.

143 *Although the company was virtually:* "Pan Am Chairman Granted Options on Million Shares," *Wall Street Journal,* April 6, 1982.

143 *The company's five labor unions:* Geoffrey Smith, "Tail Wind at Pan Am," *Forbes,* July 4, 1983, p. 42.

144 *The company had also repeatedly:* "A Recovered Pan Am Faces Tomorrow's Hurdles," *Business Week,* June 4, 1984.

144 *Within a week, Ferris:* "Pan Am Agrees to Sell United Its Pacific Unit," *Wall Street Journal,* April 23, 1985.

145 *But he also knew:* "Pan Am Indicates It Will Post Deficit of $140 Million for 1st Period, '85 Loss," *Wall Street Journal,* May 7, 1985.

146 *In a speech to a Washington:* "United Chief Calls Pan American Pacific Deal Result of Deregulation," *Aviation Week & Space Technology,* July 8, 1985, p. 39.

147 *"Carriers have become less discreet":* Aviation Daily, January 3, 1986, p. 12.

Other general sources: "The Pan Am–United Deal: 'Truly a Win-Win Situation,' " *Business Week,* May 6, 1985, p. 45; "Pan Am Routes' Sale to United Poses Problems," *Wall Street Journal,* April 29, 1985, p. 6; Colin Leinster, "Can Pan Am Survive?" *Fortune,* April 15, 1985.

CHAPTER 11: ICAHN THE TERRIBLE

PAGE

151 *With only 1 percent of TW:* Details of Odyssey's actions in *Wall Street Journal,* September 29, 1983.

154 *The airline had in 1985 posted:* Continental's results in *Aviation Daily,* February 1985.

156 *Icahn was raised an only child:* For details of Icahn's rise see Connie Bruck, *The Predator's Ball—The Junk Bond Raiders and the Man Who Staked Them* (New York: The American Lawyer/ Simon and Schuster, 1988), pp. 150–54.

158 *It was Icahn's first meeting with Meyer:* See *Aviation Daily,* May 13, 1985, p. 56.

PAGE

159 *Meyer described him as "the greediest man":* From interviews with associates of Meyer at TWA.

160 *Lorenzo was hardly TWA's ideal White Knight:* See Connie Bruck, "Kamikaze," *The American Lawyer,* December 1985, pp. 75–84.

161 *"All you want is a fast buck":* As quoted in Judith Ehrlich and Barry Renfeld, *The New Crowd* (Boston: Little, Brown, 1989), p. 299.

163 *By the next morning:* Account of Icahn-Lorenzo dealmaking from interviews with associates of Lorenzo and Icahn; Connie Bruck, "Kamikaze," pp. 75–84; Moira Johnson, *Takeover* (New York: Arbor House, 1986).

164 *Lorenzo was hailed as a visionary:* See *New York Times,* June 14, 1985.

CHAPTER 12: EMPIRE BUILDERS

PAGE

172 *"Here we've got this merger":* Burr's account of his pitch from speech to Wings Club, New York City, fall 1988.

172 *A story reported:* From interview with Burr.

173 *"That's a remarkable offer":* From *Wall Street Journal,* October 14, 1985, p. 6.

173 *"God, even Lorenzo didn't realize it":* From interview with Burr.

174 *A week before Christmas:* See "TWA-Icahn Pact Falters," *Travel Weekly,* December 26, 1985, p. 1.

176 *One tactic he used to:* Bryan's strategy described in *Aviation Daily,* January 9, 1986.

178 *the public relations department:* Draft press release dated February 24, 1986 (never issued).

178 *In the end, Bryan gave the board an ultimatum:* For a more detailed account of the sale of Eastern to Lorenzo, see Frank Borman and Robert J. Serling, *Countdown—An Autobiography* (New York: Silver Arrow Books, William Morrow and Company, 1988), pp. 427–38; Aaron Bernstein, *Grounded—Frank Lorenzo and the Destruction of Eastern Airlines* (New York: Simon and Schuster, 1990), pp. 33–53.

182 *When Burr was asked:* Account of Burr-McAdoo dispute from interviews with both men.

CHAPTER 13: THE MERGER MESS

PAGE

187 *Alone among major airline executives:* From interview with Icahn.

189 *"It wasn't just fat":* Alex Brummer, "TWA—Will It Survive the Rescue?" *Airline Business,* March 1987, p. 45.

190 *Employees quickly dubbed it "Junk from a Cart":* From interviews with Jon Proctor, Kent Scott.

191 *a type of financial legerdemain:* "The Comeuppance of Carl Icahn," *Fortune,* February 17, 1986, p. 22.

191 *"Why should I risk anything":* Ibid.

192 *The TWA and Ozark combination:* Sample fares are from "Airline Mergers: Who Gets Squeezed?" *OAG Frequent Flyer,* July 1987, p. 54.

193 *The flight attendants accused him:* Frankovitch's account repeated on an in-house videotape made by International Federation of Flight Attendants.

195 *According to a senior pilot:* From interview with Kent Scott. See also Kent Scott, "TWA Today," *Air Line Pilot,* January 1991, p. 30.

196 *The mergers-and-acquisitions fever:* For accounts of Reagan administration antitrust policies, see Roger E. Meiners and Bruce Yandle, eds., *Regulation and the Reagan Era* (New York: Holmes & Meier, 1989), esp. Chapter 5, by William F. Shughart II, "Antitrust Policy in the Reagan Administration: Pyrrhic Victories?"; Betty Bock et al., *Is Antitrust Dead?* (New York: The Conference Board, 1989).

197 *By the end of Reagan's:* See General Accounting Office June 1989 Report to Congress, titled *Airline Competition: DOT's Implementation of Airline Regulatory Authority.*

199 *The proposed combination:* See "Delta Comes Out Swinging," *Business Week,* September 22, 1986, p. 24.

200 *By early 1987, Icahn:* For accounts of Icahn's run at USAir and USAir's defense in buying Piedmont, see "Carl Icahn Is At It Again," *Business Week,* March 16, 1987, p. 42; "How USAir Cut Icahn Out," *Business Week,* March 23, 1987, p. 35.

201 *The department was in a difficult:* "USAir's Plan to Buy Piedmont Faces Resistance From Regulatory Officials," *Wall Street Journal,* September 18, 1987.

201 *Indeed,* The Wall Street Journal: "Merger Myopia," *Wall Street Journal,* October 19, 1987.

PAGE

202 *Even one of the law judges:* "USAir and Piedmont Shouldn't Merge, Agency Judge Says," *Wall Street Journal,* September 22, 1987.

202 *With Burnley facing a possible:* "Burnley Acts to Quiet Critics, Limit Fight on Confirmation for Transportation Job," *Wall Street Journal,* October 9, 1987.

202 *Later the General Accounting Office:* See *Airline Competition—DOT's Implementation of Airline Regulatory Authority* (Washington, D.C.: General Accounting Office, June 1989).

CHAPTER 14: THE BIG BANG

PAGE

203 *At Eastern's shareholders:* From tape recording made of Eastern special stockholders' meeting, November 25, 1986.

204 *When Phil Bakes:* Fountain episode from interviews with Bakes, Richard Magurno.

205 *Soon after Bakes's speech:* Examples drawn from stories appearing in the *Falcon,* Eastern's in-house newspaper in early 1987.

207 *"the least institutionalized organization":* Goolsbee's comments from Harvard Business School Case Study on Continental.

207 *"Nobody's much of a stickler":* Ibid.

208 *The folly of the former approach:* Northwest-Republic merger details covered in "Northwest and Republic: A Wedding But No Honeymoon," *Business Week,* August 18, 1986, p. 56; "Northwest's Merger Has Passengers Fuming," *Business Week,* November 24, 1986, p. 64.

210 *Burr would get about:* Burr's financial arrangements with Lorenzo from interviews (not for attribution) with former senior Texas Air executives.

212 *An unprecedented number of complaints:* "Texas Air's Rapid Growth Spurs Surge in Complaints About Service," *Wall Street Journal,* February 26, 1987.

215 *By year-end, Dole was under:* As reflected in editorials, "Free the Gridlocked Skies," *Wall Street Journal,* August 17, 1987; "The Airline Crisis," *Wall Street Journal,* October 9, 1987.

215 *Senator John Danforth told reporters:* "When Lawmakers Suffer Lousy Airline Services, They Are Able to Respond by Making New Laws," *Wall Street Journal,* March 11, 1987, p. 70.

PAGE

215 *Eastern captain Ray Davidson:* Incident cited in *OAG Frequent Flyer*, July 1987, p. 47.

216 *At Dole's behest:* "Secretary Dole Urges Joint Scheduling by Airlines to Fight Delays at Airports," *Wall Street Journal*, January 29, 1987.

216 *Airlines themselves were responsible:* "Why Do Airlines Schedule Flights at the Same Time?" *Wall Street Journal*, April 28, 1987.

CHAPTER 15: ALLEGIS

PAGE

218 *On April 30, 1987:* An account of the 1987 annual meeting is in "Allegis Weighs Greater Role for Employees," *Wall Street Journal*, May 1, 1987.

220 *So when Ferris:* John Curley, "United Airlines Hopes Pilots' Vote This Week Will Be Turning Point," *Wall Street Journal*, August 10, 1981, p. 1.

221 *Ferris got a break:* "United Airlines Gets a Break at the Bargaining Table," *Business Week*, July 2, 1984, p. 26.

222 *The airline's operations were shattered:* Harlan Byrne, "United Airlines, Pilots Union Agree to Hold Talks with Mediators in Strike," *Wall Street Journal*, May 20, 1985. Other pilot strike sources: "There's No Turning Back at United," *Business Week*, June 13, 1985; "United, Pilots Appear Ready to Deal with Prolonged Strike After Talks Snag," *Wall Street Journal*, May 28, 1985.

223 *In the middle of the pilots' strike:* "United, Pilots Appear Ready . . ." *Wall Street Journal*, May 28, 1985.

223 *First, Ferris announced:* "UAL's Westin to Sell Hotels to Partnerships," *Wall Street Journal*, June 3, 1985.

224 *A week later, UAL said:* "UAL Will Use Some of Unit's Pension Funds," *Wall Street Journal*, June 11, 1985.

224 *They settled on a price:* "RCA Agrees to Sell UAL Its Hertz Unit," *Wall Street Journal*, June 18, 1985.

224 *One-stop shopping:* For accounts of Allegis strategy, see Kenneth Labich, "United Changes Flight Pattern," *Fortune*, September 30, 1985.

225 *In the fall of 1985:* "United Airlines Orders 116 Jets from Boeing," *Wall Street Journal*, November 8, 1985.

PAGE

225 *he went after Hilton International:* "UAL to Buy Transworld's Hilton Unit," *Wall Street Journal*, December 24, 1986; "Can UAL and Its Hilton Wing Fly in Formation?" *Business Week*, January 12, 1987.

227 *In January 1987 Dubinsky:* A detailed account of the battle over Allegis's assets is in Mark Hornung, "Revolt at Allegis: How Labor and Wall Street Stopped Ferris," *Crain's Chicago Business*, November 30, 1987, p. 17.

227 *Ferris, meanwhile, met with financial:* "UAL to Change Name, Strengthen Link of Airline, Car Rental, Hotel Services," *Wall Street Journal*, February 19, 1987.

228 *The following month, word leaked out:* "Donald Trump Is Said to Acquire Holding in UAL," *Wall Street Journal*, March 13, 1987, p. 9.

228 *Trump took a swipe:* See "Rising UAL Turmoil Threatens Ferris's Job as the Chief Executive," *Wall Street Journal*, April 17, 1987, p. 1.

228 *When Donald Trump lunched:* "Talk of a Possible Takeover of UAL Is in the Air," *Wall Street Journal*, April 9, 1987.

229 *And the outlook for 1987:* "Texas Air Corp. Will Extend 'MaxSaver' Plan," *Wall Street Journal*, April 21, 1987.

229 *When the rumors:* "Talk of a Possible Takeover Is in the Air," *Wall Street Journal*, April 9, 1987; "UAL Board Backs Chairman," *Wall Street Journal*, April 20, 1987, Letters to the Editor.

229 *To further reassure Ferris:* "UAL Officials Get Golden Parachute Severance Pacts," *Wall Street Journal*, April 21, 1987.

229 *However, at the same time:* See Hornung, "Revolt at Allegis," *Crain's Chicago Business*, November 30, 1987.

229 *Then in late May:* "Coniston to Seek Control of Allegis Board, Says It Would Sell All or Part of Concern," *Wall Street Journal*, May 27, 1987.

230 *Ferris convinced the board:* "Even If Allegis Wins, the Victory Could Be Pyrrhic," *Business Week*, June 15, 1987, p. 37.

Other general sources: "The Unraveling of an Idea—How Dick Ferris' Grand Plan for Allegis Collapsed," *Business Week*, June 22, 1987, p. 42; Kenneth Labich, "How Dick Ferris Blew It," *Fortune*, July 6, 1987, p. 42.

CHAPTER 16: THE RELUCTANT FLYBOYS

PAGE

236 *Instead of managing the airline:* For accounts of Icahn's machinations see "Super Pilot or Predator?" *Barrons,* September 26, 1988; "Advanced Icahnomics," *St. Louis Post-Dispatch,* May 21, 1990; "The Terrorist of TWA," *The RiverFront Times,* February 13–19, 1991.

236 *On November 16, 1963:* From order filed with the Supreme Court of the State of New York, Appellate Division: First Department, dated New York, November 19, 1963, and accompanying affidavit filed in same court, November 15, 1963.

237 *"the advertising account guy from hell":* Adweek, October 15, 1990.

242 *"That day, TWA ceased to exist":* From interview with Kent Scott.

245 *But when he greeted Kennedy:* Account of Bakes-Kennedy encounter from interview with Bakes.

246 *"He welched on the deal":* From interview with Brian Freeman. See also Aaron Bernstein, *Grounded—Frank Lorenzo and the Destruction of Eastern Airlines* (New York: Simon and Schuster, 1990), p. 154.

247 *a new agreement that he was offering:* Account of Lorenzo's offer to pilots from interviews with pilots, and Bernstein, *Grounded,* p. 160.

247 *Meanwhile, extensive strike preparations:* From internal Eastern Airlines plan, "Strike Contingency Planning," February 1988, and interviews with former Eastern employees.

247 *Only 85 of Eastern's 1,040 flights:* Bernstein, *Grounded,* p. 162.

CHAPTER 17: END OF THE LBO

PAGE

249 *In early 1988:* Accounts of Steve Wolf's hiring and early days at United are in Barbara Marsh, "Tiger's Wolf Ideal Choice to Head United," *Crain's Chicago Business,* December 14, 1987, p. 3; Carol Jouzaitis, "Wolf Maps Flight Plan for United," *Chicago Tribune,* May 22, 1988; James Ellis, "United's New Chief is Used to Chopping and Slashing," *Business Week,* May 30, 1988; Robert Rose, "Under Its New Chief, United Airlines Begins to Pick Up Altitude," *Wall Street Journal,* July 28, 1988, p. 1; Agis Salpukas, "Steve Wolf's Big Test—United's Chief Is Saddled with Problems as American Takes the Lead," *New York Times,* January 8, 1989; "Wolf's Bane," *Forbes,* May 29, 1989;

PAGE

"Will the Carrot and Stick Work at United?" *Business Week*, February 6, 1989, p. 56. One of the few personal profiles of Wolf appeared in Mike Steere, "Up in the Air," *Chicago* magazine, May 1991.

250 *In January 1988:* Details of Crandall's restricted stock award are in AMR Corporation 10-K filings for first quarter of 1988.

251 *He was going to get married:* Details of Wolf's relationship with Delores Wallace are in Delores E. Wolf, "Mid-Career Bailout," *Across the Board*, September 1989, p. 20.

252 *Wolf immediately set about reducing:* For Wolf's budget-trimming, see "Under Its New Chief, United Airlines Begins to Pick Up Altitude," *Wall Street Journal*, July 28, 1988, p. 1.

253 *His successor, Steven Rothmeier:* See Richard Gibson, "The Autocratic Style of Northwest's CEO Complicates Defense," *Wall Street Journal*, March 30, 1989, p. 1.

254 *The suitors were soon:* See "Former Director of NWA Is Part of Suitor Group," *Wall Street Journal*, April 7, 1989, p. A4.

254 *"I want to put":* Oberstar comment is from *Travel Management Daily*, April 5, 1989, p. 1.

256 *In an early February 1989:* See "Pan Am Chief Says Firm Needs Partner for a Merger or Business Combination," *Wall Street Journal*, February 10, 1989.

256 *The idea of a Pan Am–Northwest:* Details of Pan Am's run at Northwest are in "Pan American's Effort to Buy Rival NWA Is Bold Survival Strategy," *The Wall Street Journal*, June 5, 1989, p. 1.

256 *In the end, though:* "NWA Agrees to a $3.65 Billion Takeover by Group Led by Investor Alfred Checchi," *Wall Street Journal*, June 20, 1989.

257 *Wolf's fears:* "Davis's Proposal for UAL Totals $5.4 Billion," *Wall Street Journal*, August 9, 1989.

260 *In late August, Jeffrey:* "Transportation Agency May Rein in Buy-Outs, Foreign Investments," *Wall Street Journal*, August 31, 1989.

261 *One of the callers was:* Lorenzo's phone call was described in interview with Jeffrey Shane.

261 *Secretary Skinner himself repeated:* "Skinner Warns About Debt at Airlines, Plans a Meeting with NWA's Checchi," *Wall Street Journal*, September 20, 1989, p. A8.

262 *In June 1989, for example:* *Travel Management Daily*, June 19, 1989, p. 1.

PAGE

262 *If the London route deal:* "Three Big U.S. Airlines Strive to be Big Three Carriers Abroad," *Wall Street Journal*, December 19, 1989.

262 *As economist Robert Kuttner commented:* Remark is from "Why the United Buyout Is No Great Deal for Workers," *Business Week*, October 9, 1989, p. 26.

262 *In fact, the machinists were so incensed:* From interview with machinists' adviser Brian Freeman.

263 *In early October:* "AMR Seeks SEC, Big Board Inquiries Into News Reports on Takeover Rumors," *Wall Street Journal*, October 2, 1989.

264 *Wall Street settled down:* "Battle of Titans—Crandall's American Is Unlikely Recipient of $8 Billion Trump Bid," *Wall Street Journal*, October 6, 1989, p. 1.

265 *Yet Crandall and his team:* "AMR Seeks Legislation to Stop Trump from Asking Shareholders to Oust Board," *Wall Street Journal*, October 11, 1989.

265 *Some critics contended:* For analyses of UAL 1989 buyout attempt and its failure, see "Banks Rejecting UAL Saw Unique Defects in This Buy-Out Deal," *Wall Street Journal*, October 16, 1989, p. 1; "Pilot Power," *Airline Business*, December 1989, p. 34; "Will Employee Ownership Fly?" *Airline Executive*, November 1989; Kenneth Labich, "Can United Afford to be Taken Over?" *Fortune*, September 11, 1989, p. 146; Peter Lee, "UAL: Inside the Fiasco of the Decade," *Euromoney*, November 1989, p. 58.

266 *A large number of arbitragers:* "UAL, AMR Give Arbitrageurs a Bloodbath of $500 Million," *Wall Street Journal*, October 17, 1989.

266 *Wolf and Pope watched:* "Two UAL Officers Get No Parachutes in Stock's Free Fall," *Wall Street Journal*, October 18, 1989.

266 *There were some clear winners:* "In Failed Bid for UAL, Lawyers and Bankers Didn't Fail to Get Fees," *Wall Street Journal*, November 30, 1989, p. 1.

267 *He ended up making $18 million:* "UAL Chief Is Highest-Paid U.S. Executive at $18.3 Million," *Washington Times*, April 26, 1991.

CHAPTER 18: GOING GLOBAL

PAGE

269 *He wrote about his experience:* Jan Carlzon, *Moments of Truth*, published in the United States by Ballinger Publishing Company

PAGE

1987. Reprinted in 1989 in paperback by Perennial Library, Harper & Row.

271 *First he sought:* From interview with Carlzon.

273 *That was just the beginning:* Details of SAS's investments in Continental are included in Texas Air's 1989 annual report.

273 *"It's fine if you go to bed":* From interview with senior SAS executive.

273 *The Chicago Convention created the system:* The five freedoms are: (1) the right to overfly a country; (2) the right to land in a country; (3) the right to carry passengers from your country to another; (4) the reverse of 3; (5) the right to pick up passengers in another country and carry them to a third country.

278 *By the summer of 1990, Lorenzo:* From interviews with Carlzon and other executives close to Lorenzo.

CHAPTER 19: THE VULTURES' FEAST

PAGE

280 *On a frigid New York evening:* Account of TWA Awards Dinner is from interview with Kent Scott and several other guests.

282 *Competition was taking a heavy toll:* "Pan Am and TWA, Battered by Rivals, Struggle to Survive," *Wall Street Journal,* October 18, 1988, p. 1.

283 *"there is a steadily diminishing":* Plaskett comments taken from text of speech to Wings Club, New York, September 13, 1989.

284 *sent TWA's unions into a frenzy:* see *Travel Management Daily,* December 20, 1989, p. 1.

284 *In late September, another flap arose:* "UAL Chairman Defends Profit from Buyout," *Wall Street Journal,* September 25, 1989.

284 *Pan Am carried:* "Pan Am Strives to Clip AMR's Wings in Latin America," *Wall Street Journal,* December 29, 1989.

285 *As a colleague paraphrased:* The Wolf quotation is from interview with United president Jack Pope.

285 *By 1989, Wolf was speaking publicly:* See *Travel Management Daily,* July 19, 1989, p. 1.

286 *By the second quarter:* "Pan Am Belt-Tightening Shows Up at Mealtime," *Wall Street Journal,* May 21, 1990.

286 *In May of 1990, the Pan Am shuttle:* "Pan Am Faces Hurdles in Bid to Sell Shuttle," *Wall Street Journal,* May 21, 1990.

PAGE

290 *"Frankly, I do not recall":* Copy of Crandall letter to Plaskett transmitted on PR Newswire, October 26, 1990.

292 *About a month after:* Three route acquisitions detailed in American Airlines press releases dated December 3, December 16, and December 18, 1990. See also, "TWA to Sell American Air Its U.S.-London Routes," *Wall Street Journal,* December 17, 1990.

292 *The day after:* "Pan Am Stock Soars on New Icahn Bid," *Wall Street Journal,* December 18, 1990.

293 *Things got worse:* "Merger Talks of Pan Am, TWA Stall," *Wall Street Journal,* December 26, 1990.

293 *On January 8, 1991:* "Bankruptcy Petition Is Filed by Pan Am to Get New Loans," *New York Times,* January 9, 1991, p. 1.

294 *Meanwhile, negotiations dragged on:* For detailed account of the negotiations of the United States and the United Kingdom over the right of American and United to succeed Pan Am and TWA at London Heathrow, see John Newhouse, "Air Wars," *The New Yorker,* August 5, 1991.

295 *But Bob Crandall got:* "U.S. Ruling a Setback for TWA," *New York Times,* March 15, 1991.

297 *By the beginning of August:* "Transport Chief Urges Pan Am to Consider All Reasonable Bids," *Wall Street Journal,* August 2, 1991.

299 *Captain Mark Pyle piloted:* Account of last Pan Am flight is from Mark S. Pyle, "Pan Am: The Last Clipper," *Miami Herald,* December 19, 1991.

Other general sources: "The Return of a Raider—TWA's Carl Icahn Plays Hardball With Pan Am," *Newsweek,* January 7, 1991, p. 44; "How the Whole World Is Changing—Passing the Flag," by Coleman Lollar, *Frequent Flyer* magazine, March 1991, cover story; Bridget O'Brian, "American Air Expands into Three Continents, Flexing Its U.S. Muscle," *Wall Street Journal,* June 8, 1990, p. 1.

EPILOGUE

PAGE

304 *In addition, government studies:* For a discussion of premium pricing at fortress hubs, see "The Truth About Fortress Hubs—13 U.S. Airports Are Dominated by a Single Carrier," *Frequent Flyer* magazine, October 1992, p. 16.

PAGE

305 *Two respected economists:* See Steven Morrison and Clifford Winston, "The Economic Effects of Airline Deregulation," Brookings Institution, 1986.

305 *However, critics:* See *State of the Airline Industry, 1991,* published by Transportation Trades Council of the AFL-CIO, Washington, D.C., p. 11.

305 *Some, like America West:* See *Airline Market Power: Its Impact on Competition and the Consumer,* DOT data analysis by America West Airlines, May 1991.

305 *There may have been:* "Eastern Air Agrees to Plead Guilty on Records Charge," *Wall Street Journal,* March 4, 1991.

306 *In 1989, a survey:* Yankelovich Clancy Shulman telephone survey, March 2, 1989, cited in report of Drexel Burnham Lambert Airline Safety Conference, May 1989.

306 *In a 1991 poll:* Cited in *TravelAge MidAmerica,* May 20, 1991, p. 1.

307 *A 1988 Transportation Department study:* See "Study of Airline Computer Reservations Systems," U.S. Department of Transportation, May 1988, p. 5.

307 *A lengthy 1991 investigation:* See "Winds of Change: Domestic Air Transport Since Deregulation," Transportation Research Board/National Research Council, Special Report 230, Washington, D.C., 1991.

307 *And F. Warren McFarlan:* Quotation is from *Harvard Business Review,* July–August 1990, Letters to the Editor, p. 176.

307 *On the other hand:* See *A Failed Partnership: Factors Contributing to Failures in the U.S. Airline Industry,* a study by TravelTechnics Ltd., Darryl Jenkins and Douglas Frechtling, for the International Institute of Tourism Studies (Washington, D.C.: George Washington University, October 1992), p. 1.

308 *According to the Labor Department:* As reported in "Job Security Shaky at U.S. Airlines," *USA Today,* October 20, 1992.

308 *A 1992 study by two academics:* See John R. Meyer and John S. Strong, "From Closed Set to Open Set Deregulation: An Assessment of the U.S. Airline Industry," *The Logistics and Transportation Review,* University of British Columbia, March 1992, pp. 1–21.

308 *For some airline employees:* See Hilary Rosenberg, "Playing Hardball at the PBGC," *Institutional Investor,* October 1992.

309 *The General Accounting Office, in a 1991 report:* Cited in Shirley Fockler, "The U.S. Domestic Airline Industry," *Travel & Tourism Analyst,* No. 3, 1991, pp. 5–21.

Select Bibliography

BOOKS

Banks, Howard. *The Rise and Fall of Freddie Laker*. London: Faber and Faber, 1982.

Barlay, Stephen. *The Final Call—Why Airline Disasters Continue to Happen*. New York: Pantheon, 1991.

Bender, Marylin, and Selig Altschul. *The Chosen Instrument*. New York: Simon and Schuster, 1982.

Bernstein, Aaron. *Grounded—Frank Lorenzo and the Destruction of Eastern Airlines*. New York: Simon and Schuster, 1990.

Borman, Frank, and Robert J. Serling. *Countdown—An Autobiography*. New York: Silver Arrow Books/William Morrow and Company, 1988.

Brown, Anthony. *The Politics of Airline Deregulation*. Knoxville, Tenn.: University of Tennessee Press, 1987.

Bruck, Connie. *The Predator's Ball—The Junk Bond Raiders and the Man Who Staked Them*. New York: The American Lawyer/Simon and Schuster, 1988.

Burkhardt, Robert. *CAB—The Civil Aeronautics Board*. Dulles Airport, Va.: The Green Hills Publishing Co., 1974.

Button, Kenneth, ed. *Airline Regulation—International Experiences*. New York: New York University Press, 1991.

Corbett, David. *Politics and the Airlines*. London: George Allen & Unwin, 1965.

Davies, R. E. G. *Rebels and Reformers of the Airways*. Washington, D.C.: Smithsonian Institution Press, 1987.

Davis, Sidney F. *Delta Airlines: Debunking the Myth*. Atlanta: Peachtree Publishers, 1988.

Dempsey, Paul Stephen, and Andrew R. Goetz. *Airline Deregulation and Laissez-Faire Mythology.* Westport, Conn.: Quorum Books, 1992.

Emerson, Steven, and Brian Duffy. *The Fall of Pan Am 103: Inside the Lockerbie Investigation.* New York: G. P. Putnam's Sons, 1990.

Johnson, Moira. *Takeover.* New York: Arbor House, 1986.

McCraw, Thomas. *Prophets of Regulation.* Cambridge, Mass.: The Belknap Press of Harvard University Press, 1984.

Meyer, John, and Clinton Oster, eds. *Airline Deregulation: The Early Experiences.* Boston: Auburn House, 1981.

Meyer, John, and Clinton Oster, Jr. *Deregulation and the Future of Intercity Passenger Travel.* Cambridge, Mass.: MIT Press, 1987.

Murphy, Michael A. *The Airline That Pride Almost Bought.* New York: Franklin Watts, 1986.

Nader, Ralph, and Wesley J. Smith. *Collision Course: The Truth About Airline Safety.* Blue Ridge Summit, Penn.: TAB Books/McGraw Hill, 1993.

Nance, John J. *Splash of Colors—The Self-Destruction of Braniff International.* New York: William Morrow & Co., 1984.

Newhouse, John. *The Sporty Game.* New York: Alfred A. Knopf, 1982.

Reed, Dan. *American Eagle: The Ascent of Bob Crandall and American Airlines.* New York: St. Martin's Press, 1993.

Robinson, Jack E. *Free Fall—The Needless Destruction of Eastern Air Lines and the Valiant Struggle to Save It.* New York: Harper Business, 1992.

Sampson, Anthony. *Empires of the Sky.* New York: Random House, 1984.

Serling, Robert J. *Eagle: The History of American Airlines.* New York: St. Martin's Press, 1985.

———. *From the Captain to the Colonel—An Informal History of Eastern Airlines.* New York: The Dial Press, 1980.

———. *Howard Hughes' Airline: An Informal History of TWA.* New York: St. Martin's Press, 1983.

Smith, Frank Kingston. *The Legacy of Wings—The Harold F. Pitcairn Story.* New York: Jason Aronson, 1981.

Solberg, Carl. *Conquest of the Skies—A History of Commercial Aviation in America.* Boston: Little, Brown & Co., 1979.

Taneja, Nawal K. *The Commercial Airline Industry—Managerial Practices and Regulatory Policies.* Lexington, Mass.: Lexington Books/ D. C. Heath, 1976.

Tolchin, Susan, and Martin Tolchin. *Dismantling America—The Rush to Deregulate*. Boston: Houghton Mifflin Co., 1983.

von Hoffman, Nicholas. *Capitalist Fools*. New York: Doubleday, 1992.

REPORTS AND STUDIES

Airline Economics, Inc. *State of the Airline Industry*. Washington, D.C.: January 1990.

America West Airlines. *Airline Market Power: Its Impact on Competition and the Consumer*. May 1991.

Bock, Betty, et al. *Is Antitrust Dead?* New York: The Conference Board, 1989.

Brenner, Melvin, James Leet, and Elihu Schott. *Airline Deregulation*. Westport, Conn.: Eno Foundation for Transportation, 1985.

Civil Aeronautics Board Practices and Procedures—Report of the Subcommittee on Administration Practice and Procedures of the Committee on the Judiciary of the U.S. Senate. Washington, D.C.: U.S. Government Printing Office, 1975.

The Consequences of Airline Mergers Since Deregulation—Report of the Civil Aeronautics Board and the Department of Transportation, Washington, D.C.: April 1982.

Dempsey, Paul Stephen. *Flying Blind—The Failure of Airline Deregulation*. Washington, D.C.: Economic Policy Institute, 1990.

General Accounting Office. *Airline Competition—DOT's Implementation of Airline Regulatory Authority*. Washington, D.C.: June 1989.

Hawk, Barry. "Airline Deregulation After 10 Years: The Need for Vigorous Antitrust Enforcement and Intergovernmental Agreements," *The Antitrust Bulletin*, Summer 1989, p. 267.

Jedel, Michael Jay. *Post Deregulation Strategic Employment Response of the Successful, Surviving Major Domestic Airlines: A Story Not Fully Told*. Atlanta: Institute of Personnel and Employment Relations, Georgia State University, 1990.

Jenkins, Darryl, and Douglas Frechtling. *A Failed Partnership: Factors Contributing to Failures in the U.S. Airline Industry*. Washington, D.C.: TravelTechnics Ltd. for the International Institute of Tourism Studies, George Washington University, October 1992.

Kahn, Alfred E. "Deregulation: Looking Backward and Looking Forward," *Yale Journal on Regulation*, Vol. 7, 1990, p. 325.

Levine, Michael E. "Airline Competition in Deregulated Markets:

Theory, Firm Strategy and Public Policy," Yale Journal on Regulation, Spring 1987, p. 393.

Melvin A. Brenner Associates. *Analysis of Airline Concentration Issue.* Rowayton, Conn.: July 1990.

Morrison, Steven, and Clifford Winston. "Cleared for Takeoff—The Evolution of the Deregulated Airline Industry," *The Annual Review of Travel*. American Express, 1992.

———. *The Economic Effects of Airline Deregulation.* Washington, D.C.: Brookings Institution, 1986.

Transportation Research Board/National Research Council. *Winds of Change: Domestic Air Transport Since Deregulation*, Special Report 230. Washington, D.C.: 1991.

Transportation Trades Council. *State of the Airline Industry, 1991.* Washington, D.C.: AFL-CIO, 1991.

U.S. Department of Transportation. *Study of Airline Computer Reservations Systems.* May 1988.

OTHER SOURCES

Travel Management Daily.
Travel Weekly.
Air Transport World.
Airline Business.
Company annual reports and 10-K filings.

Index